CLARENDON ARIS

*General E*
LINDSAY JL

G000129662

# ARISTOTLE
## *De Anima*

*Translated*
*with an Introduction and Commentary*
*by*

CHRISTOPHER SHIELDS

CLARENDON PRESS · OXFORD

# OXFORD

## UNIVERSITY PRESS

Great Clarendon Street, Oxford, OX2 6DP,
United Kingdom

Oxford University Press is a department of the University of Oxford.
It furthers the University's objective of excellence in research, scholarship,
and education by publishing worldwide. Oxford is a registered trade mark of
Oxford University Press in the UK and in certain other countries

Published in the United States of America by Oxford University Press
198 Madison Avenue, New York, NY 10016, United States of America

British Library Cataloguing in Publication Data
Data available

Library of Congress Cataloging in Publication Data
Data available

ISBN 978-0-19-924345-7

# ACKNOWLEDGEMENTS

Because I have had graduates and advanced undergraduates foremost in mind when preparing this translation and commentary, I have been most grateful for the feedback offered by students who kindly previewed earlier versions of this text in classes and seminars at a variety of institutions. Although they are too numerous to list by name, I thank corporately all those who read parts of the translation and commentary at the University of Colorado at Boulder, Cornell University, the Chinese University of Hong Kong, St. Louis University, the Humboldt University of Berlin, and the University of Oxford. These students have proven extremely astute in their reactions, often pressing me for greater clarity and enhanced exegetical directness. Among them I remain especially conscious of helpful feedback from Wei Cheng, Jakub Deuretzbacher, Yuuki Ohta, Sydney Penner, Rachel Singpurwalla, Nathanael Stein, and Paul Studtmann.

Two doctoral students in Oxford merit special mention. In the context of a graduate seminar on *De Anima*, Jason Carter read the entire translation and commentary with care, offering numerous corrections and suggestions for improvement. As a research assistant, Thomas Ainsworth worked minutely through the entire manuscript, issuing a long stream of highly schooled observations which resulted in a considerable number of improvements to the translation; not satisfied, he then also offered a series of incisive suggestions regarding the commentary, resulting, again, in a long list of improvements. I am most grateful to them both.

I am pleased to be in a position to acknowledge with gratitude the institutional support which permitted me to focus on this project by releasing me from other duties, whether pedagogical or administrative. Welcome support was provided by the University of Oxford, Lady Margaret Hall, Oxford, the Chinese University of Hong Kong, and TOPOI, the Excellence Cluster at the Humboldt University of Berlin. I reviewed the entire antepenultimate draft during a year in Berlin, funded partly by TOPOI and partly by the Alexander von Humboldt-Stiftung. The support of this marvellous foundation through the years has been really quite remarkable. I have no doubt that without its good offices, I would never have come to the point in life where I could offer this work for publication.

During the long period in which this book has been intermittently under production, I had the benefit of instructive feedback to presentations given to numerous learned societies and universities. The translation of the first book was read by a group of scholars at Cambridge University's May Week, at the end of which David Sedley kindly offered me written comments of his characteristically superior sort. I received similarly high-level feedback from multi-day seminars at Hokkaido University and at the Central European University, where I learned much from the acute and informed audience members.

Otherwise, I am aware of particular improvements made in response to discussions with Dominic Bailey, Charles Brittain, David Charles, Kei Chiba, Klaus Corcilius, Paolo Crivelli, Ana Laura Edelhoff, Gail Fine, John Gibert, Edward Hussey, Terence Irwin, Sean Kelsey, Colin Guthrie King, Phillip Mitsis, Graham Oddie, Robert Pasnau, Colin Shields, Richard Sorabji, Christopher Taylor, and Iakovos Vasiliou.

Some of those discussions trace back to a multi-year reading group on *De Anima* at Oriel College, Oxford, presided over by David Charles. The shifting members of that group, which included graduate students, post-doctoral students, permanent post holders in Oxford, and visiting academics from the world over, forced me to rethink many of my firmest convictions about the doctrines of *De Anima*. They also collectively reminded me that a translator of Aristotle must often play the role of a *de facto* textual critic—and accordingly, like that critic, can on occasion do little more than offer a modest conjecture.

Having hazarded such conjectures, I submitted them for review to Fred Miller, to whom I owe a special debt of gratitude. He read the entire penultimate draft of the translation and commentary with attention and learning, adroitly pointing the way forward in several difficult passages. Still greater is my debt to the editor of the Clarendon Aristotle Series. Equipped with a highly developed sense of Aristotelian prose and a deep mastery of Aristotelian philosophy, Lindsay Judson offered numerous corrections, while demanding greater clarity, depth, and fidelity, always steering me in directions that I am glad to have gone. I am permanently grateful to him for his instruction.

Finally, there is another sort of debt, distant and indirect, owed by every commentator on *De Anima* to the legion of scholars who have gone before. There are some 800 known and catalogued commentaries on *De Anima*, many of which I have freely consulted to my great edification. The monumental commentaries of earlier generations, some ancient, some medieval, and some modern, have often lain open on my desk as I was working through a puzzling passage. The vast majority of the authors of these works are no longer with us to be thanked, but I call out to them in thanks all the same. Like other students of *De Anima*, I have learned immeasurably through their efforts.

As for the disquieting thought that I offer now the 801st (or so) commentary on this text, I thank the first editor of the Clarendon Aristotle series, John Ackrill, for assuring and encouraging me with his quiet, crystalline conviction that each generation of philosophers must remake Aristotelian philosophy in its own idiom, even while striving to fathom, as some of our German friends say, *wie es eigentlich gewesen ist*.

# CONTENTS

# GENERAL INTRODUCTION

Near the beginning of his *De Anima*, Aristotle (384–322 B.C.) remarks with an arresting candour that 'Grasping anything trustworthy concerning the soul is completely and in every way among the most difficult of affairs' (*De Anima* I 1 402a10–11). This judgement is striking not least because *De Anima* is a fully mature work, most likely written near the end of Aristotle's life, during his second stay in Athens, when he was director of his own school, the Lyceum (334–323 B.C.). If that is correct, then this appraisal issues from a thinker of surpassing depth and acumen who had spent virtually all of his adult life engaged in philosophical inquiry and biological investigation, a great bulk of which took as its subject matter the nature and faculties of living beings.

Aristotle thus regards his task in *De Anima* as a formidable one. This may be due in part to his refusing to limit consideration of the soul to the human soul alone. Rather, he presumes that because the soul is a principle of life in general, any investigation into the soul (*psuchê* in Greek, or *anima* in Latin) will need to consider all animate beings, that is, all living beings, including plants and animals no less than humans. This he does in *De Anima*, even devoting some energy to determining the nature of life itself along the way. In this sense, the subject matter of this work is broad in scope, broader than either the modern discipline of psychology or contemporary philosophy of mind, with whose domains of inquiry *De Anima* has only a partial, if instructive, overlap. Aristotle seeks to uncover the nature of soul and its relation to the body; to explore perception and the perceptual faculties; to explain the character of representation in thought; to analyse thinking and the nature of mind; to assay the aetiology of human action; to characterize the nature of life; and to do all of this in a historically informed manner sensitive to the *phaenomena*, that is, to the governing appearances pertaining to living systems and their distinctively psychological traits. It is for these reasons understandable that Aristotle should find his undertaking in *De Anima* a daunting one.

# I. THE PLACE OF *DE ANIMA* IN THE ARISTOTELIAN CORPUS

Any determination of the degree to which Aristotle succeeds in meeting the demanding tasks he sets for himself in *De Anima* will be, inevitably, a matter of exegetical and critical controversy. Fortunately, whatever determinations we make, it remains clear that he brings his most sophisticated philosophical framework to bear on the issues he investigates. Judged by the terms of the psychological theory and the overarching framework within which he espouses it, Aristotle's *De Anima* clearly belongs to the last phase of his productive life. The case for treating *De Anima* as a late work of Aristotle is threefold: (i) inter-textual references to other works in the corpus recommend a relatively late date;[1] (ii) the technical vocabulary seems to place it in association with other presumptively late works;[2] and most importantly, (iii) the content of the theory propounded draws regularly upon the highly technical apparatus of hylomorphism characteristic of Aristotle's late period.[3]

---

[1] *De Anima* contains possible back references to two early Aristotelian dialogues, *De Philosophia* (404b19) and *Eudemus* (407b29); and fairly clear references to both *Gen. et Cor.* (417a1 and 423b29) and *Phys.* (417a17). Back references, or apparent back references, to *De Anima* are almost exclusively confined to works deemed to be late, primarily the *Parva Naturalia*: *De Sensu* (436a1–5, 436b10, b14, 437a18, 438b3, 439a8, a18, 440b28); *De Mem.* (449b3); *De Somno* (454a11, 455a8, a24); *De Insom.* (459a15); *De Iuv.* (467b13); *De Resp.* (474b11); as well as *Motu Anim.* (700b5, 21) and *Gen. An.* (736a37, 786b25, 788b2). There is also a clear but apparently anomalous reference to *De Anima* in a work commonly regarded as early, *De Interp.* (16a8).

[2] Crucial in this respect is the frequent use of the word 'actuality' (*entelecheia*), a term key to Aristotle's statement of his own positive view of soul and body. Strikingly, the word *entelecheia* is absent in the *Organon*. Of all Aristotle's works, it occurs most commonly in *DA* (thirty-four times), but also figures prominently in the *Phys.* (twelve times), the *Met.* (twelve times), and *Gen. et Cor.* (fifteen times). It shows up twice in *Gen. An.* and once each in *DC*, *Meteor.*, and *De Part.* The general fact of the frequency of this diction was noticed already by Zeller (1879) and emphasized by Ross as well (1961), though neither charts its frequency accurately.

[3] These criteria omit by design the vexed question of whether Aristotle's hylomorphism embraces, eschews, or is indifferent to some manner of cardiocentrism, that is a view according to which the soul has a specific bodily location, namely the heart. According to an influential study of Nuyens (1948), one can discern a clear development in Aristotle's psychology along this dimension. Nuyens agreed with Poppelreuter (1892) in holding that *De Anima* is positively

While no one of these points secures a late date for *De Anima* unquestionably, taken corporately they do suggest that the work is a mature production, one whose understanding and assessment consequently require a prior familiarity with the basic tenets of Aristotle's technical vocabulary and his most highly developed philosophical theory. Indeed, in one sense, little pertaining to a contemporary assessment of the theses propounded in *De Anima* turns crucially on the question of its dating relative to the rest of Aristotle's considerable output. It is, however, prudent to appreciate that *De Anima* draws freely on the technical terminology and apparatus developed, sometimes haltingly, in Aristotle's other theoretical works. Most important in this regard is that *De Anima* makes heavy use of the principles of *hylomorphism*, including centrally the paired notions of: (i) *form* (*eidos* or *morphê*) and *matter* (*hulê*) and (ii) *actuality* (*energeia* or *entelechia*, the latter of which is sometimes used interchangeably and sometimes not with the former) and *potentiality* (*dunamis*). It is accordingly necessary to have a ready grasp of these sometimes complex concepts before a proper appraisal of the theories of *De Anima* can be undertaken.

incompatible with cardiocentrism, which they both further understood to be an indication that it eschews that presumptively more primitive view and thus must represent a later phase of Aristotle's development. Nuyens might be criticized (and indeed *has* been criticized by Block (1961) and more recently by Tracy (1983)) on a number of grounds. First and foremost is the question of whether in *De Anima* Aristotle in fact and intentionally rejects cardiocentrism, but then also whether—whatever Aristotle's view of the matter—hylomorphism is in fact consistent with the localization of the soul, as, for instance, already in antiquity Alexander of Aphrodisias understood it to be (*DA* 23.6–24.10, 38.15–66.8, 100.13–17). Deuretzbacher (2014) considers the evidence and argues (i) that Alexander is himself a cardiocentrist; (ii) that he ascribes the same view to Aristotle's *De Anima*; and (iii) that he is right to do so—that Aristotle is himself a cardiocentrist , and so, under pains of inconsistency, must regard cardiocentrism as consistent with hylomorphism after all. Given these controversies, while the philosophical question of whether hylomorphism is compatible with any manner of localization retains a great interest, any attempt to date *De Anima* predicated upon these contentions should be set aside as at best inconclusive. As a purely philosophical matter, it is instructive, if unsurprising, that allied questions about localizations—of properties such as being alive, of thoughts, of emotions, of pains, of consciousness, and so forth—continue to exercise philosophers and psychologists down to the present day.

## II. SOME PRINCIPLES OF HYLOMORPHIC
## EXPLANATION

When approaching his investigation into the soul and its faculties, Aristotle draws upon a highly nuanced metaphysical framework whose basic tenets are easily grasped but whose applications and extensions are sometimes vexing. This is, indeed, all the more true given that in *De Anima* itself Aristotle develops and refines some of his basic technical apparatus, in some instances straining his terminology almost beyond recognition. Thus, for instance, when he puts forth his most general account, Aristotle contends that the soul is a 'first actuality of a natural organic body' (*DA* II 1, 412b5–6), that it is a 'substance as form of a natural body which has life in potentiality' (*DA* II 1, 412a20–1) and, similarly, that it 'is a first actuality of a natural body which has life in potentiality' (*DA* II 1, 412a27–8). In so speaking, Aristotle relies on a series of technical terms introduced and, in some cases, explained in his physical and metaphysical treatises, including most notably the *Physics, Metaphysics,* and *On Generation and Corruption.* Thus, the soul is a first actuality (*prôtê entelecheia*), a substance (*ousia*), and a form (*eidos*), while the body is organic (*organikon*), something having life in potentiality (*en dunamei*) and serving as the matter (*hulê*) of the soul.

When appealing to these and other like terms, Aristotle presumes that his reader is already familiar with his basic hylomorphism, the fundamental features of which are drawn from his broader explanatory schema, his *four-causal explanatory framework.*[4] As introduced and illustrated in *Physics* I 7–II 8, this framework advances a thesis about the features necessary for adequacy and comprehensiveness in explanation; it is motivated initially by the simple thought that every kind of change, whether mere alteration (as when Socrates alters from being pale to being sunburned after a day at the beach) or generation (as when Socrates first comes into existence at his birth), involves two factors: *something remaining the same* and *something gained or lost.* In the case of alteration, this is plain. Socrates is the continuing subject, while the quality lost is pallor and the quality gained

---

[4] Shields (2014), Ch. 2, offers a comprehensive introduction to Aristotle's four causes.

is being sunburned. In the case of generation, it is best to follow Aristotle's own example: a statue is generated not from nothing, but from something, say, bronze. The bronze persists and gains the shape or form of the statue. In these cases, the two factors are the matter, that which persists through change, and the form, the feature gained or lost in the change. Since Aristotle will eventually treat both perception and thought as attenuated sorts of alterations (*DA* II 5, 416b33–4), it is natural for him to appeal to the notions of matter and form in their explications.

In addition to citing material and formal causes, Aristotle also demands for completeness in explanation the specification of the two remaining causes—the final and efficient. Both notions play prominent roles in the explanatory schema of *De Anima*. Briefly, focusing first on a favourable example, an artefact, Aristotle will expect specifications of two features of, say, a computer in addition to mention of its matter and form. Because bits of plastic, metal, and silicon do not spontaneously arrange themselves into the form of a computer, an explanation of the existence of a computer must cite the agent which brought it about that the form is in the matter. This agent he calls the *efficient* or *moving cause* or the *source of motion* (*archê tês kinêseôs*). Still, knowing even the material, formal, and efficient causes does not suffice for completeness in explanation. This can be appreciated most readily by imagining an encounter with a computer of a unique and unexpected shape and material composition: we might know that the object before us is made of tungsten and ceramic, that the odd malleable dodecahedron shape was put into the material by means of an intricate mould-injecting robotic machine, while yet lacking any understanding of what the structure before us *is*. When and only when we learn that it is an ingenious voice-activated computer, functionally equivalent to an ordinary laptop, do we know what it is. We learn what it is when we learn what it is for, when we learn its function, or in Aristotle's terms, when we learn its *final cause*.

Taken altogether, then, Aristotle's explanatory schema demands the specification of the *material, formal, efficient, and final causes*. Nor does he doubt that the sort of explanation appropriate for artefacts generalizes to organisms and their parts. Indeed, he takes it as obvious that understanding, e.g., what an eye is involves appealing to its final cause: knowing that eyes are *for seeing* will prove for him an ineliminable component of any adequate explanation of the eye. That said, Aristotle does not take as his primary objective in *De Anima* the explanation of the *perceptual organs* (*aisthêtêria*); rather, he is concerned primarily with the nature of *perception* (*aisthêsis*) itself, and with the individual sensory modalities considered as capacities or faculties. He takes an interest in the organs used in perception only to the degree that a description of their characteristics may help to illuminate his primary concern with the activities of perception and thinking.[5] Their analyses, as we shall see, require technical terminology in addition to the four-causal explanatory framework already adumbrated. So too will his account of thinking, where, for reasons peculiar to that activity, Aristotle also displays considerable interest in the nature of the agent of thought, reason (*nous*).

Thus far, however, we may reasonably expect to find Aristotle appealing to his four causes when engaging in psychological explanation. This he does, relying most centrally throughout *De Anima* on the notions of matter (*hulê*) and form (*eidos* or *morphê*), for which reason his account of soul and body is referred to as a kind of *hylomorphism*.

In fact, Aristotle's positive theorizing in *De Anima* is rightly understood as consisting of three successive deployments of his general hylomorphism, each more particular and attenuated than the last: (i) he first articulates soul-body relations by claiming that soul and body are related as form and matter; (ii) he then analyses perception (*aisthêsis*) and the individual sensory modalities by appealing repeatedly to his hylomorphic account of alteration in terms of form reception; and, finally, (iii) he characterizes *thinking* or *reasoning* (*noêsis*) and *reason* (*nous*) on the same model of form reception to which he appeals in his analysis of perception, though now in terms of *intelligible* rather than sensible forms. It

---

[5] The orientation of *De Anima* thus contrasts with the more empirically involved *Parva Naturalia*, a collection of short treatises investigating living systems and their features. In those works, Aristotle understands himself to be investigating 'the phenomena common to soul and body' (*De Sensu* 436a6–8), whereas in *De Anima* he introduces as matter for investigation 'whether all affections are common to what has the soul or whether there is some affection peculiar to the soul itself' (*DA* I 1, 403a3–5), 'This,' he observes, 'is necessary to grasp, but not easy' (*DA* I 1, 403a5).

is striking how in this progression Aristotle extends his basic notions of form and matter in ways which alienate them from their elementary characterizations as, roughly, *shape* and *stuff*.

## III. SOUL AND BODY

### A. SOUL-BODY HYLOMORPHISM

Aristotle's approach to soul-body relations has stimulated interest—and has occasioned fierce exegetical and philosophical debate—since antiquity. Some of the reasons for this interest may not redound to Aristotle's immediate credit: he seems to commit himself to a parcel of theses which, while not inconsistent, do not sit easily with one another. Thus, for instance, when, after considering in detail the views of his predecessors in *De Anima* I, Aristotle turns in *De Anima* II 1 to a first introduction of his own hylomorphism, he famously dismisses as unnecessary the question of whether soul and body are one (*DA* II 1 412b6–9)—though he had evidently earlier in the same chapter already asked and answered it: they are not (*DA* II 1, 412a17). Similarly, he concludes that it is clear that the soul is not separable from the body—but then hastens to add that some of its parts may yet be, if it is indeed appropriate to say that it has parts at all (*DA* II 1, 413a3–7). He eventually, rather surprisingly, closes this same introductory chapter by wondering aloud (in a passage which has commended itself to emendation because of its evident incongruence with what has immediately preceded it) whether the soul bears the sort of relation to the body which a sailor bears to his ship (*DA* II 1, 413a8–9). This seems an odd concern for the author of hylomorphism. If he thinks that he has good grounds for denying that the soul is separable from the body, then why should he wonder how it might be like a sailor in a ship? Sailors sail ships, steer them into port, and then disembark for shore leave.

More often than not, however, the seeming incongruities in Aristotle's hylomorphism eventually prove not to be inconsistencies so much as challenges to facile first interpretations of his intended meanings. Indeed, the dominant reason Aristotle's hylomorphism has sparked exegetical controversy stems not from any initial unclarity on his part, but from an admirable form of philosophical risk-taking: Aristotle is not content to reject Platonic dualism only to embrace an expedient form of reductive materialism. On the contrary, he finds all forms of materialism articulated up to his own time explanatorily inadequate. His hylomorphism is calculated to walk a middle course between two extremes. His middle course is inevitably more nuanced than the extremes it replaces, which, however extreme they may be, nonetheless share a virtue common to all forms of uncompromising extremism: easy clarity purchased at the expense of some percentage of the phenomena. Thus, for instance, the materialists Aristotle considers have an easy time with the soul by simply identifying it with this or that element, or combination of elements. Heading in the other direction, the Platonists, recoiling from these forms of reduction, make the soul an immaterial entity, capable of existing beyond the dissolution of the body. Aristotle sees the virtues and vices of both poles; he seeks to craft a theory which embraces their strengths while eschewing their weaknesses without lapsing into the muddle of blurry compromise.

This, at any rate, presents the situation as Aristotle seems to conceive it. Hylomorphism, as he sees it, is non-reductive but also non-Platonic: it is intended to embrace the insights of the materialists without accepting their view that the soul just is this or that element, and to join Plato in contrasting the soul and body, but without inferring on that basis that the soul can exist without being embodied.

That leaves Aristotle some room for manoeuvring, though not a lot. By straddling a divide separating the least reductive forms of materialism and the most modest forms of dualism, Aristotle looks to capture the phenomena of living beings in all of their varied complexity. He takes it as given—and so accepts as *explananda*—that living things take on nutrition and grow (*DA* 434a22–434b18; cf. *Part. An.* 687a24–690a10; *Met.* 1075a16–25), that animals perceive (*De Sensu* 436b10–11), and that human beings think (*DA* 414b18, 429a6–8; cf. *Met.* 980a21). He accordingly takes it as his task to explain these activities, rather than to explain them away by reducing them to a distinct class of activities, such as material processes, or, failing that, by eliminating them altogether. At the same time, it is plain, he thinks, that the vast majority of these activities are in some sense or other matter-involving. Hence, he seeks also to explain their relation to the sorts of elements to which others theorozing before him had wanted to reduce them.

For Aristotle, the middle ground sought is soul-body hylomorphism. As applied to soul and body, hylomorphism is easy to state, but difficult to comprehend completely:

soul : body : : form : matter

The soul is the form of the body and the body the matter of the soul (*DA* II 1, 412a19–20). Together they yield one living being, just as a quantity of bronze and Hermes shape yield exactly one bronze statue of Hermes.

The initial consequences of this view, highlighted by Aristotle himself, are reasonably direct. First, he contends, given hylomorphism, the question of whether soul and body are one loses some of its force:

> It is not necessary to ask whether soul and body are one, just as it is not necessary to ask whether the wax and its shape are one, nor generally whether the matter of each thing and that of which it is the matter are one. For even if one and being are spoken of in several ways, what is properly so spoken of is the actuality (*DA* II 1, 412b6–9).

It is easy to suppose, on the basis of this contention, that it is not necessary to ask whether the soul and body are one because they so obviously are one—or at any rate yield just one thing, one living being, just as a cylindrical shape and a quantity of wax yield exactly one candle.

Note, however, that we have already two distinct grounds for dismissing as unnecessary questions of soul-body unity. The first response has it that they are one; the second has it that they *yield* one entity. The first response, however natural, seems incompatible with something Aristotle himself very plainly holds, in the same chapter of *De Anima*, that soul and body are not one (*DA* II 1, 412a17). So, if it is unnecessary to engage questions about soul-body unity, it cannot be for that reason. Perhaps, then, Aristotle's first main corollary of hylomorphism is rather that one need not ask whether soul and body are one because according to his theory soul and body come together to make just one entity, in the case of human beings, then, just one rational animal.

This may be closer to his conception, but it does not yet seem terribly persuasive. In particular, a Platonist who had decided that soul and body were not identical might then well ask whether soul and body have the same diachronic identity conditions, and whether, more to the point, the soul is such that it depends upon the body for its own existence. In point of fact, this is just what Plato did ask in the *Phaedo*; and he concluded, for better or worse, that souls were indeed capable of existing without the bodies which, in his view, were best regarded as prisons serving as temporary earthly holding cells for souls striving to escape them. If that strikes Aristotle as fanciful or foolish, then it bears noting that it is rendered at least possible by the conclusion that soul and body are not identical, a conclusion he himself evidently embraces. The question then returns to Aristotle: why is it unnecessary to ask whether soul and body are one?

One approach to this question highlights the second main consequence of Aristotle's hylomorphism, that the soul is not separable from the body. After considering its general defining features, Aristotle concludes that there is no unclarity as to whether the soul is separable from the body. It is not: 'that the soul is not separable from the body, or some parts of it if it naturally has parts, is not unclear' (DA II 1, 413a3–5). The idea here is that insofar as it is a form, the soul is unexceptionable in comparison with other forms. Granted, the form of a bronze statue is not identical with the quantity of bronze it enforms: the bronze can exist without the form, when the bronze is reshaped, and less obviously, the form can exist without just that quantity of bronze, when a bit is chipped off and then refurbished in a restoration. Still, none of this gives us any reason to suppose that when a statue is destroyed its form carries on. On the contrary, there seems to be every reason to believe that when a statue is melted down and recast into a cannon, the form of that particular statue has simply ceased to be. So, unless we are prepared to treat forms in general as capable of existing without their material bases, we should not be inclined to treat souls as exceptional cases. Hylomorphism, by itself, then gives us no reason to treat souls as separable from bodies, even if we think of them as distinct from their material bases.

This way of looking at the matter connects the two immediate inferences Aristotle draws from soul-body hylomorphism in a satisfying way. The reason that it is unnecessary to ask whether soul and body are one is not that they so obviously are (or are not) one. It is, rather, that many, including Plato, have been inclined to ask this question because of a prior interest in the possibility of *post mortem* existence for human souls. As non-reductive, hylomorphism may seem to open the door to that possibility; in suggesting that souls, like other forms, are dependent upon matter for their existence, Aristotle goes some way towards reclosing it.

Still, he does not slam the door. Instead, he hedges his conclusion about inseparability considerably. Immediately after concluding that soul and body are not separable, Aristotle appends a rider:

> Therefore, that the soul is not separable from the body, or some parts of it if it naturally has parts, is not unclear. For the actuality of some parts belongs to the parts themselves. Even so, nothing hinders some parts from being separable, because of their not being the actualities of any body (*DA* II 1, 413a3–7).

Although characteristically compressed, the argument here seeks to reserve the possibility of separability for some parts of the soul even while denying it to the soul as a whole. In so doing, it draws upon another technical feature of hylomorphism, the contention that a form is the actuality (*entelecheia*) of its matter, that the presence of the form makes some matter actually some determinate thing or other. A lump of bronze, considered in itself is potentially a statue of the Duke of Wellington; but it is equally, again considered in itself, a statue of Napoleon. It is the presence of the shape, of the Duke of Wellington or of Napoleon, which makes the matter actually a statue of the one rather than the other.

Now, Aristotle suggests, it may yet be possible that some part of the soul is not the actuality of any part of the body. Although he does not say so here, he is thinking of reason (*nous*).[6]

---

[6] On reason, see IV. C below.

## B. A PROBLEM ABOUT SOUL-BODY HYLOMORPHISM

When advancing this argument for the inseparability of soul, Aristotle makes it a sufficient condition of $x$'s inseparability from $y$ that $x$ is the actuality of $y$; and he further suggests, non-equivalently, that if $x$ is not the actuality of $y$, or any part of $y$, then $x$ is separable from $y$. The question of the degree to which these theses are cogent turns, of course, upon the nature of actualities and the conceptual or metaphysical connections Aristotle envisages between the notions of actuality and separability. That said, it is important to appreciate in the present context that in making the soul the actuality of the body, Aristotle relies upon a deeply entrenched principle of hylomorphic explanation while simultaneously opening himself to an unhappy problem about the very coherence of his preferred approach.[7]

This problem can be most readily appreciated by focusing on a simple illustration of hylomorphic explanation and by registering a difficulty about extending the same explanation to soul and body. When we focus on a statue of Hermes, we find, according to Aristotle's hylomorphic approach to change and generation, that form plays two important and non-equivalent roles. The statue changes in quality when, for example, it changes from cool to warm as the sun rises at dawn. The statue persists, but loses one *accidental form* while gaining another. Earlier though, when first cast, the lump of bronze became a statue. The statue came into existence when the bronze gained a *substantial form*. Once in existence, the statue might gain or lose any number of accidental forms; but once the bronze loses the statue shape, the statue ceases to be. Nonetheless, the bronze carries on: though it was the matter of the generation of the statue, the bronze was never essentially Hermes-shaped. Indeed, the same quantity of bronze can be now Hermes-shaped, now a distinct statue by being Pericles-shaped, and now not a statue at all but a sundial, by being sundial-shaped.

---

[7] The problem discussed in this section has received a great deal of attention in recent years. It was formulated first, and most clearly, by Ackrill (1972-3). For an overview of the literature covering the first two decades after Ackrill's challenging article, see Shields (1993). For a more recent discussion which categorizes some competing approaches, see Frey (2008).

It follows, in these cases at least, that according to the hylomorphic analysis of generation, any underlying matter is only contingently enformed by the shape it acquires when a compound is generated. Generalizing, then, one might reasonably infer that in any instance of generation, the matter comes to be enformed only contingently by a given form, because while essential to the generated compound, the form is accidental to the underlying matter. It turns out, however, that this generalization does not obtain in the case of souls and bodies, which Aristotle nevertheless seeks to subject to hylomorphic explanation. Like other living bodies, human bodies are not contingently enformed by the souls whose matter they are. On the contrary, Aristotle takes pains to insist that a body is not a body at all unless it is ensouled. So, unlike a quantity of bronze, a body cannot lose its form (= its soul) and continue in existence. For this reason, Aristotle's attempt to treat soul-body relations in hylomorphic terms may seem ill-advised.

Or, alternatively, it may seem ill-advised instead for him not to subordinate soul-body relations to the hylomorphic framework by simply allowing that bodies are contingently enformed by souls. After all, there is at the very least some linguistic oddness in the suggestion that the body is a not a body once it is unensouled. This is, however, a point upon which Aristotle insists:

> If an eye were an animal, its soul would be sight, since this would be the substance of the eye corresponding to the account. The eye is the matter of sight; if sight is lost, it is no longer an eye, except homonymously, in the way that a stone eye or painted eye is. What has been said in the case of parts must of course be understood as applying to the whole living body. For there is an analogy: as one part is to one part, so the whole perceptual faculty is to the whole of the body which is capable of perception, insofar as it is capable of perception. The body which has lost its soul is not the one which is potentially alive; this is rather the one which has a soul (*DA* II 1, 412b18–26).

Despite any apparent linguistic oddity, a body which has lost its soul, Aristotle contends, is not even potentially a body. We can call it a body, if we wish, but we must realize that we do so only in the manner in which we are prepared to call an eye in a statue an eye: it is not really an eye at all, but something which looks like an eye, in the case of a statue because it is a block of stone made to represent an eye by resembling one.

The crucial claim in all this is that a body which has lost its soul is not a body *except homonymously*. In speaking in this way, Aristotle evidently takes himself to be relying on a reasonably clear and uncontroversial case in which we call something *an F* (an eye) even though we recognize that it is not really, or not genuinely, an *F*. Our practice of calling a given non-genuine *F* an *F*, he regards as a homonymous application of the predicate, where *homonymy* is for him another technical term.[8] In this context, though, the immediate purport of its application is twofold.

First, there is the linguistic oddity already mentioned. It is an immediate consequence of Aristotle's contention that when we speak, e.g., of 'Lenin's body' on display in Red Square after his death, we are actually speaking of an item which is not numerically identical to the item we may have called 'Lenin's body,' when, for instance, offering the judgement that 'Lenin has a nice body' while observing him in the swimming pool. A careful Aristotelian may thus be prompted to correct someone claiming to have viewed Lenin's body in Red Square: 'Well, strictly speaking, it was not actually Lenin's body you saw— except homonymously.'

Be that as it may, the deeper worry concerns the second purport of Aristotle's appeal to homonymy: according to this claim, the only potentially living body is the one which is already enformed by a soul, so that, consequently, the only living body is one which is *necessarily* actually alive. If that is so, then there is no pre-existing body which is such that it comes to be ensouled (i.e. enformed by a soul) in the act of generation. If that is in turn correct, then a body is crucially unlike a lump of bronze. The role of the bronze in the generation of a statue was precisely to pre-exist as unenformed, to persist through the generation by acquiring a form, and indeed, to persist, at least possibly, after the destruction of the statue. Now Aristotle insists that a body is not like that at all. Although bronze is bronze, whether

---

[8] Aristotle's appeals to homonymy are varied, in part because he has a range of different kinds of non-equivalent conceptions at work in his critical and constructive philosophy. For a full treatment of Aristotle on homonymy, see Shields (1999).

Hermes-shaped or not, and is for this very reason well suited to be the matter for the generation of a statue explained in hylomorphic terms, a body without its form is not a body at all—except homonymously.

Reflecting on this second purport, we can push the problem to a deeper level—to the point where a contradiction looms for Aristotle. According to the hylomorphic account of generation, matter is only contingently enformed. According to the account of *De Anima*, the body is the matter of the soul, which is its form; yet bodies are necessarily, and not contingently, ensouled. So, it may appear that bodies, as matter, are both contingently and necessarily enformed by the souls whose matter they are.

In view of this threatening result it is natural to wonder why Aristotle wants to insist that the body is only homonymously a body; or, looked at from the opposite angle, it becomes natural to wonder why, if he thinks a dead body is only homonymously a body, Aristotle thinks it appropriate to treat soul-body relations in hylomorphic terms. Surely, in either case, his commitment to the homonymy of the body is the fly in the ointment. If only he would retract that claim, then the hylomorphic approach to soul and body could proceed smoothly and generate whatever other theoretical advantages that may flow from it. Indeed, one might conclude by way of pre-emption that the easiest solution to the problem identified would be simply to rescind the judgement about the body's homonymy. That would also then have the additional benefit of removing whatever linguistic oddness follows upon Aristotle's claim.

Such a pre-emptory solution proves inadvisedly expedient. For there is in the first instance little hope of any such rescission. Moreover, even a brief exploration of Aristotle's motivation for thinking of bodies as necessarily ensouled will reveal something of lasting significance about his hylomorphic analysis of soul-body relations.

On the first matter, Aristotle is not at liberty simply to retract his claim that dead bodies are only homonymously bodies. For in making this judgement, Aristotle relies upon what is for him a deeply entrenched metaphysical principle of kind individuation, a broad thesis of *functional determination*, according to which 'all things are defined by their function' (*Meteorologica* iv 12, 390a10–15; cf. *Generation of Animals* II 1,734b24–31; *Politics* i

2, 1253a19–25). This thesis states necessary and sufficient conditions for something's being a member of some kind *F* such that all and only *F* things manifest the function characteristic of that kind. So, for example, something is a tin opener if and only if it can be used to do the things a tin opener can do. No digital camera is a tin opener; rather, all and only devices which can be used to open tins are tin openers. In the context of *De Anima*, one consequence of this functional determination thesis seems to be that nothing incapable of performing the functions associated with human bodies—digesting, perceiving, thinking—will qualify as actual human bodies. Instead, something which looks like a human body but which lacks the ability to perform these functions will have more in common, in terms of kind membership, with a statue of a body than with a living body. This is why Aristotle uses the example of a statue's eye to illustrate the homonymy of *eye*. In any event, in virtue of his commitment to a functional determination thesis, Aristotle is not at liberty simply to decide that human bodies might exist unensouled: for it is only the ensouled human body which is capable of engaging in the functions characteristic of life.

Importantly, there is a second, less obvious reason for coming to believe that a body without a soul is only homonymously a body, a reason which also and independently helps to commend hylomorphism, especially as it is contrasted with Platonism. On an easy and elementary approach to soul and body, one might well, having observed that dead bodies lack something that living humans have, infer that a human being is not just a body, but a body together with a soul. We begin with a body, according to this train of thought, add to it a soul, and we have in result a living human being. Conversely, if we subtract the soul from a living being we are left with a body; and by the same token, if we subtract a body, we are left with a soul.

Aristotle's hylomorphism is unhappy with this easy, fairly pervasive way of thinking of the soul and body; his application of the homonymy principle entails that we do not begin with a body, an element, to which we add a soul, another element, and thereby generate a living animal. On the contrary, there is no body before there is an ensouled bit of matter. From the perspective of hylomorphism this is neither odd nor even linguistically jarring: what makes a single body a single body through time is precisely its being a co-ordinated set of physical activities individuated by their subordination to a single life. A body sustains material replenishment, taking on nutrition and sloughing off waste; there is no single quantity of matter which is the body. Rather, the body is that diachronic continuant, bounded in space and time, which is unified by a single principle whose presence makes the body one body and not many discrete processes. This is what Aristotle intends when he claims in *De Anima* that the human body is something *organic* (*DA* II 1, 412a28–b1, b6). He means that it is an entity in the fashion of an organ or a tool, something whose unity derives from the function or end which structures it. This end, though, is given by the presence of the soul as an organizing principle. Consequently, when there is no soul, there is no body—except, again, in the sense in which we may say that a statue has an eye, homonymously.

If the homonymy of the body is thus moored to a deeper metaphysical principle, and if this doctrine seems sensitive to some striking features regarding diachronic unity, then it is not easily or appropriately rescinded. If that is right, however, we are left with our looming contradiction. If hylomorphism demands that matter is contingently enformed and homonymy demands that bodies are necessarily ensouled, then if souls are forms, it seems as if bodies are both necessarily and contingently enformed. That is the problem with which we began.

There remains open, however, another direction of resolution. Perhaps Aristotle can yet say that there is a body which is necessarily actually ensouled, that body which we have identified as the diachronic continuant which is the human body, and another body, at a lower level, so to speak, which is only contingently enformed. In this vein, it is worth reflecting that Aristotle regularly distinguishes between the proximate and non-proximate matter of a compound of form and matter (*Met.* Δ 6, 1016a19–24; H 4, 1044a15–25; Θ 7, 1049a24–7). Non-proximate matter is the matter which underlies the matter used in the generation of some compound; and it would be true but misleading in the extreme to cite the non-proximate matter in an account of hylomorphic generation. If your house is made of bricks and mortar, then it is in one sense true, but surely misleading, to say that you live in a house made of mud. Between its being mud and its being the matter of your house, the earth and water were formed and fired into brick. So, the proximate matter of your house is brick and the non-proximate matter is mud. Similarly, on this model, the proximate matter of the human being is a body, an *organic body*, even though we may also speak of matter below the level of the organic body, the non-proximate matter. If only the body as proximate matter is necessarily enformed, then there may yet be some non-proximate matter underlying the generation of a living being which remains only contingently enformed.

Now, this much may already seem to postulate one body too many; and it may seem thus an offence to parsimony. Or it may seem plainly at odds with entrenched linguistic habit or common sense. While these and other like charges merit investigation, note that such investigation already cedes a crucial point to Aristotle's side, that hylomorphism and homonymy do not jointly generate any direct contradiction. On the contrary, a wedding of hylomorphism and homonymy in the domain of living beings yields an immediately attractive result regarding the diachronic individuation of living bodies. Aristotle assumes, quite rightly, that living bodies are non-conventional diachronic unities; and he further demands, consequently and again rightly, an account of souls and bodies capable of explaining this fact. When hylomorphism attempts such an explanation, it does so without lapsing into any immediate contradiction or conceptual confusion. This may, however, seem modest praise for the theory. That is, though, to misconstrue the current dialectical position. This response is not intended to assess the ultimate tenability of hylomorphism, but rather to open the door to such assessment by absolving the theory of an initially well-reasoned allegation of incoherence. The theory's ultimate appraisal will rest, as in the case of its competitors, on its final explanatory power.

## IV. THE FACULTIES OF THE SOUL

It is sometimes contended, misleadingly, that the Aristotelian soul is a 'set of capacities'.[9] This is misleading, first, because the

---

[9] Barnes (1971–2), Sorabji (1974). For one difficulty with proceeding in this way, see Hamlyn (1993: 96): 'it is difficult to see how the soul, if it is a set of dispositions, could be more than a necessary condition of the actual functioning of the body'.

Aristotelian soul is not a set, and more importantly, second, because it is not an aggregative entity at all (414b28–32, 432a22–b6). That said, this sort of judgement does reflect Aristotle's dominant preoccupation in the positive books of *De Anima*: he is more concerned with characterizing in detail the soul's faculties, or capacities,[10] than articulating and defending soul-body hylomorphism in the abstract. There is, however, some difficulty in determining precisely how many faculties he recognizes. Initially, he lists only four: (i) the nutritive faculty, the broadest of all faculties, which belongs to all (mortal) living beings;[11] (ii) perception (*aisthêsis*), which receives the lion's share of attention, its treatment requiring roughly one-third of the entire *De Anima*; (iii) reason (*nous*), whose ultimate status has been fiercely disputed through the ages; and (iv) locomotion, which does not command as much interest as the other three capacities (413a20–4, b16–23, 414a29–31). Aristotle eventually also introduces both *imagination* (*phantasia*, sometimes rendered as *appearance*) and *desire* (*orektikon*) as capacities, the latter in connection with his characterization of locomotion in animals. He does not strive to offer an intrinsic characterization of either.

---

[10] Depending upon how we happen to be using the terms 'capacity' or 'faculty' we might or might not be tempted to use them interchangeably: in some contexts, this seems unobjectionable, in others tendentious and problematic. In the latter case, one might, for instance, suppose that a dog has a capacity to bite without wishing to ascribe to him a biting faculty. This is so, however, only when a faculty is understood to cut more deeply than a mere ability, where a faculty is, rather, something like a deeply explanatory power, as it is, e.g., in Locke, when he says that 'The Understanding and Will, are two Faculties of the Mind' (*Essay Concerning Human Understanding* II.xix.117). In general, Aristotle's Greek uses a single word with the suffix '-*ikon*' (e.g. *aisthêtikon*) to mark powers and abilities and capacities indifferently (so, e.g., the power to perceive, an ability to perceive, or the perceptual faculty). Often it is clear what Aristotle intends. Still, it is sometimes controversial as to whether he means something deep and structural or rather something relatively superficial when using words thus suffixed. In these contexts, there is no neutral or uncontroversial way to render his Greek. In what follows, I presume that Aristotle is asking questions and making claims about the soul's faculties, understood as fundamental, explanatorily deep, or structural features of the soul, in line with Locke's diction in English. See Shields (2015) for a discussion of the terminology of 'powers', 'capacities', 'dispositions', 'potentialities', and 'faculties'. Needless to say, we should not expect regimented consistency or even crisp delineations in their applications.

[11] The qualifier 'mortal' is required because Aristotle suggests that among divine beings, reason can exist without the lower faculties (*DA* 413a31–2; cf. *Met.* 1073a23–44).

The plan of the non-critical chapters of *De Anima* tracks this list of capacities in an orderly fashion, though with digressions and polemics punctuating the flow throughout. Aristotle first considers the nutritive faculty, including the capacities for growth, decay, and reproduction, in *De Anima* II 4; perception in *De Anima* II 5–III 2, with general accounts of the entire faculty being advanced in II 5 and then again in II 12, between which chapters Aristotle takes up each of the five senses individually; imagination only briefly in *De Anima* III 3; reason in *De Anima* III 4–8; and desire in *De Anima* III 9–11, which focuses especially on the aetiology of action.[12]

## A. THE NUTRITIVE SOUL

Aristotle's interest in nutrition and the nutritive soul derives in general from his pervasive interest in biological explanation, but more locally in *De Anima* from his contention that every living thing, every ensouled compound, has at least the nutritive capacity. This capacity is 'the first and most common capacity of soul, in virtue of which life belongs to all living things' (*DA* II 4, 415a24–5). Although his reason for believing this is likely to be in some measure observationally based, it is also to some degree theoretically driven. While it may seem initially odd to suppose that a psychology should study nutrition, which might seem to lie exclusively within the ambit of the empirical biologist or physiologist, Aristotle notes that notions of eating and nutrition are in their very natures implicated in the process of living. Bare absorption is not eating, since a napkin absorbs spilt wine without drinking it; so, eating, and taking on nutrition generally, must evidently involve the absorption *for a purpose*, a purpose involving the ends of some living system or other. Further, every living creature comes into being, matures, declines, and dies. Without a faculty for nutrition, all this would be impossible (*DA* III 12, 434a22–434b18; cf. *Part. An.* 687a24–690a10; *Met.* 1075a16–25).

---

[12] Because Aristotle is primarily concerned with offering detailed positive characterizations of only the three dominant faculties of soul, we will introduce only the nutritive, perceptional, and rational souls here, leaving the presentations of imagination and locomotion to the introductions of the individual chapters where his discussions of them occur.

So, Aristotle concludes, psychology, whose scope of inquiry ranges over all living beings, must study the nutritive faculty. Part of the theoretical motivation for treating nutrition as a distinctively life-implicating process can be seen more readily in *De Generatione et Corruptione* than in *De Anima*, where, however, the same basic framework seems in place. We say that some things *get bigger*, observes Aristotle, but that other things *grow*. A pile of leaves gets bigger as more leaves are added to it, as does a building as bricks are successively set into place. If we rake two piles of leaves into one another, there may be no ready fact of the matter as to which one, if either, became bigger in the process. By contrast, when a girl eats an omelette, there is no tendency to suppose that it is arbitrary as to whether it is the omelette or the girl that has got bigger. It is the girl. She in fact has grown, because the matter of the omelette has been subordinated to her life directionality. As Aristotle says in this connection: 'The substance of the one remains unchanged, but the substance of the other (viz. the food) does not' (*Gen. et Corr.* 321a32–3).

This observation holds significance for Aristotle's account of the soul in *De Anima* insofar as it challenges a certain unsophisticated form of materialism which seeks to explain all change, including all growth, in terms of the traits and tendencies of the simple material elements. A living system exhibits not just change, but constrained and patterned growth, which is, Aristotle argues, change towards some definite goal, a goal whose attainment constitutes maturity for an organism. In this way, then, nutrition and the nutritive soul already implicate the psychologist in an appeal to final causation: limited and patterned growth, the kind of change characteristic of living systems, proceeds with reference to an end against which judgements of success or failure are appropriately made. Whereas a pile of leaves neither matures nor flourishes when made bigger, a lion cub grows in accordance with a discernible, structured directionality and for this reason can already be judged to be flourishing or failing in its own right.

This is why in *De Anima* Aristotle adopts a critical attitude towards Empedocles' explanation of growth, which is given in wholly materialistic terms:

Empedocles was not right when he added that growth occurs for plants downward, when they take root, because earth is naturally borne in this direction, and upward growth occurs because fire moves in a like manner. Nor even does he understand up and down rightly. For up and down are not the same for all things as for the universe; rather, as the head is in animals, so the roots are in plants, if it is because of their functions that one ought to say that organs are the same or different. Moreover, what is it that holds fire and earth together, even though they are borne in opposite directions? For they will be torn apart if there is nothing which hinders them. If there is something, however, this will be the soul—the cause of growing and being nourished (*DA* II 4, 415b27–a9).

So, Aristotle concludes, life is as such end-directed, and the nutritive soul provides an explanatorily ineliminable factor in capturing and explicating its directionality.


## B. PERCEPTION

Aristotle's account of perception involves him in the second of his three most central appeals to hylomorphic explanation in *De Anima*, the first having occurred in his general explication of soul-body relations. As happened with the first appeal, and as will happen again with the third, his analysis of thinking or reasoning (*noêsis*), Aristotle's invocation of hylomorphism in explaining perception proves both promising and vexing.

We begin with a simple example of change analysed hylomorphically. A grey fence is altered when it is painted white. The fence loses one form, the form whiteness, only to gain another, the form greyness. The basic model of change is given, then, in terms of *form receptivity*. Even so, the material side of the transaction places constraints on the feasible varieties of form receptivity: although a fence can be made to be grey, because it has a surface, it cannot be made to be *morose* or to be *reprogrammed*: a fence is, categorially speaking, not the right sort of subject to receive the forms requisite for these kinds of changes. Socrates might become morose, and an Apple computer might be reprogrammed to enhance its processing speed; and in each case, the subject of change has, in virtue of being the kind of entity it is, the capacity to receive the form and so to undergo the change in question.

Perception adheres in broad outline to this basic model: 'perception comes about with an organ's being changed and affected...for it seems to be a kind of alteration' (*DA* II 5, 416b33–4).[13] So, as with alteration generally, perception occurs when two reciprocally suited agents interact. When something capable of being affected by a sensible form is so affected, it alters and perception occurs. Again, though, the requisite alteration will take place only if the entities related in perception are appropriately suited to one another. An odour, for example, may affect something not capable of perceiving without perception occurring. A man in a smoke-filled tavern will smell smoke, though his wool jacket will be affected by the same smoke without perceiving it. A man, and not a jacket, has the capacity to perceive. It seems that the origin of the odour, the cigarette smoke, is the same in both cases of alteration. The alteration which qualifies as an instance of perception, or which eventuates in an instance of perception, is the one which occurs in the suitably structured patient.

Aristotle's contention about material suitability may sound initially trivial or even banal: whatever becomes actually *F* must already be possibly *F*. He intends something more, however, because a possibility is not yet a potentiality. That is, Aristotle insists that specific forms of change require the existence of suitable *capacities* in the changing subjects, where a *bona fide* potentiality requires the existence of a capacity understood as a structured ability and not a mere possibility. We might say, in a flight of fancy, that a sponge could come to be sad, because we might well imagine a cartoon sponge to speak and sing and dance.

---

[13] Some care is required here, however, since Aristotle distinguishes two grades of actuality in perception, and insists that the transition from first to second actuality is either not an instance of alteration or is a sort of alteration different from the sort which proceeds in accordance with the standard model, where one contrary (e.g. the white of a fence) is destroyed by another (the grey). See notes to 417a30 and 417b2. His point is more readily illustrated in the case of thought: there is a transition from thinking *that p* but not doing so occurrently to actually thinking *that p* at a given time, though there is no destruction of one contrary or another in the process. Thus, for instance, if asked, I will tell you that, yes, I think that the earth revolves around the sun, though I would not otherwise have been occurrently entertaining that thought; nothing seems destroyed when I move from not entertaining it to entertaining it. See also IV C below, on reason, for further discussion of this point.

If we allow for the moment that imaginability entails possibility, then we will also allow that it is possible for sponges to do these things; but we should not look upon the sponges in the sea as having such capacities. This is what Aristotle means to convey when he claims: 'the perceptual faculty is in potentiality such as the object of perception already is in actuality' (*DA* 418a3–4). Form reception results in perception only when it occurs in a living being endowed with the capacity of perception (*aisthêsis*).

So, in instances of perception, as in alteration generally, a thing capable of being affected is *enformed* by the object which affects it. Alteration, then, says Aristotle, consists in the affected things 'becoming like' the agent which affects it (*DA* 418a3–6, 424a17–21). Taken together, then, Aristotle's hylomorphic analysis of perception in terms of form reception has the following components.

> A perceiving subject $S$ perceives some sensible object **o** if and only if: (i) $S$ has the capacity $C$ requisite for receiving **o**'s sensible form $F$; (ii) **o** acts upon $C$ by enforming it; and (iii) $C$ becomes isomorphic with **o**'s sensible form by becoming itself $F$.

Note that in English, as in Greek, we may speak more or less narrowly about an 'object of perception' (an *aisthêton*). That is, we may speak of 'smelling smoke' or, more narrowly, of 'smelling an odour of smoke'. In the broad sense, we may speak indifferently of smelling or seeing smoke; though, in the narrow and stricter sense, we would not, and could not, speak of seeing an odour of smoke or of smelling the whiteness of smoke. Aristotle sometimes speaks of objects of perception broadly and sometimes narrowly, just as we do (418a25, 424a29–b31, 426a23, 431b21–3, 432a3–6). The schema provided employs the broad sense.

Although providing the general structure of Aristotle's theory of perception, this schema by itself does little to explicate the details of the theory, which in some cases prove both intricate and elusive. Fairly clearly, any eventual appraisal of Aristotle's theory will be coloured by the explications of each of these clauses. The first (i) is intended to capture the capacities, both purely passive and active, required for perception to occur in humans and other animals. The second (ii) makes plain that an object of sense enforms a sensory capacity, but does not begin to explain how this transpires. Thus, for example, one will want to know whether the bare presence of a sensible object to a functioning sensory capacity is, in Aristotle's view, sufficient for enforming, and if so, whether that much is sufficient for perception. This last query in effect invites an explication of (iii), the third and most controversial clause in Aristotle's analysis. Controversy surrounding this clause derives from the fact that it is not at all clear what is meant by Aristotle's contention that the sensory faculty is 'made like' its objects in perception; how Aristotle's hylomorphic analysis treats perception as a straightforward instance of alteration; or even why Aristotle thinks perception should be modelled in hylomorphic terms in the first place. After all, if we focus on a base case, we can agree that a white fence painted grey is made like the grey paint by being made to *exemplify* the colour grey: the fence becomes grey. Is it Aristotle's contention, then, that the sense organs are made like the objects of perception by being made to exemplify the sensible forms exemplified by those objects? This seems to be precisely what an unblinking application of the hylomorphic analysis of alteration recommends; on this approach, hylomorphism subordinates all instances of alteration to the base-case approach. This is, importantly, just what one school of interpretation of Aristotle theory of perception contends. Their approach we may call *literalism*.[14]

Literalism has some obvious advantages. Clause (iii) of our schema requires that the sensory faculty become somehow like the sensible forms of objects. According to literalism, the likeness in question is *sameness*: since shared property exemplification is the limiting case of isomorphism, it is easy to discern how, on this approach, (iii) is to be unpacked. When he says that a sensory faculty is made like its objects in perception, Aristotle means just that and nothing more or less. If it sounds crude to say that an instance of perceiving red occurs just because a red object paints my retina red, then that is only because Aristotle's theory is crude and obviously now empirically outmoded.

There are, however, some obvious difficulties pertaining to literalism as an interpretation of Aristotle's account of perception (*aisthêsis*). The first concerns the question of whether he can

---

[14] Literalism found its original proponent in Sorabji (1974). Everson (1999) offers the most detailed discussion given in literalist terms. For a comprehensive overview of the development of the debate, see Caston (2005).

actually be thought to believe, as a straightforwardly empirical matter, that my eyes become red and green and brown and orange and black when I stand before *The Fall of the Rebel Angels* by Pieter Bruegel the Elder. When I see this painting, do the shapes as well as the colours become exemplified by my eyes? Do my retinas become demon-shaped? Moving to other sensory modalities, it seems difficult to know precisely how my aural faculty comes to *exemplify* the sound of Jussi Björling singing *Ombra mai fu* or of a locomotive pulling a train out of Paddington Station. In general, it seems hard to understand how, given (i)—the claim that the sensory faculty must be of an appropriate sort to be affected—the being affected in question can amount to shared property exemplification.

Moreover, it is difficult to appreciate why on this approach, (i)–(iii) do not have additional immediately awkward results. For, if we adopt literalism, (i)–(iii) jointly seem to require that every instance of property exemplification induced by a sensible object in a being capable of perceiving accrues in an actual instance of perception. This would not seem to be the case, however. On the contrary, my flesh can become heated without my perceiving heat. Similarly, a potential perceiver can be in the presence of all manner of perceptibles without perceiving all of them, or indeed any of them. In these ways, (iii) interpreted literally has some uncomfortable results. If the response is that something more than shared property exemplification is necessary for perception, then a question emerges as to what extra condition or conditions might be added to (i)–(iii) by the literalist so that Aristotle will have an account which is at least schematically correct.

Finally, literalists have a tendency to speak as if it is the sensory organ which is made to exemplify the sensible form of an object of perception,[15] and we have so far been following them in that practice. Properly speaking, however, Aristotle is keen to distinguish the faculty of perception (the *aisthêtikon*) from the organ of perception (the *aisthêtêrion*) and to suggest that the capacity or potential (*dunamis*) for perceiving, while in the organ, is nonetheless distinct from it. One way it is distinct, according to Aristotle,

---

[15] Sorabji (1974: 49 n.22) and (1992).

is that neither the perceptual faculty nor perception itself is a magnitude (*megethos*), while the sensory organ is. Thus, he says:

The primary sense organ is that in which this sort of potentiality resides. The sense organ and this potentiality are, then, the same, though their being is different. For what does the perceiving is a certain magnitude; nevertheless the perceptual faculty is not; nor is perception a magnitude, but is rather a certain principle (*logos*) and a potentiality of that thing (*DA* 423a24–8).

According to this way of looking at the matter, perception cannot be identical with an organ exemplifying a property at a given time; for the one is a magnitude and the other is not. Consequently, a literalist interpretation of perception strains against various commitments Aristotle seems disposed to accept.

That said, there is no reason to conclude that literalism must be incorrect, or that it crucially misunderstands the kind of isomorphism captured in (iii). On the contrary, literalism, whatever its exegetical or philosophical drawbacks, has one clear advantage over some of its rivals: it explains in a plain and unflinching way what Aristotle means when he says that in perception what perceives becomes like the object of perception. Shared property exemplification is likeness par excellence.

This easy explication of isomorphism is significant in part because the second main approach to Aristotle's theory of perception, the *intentionalism* owing in modern times to the philosopher and Aristotelian commentator Franz Brentano, has a much less direct story to tell.[16] The intentionalist denies that there is good textual or philosophical reason for supposing that the kind of isomorphism relevant to (iii) in Aristotle's theory of perception is sameness of property exemplification. Rather, relying on the thought that perception is not even a magnitude, while the body exemplifying a sensible form surely is, the intentionalist concludes that the isomorphism in question somehow merely involves representation or encoding in the perceptual faculty. The idea here is akin to the way in which the binary language of a computer digitally encodes information across a variety of media. Just as a compact disc encodes without exemplifying the sounds of Mahler's Second Symphony in C Minor,

---

[16] Brentano (1867).

so the sense faculty encodes without exemplifying the sensible forms of the object of perception. Similarly, just as there is an isomorphism between the disc, a score, and a performance across a variety of media, so too is there an isomorphism involved in perception. Thus, isomorphism is not shared property exemplification but rather some manner of *sameness in structure*. This, says the intentionalist, is what Aristotle intends when he says that perception is a certain kind of *logos*, a principle, or structure, or form (*DA* 424b27–8).

The intentionalist approach has much to be said on its behalf, beginning with its ability to avoid the untoward consequences of literalism. Still, no one should rush to conclude that intentionalism is clearly to be preferred as an interpretation of Aristotle's theory of perception. To begin, one can pose to the intentionalist a question which made difficulties for the literalist and to no immediately better effect: is intentional encoding sufficient for perception? If so, why does a compact disc not perceive? Presumably, the intentionalist will respond that in the schema adopted, (ii) requires that the object of perception *cause* the perceptual faculty to encode the sensible form. That does little, however, to explain why, e.g., the air, the medium through which the sensible quality evidently moves, does not perceive. The intentionalist can then, rightly, point out that (i) requires that there be a capacity of the right sort caused to encode the form. Perhaps now, however, the intentionalist merely postpones the question of why some things are suited to perceive and other things are not. An unhappy answer, if intended as a complete answer, would be that perceptual faculties are so structured that they encode perceptible forms in a perceptual sort of way. If this is the best intentionalism has to offer, then, things will turn out as they did in the case of literalism. At this juncture intentionalism may fairly be criticized for introducing a promising approach to isomorphism only to leave unexplained (at best) some central features of perception.

It should be clear, however, that whether pursuing a literalist or an intentionalist approach to Aristotelian perception, the crucial issue to be investigated pertains to the question of how the notion of *form reception* is to be understood against the background of Aristotle's broader hylomorphism. If perceptual alteration is understood to be simply an instance of hylomorphic alteration, then literalism captures the purport of the theory. If, however, form reception in perception introduces complexities to the general hylomorphic approach to alteration, then perception is not merely an instance of hylomorphism, but an extension of that doctrine into a new and more complex domain, well beyond its comfortable base-case application. In either case, Aristotle's application of hylomorphic explanation is hardly direct or unproblematic. Just as transpired in the case of soul-body relations, an application of hylomorphism to perception offers a rich framework of explanation even while taxing that framework's resources.

## C. REASON

Aristotle's final appeal to hylomorphism in *De Anima* is also his most attenuated. He extends the model of form receptivity familiar from perception to reasoning (or thinking, *noêsis*), though the forms received are no longer perceptible (*aisthêta*) but rather thinkable or intelligible (*noêta*). Reason (*nous*, often rendered as *mind* or *intellect*) is 'the part of the soul by which it knows and understands' (*DA* III 4, 429a9–10; cf. III 4, 428a5; III 9, 432b26; III 12, 434b3). Like the other faculties of soul, reason is thus understood at least initially in broadly functional terms. However, as Aristotle signals early on in *De Anima*, reason seems somehow more substance-like than the other faculties of soul, perhaps because it is also less obviously dependent upon the body than they are. He says, for instance, 'Reason would seem to come about in us being a certain substance and not to be destroyed' (*DA* 408b18–19). When he turns to his own positive account of reason in *De Anima* III 4–6, Aristotle does seek to differentiate it from the other faculties of soul on the grounds that it is unmixed with the body and that it lacks a bodily organ, whereas the others are so mixed because they cannot function without being realized in organs (*DA* III 4, 429a24–7). Nothing digests or perceives without being bodily; evidently thinking in Aristotle's view lacks such corporeal entanglements.

Even so, the general model of form receptivity deployed in the analysis of perception re-emerges in Aristotle's account of thought. Indeed, Aristotle draws the parallel overtly: 'To be sure, if reasoning is like perceiving, it would consist in being somehow affected by the object of reason or in something else of this sort' (*DA* III 4, 429a13–15). He evidently endorses the antecedent, because he goes on to derive conclusions from the consequent. So, the same general schema obtains, given now, though, in terms of intelligible forms:

> A subject *S* thinks some intelligible object o if and only if: (i) *S* has the capacity *C* requisite for receiving o's intelligible form *F*; (ii) o acts upon *C* by enforming it; and (iii) *C* becomes isomorphic with o's intelligible form in being itself *F*.

Note in this case, however, that in neither English nor Greek does the phrase 'object of reason' (or, thought; *noêton*) enjoy the easy movement between the broad and narrow senses that occur in the case of 'object of perception' (*aisthêton*) (the difference between *smelling a cigar* and *smelling the odour of a cigar* respectively). Still, if we come around to the view that, e.g., a species has an intelligible form, but is not identical with that form, then we will be in a position to draw an analogous sort of distinction, albeit less naturally, between thinking of the species *tiger* (=broad object of thought) and thinking of the form, *being a tiger*, realized by all and only tigers (=narrow object of thought, the intelligible form properly construed). Once again, the schema presented relies on objects broadly construed, though it can be translated without loss of meaning into the terms of the narrow conception where greater precision is wanted.

In any case, Aristotle's approach to thinking parallels his approach to perception in invoking form receptivity as its crucial explanatory factor. In the case of thinking, however, he makes plain that form reception does not involve property exemplification (a fact which, arguing back from the analogy adumbrated seems to have consequences for the theory of perception as well). When one thinks of a stone, says Aristotle, 'It is not the stone which is in the soul, but its form' (*DA* III 8, 431b29–432a1; III 4, 429a27). This seems obvious enough. If the intelligible form of the stone is understood as *the form of being a stone*, then a human can hardly come to exemplify it, since only a stone exemplifies the form of being a stone and no human is a stone. It follows then, again on the assumption that the intelligible form of an object of reason is simply that object's essential form, that the form must be received not by way of a thinker's coming to exemplify that form, but rather by somehow encoding it.

Indeed, as it turns out, Aristotle's conception of *nous* precludes him from saying that reason could exemplify the form of any material entity: reason, he says, 'is not mixed with the body' (*DA* III 4, 429a24–5). Although both the precise meaning and motivation for this claim are subject to interpretive controversy, one consequence, according to Aristotle, is evidently that reason cannot have an organ, and is in this way expressly disanalogous from perception (*DA* III 4, 429a25–7). Having no organ, reason cannot be held to exemplify the sorts of forms the sense organs realize, such as themselves being hot or cold. So, the isomorphism at work in (iii) clearly cannot be shared property exemplification. Accordingly, Aristotle is reasonably understood as holding that *S* thinks some object of reason o whenever *S*'s mind is made like that object by coming to represent its defining or structural features.

Strikingly, however, now the first clause (i), that a thinking subject must have a capacity for receiving an intelligible form, a clause which seemed almost analytic as regards perception, begins to generate difficulties for Aristotle. For in the case of perception, Aristotle had maintained that the faculty has its primary residence in the sensory organ, even though the organ and the faculty need to be distinguished. By contrast, in the case of thought, as we have seen, no organ is available. So what is the capacity of thought which is made to be isomorphic with the objects of thought in thinking? It is not something residing in an organ; nor is it anything mixed with the body. Indeed, remarkably, at least before becoming active, reason is actually *nothing at all*. More precisely, as Aristotle says, reason 'is in actuality none of the things which are before it reasons' (*DA* III 4, 429a24). His motivations for arriving at this conclusion are not always transparent, but surely involve centrally his commitment to the plasticity of thought, the thesis that reason is unrestricted with respect to its range of objects. If reason is to be capable of thinking all potential objects of thought, as Aristotle contends that it is, then it cannot be anything in actuality before thinking (*DA* III 4, 429a18–22).

However this argument is ultimately to be understood, it now seems plain that in advancing it Aristotle simultaneously invokes and threatens the applicability of the hylomorphic analysis of change to thinking. On the standard model, alteration occurs when something capable of being affected comes to be affected by a form of a specified sort. Thus, some wood comes to be cut and assembled into a table, and then the surface of the table comes to be varnished. Obviously, even necessarily it is tempting to say, something pre-exists and is such as to be altered in the relevant way. Indeed, (i) enshrines just this thought. If we now learn that reason is in actuality nothing before it thinks, it strains comprehension to understand how it is altered or affected in coming to think. Again, put the other way around, if reason is unaffected and does not even exist in actuality before it is actively thinking, then it seems difficult to see why the hylomorphic model of change should be supposed a natural framework for explicating this activity.

Even so, whatever inherent difficulties there may be involved in Aristotle's appeals to hylomorphism in explicating thinking, it remains open to him to extend and develop that explanatory framework even as it is being invoked. To some extent, this seems to be Aristotle's actual practice in *De Anima*. It should be noted in this connection that hylomorphic change is not understood by Aristotle in a unidimensional way. He distinguishes between what we may call the base case of alteration, when one contrary property is destroyed and replaced by another in the course of a change, as when a grey fence is painted white, and another sort in which no destruction occurs. If a native English speaker learns German, then we say that she knows German. While in Great Britain, she rarely uses that knowledge, though when she visits Germany, she uses it regularly. While in Great Britain, we may say, she is in one way a potential and in another way an actual German speaker: although she actually has the knowledge, she is not at that time actually using it and in this way merely a potential German speaker. When she comes to use her German upon her arrival in Germany, then she actualizes her potentiality, though in the process she does not lose or have destroyed any other of her actual features. In this case, put more abstractly, nothing is destroyed, but rather that which is already dispositionally $F$ becomes occurrently $F$ by engaging in some $F$-ish activity. Significantly, it is this second kind of alteration, non-destructive alteration, to which Aristotle appeals in explicating many psychic activities. In these cases, he contends, what we have is either not an instance of alteration or 'is a different kind of alteration,' with the result that one who changes in this way 'either should not be said to be affected or there are two types of alteration' (*DA* II 5, 417b6–16).

If we approach hylomorphic explanation in psychology armed with this more expansive understanding of alteration, then some progress appears possible in understanding Aristotle's otherwise perplexing remarks about the statement that reason does not exist in actuality before thinking. Aristotle may simply be supposing that reason is akin to the most basic stuff involved in material changes, stuff which, if it exists at all, will be ultimately plastic, capable of underlying even elemental transmutations. Reason, on the hypothesis of its absolute plasticity relative to the possible objects of thought available to it, will be similar: it will be nothing in its own nature, before actual thinking begins. Once it attains some actual conceptual furnishings, then it is in a way potential still, though now actual too. Looked at from this vantage point, then, reason is in the cognitive realm what prime matter is in the material realm, something whose actual existence already involves our conceiving it in its altered state, but whose featureless character can be grasped by abstracting backwards into the state in which it is nothing actual in its own nature. Nothing incoherent threatens in this approach, since Aristotle is not committed to holding both that the mind exists in actuality before thinking and that it is in such a condition merely potential. What he holds is precisely the opposite, that reason is 'in actuality none of the things which are before it reasons' (*DA* III 4, 429a24).

At any rate, as with applications to soul-body relations and perception, hylomorphism's third and final deployment in psychology proves simultaneously illuminating and challenging. To the extent that thinking must serve the double duty of representing the world and putting a thinker into direct contact with the world's intelligible structure, Aristotle's approach to its analysis proves both challenging and promising in its very intricacy.

## V. CONCLUSION

Aristotle's psychological theory has justifiably commanded the attention of philosophers through the ages, even down to the present time. As a consequence, however, little can be said about even its most fundamental commitments without inviting scholarly dissent. In some cases, this is due to unresolved obscurities in Aristotle's own exceptionally terse manner of expression; in others, it derives from the fact that his contentions are inchoate, if richly suggestive; in still others, however, it can only be a function of the subject matter itself. Issues concerning soul-body relations, perception, and the features of intellection, including especially those pertaining to the nature of intentionality, all continue to resist consensus-building approaches. Aristotle's *De Anima* propounds theories about these matters which, though nascent, are distinctive, and which, though challenging, continue to be studied primarily because those who do the studying return again and again to find an enduring value in engaging the controversies this fruitful text inspires.

# A NOTE ON THE TEXT

This translation uses as its base text Ross (1961), which, as a reader for the Press at the time of its publication noted, updates his OCT of 1956 by offering several hundred changes. These are mainly small but judicious, and evidently arose partly in response to a review of Theiler (1958), many of whose readings he adopts, and partly as a result of Ross's own careful post-OCT review of the previously existing text of Förster (1912), whom Ross acknowledges in his Preface.

Ross's text and commentary are often criticized as having fallen below the enviable standard he himself had set in his commentaries on the *Metaphysics* (1924) and *Physics* (1936). While there are some signs of inattention in both the text and especially the commentary, where editorial lapses are sometimes unhappily pronounced, the predominantly negative verdicts on Ross's work on *De Anima* tend to obscure the unsurpassed sense of Aristotelian diction and syntax he brings to bear on his constitution of the text. Even where he does not pause to defend his preferences in anything like the detail they demand, Ross's readings nonetheless command careful consideration. If his commentary shows undue concision, the text it supports offers much to ponder.

It should be emphasized, however, that we do have a text based upon a much broader range of manuscripts than Ross or any other textual critic before him had consulted; it is, unfortunately, not widely known. This is Siwek's *Tractatus De Anima* (1965), which had the benefit of fully collating sixty-five manuscripts, arranged into nine families, as compared with the dozen or so collated by Ross and other modern editors. I have consulted Siwek with profit when reviewing textual difficulties inherent in *De Anima* and have concluded that his text should be much more widely circulated. It is unequalled in its critical apparatus and provides useful guidance to the textual difficulties of *De Anima*.

These difficulties are, alas, very numerous. I have not adopted Ross's readings in some fifty-five passages, and in dozens more I have had serious reservations—though in these cases, any alternative proposal could only be regarded as informed speculation, unmoored to any extant manuscript. As a default policy, I have tried where possible not to deviate from the dominant manuscript traditions, though neither have I followed that policy slavishly. This is because the text as we have it is replete with what Shorey (1901: 151) termed the 'not infrequent anacolutha of the *de Anima*' with its 'hopeless passages which could be cured only by extensive changes'.

It is unsurprising, then, that the text has been very highly emended by scholars of all eras, including in the modern period by Bonitz, Torstrik, Essen, Bywater, Biehl, Christ, Kampe, Susemihl, Barco, Wilson, Rodier, Hicks, and Ross himself. Each successive layer of correction reflects the scholarly sense of the emender; some regard themselves as more and some as less beholden to the manuscript tradition—which is, to be sure, replete with its own formidable complexities. (Nussbaum (1992) provides a very useful overview, omitting, though, discussion of Siwek.) In reviewing the many proposed emendations of the text, one can only proceed with cautious humility, since the ingenious creativity of one critic is as often as not reviled as incautious adventurism by another.

Here Shorey (1901) is a case in point. He rightly finds cause to commend Rodier's excellent, voluminous edition (1900) as prudently conservative, even while pausing to fault his inclusion of 'pages wasted in rejecting with sad civility the wanton emendations of Torstrik, for example' (1901: 157). By contrast, I have noticed after compiling my own readings that some 20 per cent of them adopt or adapt a suggestion of Torstrik's. One may only hope, then, heading in the other direction, that one critic's wanton ways may yet shine an instructive light on the path of another. In some cases, the hope seems warranted, because, to take but one example, the adventurous Torstrik has in some instances offered conjectural emendations on thematic grounds only to find them corroborated by significant manuscripts first collated after his death (so, e.g., at 433a21, which is supported by C, first collated by Förster).

Be that as it may, Anglophone readers need not enter into these tangled disputes to profit from a careful study of Aristotle's *De Anima*. The Clarendon Aristotle Series takes as its mission a plain, forthright exposition of Aristotle's philosophy for the engaged Greekless reader rather than the professional philologist. Still, it behoves us all, in whatever language we read it, to remember that the text of *De Anima* emerges as an unending, slow-motion committee decision: it is, consequently, a perpetual work in progress.

# DISCURSIVE OUTLINE OF *DE ANIMA*

## BOOK I

xlix

Chapter 3
- 414a29–415a13: the faculties of the soul and their priority relations

Chapter 4
- 415a14–416b31: the nutritive and generative soul

Chapter 5
- 416b32–418a6: perception, in general; perception and alteration; kinds of alteration

Chapter 6
- 418a7–25: proper, common, and co-inciding objects of perception

Chapter 7
- 418a26–419b3: sight, seeing, and the objects of sight

Chapter 8
- 419b4–421a6: hearing and the objects of hearing

Chapter 9
- 421a7–422a7: smell, smelling, and the objects of smell

Chapter 10
- 422a8–b16: taste, tasting, and the objects of taste

Chapter 11
- 422b17–424a16: touch, touching, and the objects of touch

Chapter 12
- 424a17–b3: perception in general: the reception of forms without the matter
- 424b3–18: a problem about the nature of form reception in perception

# BOOK III

Chapter 1
- 424b22–425b11: that there are only five senses

Chapter 2
- 425b12–427a16: common perception

## Chapter 3

- 427a17–b29: differentiating imagination from reason and perception
- 428a1–429a9: imagination characterized

## Chapter 4

- 429a10–b22: reason; thinking as form reception; the plasticity of reason
- 429b22–430a9: some difficulties about reason

## Chapter 5

- 430a10–25: active reason; the deathlessness of active reason

## Chapter 6

- 430a26–b31: the objects of reason; truth and falsity in thought

## Chapter 7

- 431a1–b19: fragmentary (flight and pursuit; images and thoughts; discrimination)

## Chapter 8

- 431b20–432a14: fragmentary (the soul is in a way all things; general empiricism; images and thoughts)

## Chapter 9

- 432a15–433a8: difficulties concerning the production of locomotion; desire

## Chapter 10

- 433a9–b30: the production of locomotion; the roles of desire, reason, and imagination in this production

## Chapter 11

- 433b31–434a21: desire, deliberation, and motion in imperfect animals

## Chapter 12

- 434a22–435a10: the faculties of soul and their priority relations; teleological explanation in living beings; hypothetical necessity

## Chapter 13

- 435a11–b25: compositeness in animals; the senses other than touch contribute not only to living, but to living well

# TRANSLATION

## BOOK I

### CHAPTER 1

We count cognition among the fine and honourable things, and **402a** suppose that one kind of cognition is finer and more honourable than another owing to its precision or because of its having better and more marvellous objects; and for both these reasons we may reasonably place an inquiry into the soul into the premier class of study. It also seems that research into the soul contributes greatly 5 to truth in general, and most especially to truth about nature. For the soul is a sort of first principle of animals. We aim to consider and ascertain its nature and essence, and then its properties, of which some seem to be affections peculiar to the soul itself, while others belong to animals as well because of the soul.

Yet grasping anything trustworthy concerning the soul is completely and in every way among the most difficult of affairs. The 10 general form of inquiry being common to many other areas—I mean inquiry concerning essence and what something is— perhaps it might seem to someone that there is some one method for all of the objects of inquiry whose essence we wish to ascertain, just as there is a single method of demonstration for all the properties co-incidental to them, with the result that one would 15 have to inquire what this method is. If, however, there is no single and common method for determining what something is, the task before us becomes more difficult still. For then it will be necessary to lay hold of the way for each area individually. And even if the method should be evident, whether it is demonstration or division or even some other method, the question of where one ought to begin our inquiry already involves many difficulties and quan- 20 daries, for different fields have different starting points, just as for example the fields of numbers and planes do.

It is presumably first of all necessary to determine the genus of the soul and what it is. I mean whether it is some this—that is, a substance—or a quality, or a quantity, or something in some one of the other delineated categories. Further, it is necessary to 25

determine whether it is one of the things which exist in potential-
**402b** ity or whether it is, rather, an actuality. For this makes no small
difference. One must also consider whether it has parts or is
without parts, and whether or not all souls are uniform in kind,
or if not whether they differ in species or in genus. For as things
are, those discussing and inquiring into the soul would seem to
5 consider only the human soul. And one must take care not to
overlook the question of whether there is one account of soul, as
there is one account of animal, or whether there is a different
account for each type of soul, for example, of horse, of dog, of
man, of god, while the universal animal is either nothing or is
posterior to these; and it would be the same if any other common
thing were being predicated.

Further, if there are not many souls but rather the soul has
parts, one must determine whether it is necessary to inquire first
10 into the soul as a whole or into its parts. It is also difficult to
determine which of the parts differ by nature from one another, as
well as whether one ought to inquire into the parts or their
functions first, for example, whether one ought to inquire first
into reasoning or reason, or into perceiving or the perceptual
faculty, and so on for the other parts. And if one ought to inquire
first into their functions, someone might raise a puzzle as to
15 whether one must inquire into their corresponding objects before
these, for example, into the objects of perception before the
faculty of perception, and the objects of reason before reason.

It would seem that not only is ascertaining what a thing is
useful for considering the causes of the properties of substances,
as, for example, in mathematics ascertaining what straight and
curved are, or what a line and plane are, is useful for observing
20 how many right angles the angles of a triangle equal, but also,
conversely, that ascertaining the properties of a substance plays a
great part in knowing what a thing is. For when we can render an
account of all or most of the properties according to imagination,
we will also then be able to speak best about the substance. For
25 the starting point of every demonstration is what a thing is, so
that those formulas which do not lead us to ascertain the properties of a substance, or at least to know of them in a ready sort of
**403a** way, will clearly and in every case be dialectical and vacuous.

There is also a puzzle about the affections of the soul, concerning whether all are common to what has the soul as well or

whether there is something peculiar to the soul itself. This it is necessary to grasp, but not easy. It seems that in most cases the 5 soul neither is affected nor acts without the body, as, for instance, with being angry or confident or appetitive, or, generally, with perceiving; reasoning, however, would seem most of all to be peculiar to it, but if this is a sort of imagination, or not without imagination, it would not be possible for even this to be without the body. If, then, some one of the functions or affections of 10 the soul is peculiar to it, it would be possible for the soul to be separated; but if there is nothing peculiar to it, it would not be separable. Rather, it will be just like the straight, insofar as it is straight: though it has many properties, for example touching a bronze sphere at a point,[1] nevertheless, when it is separated, the[2] straight will not touch the sphere in this way; for it is not something separable, since it always involves some body. 15

And it would seem that all the affections of the soul involve the body—anger, gentleness, fear, pity, courage, as well as joy, and loving and hating. For at the same time as these, the body is affected in some way. This is shown by the fact that sometimes, even though strong and evident affections are present, we are not 20 provoked or made afraid, while at other times we are moved by something small and obscure, whenever the body is agitated and in the condition it is in when angry. This is even clearer from the fact that sometimes though nothing frightful is present, people come to have the affections of a frightened person. If this is so, it is clear that the affections are accounts in matter. Consequently, 25 definitions will be of this sort, for example: 'being angry is a sort of motion of a body of such a sort, or of a part or capacity of a body, brought about by this for the sake of that.' And for these reasons, a consideration of the soul, either all souls or this sort of soul, is already in the province of the natural scientist.

The natural scientist and the dialectician would define each of these affections differently, for example, what anger is. The dia- 30 lectician will define it as desire for retaliation, or something of this sort, while the natural scientist will define it as boiling of the blood and heat around the heart. Of these, one describes the **403b** matter and the other the form and the account. For this is the account of the thing, but it is necessary that it be in matter of this sort if it is to exist. It is just as if the account of a house is of this sort—that it is a shelter capable of guarding against destruction

5 by wind, rain, and heat: one will say that it is stones and bricks and timber and another will say that it is the form in these things, for the sake of which these things are. So who among them is the natural scientist? Is it the one who knows about the matter but is ignorant of the account? Or the one who knows only about the account? Or is the natural scientist rather the one concerned with what comes from both of these? In that case, who is each of the other two? Or is no one concerned with the inseparable affections 10 of matter in so far as they are not separable?³ But the natural scientist is concerned with all those things which are the functions and affections of this sort of body and of this sort of matter. Someone else deals with things not of this sort, perhaps some of them concern some craftsman or other, for example, a carpenter or a doctor; but among affections which are not separable, some, in so far as they are not affections of this sort of body and are 15 from abstraction, concern the mathematician, and others, the separate ones, the first philosopher.

But it is necessary to return to the point where our discussion began. We were saying, then, that the affections of the soul are in this way inseparable from the natural matter of animals, at any rate in so far as they are of the sorts which are present as anger and fear are, and are unlike line and surface.

### CHAPTER 2

**403b20** It is necessary as we inquire into the soul—even as we are going through the problems which those making progress must solve—to collect the opinions of those of our predecessors who have expressed views about the soul, so that we may embrace what has been said rightly, and if anything has not been said rightly, that we may guard against it.

The starting point of this inquiry is to set out those things which seem most of all to belong to the soul by nature. What is ensouled 25 seems to differ from what is not ensouled chiefly in two respects: motion and perception. These are also very nearly the two features of the soul which we have taken over from our predecessors. For some of them say that the soul is most of all and primarily what initiates motion; thinking that what is not in motion itself

cannot move something else, they supposed the soul to be one of 30
the things which are in motion.

On this basis, Democritus says that the soul is a sort of fire and
heat. For the shapes and atoms being infinite, he says that the 404a
spherical ones (like the so-called motes which appear in shafts of
light coming in through windows) are fire and soul. Among the
atoms, he says the 'wholeseed' is the element of all of nature (just
as Leucippus does), and of these he says the spherical ones are the 5
soul, because, being of such a shape, they are most of all able to
slide through everything and move the rest, by being themselves
in motion too. In so speaking, they suppose that the soul is what
provides motion to animals. It is for this reason that they also say
that the mark of life is breathing. For when what surrounds a 10
body contracts it and squeezes out those figures providing motion
to animals because of their never remaining still, help comes from
without when other shapes of this sort enter in breathing. For
these hinder the ones still present in animals from being expelled,
by counteracting contraction and hardening. And they continue 15
to live so long as they are able to do this.

It also seems that what was said by the Pythagoreans contains
the same thought. For some of them said that the motes in the air
are the soul, and others that it is what moves these motes. They
spoke of these because they are seen to be continuously moving,
even when the air is perfectly still. 20

Also drawn to this same thought are those who say that the
soul is what moves itself. For all of these seem to have supposed
that motion is most characteristic of the soul, and that all other
things are moved because of the soul, while it is moved by itself,
because of their never seeing anything initiate motion without
itself being in motion.

In a similar way, Anaxagoras too says that the soul is what 25
causes motion, and with him is anyone else who claims that
reason set the whole universe in motion. But he is not in complete
agreement with Democritus, since the latter made soul and reason
absolutely the same. For he said that what is true is what appears,
for which reason he thought Homer wrote well when he said that
Hector 'lay with his thoughts elsewhere'. He does not employ 30
reason as a particular capacity concerned with the truth, but says
that the soul and reason are the same. Anaxagoras is less clear 404b
about them; for in many places, he says reason is the cause of

5

beauty and rightness, and yet in other places he says that it is the same as the soul. For he says that it belongs to all animals, great and small, noble and base. But reason—at any rate what is called
5 reason in the sense of intelligence—does not appear to belong similarly to all animals, nor even to all humans.

Those who focused on the ensouled in terms of being in motion supposed the soul to be what is most productive of motion; those who focused on the ensouled in terms of knowing and perceiving
10 the things which are speak of the soul in terms of first principles— some of them, positing a plurality of first principles, say that the soul is these, while others, positing one, say that it is this.

Thus Empedocles makes the soul from all the elements, but also says each of them is a soul, speaking in this way:

> For by earth we see earth, by water water
> By aether godlike aether, and yet by fire annihilating fire,
> 15    By love love, and strife by sad strife.

In the same way, Plato, in the *Timaeus*, makes the soul from the elements; for he says that like is known by like, and that things come from first principles. Similarly, in the work *On Philosophy* it
20 was determined that the animal itself is from the idea of the one itself and the primary length, breadth, and depth, and that the others come about in a similar way. He put it in yet another way: reason is the one; knowledge the two (for it goes in one way to one point); opinion the number of the plane; and perception the number of the solid. For while the numbers were said to be the
25 forms themselves and the first principles, they are from the elements, and some things are judged by reason, some by knowledge, some by opinion, and some by perception, and these numbers are the forms of things.

Moreover, since the soul has seemed to be both productive of motion and in this way cognitive, some have entwined these
30 together, declaring the soul to be a self-moving number.

People differ, however, concerning the first principles, as to what they are and how many they are; but the greatest differences are between those who make them corporeal and those who make
**405a** them incorporeal, and between these and those who mix the corporeal and incorporeal together and declare the first principles to be from both. People also differ concerning their number, some saying there is one and others more.

They provide accounts of the soul consequent upon these differences. For they supposed what is productive of motion in its own nature to be counted among the primary things—and not unreasonably. On this basis it seemed to some to be fire. This is the most fine-grained and the most incorporeal of the elements; further, it is both in motion and moves other things in a primary way.

Democritus spoke more subtly than others when revealing the reason for both of these things. For he says that the soul is the same as reason, and that this is among the primary and indivisible 10 bodies, and that it is productive of motion because of their fineness and shape. And he says that among shapes the spherical is most mobile, and that both reason and fire are of this sort.

Anaxagoras seems to say that soul and reason are different, just as we said earlier; but he treats them both as having one nature, except insofar as he posits reason most of all as a first principle. 15 At any rate, he says that it alone among things which exist is simple and both unmixed and pure. He assigns both to the same first principle, knowing and moving, that is, by saying that reason moves the whole universe.

Thales too, on the basis of what is related about him, seems to have supposed the soul to be something productive of motion, if 20 indeed he said that the magnet has a soul because it moves iron.

Diogenes, just like some others, says that it is air, supposing this to be the most fine-grained of all things and the first principle; and it is because of this that the soul both knows and moves— insofar as it is primary and all else comes from this, it knows, and insofar as it is finest, it is productive of motion.

Heraclitus claims that the soul is the first principle, if indeed it 25 is the rising vapour from which other things are constituted; and he says that it is the most incorporeal and is always in flux. And what is in motion is known by what is in motion; for he thought, as did many others, that what exists is in motion.

Alcmaeon seems to have made suppositions about the soul similar to theirs. For he says that the soul is immortal, because 30 of its resembling the immortals. And he says that this belongs to it on the grounds that it is always in motion; for all divine things too are always continuously in motion—the moon, the sun, the stars, and the whole of heaven.

Among the cruder thinkers, some, like Hippo, declared the soul **405b** to be water. They seem to have been persuaded on the basis of

seed, because the seed of all things is moist. He even objects
against those who claimed that the soul is blood, that seed is
5 not blood, while seed is the primary soul. But others, like Critias,
declared the soul to be blood, supposing perception to be most
characteristic of soul and this to belong to soul because of the
nature of blood.

All of the elements have found a proponent, except earth. No-
one has declared the soul to be earth, except insofar as some have
10 said that the soul is or is from all of the elements.

In summary, then, they all define the soul by three things:
motion, perception, and incorporeality; and each of these is
referred back to the first principles. For this reason, even those
who define it by knowing make it an element or from the elements, speaking in a manner similar to one another, with one
15 exception. For they say that like is known by like; for since the
soul knows all things, they constitute it from all of the first
principles. Those who say that there is some one cause and one
element assume the soul too is one, e.g. fire or air; those who say
the first principles are more than one also make the soul more
20 than one as well. Only Anaxagoras says that reason is unaffected
and that it has nothing in common with any of the other things.
How or by what cause it knows, if it is of such a sort, he did not
say; nor is it clear from what he said. Those who recognize pairs
of opposites among the first principles also constitute the soul
from opposites, while those who recognize one or the other of the
25 opposites, for example the hot or the cold or something else of this
sort, likewise assume the soul to be some one as well. For this
reason, they even take a cue from words: those who say that the
soul is the hot say that living is so named because of this, while
those who say that the soul is the cold say that it is so-called
because of respiration and its cooling effect.

These, then, are the views handed down to us about the soul, as
30 well as the reasons why they are advanced.


## CHAPTER 3

**405b31** We ought first to inquire into motion. For it is presumably not
**406a** merely false to say that its essence is of the sort claimed by those
who say that the soul moves itself, or is able to move itself, but it

is, rather, impossible that motion belong to the soul. First, that it is not necessary that what initiates motion is also itself in motion has already been stated. Moreover, everything in motion is so in either of two ways: in virtue of another or in virtue of itself. By 'in 5 virtue of another' we mean whatever is moved by being in something which is in motion, as for instance sailors are; for they are not moved in the same way as the ship is—the one is moved in virtue of itself and the other by being in what is in motion. This is clear with regard to their parts. For the proper motion of the feet is walking, as it is of humans as well. But this does not belong to sailors. Hence, given that being in motion is spoken of in two 10 ways, we are now investigating whether the soul is moved, and shares in motion, in virtue of itself.

There being four types of motion—locomotion, alteration, decay, and growth—the soul would move in respect of one, or some, or all of these. If it is moved non-co-incidentally, then motion would belong to it by nature; but if so, so too would 15 place, for all of the motions mentioned are in place. Further, if it is the case that the essence of the soul is to move itself, being in motion will not belong to it co-incidentally, as it does to white or to three cubits long. For these things too are moved, but co-incidentally, since that to which they belong, the body, is what 20 is moved. For this reason, neither does place belong to them; but it will belong to the soul, if indeed it partakes of motion by nature.

Further, if it is moved by nature, then it would be moved by force; and if it were moved by force, then also by nature. The situation is the same with respect to rest. For something rests by 25 nature in the state into which it is moved by nature; and similarly, something rests by force in the state into which it is moved by force. But it will not be easy to provide an account of the sorts of forced motions and rests that are to belong to the soul—not even for those willing to fabricate one.

Further, if it is moved upwards, it will be fire, but if downwards, earth; for these are the motions belonging to these bodies. And the same argument obtains concerning those in between.

Further, since it is evident that it moves the body, it is reason- 30 able that it impart those motions in terms of which it is itself moved. If so, it will also be true to say, conversely, that the motion in terms of which the body is moved the soul has as well. The body, however, is moved by locomotion, with the result **406b**

that the soul would change in place,[4] either as a whole or with respect to its parts. If this is possible, then it would also be possible for the soul to enter back into the body once it has left
5 it. And upon this would follow the resurrection of the dead among animals.

The soul could be moved co-incidentally, by another, for an animal could be knocked off course by force. It is not necessary for that which is moved by itself, in its essence, to be moved by another, except and unless it is moved co-incidentally, just as it is not necessary for that which is good in virtue of itself to be good for the sake of something else, or for what is good because of itself
10 to be good because of something other.

One should say that the soul is most of all moved by perceptual objects, if indeed it is moved. Moreover, if in fact the soul moves itself, it would itself be moved as well. So, if every motion is a dislodging of what is moved insofar as it is moved, the soul too would be dislodged from its essence, if, that is, it does not move
15 itself co-incidentally, but motion belongs to its essence in virtue of itself.

Some say that as the soul is in motion; it moves the body in which it is, e.g. Democritus, speaking in a manner much like the comic playwright Philippus. For Philippus claims that Daedalus made his wooden Aphrodite move by pouring liquid
20 silver into it. What Democritus says is similar: he claims that since the indivisible spheres are in motion, because it is their nature never to remain still, they draw the whole body along with them and set it in motion. But we will pose the question of whether this same thing also causes the body to come to be at rest. How it will do so is difficult or even impossible to say. In general, the soul does not appear to initiate motion in
25 animals in this way, but rather through some sort of decision and reasoning.

In the same way, Timaeus offers a physical account of how the soul moves the body: by being in motion itself, the soul moves the body because of its being entangled with it. For having constituted the soul out of the elements and having divided it in accordance with the harmonic numbers so that it might have an innate perception of harmony and so that the whole universe might be
30 borne in harmonious orbits, he bent the straight into a circle. And having divided the one circle into two circles intersecting at two

points, he again divided one of them into seven circles, so that the **407a**
orbits of heaven were the motions of the soul.
First, then, it is not right to say that the soul is a magnitude.
For it is clear that he wishes this sort of soul, the soul of the
universe, to be what is sometimes called reason, since it is at any
rate surely neither such as to be perceptual nor such as to be 5
appetitive, for the motion belonging to these is not circular. But
reason is one and continuous in the way that reasoning is, and
reasoning is one as the objects of thought are: these are one
successively, as numbers are, not as a magnitude is. This is why
reason is not continuous in this way, but is either without parts or
is continuous in a way other than the way a magnitude is.
For how will it reason if it is a magnitude? With just any of its 10
parts, or with a part[5] in virtue of its being a magnitude or in
virtue of its being a point (if, that is, one ought to call a point a
part)? If, then, it is in virtue of its being a point, and these are
infinite, it is clear that these will never run out; but if it is in
virtue of its being a magnitude, it will very often or endlessly
reason about the same thing. But it is evidently possible to 15
reason about something only once. If it suffices for just any of
its parts to make contact, why is it necessary for it to be moved
in a circle, or for it to have magnitude at all? But if it is
necessary to reason by making contact with the whole circle,
what does contact consist in for the parts? Further, how will it
reason about what has parts with what has no parts or what has
no parts with what has parts?
It is necessary that this circle be reason, for the motion of 20
reason is reasoning, while that of a circle is revolving. If, accordingly, reasoning is revolving, the circle whose reasoning is this
sort of revolving would be reason. What, then, will it always
reason about? For it is necessary that it do so, if indeed the
revolving is everlasting; for there are limits to practical reasoning,
since all instances of it are for the sake of something other, while
theoretical reasoning is defined in a way similar to the accounts. 25
For every account is either a definition or a demonstration.
Demonstration is from a starting point and has, in a way, an
end: the conclusion or inference. If, though, a demonstration does
not reach a conclusion, it will at any rate not return back again to
its starting point, but will forever take up another middle and
extreme term and move straight ahead, whereas a revolution

30 returns back again to its starting point. And definitions are all
delimited.

Further, if the same revolution recurs many times, it will be
necessary to reason about the same thing many times.

Further, reasoning is more like resting or dwelling upon something than like moving; and the same holds for a syllogism.

Moreover, what is not easily accomplished, but forced, is surely
**407b** not blessed. If motion is not essential to it,[6] it would be moved
contrary to its nature. It is also toilsome for it to be mixed with the
body and incapable of being separated from it; and that is additionally to be avoided, if it is indeed better for reason not to be
5 with the body, just as is customarily asserted and widely agreed.

And the cause of heaven's being borne in a circle is unclear. For
the essence of the soul is not the cause of its being borne in a circle;
rather, its being moved in this way is co-incidental. Nor is it the
body; on the contrary, the soul is rather the cause for that.
Moreover, it is not even said that this is better. Still, it ought to
10 have been the case that god made the soul be borne in a circle
because of this: it is better for it to be in motion than to remain
still, and better for it to be moved in this way rather than in some
other.

Since this sort of inquiry is more appropriate to other writings,
let us set it aside for now.

But something absurd turns out for this account as for most
15 others concerning the soul, since they conjoin the soul to the body
and place it in the body without articulating in addition the cause
of this or the condition of the body. This, however, would seem to
be necessary; it is because of their commonality that one acts
while the other is affected, and that the one initiates motion and
the other is in motion. None of this belongs to things which just
happen to be related to one another.

20     These accounts merely endeavour to say what sort of thing the
soul is without articulating anything further about the body
which is to receive the soul, as if it were possible, as according
to the Pythagorean myths, for just any soul to be outfitted in just
any body. For each body seems to have its own peculiar form and
shape, and what they say is almost the same as if someone were to
25 say that carpentry could clothe itself in flutes; for it is necessary
that the craft make use of its tools, and that the soul make use of
its body.

## CHAPTER 4

There is also another opinion handed down concerning the soul, **407b26** one which is no less persuasive to many than those already mentioned, and one given over to strict scrutiny in those discussions held corporately: people say that the soul is a sort of 30 attunement. For they say that an attunement is a blending and a compounding of opposites, and that the body is composed out of opposites.

And yet an attunement is a certain proportion of things mixed together, or a compounding of them, and a soul can be neither of these. Further, it does not belong to an attunement to initiate motion, but virtually everyone assigns this attribute more than any other to the soul. Rather, it is more in tune with the facts to **408a** speak of attunement in the case of health, or bodily virtues in general, than it is in the case of the soul. This would become most evident if someone tried to ascribe the affections and actions of the soul to some sort of attunement; for it is difficult to bring these into attunement.

Further, if we may speak of attunement by focusing on its two 5 main varieties, one, the most proper, pertains to a compounding of magnitudes, in things with motion and position, and it is a compounding of them whenever they are tuned so tightly that they admit of nothing of the same kind, and then the other to a proportion of the things which are mixed. In neither of these uses is it reasonable to call the soul an attunement. The first use, where 10 an attunement is a compounding of parts of the body, is exceedingly easy to criticize. For there are many different compoundings of parts and they may be compounded in many different ways. Of what part, then, should one suppose that its compounding is reason? Or the perceptual faculty? Or the appetitive faculty? And compounded how? And it would be similarly absurd for the soul to be the proportion of a mixture. For a mixture of elements does not have the same proportion for flesh and for bone. It will turn out, 15 then, that a thing has many souls, all over its body, if all of its parts are compounded from the mixed elements, while the proportion of the mixture is an attunement, that is, a soul.

One might well put this question to Empedocles, for he says that each of these is in a certain proportion: is the soul a 20

13

proportion or is it rather something more, something which comes to be in the parts? Further, is Love the cause of any chance mixture or of the mixtures which are proportional? If the latter, is Love the proportion or something more, beyond the proportion? These views, then, have these sorts of difficulties. Still, if the
25 soul is something other than a mixture, why is it that the soul is destroyed at the same time as the being of flesh and of the other parts of an animal? Additionally, if it is indeed not the case that each of the parts of the body has a soul of its own, as they will not if the soul is not the proportion of a mixture, what is it that perishes when the soul departs?

Consequently, that the soul can be neither an attunement nor
30 borne in a circle is clear from what has been said. It is the case, though, that it is moved co-incidentally, as we have said, and that it moves itself, for example when that which it is in is moved, or when this is moved by the soul. Otherwise, it could not be moved in respect of place.

Someone might more fairly raise a difficulty concerning how the soul is in motion, by focusing on these sorts of considerations:
**408b** we say that the soul is pained and pleased, is confident and afraid, and further that it is angry and also that it perceives and thinks. But all of these seem to be motions. On this basis, one might suppose that the soul is in motion. But this is not necessary. For
5 let it be the case that being pained or pleased or reasoning are motions, and that each of these counts as being moved, and that the movement is effected by the soul—for instance that being angry or afraid is the heart's being moved in such and such a way, while reasoning is presumably either this or something else moved,[7] and this comes about in some cases in virtue of some-
10 thing's being in motion in respect of place and in other cases in virtue of alteration. (Questions regarding what sorts of motions and how they occur are a matter for another discussion.) Yet[8] saying that the soul is angry would be like saying that the soul weaves or builds. For it is perhaps better not to say that the soul pities or learns or thinks, but that the human being does these
15 things with the soul; and this is not insofar as there is motion in the soul, but rather because motion sometimes reaches as far as the soul, and sometimes proceeds from it. Perception, for instance, is from these objects, whereas recollection is from the soul, ranging over the motions or traces in the sense organs.

But reason would seem to come about in us as a certain substance and not to be destroyed. For it would be destroyed principally by the impairment of old age, but in fact things turn 20 out for it just as they do for the sense organs. For if an old man were to receive an eye of the sort which the young have, he would see just as a young man sees. Consequently, old age occurs not because of the soul's having been affected in a certain way, but rather because that in which it is has been affected, just as in drunkenness and illness. So too reasoning and contemplating wither away when something else within is destroyed, but are 25 themselves unaffected. Reasoning and loving or hating are not affections of reason, but rather of that which has reason, insofar as it has it. Accordingly, when this is destroyed, one neither remembers nor loves. For these did not belong to reason, but to the common thing, which has perished. But reason is presumably something more divine and unaffected.

Consequently, that the soul cannot be moved is evident from 30 these considerations. But if it is not moved in general, it is clear that it is not moved by itself.

Of the claims discussed, very much the most irrational is the one saying that the soul is a number which moves itself. For first of all it faces the impossibilities resulting from the soul's being moved, and then also others peculiar to saying that it is a number. **409a** For how is one to reason of a unit as something being moved? And by what? How indeed, when it is something without parts and undifferentiated? For if it is capable of initiating motion and is itself capable of being moved, it must be differentiated.

Further, since they claim that a line when moved makes a plane, and a point a line, the movements of the units will also 5 be lines; for a point is a unit having position, and a number belonging to a soul already is somewhere and has position. And if someone subtracts a number, or a unit, from a number, what remains is a different number. But plants and many animals, when divided, continue living and seem to have a soul which is the same in species.

It would seem to make no difference whether we are speaking 10 of units or of tiny little bodies. For if points should come to be out of Democritus's tiny spheres, with only their quantity remaining, there will be something in each thing,[9] both what moves and what is moved, just as they will be in what is continuous. For this

observation does not result because of these spheres differing in
15 size or by being small, but solely from their being a quantity. For
this reason, it is necessary that there be something to move the
units.

If in an animal the soul is what initiates motion, the soul will be
what initiates motion in the number too, so that soul will not be
both what initiates motion and what is moved, but only that
which initiates motion. How then can this be a unit? For there
must be some difference which belongs to one of them in relation
20 to the others; but what difference could there be in the case of a
unit point except position?

If, on the one hand, the units and points in the body are
distinct, the units will be in the same place as the points, for
each will occupy the space of a point. And yet, if there are two
units in the same place, what prevents there being an infinite
number? For things whose place is indivisible are themselves
25 indivisible. But if on the other hand, the points in the body are
the number of the soul, or if the soul is the number of the points in
the body, why will it be the case that not all bodies have a soul?
For there seem to be points in all bodies, and an infinite number
of them.

Further, how can points be separated or released from their
30 bodies, unless at any rate lines are divided into points?[10]

It turns out, as we said, that taken one way this says the same as
those who suppose that the soul is some sort of fine-grained body,
**409b** but that taken another way—in the way Democritus claims that
the body is set in motion by the soul—it has its own peculiar
absurdity. For if indeed the soul is everywhere in a perceiving
body, it is necessary that there will be two bodies in the same
place, if the soul is some sort of body. Further, for those who say
that the soul is a number, there will be many points in a single
5 point, or[11] every body will have a soul, unless some different
number comes to be in the body and it is something other than
the points present in the body. It turns out too that the animal is
moved by the number, in just the way we said Democritus moves
it. For what difference is there in speaking of little spheres or big
units, or generally, of units being borne about? For in either case
10 it is necessary that one move the animal by means of these things
being moved.

These, then, and many others of the same sort, are the results for those who entwine motion and number into the same thing. For not only is it impossible for this sort of thing to be a definition of the soul: it cannot even be a property of it. This would be clear if someone endeavoured to specify the affections and actions of 15 the soul based on this account—like calculations, perceptions, pleasures, pains, and other things of this sort. For, as we said earlier, it is not easy to divine what might be said about these on the basis of their claims.

## CHAPTER 5

Three ways of defining the soul have been handed down. Some **409b19** have declared it to be what is most productive of motion because 20 it moves itself; others make it the most fine-grained or the most incorporeal body of all. These views contain certain difficulties and inconsistencies; we have pretty well recounted them. It remains to investigate what is meant by saying that the soul is from the elements.

They say this so that the soul may perceive and come to know 25 each of the things which exist. Of necessity, then, it turns out that there are necessarily many impossibilities in this account. For they maintain that one comes to know like by like, just as if they were supposing that the soul and the things it knows are the same. But elements are not the only things. There are many other things as well—the things which are constituted from the elements which are, rather, perhaps infinite in number. Let it be the case that the soul knows and perceives those things from 30 which each of these is. Still, by what means will it come to know or perceive the composite, for example, what god is, or what man or flesh or bone is? And it is the same for any other of the compounds. For it is not the elements standing in just any **410a** condition which each of these is, but rather their standing in some particular proportion and arrangement, just as even Empedocles says of bone:

The kind earth in broad beds
Took two parts of eight of sunlight and of water, 5
And four of fire; thus white bones came to be.

17

There is, then, no advantage to there being elements present in the soul, unless there are also proportions and an arrangement. For each element will know its like, but not bone or man, unless these
10 are also present. And that this is impossible it is not even remotely necessary to say. For who could raise a difficulty as to whether there is present in the soul a stone or a man? And the point holds similarly for the good and the not good, and in the same way for other things.

Further, given that being is spoken of in many ways (for it signifies some this, or a quantity, or a quality, or some other of the
15 delineated categories), will the soul be from all of these or not? But the elements do not seem common to them all. Then will it be only from those belonging to substances? How then will it know each of the others? Or will they claim that the genera of each of the categories will be elements and first principles peculiar to each, from which the soul is to be constituted? Then the soul
20 will be a quantity and a quality and a substance. But it is impossible that from the elements of quantity a substance, and not a quantity, will come to be. These and other such are the results of saying that the soul is from them all.

It is, moreover, absurd to say that like is unaffected by like, but that like is perceived by like and that one knows like by like. Yet
25 they maintain that perceiving is a sort of being affected or being moved; and the same holds for both reasoning and knowing.

There are many problems and pitfalls in saying, as Empedocles does, that each thing is known by bodily elements, in relation to what is like it,[12] as what was just said bears witness. For it seems
30 that whatever in the bodies of animals is made purely of earth, for
**410b** example bones, sinews, and hair, perceives nothing, with the result that it perceives nothing even of what is like it, although this would fit the terms of the argument. Further, more ignorance than understanding will belong to each of these principles, since each will know one thing but be ignorant of many; for every one will be ignorant of all the others.

It also turns out, at least for Empedocles, that god will be the
5 most unintelligent of all: god alone will fail to know one of the elements, strife, whereas mortals will know them all, since each one is from them all.

In general, why is it that not everything which exists has a soul, since everything is either an element, or from one, several, or all of the elements? For it is necessary that each one know either one, or some, or all of them. And one might also raise a difficulty: 10 whatever is it that unifies the elements? For the elements are surely like matter, and what keeps them together—whatever it is—is the most sovereign. And it is impossible that there be something superior to the soul, or dominant over it; and still less is this possible in the case of the reason. For it is reasonable to suppose that the reason is by nature most ancient and sovereign; yet they assert that the elements are primary among things 15 which exist.

Neither those who say that because of its knowing and perceiving what exists the soul is from the elements, nor those who say that it is what is most productive of motion, speak of the soul as a whole. Not all perceiving beings are productive of motion: for it appears that among animals some are stationary with respect to 20 place. Yet it surely seems that among motions it is in terms of this one alone that the soul moves the animal. The case is similar for whoever makes reason and the perceptual faculty from the elements: for it appears that plants, which do not have a share in perception, are alive, and that among animals, many do not have thought.[13]

But if someone were to bypass these points and maintain that 25 reason is a certain part of the soul, and likewise the perceptual faculty, he would not in that case be speaking universally of the soul as a whole, nor of any one complete soul. This argument pertains to the so-called Orphic poems as well. For they claim that the soul enters in from the universe with breathing, borne by the winds, though this cannot turn out to be the case for plants, 30 nor for some animals, if indeed not all animals draw breath. This **411a** has escaped those who adopted this view.

If, however, it is necessary to make the soul from the elements, it is not necessary that it be from all of them, since one member of a pair of contraries suffices to discern both itself and its opposite. For we know both the straight and the curved by means of what is 5 straight, a ruler being the arbiter of both, while the curved is such of neither itself nor the straight.

And some claim that the soul was mixed into the very universe, for which reason, perhaps, even Thales thought that everything is full of the gods. But this contains some difficulties. Why is it that the soul which is in air or fire does not make an animal, while it 10

does when in mixed elements? Why is this so, even though the soul seems better when in air or fire? And one might further inquire why it is that the soul in the air is better and more deathless than the soul in animals. The alternatives are absurd and
15 irrational: to say that fire or air is an animal is beyond reason, while to deny that they are animals when there is a soul present in them is absurd.

They seem to have supposed that the soul was in the elements because the whole universe is one in kind with its parts. The consequence is that it is necessary for them to say that the soul too is one in kind with its parts, if it is by means of there being in animals something taken in from the surrounding environment
20 that animals become ensouled. If air, when scattered, is of one kind, but the soul is anhomoeomerous, it is clear that some part of soul will be present, while some other part will not. It is necessary, therefore, either that the soul be homoeomerous or that it not be present in just any portion of the universe.

So it is evident from what has been said that knowing does not
25 belong to the soul because of its being from the elements; nor is the soul rightly or truly said to be moved. But since knowing belongs to the soul, as do both perceiving and believing, as do, further, being appetitive and wishing and desires in general, while motion in respect of place comes to be in animals as effected by the soul, as, further, do growth and maturity and decay, we
30 should ask whether each of these belongs to the soul in its entir-
**411b** ety. That is, is it by the whole soul that we think and perceive and are moved and both do and experience each of the others, or do we do different things with different parts of the soul? Again, does living depend on some one of these parts, or on several, or on all? Or is it due to some other cause?
5   To be sure, some say that the soul has parts and that reasoning is by means of one part and desiring by means of another. What, then, holds the soul together, if it naturally has parts? For it is surely not the body; on the contrary, the soul seems rather to hold the body together. At any rate, when the soul has departed, the body disintegrates and putrefies. If, then, something else makes
10 the soul one, that, more than anything else, would be soul; and then one will again need to inquire whether it is one or many-parted. For if it is one, why will the soul too not be one straight-away? If it has parts, the argument will once again inquire into

what it is which holds it together, and thus it will proceed ad infinitum.

Someone might also pose a difficulty concerning the parts of the soul: what capacity does each have in the body? For if the 15 entire soul holds together the whole body, it will also be appropriate for each of its parts to hold together a certain part of the body. This, however, seems impossible. For what sort of part will reason hold together? And how? It is difficult even to fabricate an answer.

It also appears that plants live when divided, as do, among animals, some of the insects; so that each has a soul which is the 20 same in form, if not also in number. For each of the parts has perception and moves with respect to place for some time. If they do not continue to do so, there is nothing odd in that: they do not have the organs they need in order to preserve their nature. Nonetheless, all of the parts of the soul are present in each of 25 the parts, and the parts of the soul are the same in kind with one another and with the entire soul, with one another inasmuch as they are not separable, and with the entire soul inasmuch as it is not divisible.

It also seems that the first principle in plants is a sort of soul; for animals and plants have this alone in common, and this exists separated from the perceptive first principle, though nothing 30 lacking this has perception.

# BOOK II

## CHAPTER 1

**412a1** Let this much be said about what has been handed down concerning the soul by our predecessors. Let us start anew, as if from the beginning, endeavouring to determine what the soul is and
5 what its most common account would be.

We say that among the things that exist one kind is substance, and that one sort is substance as matter, which is not in its own right some this; another is shape and form, in accordance with which it is already called some this; and the third is what comes from these. Matter is potentiality, while form is actuality; and
10 actuality is spoken of in two ways, first as knowledge is, and second as contemplating is.

Bodies seem most of all to be substances, and among these, natural bodies, since these are the principles of the others. Among natural bodies, some have life and some do not have it. By 'life' we mean that which has through itself nourishment, growth, and decay.

15 It would follow that every natural body having life is a substance, and a substance as a compound. But since it is also a body of this sort—for it has life—the soul could not be a body; for the body is not among those things said of a subject, but rather is spoken of as a subject and as matter. It is necessary, then, that the
20 soul is a substance as the form of a natural body which has life in potentiality. But substance is actuality; hence, the soul will be an actuality of a body of such as sort.

Actuality is spoken of in two ways, first as knowledge is, and second as contemplating is. Evidently, then, the soul is actuality as knowledge is. For both sleeping and waking depend upon the
25 soul's being present; and as waking is analogous to contemplating, sleeping is analogous to having knowledge without exercising it. And in the same individual knowledge is prior in generation. Hence, the soul is the first actuality of a natural body which has life in potentiality.

22

This sort of body would be one which is organic. And even the **412b** parts of plants are organs, although altogether simple ones. For example, the leaf is a shelter of the outer covering, and the outer covering of the fruit; and the roots are analogous to the mouth, since both draw in nourishment. Hence, if it is necessary to say something which is common to every soul, it would be that the 5 soul is the first actuality of an organic natural body.

For this reason it is also unnecessary to inquire whether the soul and body are one, just as it is unnecessary to ask this concerning the wax and the shape, nor generally concerning the matter of each thing and that of which it is the matter. For while one and being are spoken of in several ways, what is properly so spoken of is the actuality.

It has now been said in general what the soul is: the soul is a 10 substance corresponding to the account; and this is the essence of this sort of body. It is as if some tool were a natural body, e.g. an axe; in that case what it is to be an axe would be its substance, and this would also be its soul. If this were separated, it would no longer be an axe, aside from homonymously. But as things are, it is an axe. For the soul is not the essence and 15 organization (*logos*) of this sort of body, but rather of a certain sort of natural body, one having a source of motion and rest in itself.

What has been said must also be considered when applied to parts. For if an eye were an animal, its soul would be sight, since this would be the substance of the eye corresponding to the account. The eye is the matter of sight; if sight is lost, it is no 20 longer an eye, except homonymously, in the way that a stone eye or painted eye is.

What has been said in the case of parts must of course be understood as applying to the entire living body. For there is an analogy: as one part is to one part, so the whole perceptual faculty is to the whole of the body which is capable of perception, insofar as it is capable of perception. The body which has cast off its soul 25 is not a being which is potentially such as to be alive; this is rather the one which has a soul. The seed, however, and the fruit, is such a body in potentiality.

Hence, as cutting and seeing are actualities, in this way too is waking an actuality; and as sight and the potentiality of a tool **413a** are, in this way too is the soul. The body is a being in potentiality.

But just as an eye is a pupil and sight, so in this case too an animal is the soul and the body.

Therefore, that the soul is not separable from the body, or some
5 parts of it if it naturally has parts, is not unclear. For the actuality of some parts belongs to the parts themselves. Even so, nothing hinders some parts from being separable, because of their not being the actualities of a body.

It is still unclear, however, whether the soul is the actuality of the body in the way that a sailor is of a ship.[14]

Let the soul, then, be defined in outline in this way and
10 sketched out.


CHAPTER 2

**413a11** Because what is sure and better known as conforming to reason comes to be from what is unsure but more apparent, one must try to proceed anew in this way concerning the soul. For it is not only necessary that a defining account make clear *the that*,
15 which is what most definitions state, but it must also contain and make manifest the cause. As things are, statements of definitions are like conclusions. For example: 'what is squaring? It is an equilateral rectangle being equal to an oblong figure.' But this sort of definition is an account of the conclusion: the one who states that squaring is the discovery of a mean states
20 the cause of the matter.

We say, then, taking up the beginning of the inquiry, that what is ensouled is distinguished from what is not ensouled by living. But living is spoken of in several ways. And should even one of these belong to something, we say that it is alive: reason, perception, motion and rest with respect to place, and further the motion
25 in relation to nourishment, decay, and growth.

For this reason, even plants, all of them, seem to be alive, since they seem to have in themselves a potentiality and a principle of such a sort through which they grow and decay in opposite directions. For it is not the case that they grow upwards but not downwards; rather they grow in both directions and in all ways—
30 those, that is, which are always nourished and continue to live as long as they are able to receive nourishment.

This can be separated from the others, but among mortal beings the others cannot be separated from this. This is evident in the case of plants. For no other capacity of soul belongs to them.

Being alive, then, belongs to living things because of this prin- **413b** ciple, but something is an animal primarily because of perception. For even those things which do not move or change place, but which have perception, we call animals and not merely alive. The primary form of perception which belongs to all animals is touch. But just as the nutritive capacity can be separated from touch and 5 from the whole of perception, so touch can be separated from the other senses. By nutritive we mean the sort of part of the soul of which even plants have a share. But all animals evidently have the sense of touch. The reason why both of these turn out to be the case we shall state later.                                                    10

For now let just this much be said: the soul is the principle of the things mentioned and is delimited by them, namely, nourishment, perception, thought, and motion. In some cases, it is not difficult to see whether each of these is a soul or a part of a soul, and if a part, whether in such a way as to be separable in account alone or also in place; but in other cases there is a 15 difficulty. For just as in the case of plants, some, when divided, evidently go on living even when separated from one another, there being one soul in actuality in each plant, but many in potentiality, so we see this occurring in other characteristics of the soul in the case of insects cut into two. For each of the parts 20 has perception and motion with respect to place, and if perception, then also imagination and desire; for wherever there is perception, there is also both pain and pleasure; and wherever these are, of necessity there is appetite as well. But concerning reason and the capacity for contemplation nothing is yet evi- 25 dent but it seems to be a different genus of soul, and this alone admits of being separated, in the way the everlasting is from the perishable.

It is evident from these things, though, that the remaining parts of the soul are not separable, as some assert. That they differ in account, however, is evident; for what it is to be the perceptual faculty is different from what it is to be the faculty of belief, if 30 indeed perceiving differs from believing, and so on for each of the other faculties mentioned.

25

Further, all of these belong to some animals, and some of them to others, and only one to still others. And this will provide a
**414a** differentiation among animals. It is necessary to investigate the reason why later. Almost the same thing holds for the senses: for some animals have them all, others have some of them, and others have one, the most necessary, touch.

That by which we live and perceive is spoken of in two ways,
5 just as is that by which we know. We speak in one case of knowledge and in the other of the soul, because we maintain that we know by means of each of these. Likewise, we are healthy in one way by health and in another way by some part of, or the whole of, the body.[15] On one of these ways of speaking, knowledge and health is each a shape, a sort of form, an organization (*logos*), and so as to be an actuality of what is capable of
10 receiving them—in the one case of what is capable of knowledge and in the other of what is capable of health. For the actuality of productive things seems to reside in what is affected and is disposed to receive it.

Consequently, the soul is in the primary way that by which we live and perceive and think, so that it will be a sort of organization (*logos*) and a form, but not matter and a substrate. For substance
15 is spoken of in three ways, just as we said, of which one is form, another matter, and another what is from both; and of these the matter is potentiality and the form actuality. Since what is from both is an ensouled thing, the body is not the actuality of the soul, but the soul is the actuality of some body.

For this reason, those to whom it seems that the soul is neither without body nor some kind of body understand things rightly.
20 For it is not a body, but is something belonging to a body; and because of this it is present in a body, and in a body of this sort— not as our predecessors supposed when they fitted the soul into the body without additionally specifying in which body or in which sort, even though it appears that whatever happens to show up does not receive whatever it happens upon. It happens
25 rather in this way, in conformity with reason: the actuality of each thing comes about naturally in what has it in potentiality, that is, in its appropriate matter.

That, then, the soul is a kind of actuality and an organization (*logos*) of what has a potentiality to be of this sort, is evident from these things.

## CHAPTER 3

Among the capacities of the soul, all belong to some, to others **414a29** some of them belong, and to still others only one belongs. The **30** capacities we mentioned were: the nutritive faculty, the perceptual faculty, the desiderative faculty, the faculty of motion with respect to place, and the faculty of understanding. The nutritive faculty alone belongs to plants; both this and the perceptual faculty belongs to others. But if the perceptual faculty, then also **414b** the desiderative faculty: desire is appetite, spirit, and wish. And all animals have at least one kind of perception, touch. And that to which perception belongs, to this belongs also both pleasure and pain, as well as both the pleasurable and the painful; and to those things to which these belong also belongs appetite, since **5** appetite is a desire for what is pleasurable. And further they have perception of nourishment; for touch is perception of nourishment, since all living things are nourished by dry, wet, hot, and cold things, and touch is perception of these. Touch is perception of other sensibles co-incidentally. For neither sound nor colour **10** nor smell contributes anything to nourishment, whereas flavour is among the objects of touch.

Hunger and thirst are appetites—the first sort, hunger, for the dry and the hot, and the second sort, thirst, for the wet and the cold. Flavour is a sort of seasoning of these.

It will be necessary to clarify these matters later. For now let this much be said: to those living things which have touch, desire **15** belongs as well. But regarding imagination things are not clear. One must inquire into that later.

In addition to these things, a capacity to move with respect to place belongs to some things; and to others both the faculty of understanding and reason, for example to humans and to anything else there may be of this or of a more elevated sort.

It is clear, then, that in the same way there could be one **20** account for both soul and figure. For in the one case a figure is nothing beyond a triangle and the others following in a series, and in the other a soul is nothing beyond the things mentioned. There could, however, in the case of figures be a common account which fits them all, though it will be peculiar to none; and the same holds in the case of the souls mentioned. For this reason, it is ludicrous **25** to seek a common account in these cases, or in other cases, an account which is not peculiar to anything which exists, and which does not correspond to any proper and indivisible species, while neglecting what is of this sort. Consequently, one must ask individually what the soul of each is, for example, what the soul of a plant is, and what the soul of a man or a beast is.[16]

What holds in the case of the soul is very close to what holds
30 concerning figures: for in the case of both figures and ensouled things, what is prior is always present potentially in what follows in a series—for example, the triangle in the square, and the nutritive faculty in the perceptual faculty. One must investigate
415a the reason why they are thus in a series. For the percepual faculty is not without the nutritive, though the nutritive faculty is separated from the perceptual in plants. Again, without touch, none of the other senses are present, though touch is present without
5 the others; for many animals have neither sight nor hearing nor a sense of smell. Also, among things capable of perceiving, some have motion in respect of place, while others do not. Lastly, and most rarely, some have reasoning and understanding. For among perishable things, to those to which reasoning belongs all the remaining capacities also belong, though it is not
10 the case that reasoning belongs to each of those with each of the others. Rather, imagination does not belong to some, while others live by this alone. A different account will deal with theoretical reason.

It is clear, therefore, that the account of each of these will also be the most appropriate account concerning the soul.

## CHAPTER 4

415a14 It is necessary for anyone who is going to conduct an inquiry into
15 these things to grasp what each of them is, and then to investigate in the same way things closest to them as well as other features. And if one ought to say what each of these is, for example, what the intellective or perceptual or nutritive faculty is, then one should first say what reasoning is and what perceiving is, since actualities and actions are prior in account to potentialities. But
20 if this is so, and their corresponding objects are prior to them,[17] it would for the same reason be necessary to make some

determinations about, for instance, nourishment and the objects of perception and reasoning.

The result is that one must speak first of nourishment and generation; for the nutritive soul also belongs to the others as well. This is both the first and most common capacity of the soul, 25 in virtue of which living belongs to all living things, a capacity whose functions are generating and making use of nutrition. For the most natural among the functions belonging to living things, at least those which are complete and neither deformed nor spontaneously generated, is this: to make another such as itself, an animal an animal and a plant a plant, so that it may, insofar as it is able, partake of the everlasting and the divine. For that is **415b** what everything desires, and for the sake of that everything does whatever it does in accordance with nature. ('That for the sake of which' is spoken of in two ways: that on account of which and that for which.) Since, then, these things are incapable of sharing in the everlasting and the divine by existing continuously (because among perishable things nothing can remain the same and one in number), each has a share insofar as it is able to partake in this, 5 some more and some less, and remains not itself but such as it is, not one in number but one in form.

The soul is the cause and principle of the living body. As these things are spoken of in many ways, so the soul is spoken of as a cause in the three of the ways delineated: for the soul is a cause as 10 the source of motion, as that for the sake of which, and as the substance of ensouled bodies.

That it is a cause as substance is clear: for substance is the cause of being for all things, and living is being for living things, while the cause and principle of living is the soul. Further, actuality is the organization (*logos*) of that which is potentially.

It is evident that the soul is a cause as that for the sake of which: 15 just as reason acts for the sake of something, in the same way nature does so as well; and this is its end. And in living beings the soul is naturally such a thing.[18] For all ensouled bodies are organs of the soul—just as it is for the bodies of animals, so is it for the bodies of plants—since they are for the sake of the soul.[19] 'That 20 for the sake of which' is spoken of in two ways: that on account of which and that for which.

Moreover, the soul is also that from which motion in respect of place first arises, though this capacity does not belong to all living

things. There are also alteration and growth in virtue of the soul;
for perception seems to be a sort of alteration, and nothing
25 perceives which does not partake of the soul. The same holds
for both growth and decay; for nothing which is not nourished
decays or grows naturally, and nothing is nourished which does
not have a share of life.

Empedocles was not right when he added that growth occurs
**416a** for plants downwards, when they take root, because earth is
naturally borne in this direction, and upward growth occurs
because fire moves in a like manner. Nor even does he understand
up and down rightly. For up and down are not the same for all
things as for the universe; rather, as the head is in animals, so the
roots are in plants, if it is because of their functions that one ought
5 to say that organs are the same or different. Moreover, what is it
that holds fire and earth together, even though they are borne in
opposite directions? For they will be torn apart if there is nothing
which hinders them. If there is something, however, this will be
the soul—the cause of growing and being nourished.

The nature of fire seems to some to be without qualification the
10 cause of nourishment and growth, since among bodies fire alone
is evidently something which is nourished and grows. On this
basis, one might suppose fire to be what accomplishes this in
plants and animals. It is, however, a sort of co-cause, and most
surely not a cause without qualification; the cause is, rather, the
15 soul. For fire's growth is without limit, so long as there is something combustible. By contrast, for all things naturally constituted, there is a limit and an organization (*logos*) of both size and
growth. These things belong to the soul, and not to fire, and to the
organization (*logos*) rather than to the matter.

Since the same capacity of soul is both nutritive and generative,
20 it is necessary to determine what concerns nutrition first; for it is
in virtue of this function that it is marked off from the other
capacities. Nutrition seems to be from a contrary to its contrary,
though not from every contrary to every contrary, but only those
contraries which have not only generation from one another but
also growth. For many things are generated from one another,
but not all of them are quantities, as, for example, the healthy
25 from the sick. Nor even among growing contraries does it appear
that nourishment is reciprocally one from the other: whereas
water is nourishment for fire, fire does not nourish water. Now

then, in the case of simple bodies it seems most true that the one is nourishment and the other nourished.

Yet there is a difficulty. Some say that like is nourished by like just as like grows by like. By contrast, as we said earlier, it seems 30 to others that contrary is nourished by contrary, since like is unaffected by like, and that nourishment changes, and is digested, while every change is into its opposite or an intermediary. Further, nourishment is in some way affected by what is nourished, but what is nourished is not affected by nourishment, just as a 35 carpenter is not affected by the matter, but it is affected by him. **416b** The carpenter changes only from idleness into activity.

It makes a difference whether nourishment is what is added last or first. If it is both, in one instance undigested and in the other digested, it would be possible to call either nourishment. For 5 insofar as it is undigested, contrary is nourished by contrary; and insofar as it is digested, like is nourished by like. As a consequence, evidently each side will be in one way correct and in another way incorrect.

Since nothing which does not partake of life is nourished, what is nourished would be the ensouled body, insofar as it is ens- 10 ouled, with the result that nourishment is relative—and not co-incidentally—to what is ensouled.

There is a difference, however, between being nourishment and being able to produce growth in something. For insofar as an ensouled thing is a particular quantity, something is capable of producing growth in it, while insofar as it is some this and a substance, something is nourishment for it. For what is ensouled preserves its substance and exists as long as it is nourished; and it is capable of generating not the very thing which is nourished, but 15 rather something like what is nourished, since its substance already exists and nothing generates itself, but rather preserves itself.

Consequently, this principle of the soul is a capacity of the sort which preserves the thing which has it, as the sort of thing it is, while nutrition equips it to be active. Hence, whatever has been deprived of nutrition cannot exist.

Since it is right to name each thing after its end, and here the end is to generate another such as itself, it would be right to call this primary soul *generative* of another such as itself.[20]

Since these are three things—what is nourished, that by which 20 it is nourished, and what nourishes—that which nourishes is the

primary soul; that which is nourished is the body which has the
25 primary soul; and the nourishment is that by which it is nourished. And that by which something nourishes is twofold, just as
that by which one steers is both the hand and the rudder, the one
both producing movement and itself moving, and the other
merely moving. It is necessary that all nourishment be able to
be digested; and what is hot effects digestion. For this reason,
everything ensouled has heat.
30   So, it has been said in outline what nourishment is. It is to be
made completely clear later, in the appropriate discussion.


## CHAPTER 5

**416b32** With these things determined, let us discuss what is common to
\*      the whole of perception. Perception arises in both being moved
and being affected, just as was said; for it seems to be a kind of
**417a** alteration. Some also say that like is affected by like; and we have
said how this is possible or impossible in our general discussions
on acting and being affected.

There is a puzzle as to why there is no perception of the senses
themselves, and why they do not produce perception without
external objects, even though present in them are fire, earth, and
5 the other elements of which there is perception either in themselves or in respect of their co-incidental properties. It is clear,
then, that the perceptual faculty is not actual, but only in potentiality; for this reason it does not perceive, just as what is combustible does not burn by itself without something capable of
burning it. For otherwise it would burn itself, and would have
no need of any actually existing fire.

10   Since we speak of perceiving in two ways—for we speak of that
which potentially hears or sees as hearing and seeing, even if it
should happen to be sleeping, and also of that which is already
actively seeing or hearing—perception will also be spoken of in
two ways, in one case as potential and in the other as actual; and
the same for the object of perception, in one case as potential and
in the other as actual.

First, then, let us speak as if being affected and being moved
15 and being actual were the same; for motion is a kind of actuality,
however incomplete, as was said in other writings. Everything is

affected and moved by what is capable of producing such a result and is in actuality. There is, accordingly, a sense in which like is affected by like and there is a sense in which unlike is affected by unlike, just as we have said; for something unlike is affected, but 20 once affected it is like.

One must also draw a distinction concerning potentiality and actuality. For we have just now been speaking of them without qualification. In the first case, something is a knower in the way in which we might say that a human knows because humans belong to the class of knowers and to those things which have knowledge; but in the second case, we say directly that the one who has 25 grammatical knowledge knows. These are not in the same way potential knowers; instead, the first one because his genus and matter are of a certain sort, and the other because he has the potential to contemplate whensoever he wishes, so long as nothing external hinders him. Yet another sort of knower is the one already contemplating, who is in actuality and strictly knowing this *A*. In the first two cases, then, those knowing in potentiality 30 come to be knowers in actuality, but the first one by being altered through learning, with frequent changes from a contrary state; and the other, from having arithmetical or grammatical know- **417b** ledge and not actualizing it to actualizing in another way.

Nor is being affected unqualified. Rather, in one way it is a kind of destruction by a contrary, and in another way it is rather a preservation of what is in potentiality by what is in actuality, and of what is like something in the way potentiality is in relation to 5 actuality. For whenever the one who has knowledge comes to contemplate, he is either not altered, since this is a progression into the same state and into actuality, or his is a different kind of alteration. For this reason, it is inappropriate to say that one who understands is altered whenever he understands, in just the way it is inappropriate to say that the builder is altered when- ever he builds. Hence, leading one who thinks or understands 10 into actuality from potentiality is not teaching, but properly has some other name; whereas the one who, from being in potenti- ality, learns and receives knowledge from one who is in actual- ity, and able to teach, either should not be said to be affected or there are two types of alteration, one a change towards conditions of privation and the other towards positive states 15 and a thing's nature.

In what is capable of perceiving, the first change is brought about by the parent; what is born also already has perception, just as we have knowledge. Actually perceiving is spoken of in a way similar to contemplation. But there is a difference: what is capable
20  of producing this actuality, the object of sight and hearing and so on for the remaining objects of perception, is external. The reason is that actual perception is of particulars, whereas knowledge is of universals, which are in a sense in the soul itself. Consequently, reasoning is up to oneself, whenever one wishes; but perceiving is
25  not up to oneself, since it is necessary for the object of perception to be present. This holds in the same way for the types of knowledge which concern objects of perception, and for the same reason, namely that the objects of perception are particulars and are external.

There may come an appropriate time later to clarify these
30  things. For now, let this much be distinguished: that what is spoken of as being in potentiality is not without qualification, but rather in the first case as when we say that the child is potentially a general, and in the second, as when we say this of someone who is at the right age; and it is in this way that we speak
**418a**  of what is capable of perceiving. Since the difference between these has no name, though the boundary between them has been drawn—that they are different and how they are different—it is necessary to use 'being affected' and 'being altered' as though they were the appropriate names.

What is capable of perceiving is in potentiality such as the object of perception is already in actuality, as was just said.
5  Hence, it is affected while being unlike what affects it, but when it has been affected, it has been made like it and is such as what affected it is.


CHAPTER 6

**418a7** In the case of each sense, it is necessary to speak first about perceptible objects. Perceptible objects are spoken of in three ways: in two cases we say perceptible objects are perceived in their own right, and in one co-incidentally. Of the first two, one
10  is exclusive to an individual sense and the other common to them all.

By exclusive I mean what cannot be perceived by another sense and about what one cannot be deceived. For example, sight is of colour, hearing is of sound, and taste is of flavour, whereas touch has a number of different objects. In any case, each sense discerns these and is not deceived that there is colour or that there is 15 sound—as opposed to what or where the coloured or sounding thing is. Accordingly, these sorts of objects are said to be exclusive to each sense.

Common objects include motion, rest, number, shape, and magnitude, since these sorts of objects are exclusive to no one sense but are, rather, common to them all. For in some cases movement is an object of perception for both touch and sight.

Something is said to be an object of perception co-incidentally 20 if, for example, the white thing should be the son of Diares. There is co-incidental perception of him, because he coincides with the white thing, of which there is perception. For this reason, one is not affected by an object of perception insofar as it is such a thing as the son of Diares.

Among things perceived in their own right, exclusive objects are properly perceptible objects; and it is to these that the essence of each sense is naturally relative.                    25

### CHAPTER 7

That of which there is sight is the visible. The visible is both **418a26** colour and something which it is possible to describe in words, but which has no name. (What we mean will be clear as we proceed.)

The visible is colour, and that which is on the surface of what is visible in its own right—in its own right not by definition, but because it contains within itself the cause of its being visible. 30 Every colour is capable of setting in motion that which is actually **418b** transparent; and this is its nature. Consequently, nothing is visible without light. Rather, the colour of each thing is always seen in light.

Accordingly, one must say first what light is. There is, to be sure, the transparent. By *transparent* I mean that which is visible, not strictly speaking in its own right but due to the colour of 5 something else. Of this sort are air, water, and many solids; these

are not transparent insofar as they are air or water, but because there is an indwelling nature which is the same in them both, as well as in the everlasting body above. And light is the actuality of
10 this, the transparent, insofar as it is transparent. Where this is there is also, potentially, darkness. Light is a sort of colour of the transparent, whenever it is made in actuality transparent by fire or something that is like the body above; for something one and the same belongs to this and to fire.

We have said, then, what the transparent is and what light is:
15 light is neither fire nor in general a body nor an effluence from any body, since in that case it too would be a body. Rather, it is the presence of fire or something of this sort in the transparent. For two bodies cannot be in the same place at the same time. Further, darkness seems to be the contrary of light. It is also the case that darkness is the absence of this sort of positive state from the
20 transparent; the result is plainly that its presence is light.

Empedocles was wrong, together with anyone else who characterized light as something borne along and as extending[21] for a time between the earth and what surrounds it, but as escaping our notice. For this is contrary to what reason makes clear and also to
25 the phenomena: it might escape our notice in a short interval, but it is too much to ask that it should escape our notice over the distance from east to west.

It is also the case that the colourless is capable of receiving colour, and the soundless sound. The transparent is colourless, as is the invisible, or what is barely seen, as a dark thing seems. The
30 transparent is this sort of thing—not when it is in actuality transparent, but when it is potentially so. For the same nature is sometimes darkness and sometimes light.

**419a**    It is not the case that all visible things are in light; rather, only the colour proper to each thing is. For some things are not seen in the light, but produce perception in the dark, for example, things appearing fiery and glowing (there is no one name for them), for
5 example mushrooms, horn,[22] and the heads, scales, and eyes of fish; the colour proper to none of these is seen. The reason why these are seen requires another discussion.

For now, this much is evident: what is seen in light is colour, which, accordingly, is not seen without light. For being colour is the same as being capable of setting in motion what is actually
10 transparent,[23] and the actuality of the transparent is light.

Evidently an indication of this: if someone should place what has colour upon the eye itself, it will not be seen. Rather, colour moves the transparent, e.g. air, and the sensory organ is moved by this, which is continuous.

Democritus is wrong to think that if the intervening medium 15 were a void, even an ant in heaven would be seen clearly. For this is impossible, since seeing comes to be when what is capable of perceiving is affected by something. Hence, while it is impossible that it be affected by the very colour seen, what remains, surely, is that it be affected by the intervening medium. Consequently, there must be an intervening medium. If it were a void, it is not 20 that things would not be seen clearly, but rather that nothing would be seen at all.

The reason why it is necessary that colour is seen in the light has been stated. Fire is seen in both, in darkness and in light, and this too is of necessity. For it is by this that the transparent comes to be transparent.

The same account also pertains to sound and odour. For 25 neither of these produces perception when touching the sensory organ. Rather, an intervening medium is moved by odour or sound, and each of the sensory organs is moved by this. Whenever one puts something sounding or something with an odour upon the sensory organ itself, it will not produce perception. Things are similar concerning touch and taste, though this does not appear 30 to be so; the reason why will be clear later.

The intervening medium for sound is air, while that of odour is nameless. For there is a quality common to air and water, which, present in them both, is to what has odour as the transparent is to colour. For evidently even animals living in water have percep- 35 tion of odour. But man, together with all land animals that **419b** breathe, cannot smell when not breathing. The reason for these things will also be stated later.

CHAPTER 8

Now, let us first determine the facts concerning sound and hear- **419b4** ing. There is sound in two ways, as something actual and as a 5 potentiality. We deny that some things have sound, e.g. sponge and wool, and affirm that other things have it, e.g. bronze and whatever is solid and smooth, because they can make sound (that is, each can produce an actual sound between itself and the organ of hearing).

10 Actual sound always occurs as the sound of something, in relation to something, and in something; for what produces it is an impact. Accordingly, it is also impossible for sound to occur when there is just one thing, since what strikes and what is struck are different, so that what makes a sound does so in relation to something. And without movement, no impact occurs. Still, as we said, it is not an impact of whatever happens to be around; for if one were to strike wool, no sound would be made. Rather, it is 15 bronze and whatever is smooth and hollow; bronze because it is smooth, while hollow things produce many impacts after the first by reverberating, since what has been set in motion is unable to escape.

Further, sound is heard in air, and in water, though less so. But it is not the case that either air or water is chiefly responsible for sound; rather, it is necessary that there be an impact of solid 20 objects with one another and with the air. This occurs when impacted air remains and is not dispersed. Accordingly, whenever air is impacted swiftly and violently, it makes a sound. For the motion of what does the striking must outpace the dissolution of the air, just as if someone were to strike a swiftly moving pile or string of sand.

25 An echo occurs whenever air, having become a unit because a confining receptacle precludes its dispersing, rebounds like a ball. It seems likely that an echo always occurs, though it is indistinct, since things surely turn out in the case of sound as they do in the case of light. For light is always reflected (for otherwise light 30 would not come to be everywhere; rather, there would be darkness outside of what is lit by the sun), though it is not reflected as it is from water, bronze, or any other smooth objects, so as to produce a shadow, by which light is bounded.[24]

The void is rightly said to be chiefly responsible for hearing: the air seems to be a void, and it is this which produces hearing, whenever it is moved as something unified and continuous. But because of its being friable no sound occurs, unless what is 420a impacted is smooth. In that case, the air comes to be unified all at once, because of the surface, since the surface of a smooth object is unified.

What is capable of producing sound, then, is that which is capable of moving continuously unified air up to the organ of hearing. Air is congenital to the organ of hearing; because the air is unified,[25] when the outside air is in motion, the inside air is moved. Consequently, it is not everywhere that an animal hears; 5 the air does not penetrate everywhere, since it does not have air everywhere. Rather, the part which is going to be moved has air.[26]

By itself, air is soundless, because of its being easily dispersed; but whenever it is prevented from dispersing, its movement is sound. The air inside the ears has been encased, in order to be unmoving, so that it can accurately perceive all the variations of 10 motion. And it is because of these things that we also hear in water, seeing that the water does not penetrate the very air which is congenital to the organ of hearing; or, rather, it does not even penetrate into the organ of hearing, because it is spiralled. Whenever that does happen, one does not hear; nor does one hear when the tympanic membrane is worn out, just as obtains as well for the eye's cornea.[27] And the ear's resonating as a horn does is no 15 indication of whether we hear or not;[28] for the air internal to the ear is forever moving with its own motion, whereas sound is foreign to the ear and not private. And because of this some people say that hearing occurs by means of what is void and resonating, because we hear by means of what has bounded air within it.

Which makes a sound: the thing struck or the thing which 20 strikes? Or is it in fact both, each in a different way? For it is also the case that sound is the motion of what is potentially moved in the way that things which rebound from smooth surfaces rapped by someone are. But surely, as was said, not every case of striking and being struck makes a sound, e.g. if a needle were to knock against a needle. Rather, it is necessary that the thing struck be smooth, so that a mass of air is rebounded 25 and vibrated.

The varieties of things which make sound are made clear in actual sound. For just as colours are not seen without light, so sharp and flat are not heard without sound. The sharp and flat are spoken of in a way transferred from tangible things: for what is sharp moves perception greatly in a short time, whereas the flat 30 moves it a little in a long time. The sharp is not just quick, nor the

flat slow; rather, the one sort of motion comes about because of
**420b** quickness, and that of the other because of slowness. And this
seems to have an analogue in what is sharp and blunt in the case
of touch: the sharp, for instance, pierces, while the blunt, for
instance, forces, because in one case the motion is short and
in the other long, so that the one turns out to be quick and the
other slow.

5     Let so much be determined about sound. Voice is a certain sort
of sound, one belonging to the ensouled; for nothing without a
soul is vocal, but is instead said to vocalize by way of likeness, e.g.
a flute, lyre, or any other soulless thing with register, melody, and
articulation. That is reasonable, since voice has these as well.
Many animals lack voice, for example, both the bloodless and,
10 among those with blood, fish (something which is also reasonable,
since sound is a certain sort of movement of air). Those fish which
are said to have voices, e.g. those in the Achelous, make sounds
with their gills or some other such part, whereas voice is not a
sound originating from just any random part of an animal.
Rather, since everything makes sound when something is struck
15 and something strikes in something, which is the air, it would be
reasonable that only those animals which draw in air have a
voice. For nature at that point makes use of the inhaled air for
two functions, just as it uses the tongue for both taste and articulation. Of these, taste is the necessary one (for which reason it also
belongs to more animals), while the power of speech is for the
20 sake of well-being. In the same way, nature uses breath both
for internal heating, since, for a reason to be stated elsewhere,
that is necessary, and also for the voice, so that one may attain
well-being.

The organ for breathing is the windpipe; this part exists for the
sake of the lung. For it is in virtue of this part that land animals
25 have more heat than other animals. The area around the heart
also needs breath in a primary way. It is accordingly necessary
that the air comes in by being breathed in.

Consequently, voice is an impact, effected by the soul in these
parts, of the inhaled air upon what is called the trachea. For, as
30 we have said, not every sound belonging to an animal is voice: it is
also possible to make a sound with the tongue or as those who
cough do. Rather, it is necessary for what does the striking to be
ensouled and to proceed with a definite imagination, since it is

certainly the case that voice is a definite significant sound, and not merely that of inhaled air, as in a cough. Rather, with this air an animal strikes the air in the trachea against the trachea itself. As **421a** evidence of this: it is not possible to vocalize while inhaling or exhaling, but only when holding one's breath. For it is with this air that the one holding his breath initiates motion. This is evidently why fish have no voices: they do not have windpipes. They do not have this part because they do not take in air or inhale. The 5 reason why is a separate discussion.


CHAPTER 9

Matters concerning smell and the object of smell are less easy to **421a7** determine than those that have already been discussed: it is not clear what sort of thing smell is, not in the way that it is in the cases of sound and colour. The reason for this is that we do not have this sense with precision, but are inferior to many animals. 10 For humans smell things weakly and do not perceive any object of smell without its being painful or pleasant, because the sensory organ is imprecise. It is also likely that hard-eyed animals perceive colours in this way, and that the variations among colours are not especially clear for them, excepting those which do and do 15 not inspire fear. So too is the human race when it comes to smells.

For smell seems analogous to taste, and the kinds of flavours are similarly analogous to the kinds of smell, but we have a more precise sense of taste because of its being a sort of touch, and this is the sense which is most precise in humans. For in the other 20 senses humans are surpassed by many other animals, whereas in the case of touch humans differ from the others in being by a long measure more precise. Humans are, accordingly, the most intelligent of animals. As an indication of this: in the human race, natural aptitude depends upon this sensory faculty but not upon any other. For whereas those with hard flesh have no natural 25 aptitude for thought, those with delicate flesh do.

It is also the case that just as some flavours are sweet and others bitter, so it is with smells, though in some cases smell and flavour correspond (I mean the sort of thing with a sweet smell and a sweet flavour), and in other cases they are opposite one another. Similarly, smells are also pungent, grating, sharp, or 30 oily. But just as we said, because smells, unlike flavours, are not especially clear, they have taken their names from things by way

**421b** of likeness:[29] a sweet smell from saffron or honey, and a pungent smell from thyme or other things of this sort, and in the same way in other cases.

It is also the case that smell is like hearing and each of the other senses: hearing is of the audible and inaudible; sight is of the
5 visible and invisible; and smelling is of the scented and unscented. Some things are unscented on account of its being generally impossible that they have a smell and others because of their having a slight or weak smell. And the same may be said for the untasteable.

It is also the case that smelling takes place through a medium like air or water; for water animals, those with blood and those
10 without alike, also seem to perceive smell, just as those in the air do. For some of these come upon food from far away, having been guided by smell.

For this reason, there appears to be a problem: if all things smell in a similar way, and yet a human smells when inhaling, though when he is not inhaling but rather exhaling or holding his
15 breath he does not smell, neither from afar nor from what is near, not even if something scented has been placed on the inside of his nostril. And while it is common to all animals that something placed upon the sensory organ itself is imperceptible, it is peculiar to humans to fail to perceive without inhaling. (That is clear from
20 experiments.) The result is that bloodless animals, since they do not inhale, would have some other sense beyond those already mentioned. But that is impossible, if it is smell they perceive; for the perception of an object of smell, both the malodorous and the aromatic, is smelling. Moreover, strong smells which are evidently destructive to them are the very ones which are destruc-
25 tive to humans: bitumen, sulphur, and that sort of thing. It is necessary, then, that they smell, but not by inhaling.

It is likely that in humans this sensory organ differs from that of the other animals, just as their eyes do from those of the hard-eyed animals. For humans have eyelids as protection and as a case, as it were; without moving them or drawing them up, a
30 human does not see. Hard-eyed animals, however, have nothing of this sort, but see straightaway what comes to pass in the transparent. It is similarly likely that the sensory organ for smell

in some is uncovered, like the eye, but in those which take in air it **422a**
has a covering which is drawn back when they inhale, the veins
and passageways being dilated. And because of this, animals
which inhale do not smell in water; for it is necessary that they
smell while inhaling, something it is impossible to do in water.    5
  It is also the case that smell belongs to what is dry, just as
flavour belongs to what is moist, and the sensory organ for smell
is potentially of such a sort.


### CHAPTER 10

An object of taste is something tangible; and it is for this reason **422a8**
not perceptible through the medium of a foreign body, since
touch does not come about this way.[30] And the body in which 10
the flavour is, the object of taste, is in moisture, which is its
matter. This is something tangible. Consequently, even if we
were in water, we would perceive something sweet which had
been thrown into it; but our perception would not be through a
medium, but by something's having been mixed with the water,
just as in the case of a drink. Colour is not seen in this way, by
having been mixed, nor by means of emanations. Hence, nothing 15
is present as a medium; but as colour is the object of sight, so
flavour is the object of taste. Nothing produces the perception of
flavour without moisture; rather, it is what has moisture in actuality or in potentiality, as something salty, for example, does. For it
is both itself easily dissolved and also melds with the tongue.
  Sight is of the visible and the invisible (for darkness is invisible, 20
and sight discriminates this too), and, moreover, of that which is
overly bright (for this too is invisible, though in a different way
from that in which darkness is); similarly, hearing is of both
sound and silence, the one as something heard and the other as
something unheard, and of very loud sound in the way that sight
is of what is very bright (for just as a small sound is inaudible, so 25
too, in a certain way, is a great and violent sound). What is
invisible is so called in one way when something is completely
invisible, just as in other cases where something is impossible, but
in another way, when something happens to lack or have only
slightly what it naturally has,[31] as in the cases of what is footless
or pipless. In the same way, then, taste is of the tasteable and of

30 the untasteable (this being what has a slight or weak flavour, or what is destructive to the sense of taste).

The starting point seems to be the drinkable and the undrinkable, since taste is in a certain way of both, in the one case of something weak and destructive, while in the other it is natural.[32] It is also the case that what is drinkable is common to touch and taste.

**422b** Since the tasteable is something moist, its sensory organ must be neither moist in actuality nor incapable of being moistened. For taste is something affected by the object of taste insofar as it is an object of taste. It is necessary, then, that the sensory faculty of taste, though it is not itself something moist, be capable of being 5 moistened and of being preserved when moistened. As an indication of this: the tongue perceives when it is neither completely dry nor excessively wet. In the latter case, this is in virtue of touching the moisture first there,[33] just as when someone who has tasted a strong flavour then tastes another flavour, and as happens, for example, to the sick: everything seems bitter, because of their perceiving with a tongue full of moisture of that sort.

10 As in the case of colours, the simple flavours are opposites: sweet and bitter. Standing alongside the one is the oily and the other the salty; and between these are the pungent, the grating, the sour, and the sharp—for these seem to be pretty much the variations among flavours. Consequently, what is capable of 15 tasting is this sort of thing in potentiality, while the object of taste is what is capable of making it so in actuality.


CHAPTER 11


**422b17** The same account holds for touch and the tangible. For if touch is not one sense, but several, then it will be necessary for there to be several perceptible objects of touch as well. But there is a diffi- 20 culty whether these are several or one, and another difficulty concerning what sensory organ belongs to the capacity of touch—whether this is flesh and something analogous in the other animals, or not, or if flesh is rather a medium, with the primary sensory organ being something else, something internal.

Every sense seems to be of a single pair of contraries: sight of 25 white and black; hearing of high and low; taste of bitter and sweet. But among the objects of touch are included many pairs of contraries: hot and cold, dry and wet, hard and soft, and whatever else is of this sort.

There is a solution for at least this difficulty, namely that in the case of the other senses there are also several pairs of opposites. For example, in spoken sound there is not only highness and lowness, but also loudness and softness, and smoothness and 30 roughness of voice, as well as other things of this sort. There are also other such variations in the case of colour. Still, it is not yet clear what one thing is the substrate for touch, as sound is for hearing.

Regarding whether the sensory organ for touch is internal or is not, or is rather the flesh immediately: it does not seem to count as **423a** evidence that perception occurs at the same time as things are handled. For even as things are, if someone had made a sort of membrane and were to stretch it around the flesh, it would communicate the sensation in the same way, immediately when touched. Even so, it is clear that there is no sensory organ in this (though if it were to become naturally attached, the perception 5 would pass through it still more quickly). Consequently, this sort of bodily part seems related to us as the air around us would be if it were to become naturally affixed to us. For then we would have thought that we perceived sound and colour and smell by some one thing, and that sight and hearing and smelling were one individual sense. As things are, though, because that through 10 which motions come about is detached from us, the organs mentioned are patently different. But in the case of touch, this is, as things stand, unclear.

For it is not possible for an ensouled body to be constituted out of air or water, since it is necessary that it be something solid. It remains, then, that it is a mixture of earth and these, as flesh and its analogue tend to be. Consequently, it is necessary 15 that the body be a naturally attached medium belonging to the faculty of touch, through which perceptions, which are several, come about. That they are several is clear from touch in the case of the tongue: it perceives all objects of touch at the same part as it perceives flavour. If, then, the remaining flesh were to perceive flavour, taste and touch would seem to be one and the same 20 sense; but as things are, they are two, because of there being no interchangeability.

Someone might raise a difficulty: every body has depth; and this is the third dimension; yet when between two bodies there is another body, these cannot touch one another; and what is wet or
25 moist does not occur without body, but instead either is or contains water; and it is necessary that things which touch each other in water have water between them, since they are not dry at their edges, when their extremities are full of water. If this is true, it will be impossible for them to touch one another in water; in the same way, they will not be able to touch one another in the air either. (For air is related to the things in air in a manner similar to
30 the way water is related to things in water, though this is more likely to escape our notice, just as it will more likely escape the notice of animals living in water if something moist touches
**423b** something moist.) The difficulty is then whether perception in all cases proceeds similarly, or whether different cases proceed differently, just as it now seems that while taste and touch occur by means of touching, the others occur at a distance.

But this is not the case. Rather, we perceive the hard and the soft through other things, just as we do that which can sound, as
5 well as the objects of sight and smell. But we perceive some of these from afar, and others from up close, for which reason it escapes our notice—since we do perceive all things through some intermediary, though in some cases this escapes our notice. Even so, just as we also said earlier, even if we were to perceive all tangible things through a membrane without noticing that it lay
10 between us and them, we would be in much the same condition as we are now, in fact, in water and air. For we now suppose ourselves to touch the objects themselves, with nothing happening through an intermediary.

Still, the object of touch differs from the objects of sight and hearing, since we perceive these latter because the medium affects us in some way, whereas we perceive the objects of touch not in virtue of having been affected by the medium but simultaneously
15 with the medium, as when someone is struck through a shield. For it is not the case that the shield hit its wearer after it was struck; rather, both co-incided in being struck simultaneously.

In general, it would seem that flesh and the tongue are related to their sensory organ just as, in each case, air and water are related to sight, hearing, and smelling. When the sensory organ
20 itself has been touched, no perception could occur in either this or

that case, as if, for example, someone were to place a white body upon the surface of the eye. In this way too it is clear that the capacity to perceive an object of touch is internal. It would turn out here just as it has in the other cases: one does not perceive things placed upon the sensory organ, but one does perceive what 25 is placed upon the flesh. Consequently, flesh is the medium pertaining to the faculty of touch.

The objects of touch are then the distinguishing features of a body insofar as it is a body. By distinguishing features I mean those which characterize the elements which we spoke about earlier in our writings on the elements: hot and cold, dry and wet. The sensory organ for these, that which is able to touch, and 30 that in which the sense called touch primarily belongs, is that part which is potentially such as these are. For perceiving is a sort of **424a** being affected; consequently, the thing which acts makes that which is in potentiality such as it is itself in actuality.

Accordingly, we do not perceive what is hot and cold, or hard and soft, in measures equal to ourselves, but only excesses, since perception is a sort of a mean between the contraries present in 5 perceptible objects. And because of this it discriminates perceptible objects; for the mean is capable of discriminating, since it comes to be, relative to either one or the other, its opposite extreme. And just as it is necessary for what is going to perceive white and black to be neither of these in actuality, but both in potentiality (and so on for the other cases), so too in the case of 10 touch it must be neither hot nor cold.

Further, just as sight was in a certain way of the visible and the invisible, and as the remaining senses were similarly of opposites, so too is touch of the tangible and the intangible. The intangible includes both that which has an extremely faint distinguishing feature of tangible things, e.g. the air, and the excesses among tangible things, just as those which are destructive are.

What pertains to each of the senses, then, has been described 15 in outline.

CHAPTER 12

It is necessary to grasp, concerning the whole of perception gener- **424a17** ally, that perception is what is capable of receiving perceptible

20 forms without the matter, as wax receives the seal of a signet ring without the iron or gold. It acquires the golden or the metallic seal, but not insofar as it is gold or metal. In a similar way, perception is also in each case affected by what has the colour or taste or sound, but not insofar as each of these is said to be something, but rather insofar as each is of a certain quality, and corresponding to its proportion.

The primary sense organ is that in which this sort of potential-
25 ity resides. The sense organ and this potentiality are, then, the same, though their being is different. For what does the perceiv-ing is a certain magnitude; nevertheless being capable of percep-tion is not; nor is perception a magnitude, but is rather a certain proportion and a potentiality of that thing.

It is evident from these considerations why excesses in the objects of perception destroy the sensory organs. For should a
30 motion be too strong for the organ, then the proportion—and this is the sense—is destroyed, just as the attunement and the tone are destroyed when the strings of an instrument are thumped.

And this is why plants do not perceive, even though they have one psychic part and are affected in a way by the objects of touch,
**424b** since they are cooled and heated. The reason is that they do not have a mean, nor do they have the sort of principle for receiving the forms of perceptible things; rather, they are affected with the matter.

Someone might raise a difficulty as to whether what cannot smell can be affected by odour in any way, or what cannot see
5 by colour, and similarly for the other senses. If the object of smell is odour, if it produces anything, then odour produces smelling, so that nothing incapable of smelling can be affected by odour; and the same argument applies to the other senses. Nor can what is capable of perceiving perceive, except insofar as it is in each case capable of perceiving. This is also immediately clear in this way: neither light and darkness nor sound nor
10 odour affects bodies in any way; rather, that in which they are does. For example, it is the air accompanying thunder which splits timber.

Still, tangible things and flavours affect bodies. For if they did not, what would affect or alter things without souls? Then, will the other objects of sense also affect bodies? Or is it rather not the case that every body is capable of being affected by odour and

sound, and that those so affected are indeterminate, and do not 15
remain, like the air, for example (for it smells just as if it were
affected in a certain way)?

What, then, is smelling beyond being affected by something?
Or is smelling also perceiving, whereas the air which is affected
quickly becomes something perceptible?

# BOOK III

## CHAPTER 1

**424b22** That there is no other sense beyond these five (I mean these: sight, hearing, smelling, taste, and touch) one might feel confident on the basis of the following considerations. For as things are we 25 have perception of everything of which touch is the sense (for all qualities of the tangible, as tangible, are perceptible by us by means of touch); and it will be necessary, if indeed some sense is left out, that some sensory organ is also left out. And anything which we perceive by handling them is perceptible by means of touch, which we do possess, while anything we perceive through 30 media and not by handling them we perceive by means of the simple bodies (I mean, for example, air and water). And this being so, the result is that if two things differing from one another in genus are perceptible through one medium, it will be necessary that one who possesses this sort of sensory organ be able to perceive them both (for example, if a sensory organ is made of air and it is also the case that air is the medium of both sound **425a** and colour); if, however, there is more than one medium for the same thing (for example, both air and water are the media of colour, since both are transparent), then the one who possesses only one or the other of these will perceive whatever is perceptible through both. The sensory organs are made of only two of the simple bodies: air and water. (For the pupil is made of water, the organ of hearing of air, and the organ of smelling 5 of one or the other of these.) Fire belongs either to none of them or to all in common, since nothing can perceive without heat, while earth belongs either to none or is mixed exclusively and especially into touch. It remains, consequently, that no sensory organ remains beyond those of water and air, and certain animals do in fact have these.

Hence, all the senses are possessed by those animals which are 10 neither imperfect nor defective (for even the mole evidently possesses eyes beneath its skin). Consequently, unless there is some other body as well as a quality belonging to none of the bodies here now, no sense would be left out.

Moreover, there cannot be some special sensory organ for the common objects, which we perceive co-incidentally by each sense— for example, motion, rest, shape, magnitude, number, and unity.[34] 15 For all of these we perceive by motion: for example, we perceive magnitude by motion (and consequently, shape, since shape is a sort of magnitude); something at rest in virtue of its not being moved; number in virtue of the lack of continuity as well as by the peculiar objects of perception (since each sense perceives one thing).

Consequently, it is clear that there cannot be any special sense 20 for these, for instance, for motion. For in this way things will be just as they are now when we perceive the sweet by sight: this occurs because we as a matter of fact have a perception of them both, by which we come to know them at the same time when they occur together. Otherwise, we would never perceive such things other than co-incidentally. For example, we perceive the son of 25 Cleon not because he is the son of Cleon, but because he is a white thing, and it is co-incidental to this white thing to be the son of Cleon.

We have common perception of the common objects, however, and a not co-incidental one. Thus these are not exclusive objects; otherwise, we would not perceive them in any way other than in the way just mentioned that we see the son of Cleon.[35]

The senses perceive one another's exclusive objects co-inciden- 30 tally, not insofar as they are the senses they are, but insofar as they are one, whenever perception occurs of the same thing at the **425b** same time, for example of bile that it is bitter and yellow (for it most surely does not belong to another sense to say that the two are one). This is also why one is deceived when, should something be yellow, one thinks it is bile.[36]

Someone might ask for the sake of what we have several senses, and not one only. Or is it so that the accompanying common 5 things (e.g. motion, magnitude, and number) will be less likely to escape our notice? For if there were only sight, and if it were of white, such objects would more likely escape our notice and it would seem that all things were the same because colour and magnitude concurrently accompany one another. As things are, since the common objects are also present in some other sense 10 object, this makes clear that each of them is something distinct.

51

## CHAPTER 2

**425b12** Since we perceive that we are seeing and hearing, it is necessary that one perceives that one sees either by sight or by some other sense. But then the same sense will be of sight and of the under-
15 lying colour, with the result that either there will be two senses of the same thing or a sense will be of itself. Further, if the sense which perceived sight were to be other than sight, then either this will carry on into infinity or there will be some sense which will be of itself, with the result that one should grant this in the case of the first sense.

But this contains a difficulty: if perceiving by sight is seeing and what is seen is either colour or what possesses colour, if one is to see that which sees, then that which sees will have colour in a primary way.

20 It is evident, then, that perceiving by sight is not one thing; for even when we are not seeing, we discriminate light and darkness by sight, though not in the same way. And, moreover, that which is seeing is in a sense coloured. For the sensory organ is in each case receptive of the object of perception without its matter; and for this reason, even when the objects of sense have gone away,
25 perceptions and imaginings remain in the sensory organs.

The actuality of the object of perception and of the senses are one and the same, but their being is different. I mean, for example, actual sound and actual hearing. For it is possible for someone who has hearing not to be hearing; and what has sound is not always making a sound. But whenever what is able to hear is in actuality
30 hearing and whatever is able to sound is sounding, then actual hearing and actual sounding come about simultaneously. One could say of these that the one is hearing and the other sounding.

If, then, the motion (both acting and being acted upon) is in
**426a** the thing which is being acted upon,[37] it is necessary that both the sound and the actual hearing be in something potential. For the actuality of what produces and causes motion comes about in
5 the thing which is affected—for which reason it is not necessary that what initiates motion be in motion. Hence, the actuality of what is capable of making a sound is sound or sounding, and the actuality of what is capable of hearing is hearing or listening. For hearing is twofold; and sound is twofold.

The same account also applies to the other senses and sensible objects. For just as both acting and being affected are in what is affected, but not in what is acting, so also is the actuality of the 10 sensible object and of what is capable of perceiving in what is capable of perceiving. But while in some cases each has a name, e.g. sounding and hearing, in others one or the other is without a name. For the actuality of sight is called seeing, while the actuality of colour has no name, and tasting is the actuality of what is able to taste, while the actuality of flavour has no name.

And since there is one actuality of the sensible object and what 15 is capable of perceiving, though their being is different, it is necessary that what is spoken of in this way as hearing and sounding perish or be preserved at the same time, and so also for flavour and tasting, and similarly for the other cases. But this is not necessary for those things spoken of as potential.

Still, the earlier natural philosophers did not speak well on this 20 point, because they supposed that nothing is white or black without sight, nor is there flavour without tasting. For though they were in one way right, in another way they were not right, since both perception and perceptible objects are spoken of in two ways, in some cases as potential and in others as actual. What was said by them applies to the latter, but does not apply to the 25 former. They, however, spoke without qualification about matters which are spoken of only with qualification.

If voice is a sort of concord, and voice and hearing are in a way one, and a concordance is a proportion, it will be necessary that hearing too will be a certain proportion.[38] It is also for this reason 30 that each of the excesses, both high and low, destroys hearing. 426b Similarly, since perception is a sort of proportion, excess in flavour also destroys taste, in colours exceeding radiance or murkiness destroys sight, and in smelling it is a strong smell, whether sweet or bitter. Accordingly, things are pleasant when, though pure and unmixed, like the acidic or the sweet or the salty, 5 they are brought into a proportion, since then they are pleasant; and in general what is mixed, a concordance, is pleasant rather than the high or the low, and in the case of touch it is what can be heated or cooled. Perception is the proportion, and excesses cause pain or destroy it.[39]

Hence, each perception is of an underlying perceptible object, is present in the sensory organ insofar as it is a sensory organ,

10 and discriminates the variations of its underlying  object of perception, e.g. sight discriminates white and black; taste, sweet and bitter; and so things stand for the others. Since we discriminate white and sweet and each of the other objects of perception in relation to one another, what is it by which we perceive that they differ?[40] It is necessary, to be sure, that this is by perception, since they are perceptible objects. And it is in this

15 way clear that flesh is not the ultimate sensory organ; for it would then be necessary for that which discerns to do so by touching its object.[41]

Nor, indeed, is it possible for separate things to discern that white is something other than sweet; rather, it is necessary for both to be manifest to some one thing. For otherwise, if I were in this way to perceive one thing and you another, it would be clear that they were different from one another. Rather, it is necessary

20 for one thing to say that they are different; since sweet is different from white. So then, the same thing says this. Consequently, as one makes a declaration, so one both thinks and perceives. It is clear, therefore, that it is not possible to discern separate things with what is separate.

Nor, further, on this basis, is this possible in separate times, therefore. For just as the same thing says that the good and the

25 bad are different, so also when it says that the one is different from the other, it also says that the other is different from the one: the *when* here is not co-incidental. I mean, that is, I do not now say that they are different, without saying that they are different now. Rather, one proceeds thus: saying it now and saying they are different now—so, simultaneously. Consequently, it is a non-

30 separate thing in a non-separate time.

Yet it is surely impossible for the same thing, in so far as it is indivisible, and in an indivisible time, to be moved simultaneously with opposite motions. For if something is sweet, it moves per-

427a ception or thought in a certain way, while what is bitter moves these in an opposite way, and what is white differently again. So then is that which discriminates simultaneously indivisible in number and non-separate, yet in its being something separate? To be sure, there is a way in which what is divisible perceives what has been divided, but there is also a way in which it does so insofar as it is indivisible; for while it is divisible in its being, it

5 is indivisible in place and in number.

Or is that impossible? For the same thing, something indivisible, is potentially opposite things, though it is not so in its being, but rather is divided by being actualized, and cannot simultaneously be white and black, with the result that it cannot be affected by their forms, if perception and thought are something of this sort.

Rather, it is like what some call a point: it is both indivisible 10 and divisible, insofar as it is either one or two.[42] Hence, insofar as it is something indivisible, what discriminates is one thing and it discriminates simultaneously, while insofar as it is divisible, it uses the same token simultaneously twice over. Hence, insofar as it uses the same limit twice, and discriminates two separate things, there is a sense in which it discriminates separately; but insofar as it uses one, it discriminates one thing and does so simultaneously.

Concerning the principle in virtue of which we say that an 15 animal is capable of perception, let it be determined in this way.

## CHAPTER 3

People define the soul principally by two differentiae: motion with **427a17** respect to place; and reasoning, discriminating, and perceiving.[43] Both reasoning and understanding seem to be a sort of perceiving, for in both these cases, the soul discriminates something and 20 comes to know things that are. The ancients, indeed, say that understanding and perceiving are the same, as even Empedocles said, 'For the wisdom of human beings grows in relation to what is present to them,' and in other writings, 'Whence different understandings ever present themselves to them.' What was said by Homer tends in the same direction as these, 'For such is 25 reason.' For all of these suppose that reasoning is corporeal, just as perceiving is, and that both perceiving and understanding are of like by like, just as we determined at the outset of our writings.

Even so, they ought also at the same time to have said something about error, since this is the more typical state in animals **427b** and the soul spends more time in this condition. For this reason it is necessary either, as some say, that all appearances are true, or that error is contact with what is unlike, since this is the opposite

5 of coming to know like by like. It seems, however, that both error
and knowledge of opposites are the same.

In view of all that, therefore, it is evident that perceiving and
understanding are not the same. For all animals have a share of
the one, but only a few of the other. Nor, moreover, is reasoning,
in which there is a right and a wrong—understanding and know-
10 ledge and true belief being right, and the opposites of these being
wrong—nor is this the same as perceiving. For perception of
exclusive objects is always true, and belongs to all animals,
whereas reasoning can also be false, and it belongs to nothing
which lacks reason.

For imagination is different from both perception and reason-
15 ing, and it does not come about without perception, and without
this there is no conceiving.

It is evident that imagination is also not conceiving.[44] For in
this case, the affection is up to us, whenever we wish (for it is
possible to produce something before one's eyes, as those who
produce images and arrange them in mnemonic systems do),
20 whereas believing is not up to us, since it is necessary that it be
true or false. Moreover, whenever we come to believe something
terrible or frightful, we are correspondingly affected right away,
and similarly with something audacious. But in the case of
imagination, we are just as if we had seen the terrible or audacious
things in a picture.

25 There are also varieties of conceiving itself: knowledge and
belief and understanding and the opposites of these. Let there
be another account concerning the variations among them.

Concerning reasoning: since it is something other than perceiving, and both imagination and conception seem to belong to it, it
is necessary for those who have first characterized imagination
**428a** then to speak of the other. So, if imagination is that in virtue of
which we say that a particular image comes about for us, and we
refrain from speaking metaphorically, will it be one of these: a
capacity or state in virtue of which we discriminate and issue
truths or falsehoods? Such faculties or states are perception,
5 belief, knowledge, and reason.

That it is not perception, then, is clear from the following. For
perception is either a potentiality or an actuality, such as sight
and seeing; yet something may also appear even when neither of
these is present, as in sleep. Further, perception is always present,

though imagination is not. If these were the same in actuality, it would be possible for imagination to belong to all beasts; but this 10 does not seem to be the case. For instance, it belongs to the ant or the bee, but not to the grub. Further, perceptions are always true, whereas imaginings are for the most part false. Again, we do not say that this appears to us to be a man whenever we are in a state of actuality accurately in relation to the perceptual object, but rather whenever we do not perceive clearly whether it is true or false. And there is also what we said earlier, that visual images 15 appear even to those whose eyes are closed.

Nor, moreover, is it the case that imagination is counted among those things which are always true, such as knowledge and understanding; for it is the case that imagination is false as well.

It remains, then, to see if it is belief, since belief too is both true and false. But conviction follows upon belief (since no one can 20 believe something which does not seem convincing); yet no beast has conviction, though many of them have imagination. Further, every case of belief implies conviction, while conviction implies being persuaded, and persuasion implies reason; yet among the beasts some have imagination, but none has reason.[45]

It is evident, then, that imagination could be neither belief 25 accompanied by perception, nor belief acquired through perception, nor an interweaving of belief and perception, both because of these reasons and because belief will be of nothing other than the object of perception, if indeed there is one. I mean that imagination will be the interweaving of a belief regarding, and a perception of, something white—since it surely will not come from a belief regarding something good and a perception of 30 something white. For then imagining will be believing, non- **428b** co-incidentally, the very thing one perceives. Yet things do appear falsely even among those things concerning which one has at the same time a true conception: for instance, although the sun appears to be one foot across, one is convinced that it is larger than the inhabited world. This results, then, either in our having rejected the 5 true belief which we had concerning that thing, even though the thing remains as it was and we have neither forgotten anything nor been persuaded of anything new, or, if the true belief still stands, then the same belief must be both true and false. (Otherwise, it could have become false, seeing that it might have escaped our notice that the thing had changed over.) Consequently, imagination is neither any one of these nor something from them.

10     Still, since it is possible when something is set in motion for something else to be moved by it, and since imagination seems to be a sort of motion and not to occur without perception, but rather to occur in things which are perceiving and to be of those things of which perception is, and since it is possible for motion to be effected by the actuality of perception, which motion is necessarily similar to the perception, this motion would be neither 15 possible without perception nor could it belong to things which are not perceiving; and it is possible for what has imagination both to act and be affected in many ways in accordance with it, and for it to be either true or false. This result is due to the following: perception of exclusive objects is true, or is subject to falsity in the smallest degree. Second, perception is of something's 20 being an attribute of something;[46] and already here it is possible to be mistaken. For one is not mistaken *that there is white*; but if one says that this or that other thing is what is white, one is mistaken. Third, perception is of the common objects which follow upon the attributes to which the exclusive objects belong (I mean, for instance, motion and magnitude, which are attributes of the objects of perception), concerning which there is already, 25 most of all, deception in the realm of perception.

The motion resulting from these three kinds of perception, the motion effected by the actuality of perception, will differ: the first, when the perception is present, is true; the others can also be false, whether the perception is present or absent, and most of all when the object of perception is far away.

30     If, then, nothing other than imagination has the features men-
**429a** tioned (and this is what was claimed), then imagination would be a motion effected by actual perception.

Since sight is the principal sense, the name imagination (*phantasia*) was derived from light (*phaos*), because without light it is not possible to see.

Because instances of imagination persist and are similar to per-
5 ceptions, animals do many things in accordance with them, some because they lack reason, e.g. beasts, and others because their reason is sometimes shrouded by passion, or sickness, or sleep, e.g. humans.

Concerning imagination, what it is and why it is, let so much be said.

## CHAPTER 4

Concerning the part of the soul by which the soul both knows and **429a10**
understands, whether it is separable or is not separable in magnitude but only in account, it is necessary to consider what its
differentia is and how reasoning ever comes about.

To be sure, if reasoning is like perceiving, it would consist in
being somehow affected by the object of reason or in something else
of this sort. It is necessary, therefore, that it be unaffected, yet 15
capable of receiving the form; that it be of this sort potentially but
not be this; and that it be such that just as the perceptual faculty is to
the objects of perception, so reason will be to the objects of thought.

It is necessary, then, since it reasons all things, that it be
unmixed, just as Anaxagoras says, so that it may rule, that is, so
that it may know; for the interposing of anything alien hinders 20
and obstructs it. Consequently, its nature must be nothing other
than this: that it be potential.

Hence, that part of the soul called reason (and by *reason* I mean
that by which the soul reasons and conceives) is in actuality none
of the things which are before it reasons; nor is it, accordingly,
reasonable for it to be mixed with the body, since then it would 25
come to be qualified in a certain way, either cold or hot, and there
would be an organ for it, just as there is for the perceptual faculty.
As things are, though, there is none.

Therefore, they speak well, further, who say that the soul is a
place of forms—except that it is neither the whole soul, but
rather the rational soul, nor the forms in actuality, but rather
in potentiality.

That the unaffectedness of the perceptual and rational faculties
is not the same is evident in the case of the perceptual organs and 30
perception. For perception cannot perceive when coming from an
intense object of perception, for instance a sound when coming **429b**
from loud sounds, nor when coming from strong colours or
odours can it see or smell. By contrast, when it reasons some
intense object of reason, reason reasons inferior things not to a
lesser degree but rather to a greater. For the perceptual faculty is
not without the body, whereas reason is separate. 5

Whenever it becomes each thing in the manner in which one
who knows in actuality is said to do so (this occurs whenever one

is able to move to actuality through oneself), even then it is somehow in potentiality, not, however, in the same way as before learning or discovering. And then it is able to reason through itself.

10 Since a magnitude and being a magnitude differ, as also water and being water differ (and thus for many other cases, though not all, since in some cases they are the same), one discerns flesh and being flesh either by means of different things or by means of something in a different condition. For flesh is not without matter, but is rather just as the snub: a this in a this. One discerns by 15 means of the perceptual faculty the hot and the cold, those things of which flesh is a proportion.[47] But it is by means of something else, something either separate or something which is as a bent line is to itself when it has been straightened out, that one discerns being flesh.

Further, in the case of things which are by abstraction, the straight is as the snub is, since it is with extension. The essence though, if it is the case that being straight and the straight 20 differ, is something else. For let it be two: then one discerns it either by different things or by something in a different condition. Generally, then, as things are with respect to things separate from matter, so too are they with respect to things concerning reason.

Someone might raise a difficulty: if reason is simple and unaffected and has nothing in common with anything, just as Anaxagoras says it is, how will it reason, if reasoning is to be 25 being affected somehow (since it is insofar as something common belongs to both that one thing seems to act and the other to be affected)? And there is a further difficulty: is it itself an object of reason? For either reason will belong to other things, if it is an object of reason itself not in virtue of something else, and the object of reason is one in form, or it will be something mixed with it which makes it an object of reason just as other things are.

Or else being affected in virtue of something common is as discussed earlier: that reason is in a certain way in potentiality the 30 objects of reason, though it is nothing in actuality before it 430a reasons—in potentiality just as in a writing tablet on which nothing written in actuality is present, which is just what turns out in the case of reason.

And it is itself an object of reason just as other objects of reason are. For whereas in the case of those things without matter what reasons and what is being reasoned about are the same, since theoretical knowledge and what is known in this way are the same 5 (though one must inquire into the cause of its not always reasoning), in the case of those things which have matter it is each of the objects of reason in potentiality.

Consequently, reason will not belong to those things (since it is without their matter that reason is a potentiality of these sorts of things), though it will belong to reason to be an object of reason.

## CHAPTER 5

Since in all of nature there is something which is the matter for **430a10** each kind of thing (and this is what is all those things in potentiality), while something else is their cause, i.e. the productive one, because of its producing them all as falls to a craft in relation to the matter, it is necessary that these differences be present in the soul.[48] And there is one sort of reason by coming to be all things, and another sort by producing them all, as a kind of positive state, 15 like light. For in a certain way, light makes colours which are in potentiality colours in actuality.

And this reason is separate and unaffected and unmixed, being in its essence actuality. For what acts is always superior to what is affected, as too the first principle is to the matter.

[Knowledge in actuality is the same as the thing, though in an 20 individual knowledge in potentiality is prior in time, though generally it is not prior in time.][49]

But it is not the case that sometimes it reasons and sometimes it does not. And having been separated, this alone is just what it is, and this alone is deathless and everlasting, though we do not remember, because this is unaffected, whereas passive reason is perishable. And without this, nothing reasons. 25

## CHAPTER 6

Reasoning of indivisible things is among the things concerning **430a26** which there is no falsity, while among those where there is both

falsity and truth there is already some combining of thoughts, as a unity from them. As Empedocles said, 'Where there sprang the neckless heads of many things,' thereafter combined by love, so too these, having been separate, are combined, for instance, the
30 incommensurable and the diagonal.
**430b**    Should reasoning be of what has gone before or what will be, then one combines time as well in the conceptions.[50] For falsity is always in combining. For even if one says the white is not white, one has combined white and not white.[51] It is also possible, though, to maintain that all are instances of division. In any case, however, it is surely not only true or false that Cleon is
5 white, but also that he was or will be. What produces a unity in each case is this: reason.
   Since the undivided is spoken of in two ways, either in potentiality or in actuality, nothing precludes one's thinking what is undivided whenever one thinks of a length (for this is undivided in actuality), or thinking in an undivided time, since time is divided and undivided in a manner similar to a length. It is not possible to say what one was thinking in the case of each half, since if the whole
10 has not been divided, there are no halves, except in potentiality. And if one thinks each of the halves separately, one also divides the time simultaneously, and then the half times were similar to lengths. But if it is thought of as made up of both halves, it is also thought of in the time corresponding to both of its halves.
   One thinks what is undivided not in quantity but in form in an
15 undivided time and with an undivided part of the soul.[52]
   But what one thinks and the time in which one thinks it are co-incidentally divided and not insofar as they are these things, but insofar as they are these things, they are undivided. For present in them is something undivided, though perhaps not something separate, which makes them one with respect to time and length. And
20 this is similar in every case of continuity, of both time and length.
   A point and every division—and whatever is in this way undivided—are revealed just as a privation is. And the account is similar in other cases, for instance how one comes to know bad or black; for in a certain sense one comes to know them by means of their opposites. For it is necessary that the one who comes to know is in potentiality and that these be present.[53] If, though, there is nothing opposite to something, then this knows itself and
25 is an actuality and is separate.[54]

It is also the case that every assertion, just as every denial, says one thing of another, and is true or false. But not every instance of reason does; rather reason directed to what something is with regard to its essence is true, and does not say one thing of another. Rather just as the seeing of an exclusive object is true, while whether the white thing is a man or not is not always true, so things are with respect to whatever is without matter. 30

CHAPTER 7

Knowledge taken as actual is the same as the thing, though in an **431a1** individual potential knowledge is prior in time, though it is not prior even in time generally, since it is the case that everything which comes to be does so from something existing in actuality.

It is evidently the case that the object of perception is what turns the perceptual faculty into something actual from being in 5 potentiality. For it is neither affected nor altered. Consequently, this kind is different from motion, since motion is the actuality of something incomplete, whereas unqualified actuality, that of something complete, is something else.

Perception is similar, then, to bare assertion and to thinking. But whenever there is something pleasant or painful, it by, so to speak, affirming or denying, pursues or avoids. And it is the case 10 that being pleased and being pained are the actualization of the mean of the perceptual faculty in relation to what is good or bad insofar as they are such.

And avoidance and desire are the same, in respect of their actuality; and the capacity for desire and the capacity for avoidance do not differ either from one another or from the perceptual faculty, though they do differ in being.

Images belong to the rational soul in the manner of percep- 15 tions, and whenever it affirms or denies that something is good or bad, it pursues or avoids. Consequently, the soul never thinks without an image.

Just as the air brought the pupil into a certain state, and the pupil something else, so hearing proceeds similarly. But the ultimate capacity is one, and the mean too is one, though its being is more than one.

20      What it is by which one discriminates how the sweet and the hot differ has been said earlier, but one must say it again in this way. For there is something one, as a boundary is such, and these too (being one by analogy and in number) stand in relation each to the other as those stand to one another. For what is the difference between puzzling how one discriminates things not of the same kind and opposites, like white and black?[55] Let A,

25      the white, stand in relation to B, the black; and let C stand in relation to D, as those are in relation to one another, with the result that they would be, converting as appropriate, one. If, therefore, CA were to belong to one thing, so this will be in the same condition as that to which DB belongs: though one and the same, their being would not be the same—and similarly with respect to those. The same account would hold if A were the sweet and B the white.

**431b1**      The rational faculty thinks some forms in images, and just as it is in these that what is to be pursued and what avoided are distinguished by it, so even outside of perception, whenever one is presented with images, one is moved. For instance, one who

5      perceives a beacon, because it is fire, and by common perception sees it moving, and recognizes that it is an enemy's. Sometimes, on the basis of images or thoughts in the soul, just as if seeing them, one calculates and plans future things with reference to things which are present. And whenever one says *there is the sweet* or *the painful*, in that case one avoids or pursues, and in general

10      will do some one thing.

And truth or falsity outside the sphere of action are also in the same genus as the good and the bad, though to be sure in one case they differ unqualifiedly and in the other relative to a person.

One thinks other things spoken of in abstraction just as if one were to think of the snub not as the snub, but rather as something

15      separate,[56] as the concave without the flesh in which the concave is. One thinks mathematical things in this way: though not existing as separate entities, one thinks of them as separate whenever one thinks of them just as they are.

In general reason, taken as actual, is the same as things. We must consider later whether or not it is possible for it when it is not itself separated from magnitude to think something belonging to the class of things which are separated.

## CHAPTER 8

Now, then, by way of summarizing the things which have been **431b20**
said concerning the soul, let us say again that the soul is in a sense
all existing things; for what exists is either objects of perception or
objects of reason; and knowledge is in a way the objects of
knowledge, and perception the objects of perception. Yet how
this is so must be investigated.

Knowledge and perception are divided with reference to
things: when in potentiality to those in potentiality and when 25
in actuality to those in actuality. The soul's perceptual faculty
and faculty of knowledge are these things in potentiality, the
one the object of knowledge and the other the object of perception.[57] It is necessary that they be either these things themselves
or their forms. It is certainly not the things themselves, however:
for the stone is not in the soul, but rather its form. Conse- **432a**
quently, the soul is just as the hand is; for the hand is a tool of
tools, and reason is a form of forms, and perception a form of
the objects of perception.

Since there is nothing beyond perceptible magnitudes, as it
seems, nothing separate, the objects of reason are in perceptible 5
forms, both those spoken of in abstraction and all those which are
states and affections belonging to the objects of perception. And
because of this, one who did not perceive anything would neither
learn nor understand anything, and whenever one contemplates,
one necessarily at the same time contemplates a sort of image; for
images are just as perceptions are, except without matter.

But it is also the case that imagination differs from assertion 10
and denial, since what is true or false is an interweaving of
thoughts. What, though, will differentiate the first thoughts
from images? Indeed, even the others are not images, but they
are not without images.[58]

## CHAPTER 9

Since the soul of animals has been defined in respect of two **432a15**
capacities, first the faculty of judgement, which is the work of
thought and perception, and further by its initiating locomotion,

it is necessary to make an inquiry into the initiation of motion, letting just so much be determined regarding perception and reason. It is necessary to inquire into whatever it is in the soul which initiates motion: whether it is just some one part of the soul,

20 being separate in either magnitude or account, or the whole soul; and if it is some one part, whether it is something special, beyond those customarily mentioned and already discussed, or whether it is some one of them.

There is an immediate difficulty concerning both how one ought to speak of the parts of the soul and how many there are. For in a certain way there appears to be an indefinite number of them: and it is not only according to those who, when distinguish-

25 ing them, mention the rational and the spirited and appetitive faculties, but also those who mention the rational and the irrational parts. For according to the differentiating features on account of which they separate them, other parts seem to have an even greater contrast than these, about which we have even now been speaking: the nutritive faculty, which belongs to plants

30 and to all animals, and the perceptual faculty, which one could not easily set down as either the irrational or the rational part.

**432b** Further, there is the imaginative faculty, which differs from them all in being, though there is considerable difficulty in saying—if one is going to posit separate parts of the soul—with which of the others it will be the same or from which of the others will it differ.

And in addition to these there is the faculty of desire, which would seem to differ from them all in account and in its potenti-

5 ality. And it is definitely absurd to break this up, because wish comes to be in the rational faculty, while appetite and spirit come to be in the irrational part, and if the soul is threefold, there will be desire in each part.

In any case, concerning the discussion now under way: what is it that initiates an animal's locomotion? For what belongs to all, namely the faculties of reproduction and nutrition, would seem to

10 impart what belongs to all, motion in respect of growth and decay.

(It is necessary to inquire later into breathing in and out, and concerning sleep and waking, since these too present a great difficulty.)

But concerning locomotion, it is necessary to consider what imparts the motion involved in an animal's going anywhere. That

15 it is not the nutritive capacity is clear, since this motion is always

for the sake of something, and occurs along with imagination and desire; for nothing is moved, other than by force, which is not desiring or fleeing something. Moreover, even plants would then be mobile and would have some organic part for this motion. Nor, similarly, is it the perceptual faculty. For there are many among the animals which have perception but remain fixed and 20 immobile until the ends of their lives. If, then, nature neither does anything in vain nor leaves out anything necessary (except in the defective or incompletely developed—these sorts of animals, though, are complete and not defective, an indication of which is that they are capable of reproduction and have maturity and decline), the consequence is that they too would have the organic 25 parts pertaining to their going anywhere.

Yet neither is the rational faculty or what is called reason what initiates motion, for the faculty of contemplation does not contemplate what is to be done, nor does it say anything at all about what is to be pursued or avoided, while motion always belongs to one who is avoiding or pursuing something. Nor is it the case, whenever it does contemplate something of this sort, that it thereby directly commands fleeing or pursuing. For instance, it 30 often considers something fearful or pleasant, but it does not command being afraid, though the heart is moved, or should it 433a be something pleasant, some other part. And, moreover, even when reason does command and thought does say to flee or pursue something, one is not moved, but acts in accordance with appetite, as, for instance, the incontinent man does. And generally we see that one with medical knowledge does not heal, there being something else—not his knowledge—in charge of his 5 acting in accordance with his knowledge.

Nor even is desire in charge of this motion, since continent people, though they experience desire and appetite, do not act as desire bids, but instead follow reason.

CHAPTER 10

In any case, these two appear to initiate motion: desire and 433a9 reason—if one were to posit imagination as a sort of reasoning. 10 For many follow imaginings contrary to knowledge, and in the other animals there is neither reasoning nor calculating, though

there is imagination. Accordingly, both of these initiate locomotion: reason and desire—the reason which engages in calculation
for the sake of something and is practical, and which differs from
15 the contemplative reason with respect to its goal. And desire, too,
is always for the sake of something, since desire is for something,
and this is the starting point of practical reason, while its final
stage is the beginning of action.

Consequently, it is reasonable that these two appear to be what
initiates motion: desire and practical thought. For the object of
desire initiates motion and because of this thought initiates
motion, because its starting point is the object of desire. And
20 whenever imagination initiates motion, it does not do so without
desire.

And so there is one thing initiating motion: the faculty of
desire. For if there were two things which initiated motion—
reason and desire—they would do so according to some common
form. But as things are, reason apparently does not initiate movement without desire (since wish is desire, and whenever something
is moved in accordance with calculation, it is also moved in
25 accordance with wish), whereas desire also initiates motion
opposed to calculation; for appetite is a kind of desire.

Reason, then, is in every instance correct, while desire and
imagination are both correct and not correct. Consequently, the
object of desire always initiates motion; but this is either the good
or the apparent good—not every good, but the good concerned
with what can be done, since what can be done is contingent and
30 can be otherwise.

It is evident, then, that what is called desire is the sort of
**433b** capacity in the soul which initiates motion. For those who distinguish parts of the soul, there will turn out to be a great many, if
they distinguish and separate them in accordance with their
potentialities: the faculties of nutrition, perception, thought, and
deliberation, and, further, a faculty of desire. For these differ
from one another to a greater extent than do the faculties of
appetite and spirit.

5 Since, however, desires arise opposite to one another, and this
occurs whenever rationality and the appetites are opposed, and
this comes about in those with a perception of time (since reason
encourages a pulling back because of what is going to happen,
whereas appetite operates because of what is already present,

since a present pleasure appears to be an unqualified pleasure, and an unqualified good, because of its not seeing what is going to happen)—it follows that what initiates motion is one in kind: the 10 faculty of desire insofar as it is a faculty of desire. But first of all is the object of desire, since this initiates motion without being moved, by being thought of or imagined. In number, though, the things initiating motion will be more than one.

Since there are three things, first, what initiates motion, second, that by which it initiates motion, and further, third, what is moved, and that which initiates motion is twofold, in the one instance being unmoved and in the other initiating motion while 15 being moved, there is: something unmoved, the good concerned with what can be done; something initiating motion while being moved, the faculty of desire (for what is moved is moved insofar as it is desiring, and desire, when in actuality, is a kind of motion); and what is moved, the animal.

The instrument by which desire initiates motion is already something bodily; accordingly, it is necessary to examine it 20 among the functions common to body and soul. For now, though, to summarize: something initiates motion instrumentally when the starting point and the end point are the same, for instance, in a hinge—since here the convex is the end point and the concave the starting point (for which reason the one is at rest and the other is moved), and though differing in account, they are inseparable in magnitude. For all things are moved by pushing 25 and pulling; consequently, it is necessary, just as in the case of a circle, for something to remain fixed and for the motion to begin from there.

In general, as has been said, insofar as an animal is capable of desire, it is, in virtue of this, capable of moving itself; but it is not capable of desire without imagination. And all imagination is either rational or perceptual. And in this latter, then, the other animals have a share as well. 30

CHAPTER 11

It is also necessary to consider what initiates motion in imper- **433b31** fectly developed animals, those whose perception is limited to touch; whether or not it is possible for them to have imagination **434a**

and appetite. For they appear to have pleasure and pain in them; but if they have these, then it is necessary that they have appetite as well. But how could they have imagination in them? Or rather, just as they are moved indeterminately, these things are present in
5 them, but present indeterminately.

Hence, as was said, while perceptual imagination belongs to the other animals, deliberative imagination belongs to rational animals (since whether one is to do this or that is already the work of reasoning—and it is necessary that measuring take place by one thing, inasmuch as one pursues what is greater and can, consequently, make one out of many images).
10   This is why they do not seem to have belief: because they do not have the imagination arising out of reasoning.[59] Consequently, desire does not have a deliberative faculty. Sometimes this desire overpowers that desire and initiates motion, and sometimes that one overpowers this one and initiates motion, like one ball overpowering another,[60] so one desire overpowers another desire, whenever incontinence occurs. The top desire always naturally
15 dominates and initiates motion, so that three motions are already initiated. The faculty of knowledge is not moved, however, but remains fixed.

Since the one conception and proposition is universal, and the other is of what is particular (since one says that a certain sort of man must do such and such a thing, and the other says that *this* is such and such a thing, and *I* am that sort of man), this latter belief—not the universal one—initiates motion; or, both do, but
20 this first is more at rest, and the second is not.

CHAPTER 12

**434a22** It is necessary, then, that anything which is alive and has a soul has a nutritive soul from its generation until its destruction. For it is necessary that whatever is generated have growth and also maturity and decline, and these are impossible without nutrition;
25 consequently, it is necessary that the nutritive soul be present in all things which grow naturally and decline. But perception is not necessary in all living things: indeed, neither those things having a simple body nor those incapable of receiving the form without the matter can have it.

It is, however, necessary that an animal have perception—for 30 without this nothing could be an animal, if nature does nothing in vain.[61] For everything existing by nature is for the sake of something, or else will be concomitant with something which is for the sake of something. Any body capable of going anywhere and yet lacking perception would perish and not reach its end, which is the work of nature. For how will it be nour- **434b** ished? Nourishment comes to sessile animals from the areas where they naturally occur; and a body cannot have a soul and reason capable of discriminating without having perception, if it is not sessile and generated—nor moreover if it is ungenerated. For why will it have it?[62] Or will it be due to its being 5 better for either the body or the soul? But as things are, neither of these is the case. For the soul will not then reason better, and nor will things be better for the body because of this. Consequently, no non-sessile body has a soul without also having perception.

Moreover, if it indeed has perception, it is necessary that its body be either simple or mixed. Yet it cannot be simple. For it will 10 not have touch, but it is necessary that it have this. This is clear from the following. Since an animal is an ensouled body, and every body is tangible, necessarily the body of the animal must be capable of touch if the animal is going to survive.[63] For the other senses perceive through other things, for instance, smelling, see- 15 ing, and hearing; but when making contact, if it does not have perception, it will not be able to flee some things and take hold of others. But if this is so, the animal will not be able to survive. Accordingly, taste is like a sort of touch; for taste is of nourishment, and nourishment is a tangible body. But sound and colour and scent do not nourish; nor do they bring about growth or 20 decay. Consequently, it is necessary that taste be a sort of touch, because of its being the perception of what is tangible and capable of nourishing.

While these senses are necessary to an animal, and it is evident that an animal cannot be without touch, the other senses are for the sake of doing well and do not belong to just any chance kind of animal—though it is necessary that they belong to some, for 25 instance, to any one of them capable of going anywhere. For if it is going to survive, it is not only necessary that it perceive when making contact, but also from a distance.

This would occur if it could perceive through a medium, with the medium being affected and moved by the object of perception and the animal by the medium. For just as what initiates motion
30 in place makes something change up to a point, and when something, having pushed something else brings it about that it pushes, and there is a motion through an intermediary, and the first thing initiating the motion pushes while not being pushed, and the final one alone is pushed but does not push, and the middle one both
**435a** pushes and is pushed (and the ones in the middle are many), so too is it in the case of alteration, except that what is altered remains in the same place.[64] For instance, if someone were to dip something into wax, the wax would be moved up to the point where he had dipped it, whereas a stone is not moved at all, while water is moved up to a distant point and air up to the furthest point—and if it remains and is something unified it both acts and is affected.
5 For this reason as well, as regards reflection, rather than saying that sight goes out and is then reflected back, it is better to say that the air is affected by the shape and colour up to the point where it would be unified. In the case of what is smooth, it is unified; accordingly, this in turn moves sight, just as if a seal in wax were
10 to penetrate through to its outer surface.


CHAPTER 13

**435a11** That, then, the body of an animal cannot be simple is evident—I mean, for instance, something fiery or airy. For without touch it can have no other sense (for every ensouled body is capable of
15 touch, just as was said). Elements other than earth can bring about sensory organs, but these all produce perception by perceiving through something else, that is, through a medium, whereas touch occurs by touching objects of touch[65]—whence its name. And indeed, the other sensory organs also perceive by touch—but through something else. Only touch seems to perceive
20 through itself. Consequently, none of these sorts of elements could be the body of an animal. Nor, indeed, could an earthen one. Touch serves as sort of mean of all the objects of touch, and the sensory faculty is receptive not only of the differentiations belonging to earth, but also of hot and cold and all the objects of

touch. And this is why we do not perceive with bones or hair or
parts of this sort, because they are of earth.                    25

This is also why plants do not have perception: because they **435b**
are of earth, and none of the other senses can be present without
touch, while this sensory faculty is neither of earth nor of any one
of the other elements.

It is evident, then, that of necessity animals deprived of this
sense alone will die. For nothing having this can fail to be an 5
animal, nor does what is an animal need any sense other than this.
And because of this, whereas other objects of perception do not
destroy an animal by being excessive—for instance colour and
sound and scent—but only the sensory organs (unless co-incidentally if, for instance, a sound should happen at the same time as a 10
thrusting or a blow); and there are things set in motion by objects
of sight and by scent which destroy touch. And taste destroys
insofar as it turns out at the same time to be something capable of
coming into contact. An excess in the objects of touch, on the
other hand (for instance cases of hot or cold or hard) will destroy
the animal. For an excess in any object of perception will destroy 15
the sensory organ, so that an object of touch will destroy touch,
and an animal is defined by touch; for it was shown that an
animal cannot be without touch. For this reason, an excess in
the objects of touch destroys not only the sensory organ, but the
animal as well, because this alone an animal must have.

As we have said, the other senses an animal has not for the sake 20
of existing, but for the sake of existing well: for instance sight,
because it lives in air or water, or generally in the transparent, so
that it sees; taste, because of pleasure and pain, so that it may
perceive and desire and be set in motion;[66] and hearing so that
something may be signified to it.[67]

# TEXTUAL NOTES AND VARIANT READINGS

1. 403a13–14: Retaining χαλχῆς, unnecessarily secluded by Ross as insufficiently mathematical to serve as a suitable illustration.
2. 403a15: Accepting Ross's conjectured τι, in variance to the common manuscript readings of τό.
3. 403b9: Retaining ἔστι τις with the common manuscript reading, against Ross's emendation to ἔστιν.
4. 406b2: Reading κατὰ τόπον, as conjectured by Bonitz, for κατὰ τὸ σῶμα, read in common by the ms. and accepted by Ross.
5. 407a11: Reading πότερον ὁτῳοῦν μωρίῳ with E.
6. 407b1/406a33: Retaining μὴ with the mss., against ᾗ, conjectured by Torstrik and adopted by Ross.
7. 408b9: Reading ἢ τοῦτο ἴσως ἢ ἕτερόν τι. The manuscript here is in a difficult state.
8. 408b11: Reading δέ rather than δή, with the dominant manuscripts.
9. 409a13: Reading τι, setting aside Ross's brackets as unnecessary.
10. Ross's text accepts the chapter division followed by most modern editions. I have preferred the pre Renaissance division. See note to 409a31–b18.
11. 409b5: Reading ἤ with the ms. over καί, conjectured by Torstrik and accepted by Ross.
12. 410a29: Reading πρός, τὸ ὅμοιον with the manuscripts, against Ross's conjecture of πρός, τῷ ὁμοίῳ, which comes with support from Sophonias and perhaps from the paraphrase of Philoponus.
13. 410b23–4: The manuscripts agree on φορᾶς οὐδ', which was secluded by Torstrik for defensible reasons; the translation reflects his seclusion. The translation also reflects the manuscript reading of πολλὰ over τὰ πολλά at 410b24.
14. 413a9: Rejecting Ross's interpolation of ᾗ.
15. 414a7: Omitting ᾧ, secluded by Bywater.
16. The text is here transposed for clarity's sake. The sentence at 414b28–32 has been made to follow 414b32–3, which is evidently the conclusion of the train of thought leading to 414b28. The transposed sentence itself appears immediately connected with 414b33ff.

It is therefore preferable not to follow Ross in treating 414b28–32 as a mere parenthetical intrusion.

17. 415a21: Omitting δεῖ τεθεωρηκέναι with W.
18. 415b18: Reading ζῶσιν with J^c, O^c, H^c, and V.
19. 415b18: Reading τὰ ἔμψυχα with Torstrik, deriving some support from Φ^p.
20. This translation, following a suggestion of Torstrik, transposes 416b23–5 to 416b20.
21. 418b22: Reading τεινομένου with CVe, over γιγνομένου.
22. 419a5: Reading κέρας over κρέας (flesh, or a body, i.e. a corpse); the mss. are split on this matter. Renehan (1996) offers a spirited argument for κρέας.
23. 419a9: Reading αὐτὸ for αὐτῷ with W, following Barco.
24. 419b33: Reading ὁρίζεται for the ms. ὁριζόμενον, following a suggestion of Torstrik.
25. 420a4: Reading διὰ τὸ ἕνα ἀέρα εἶναι with Steinhart, for the ms. διὰ τὸ ἐν ἀέρι εἶναι.
26. 420a7–8: The text here is plainly corrupt. The translation reflects a reading of ἀλλὰ τὸ κινησόμενον μέρος, while deleting καὶ ἔμψυχον. This partly takes up a suggestion of Torstrik, but also rejects part of his conjecture.
27. 420a15: Deleting ὅταν κάμῃ, which is present in UΦ^c but not in CPe.
28. 420a15: The translation reflects the acceptance of an unattested conjecture of Ross, ἀλλ' οὐ for the ms. ἀλλὰ καὶ.
29. 421a32: Accepting Ross's seclusion of ἀπὸ τούτων.
30. 422a10: Reading ἡ ἀφή with the dominant ms. tradition for Ross's unnecessary emendation to τῇ ἀφῇ.
31. 422a28: The translation reflects a reading of τὸ δ' ἐὰν πεφυκὸς ἔχειν μὴ ἔχῃ ἢ φαύλως, conjectured by Ross. The text is uncertain.
32. 422a33–4: Reading ἀμφοτέρου with Trendelenberg for the ms. ἀμφότερα, and omitting τῆς γεύσεως as a likely gloss.
33. 422b6: The translation accepts Ross's suggestion of αὕτη γὰρ ἀφῇ, though the reading is without ms. support.
34. 425a16–17: Adding ἑνὸς to the list, following CESUV^l XΦ^c.
35. 424a29–30: Deleting Ross's unnecessary excision.
36. 425b3: Deleting καὶ^2.
37. 426a2–3: Reading ποιουμένῳ for κινουμένῳ.
38. 426a28: Deleting the words καὶ...αὐτό, rightly secluded by Torstrik.
39. 426b7: Accepting Bywater'suggestion of λυπεῖ for λύει. The suggestion has good ms. support, though cf. 424a30–1.
40. 426b14: Reading τινι with CES^lΣ for τινί SUX.

41. 426b16: Reading αὐτοῦ with the ms., in place of αὐτό, preferred by Ross, following Essen.
42. 427a10: Accepting Biehl's conjecture of ἢ μία ἢ δύο.
43. 427a18: Reading κρίνειν, against Ross's suggested φρονεῖν.
44. 427b16: Reading φαντασία with C² U² S¹ and secluding νόησις with Madvig. Effectively the same meaning results from simply secluding νόησις.
45. 428a22–4: Setting aside Ross's seclusion.
46. 428b19–21: Reading τοῦ ᾧ with W, and rejecting Bywater's transposition, which has been followed by Ross.
47. 429b15: Omitting καί² with C¹.
48. 430a10: Accepting Ross's excisions of ὥσπερ and τι.
49. 430a19–22: The brackets here differ from those of Ross, who extends them one sentence further, into 430a22. The sentence bracketed is doubtful because it occurs again at 431a1–3, where it makes better sense, if only marginally.
50. 430b1: Retaining καί, but accepting Torstrick's conjecture of συντίθησι for συντιθείς.
51. 430b2–3: Accepting Ross' interpolation of φῇ, τὸ λευκὸν καί.
52. 430b14–15: Reading τὸ δὲ... τῆς ψυχῆς in this location. Bywater contended, perhaps correctly, that this paragraph should be transposed and inserted into 430b20 after μήκει.
53. 430b24: Accepting Förster's (somewhat desperate) conjecture of ἐκεῖνα.
54. 430b25: Deleting τῶν αἰτίων, and rejecting Torstrik's suggested replacement of τῶν ὄντων.
55. 431a24: The translation reflects reading μή, included by Ross, but which has only divided ms. support.
56. 431b14: Reading κοῖλον ἐνόει, ἄνευ.
57. 431b27–8: Reading τὸ μὲν ἐπιστητὸν τὸ δὲ αἰσθητόν.
58. 432a13: Reading τἆλλα for ταῦτα, an unnecessary emendation, supported, though, by Θ.
59. 434a11: Secluding Cornford's αὕτη δὲ κινεῖ with Bywater, and omitting the ms. αὕτη δὲ ἐκείνην.
60. 434a13: Reading σφαῖρα σφαῖραν with Essen.
61. 434a28–30: The translation reflects Ross's reasonable transposition of ll. 28–29 to 30.
62. 434b5: Omitting οὐχ, following LSUΦᶜ.
63. 434b12–13: Deleting ἅπτον... ἁφῇ in b12–13 and καί in b13.
64. 435a2: Reading ἀλλοιοῦται with Trendelenberg, in place of Ross's ἀλλοιοῖ, which is, though, well attested.
65. 435a17: Reading τῶν ἁπτῶν with y.
66. 435b23: Omitting τὸ ἐν τροφῇ with W.
67. 4–25: Secluding γλῶτταν δὲ... ἑτέρῳ, with Torstrik.

# COMMENTARY

## BOOK I

### CHAPTER 1

**Introduction to I 1**

Aristotle begins by emphasizing the soul's importance and by recounting the kinds of difficulties which beset its study. He makes prominent two related difficulties, both broadly methodological: (i) the appropriate form of inquiry to be attempted is underdetermined at the outset; and (ii) the starting point of the inquiry, whatever its form, is in consequence difficult to ascertain. It is striking how quickly these methodological questions give way to speculation about the separability of the soul. This is not accidental, since scientific inquiry aims at demonstration, and any demonstration concerning the soul begins with a statement of what the soul is essentially. Questions about the soul's essence in turn involve controversies about whether its attributes are necessarily embodied. This, then, explains Aristotle's opening perplexity: the form of inquiry appropriate to the subject matter is partly a function of the kind of entity the soul turns out to be essentially, but that we cannot know before undertaking an inquiry into its nature.

The themes of this first, agenda-setting chapter recur throughout *De Anima*. Accordingly, understanding the programme of the entire work requires an appreciation of the difficulties and issues as Aristotle conceives them in this introductory chapter. It also requires an understanding of Aristotle's conception of science (*epistêmê*) and demonstration (*apodeixis*), including his views on how the various sciences are organized and individuated from one another.

Like Plato, Aristotle regularly orders the forms of mental activity hierarchically: sense perception is the most common, followed in order by memory, experience, craft knowledge, and finally scientific knowledge and understanding (*APo.* 99b34–100a9, *Met.* 980a27–981a12). He elsewhere distinguishes between practical, productive, and theoretical sciences (*Top.* 145a15, 157a9–10; *EN* 1139a27), and further discriminates among lower and higher theoretical sciences: natural science, mathematics, and first philosophy or theology, in ascending order (*Met.* 1026a6–18, 1064b1–6).

Part of his classification of the sciences turns on whether their objects are separate (*chôriston*), which proves to be a complex and technical matter for him. Given its general importance in *De Anima*, it is important to bear it in mind that Aristotle uses the term 'separate' (*chôriston*) in several different ways, and that he does not always indicate which sense he has in view when making claims about the separation of soul or its faculties, including most notably reason (*nous*). In general, separation may be spatial, definitional, or unqualified (*haplôs*), where unqualified separation indicates a capacity for independent existence (*Gen. et Cor.* 317b10, 329a25; *Met.* 1019a1–4, 1028a33–4, 1042a29; *EN* 1102a28–32). Fine (1984) offers a detailed account of separation in Aristotle's metaphysics; Miller (2012: 308–14) offers a crisp and comprehensive overview of the varieties of separation in Aristotle, with a special focus on their application in *De Anima*. He reviews inter alia the significant suggestion of Caston (1999) that in addition to the varieties of separation just listed, Aristotle recognizes in *De Anima* a distinct sort, namely taxonomical separation. For the notion of taxonomical separation and its possible role in Aristotle's conception of reason, see commentary to 430a22–5 in III 5.

In the present chapter, these distinctions colour the question of where the study of the soul fits in Aristotle's schema of sciences, since the answer to that question will be partly determined by whether, and, if so, in which way, the soul is separate. At various junctures, Aristotle reflects on the question of how psychology qualifies as a theoretical science. He tentatively introduces psychology as a form of natural science, but does not, contrary to the view of many contemporary commentators (typical is Ross (1961: 16)), in fact state unequivocally that this is so. Aristotle's unwillingness to offer a determinate and fully general ruling on this question has two sources. First, Aristotle appears undecided about whether, or, if so, how, the soul qualifies as separate (*chôriston*), but the assignment of psychology to one or another branch of theoretical science turns on precisely this question. Second, in typical fashion, before offering his own positive theories Aristotle prefers to survey the *endoxa*, the credible opinions handed down on his topic of inquiry (cf. *Top.* 100a29–30; *Phys.* 189a31–2; *EN* 1097b8; *Met.* 995b24). Accordingly, most of *De Anima* I is taken up with considerations of the views of Aristotle's predecessors, views which include a full range of opinions on the question of separation.

Some thinkers before Aristotle conceived of the soul as some manner of material body (e.g. the atomists); others regarded it as an immaterial entity capable of existing without the body (Plato); and still others regarded it as a kind of mathematical entity (some unnamed theorists, presumably including Xenocrates, 404b28–30 and 408b31–2; cf. *APo.* 91a35–b1). On some of these approaches, the soul is unqualifiedly separate (*chôriston haplôs*); on others it is only qualifiedly separate, perhaps separate only in definition (*chôriston logô(i)*); while in others it appears to be not at all separate. If, for instance, the soul simply *is* so many atoms swirling in the void, then it is hardly separable from those atoms. The same holds for any identification of the soul with the elements, whether taken individually or in combination; views of this sort are not recounted by Aristotle until the next chapter (see note to 404b30–405b10). Since in Aristotle's terms, his various predecessors implicitly answered the question of the appropriate home for the study of soul in different and incompatible ways, at this stage of his inquiry, any definite opinion on the appropriate branch of study for psychology might reasonably be regarded as pre-emptory. For more on the role of separation (*chôriston*) in this chapter, see note to 403a3–27; for more on the home of psychology in Aristotle's division of the sciences, see note to 403a27–b16 and also Shields (2015).

These difficulties about separation aside, one should also reflect more generally on the degree to which Aristotle's remarks about the soul in this chapter are committal or propaedeutic: in endoxic or aporetic contexts it is often difficult to determine when Aristotle is speaking *in propria persona* and when he is not. Although in some such contexts it seems perfectly appropriate to understand him as venturing a view of his own even as he recounts the opinions of others, such conclusions are often delicate and easily disputed. So, for this reason too, some measure of caution is warranted when seeking to ascribe positive doctrine to Aristotle on the basis of the several striking remarks he offers in this chapter.

**402a1-4: The Subject of Inquiry and its Importance:** Aristotle thinks that cognition (*eidêsis*) in general is a fine thing, but that some forms of cognition are finer than others in virtue of their precision or the elevated status of their objects. The word 'cognition' (*eidêsis*; 402a1) is unattested before Aristotle and it is probable that he himself coined it for use as a generic term here. In any event, he apparently intends 'cognition' to cover the various forms of knowing and coming to know recognized in the *De Anima* and elsewhere.

Aristotle points out that one kind of knowing is better in virtue of its being more exact (cf. *Top.* 157a8–9). Sometimes this judgement is explicated by reference to the objects of the science in question (*Met.* 982a25–6). In other places, Aristotle relies on the status of the premises of the demonstrations employed by an exact science, where those which rely on necessary premises qualify as exact and those which do not are not (*Met.* 1064a4–7; *EN* 1094b11–27). Theoretical sciences rely on necessary premises, or at least on premises which capture natural regularities, things which happen either of necessity or usually or, in Aristotle's preferred locution, 'for the most part' (*hôs epi to polu* (*APo.* I 30; *Met.* 1026b27–1027a15; cf. *EN* 1094b19–27, 1139b14–19). Such occurrences are usual in a more than merely statistical sense, involving deviations from natural regularities. The best sort of knowing tracks what happens of necessity, or at least for the most part in this strong sense.

By introducing the study of soul as belonging to the first rank of science, Aristotle thus intends more than the general judgement that studying the soul is an eminently worthy activity. He also means, more precisely, that such study is a form of theoretical science. One question for the remainder of the chapter concerns whether it qualifies as theoretical by being a branch of natural science or as a form of first philosophy. On the importance of this question, see the Introduction to this chapter and the note to 403a27–b16.

**402a4-7: The Contributions of this Study to Other Inquiries:** Study of the soul is certainly relevant to other disciplines. Appeals to its nature help inform, among others, investigations into ethics and politics (*EN* 1102a17–19, 23–4; on the importance of the study of soul for ethics, see Irwin (1980) and Shields (2015)).

At the same time, suggests Aristotle, its most immediate contributions are to the physical sciences. He grounds this judgement in the claim that the soul is a source or principle (*archê*) of animals, presumably of animal life, by which he means that the most distinctive features of animal life, including nutrition, growth, self-motion, perception, imagination, and, in humans, thought, are explained by appeal to the activities of the soul. Aristotle makes this more explicit later, at 413b11–13, where it is also made clear that souls are not restricted to animals, but are present in all living things, including plants, and at 415b8–16a18, where the various ways in which the soul is a source or principle (*archê*) of life are distinguished.

**402a7–10: The Aims of this Study:** The first aim of the study is to ascertain the nature (*phusis*) and essence (*ousia*) of the soul. Aristotle uses these terms in closely connected ways here, as he very often does elsewhere, since the essential features of something, those which are necessary, invariant, and explanatorily basic, constitute that thing's nature (*Part. An.* 646a25; *Phys.* 193a9; *Met.* 1014b36, 1019a2, 1064b11). Still, as a linguistic matter, Aristotle speaks of nature (*phusis*) in a variety of different ways, sometimes technically and sometimes in a more relaxed manner, corresponding in broad outline to the many English uses of the term 'nature': some uses are normative and some not; some pick out the natural world in its totality and others signify rather the inherent character or basic defining feature of some individual thing within the broader world. In this latter usage, Aristotle will say that some part of nature, perhaps a human being, *has* (*echein*) a nature, which is its essence. In the current passage, Aristotle clearly has this second, narrow sense in mind. His use is, however, more technical than its closest English parallel, because it carries the suggestion that the soul *has* an essence, in addition to *being* the essence of the human animal (cf. *Met.* 1015a10–11).

It is also relevant to the investigations of *De Anima* that Aristotle has a special notion of nature (*phusis*), such that whatever has a *phusis* has its own internal source or principle (*archê*) of motion; Aristotle develops this notion of a nature (*phusis*) in several passages, especially when he is distinguishing living beings from artefacts (*Phys.* 192b13–15; *Met.* 1015a13–15, 1070a6–9).

In acknowledging that it falls to him to ascertain the essence of the soul, Aristotle is responding to a demand of scientific explanation as he conceives it, because a statement of something's essential properties is the starting point of every demonstration (*apodeixis*) in science (*epstêmê*) (*A. Po.* 75a42–b2). In order to discharge his purely scientific explanatory duties, Aristotle sets out to capture what belongs to the soul in its own right (*kath' hauto*), and to specify a fully general answer to the question: What is the soul?

Importantly, one central issue pursuant to this question concerns whether some or all of its properties belong to the soul alone or whether they all belong to the ensouled animal. This will prove to be an important and tricky question for Aristotle, one with significant consequences about the separability of the soul (see note to 403a3–27 below for a discussion of this matter). Two points are noteworthy at this stage of the inquiry: (i) in posing the question this way, Aristotle takes it as given that some psychic properties are without question properties of the ensouled entity, the whole animal or plant; and (ii) still, it seems at least initially that some may be exclusive (or peculiar, *idion*) to the soul and so not appropriately regarded as properties of the animal as a whole.

In addition to offering an account of the soul's essence, one also needs, says Aristotle, to characterize its 'properties' (*hosa sumbebêke;* 402a8). Most often, when Aristotle uses the term 'property' (*sumbebêkos*), it is more or less equivalent to 'accident' or 'co-incident', as it is a property of Alcibiades that he is feeling merry this evening. (The rendering 'co-incident', which is favoured in the translation, is a bit artificial, but is intended to capture the fact that various features of an entity or aspects of an event may co-incide with one another without that being accidental or unplanned. Our plans to attend the opera tonight may co-incide even though they are independent of one another and their co-inciding is neither welcome nor unwelcome.) Sometimes, though, especially in contexts where it is connected with demonstration, the term 'property' (*sumbebêkos*) is used in a highly technical manner. In this more technical sense, something is a property when it follows of necessity from a thing's essence without being part of that essence—e.g. a triangle has the property of having interior angles equalling two right angles, or Alcibiades has the property of being able to process novel syntax. In the current passage, Aristotle has the more technical notion in mind, as becomes clear in virtue of the examples he gives at 402b20 (cf. *APo.* 73b30–74a3, 74a25–b4). So, he accepts it as his task to specify the necessary but non-essential features of the soul as well as its essential features.

**402a10–22: Procedures and Starting Points Appropriate to this Study:** The dominant aim of the study is to state the soul's essence. Because science aims for essence-specifying definitions, one might assume that there is a single method of investigation appropriate to all forms of scientific inquiry, a method which leads to the discovery of the essential features of entities in any arbitrarily selected domain. Aristotle queries this assumption: perhaps different scientific domains, though equally concerned with essence, require distinct forms of investigation. If so, an inquiry into the soul is immediately hampered by the prior question of which form of essence-seeking method ought to be employed in its investigation. Further, and in any case, even when the question of the appropriate form of inquiry is settled, there remains the issue of the appropriate starting point for the study of soul, since different sciences require different first principles (*archai*).

Aristotle does not settle these questions of method here. He mentions two approaches to inquiry familiar from Plato and from his own philosophy of science: demonstration (*apodeixis*) and division (*diairesis*) (for the Platonic background, see *Phaedrus* 265d; *Philebus* 15a–16b; *Statesman* 287c; *Soph.* 218e–231e; on Aristotle's criticisms of and refinements to Platonic division, see *APr.* I 31, *APo.* II 5–6, 13, *PA* I 2–3; on Aristotelian demonstration, see *APo.* I 2). And he allows, somewhat offhandedly, that there might be 'some other method' (*tis allê methodos*; 402a20) to be followed. In this passage Aristotle does not intend to decide among these alternatives. Instead, he is primarily pointing out that even if one settles upon the appropriate method for studying the soul, there remains the formidable difficulty of determining the starting points appropriate to the method selected relative to the discipline in which it is to be deployed.

Aristotle's concern about starting points, or first principles, reflects his contention that scientific knowledge be expressed in the form of demonstration, which proceeds from axioms which are necessary, explanatory, and better known than the propositions derived from them by means of a deduction (*apodeixis*) (cf. *APo.* 71b16–25). The first principles of a given science are not themselves proven by the science whose first principles they are. Instead, the science accepts them as axiomatic, even though one might wish to query or defend them from outside the science. Such first principles will typically make use of non-trivial definitions, the sort which state the essence of the kind under consideration (*Top.* 101b38), canonically by placing the *definiendum* into a genus and differentiating it from other species in that same genus (*Top.* 141b26), e.g. 'man is a rational (*differentia*) animal (*genus*)'. To look forward to the positive account of soul in *De Anima* II 1, it seems plain that we are not given a definition of soul expressed in this canonical form, though it does not follow that he fails to give a definition which qualifies 'as an account revealing why something is' (*APo.* 93b34), which is the sort he says he required for scientific demonstration.

In any event, Aristotle is not here attempting to straitjacket the possible forms of definition we might offer of the soul so much as exploring the varieties of approach to its study open to him. In this connection, he raises a cautionary note to the effect that although we need to become clear about the category to which the soul belongs, our doing so will not amount to a statement of its essence. He makes this clear by deploying an illustration involving numbers and planes, the point of which he does not expressly state. Presumably he is drawing upon his conviction that while both numbers and planes are kinds of quantity, one, number, is discrete, while the other, a plane, is continuous (*Cat.* 4b20–5). In the present context, this serves to illustrate that it may be possible for us to determine the category to which the soul belongs without thereby settling the question of the first principles of demonstrations involving it. Taking this to be the purport of Aristotle's illustration, we might ascertain, for example, that time belongs in the category of quantity (*poson*), without first having decided whether time is discrete or continuous, something surely we must know if we are to understand its nature fully. Consequently, even if we have grasped the categorial facts about time, we may not yet be in a position to display its essence or to construct demonstrations involving it.

Similarly, then, we might determine that the soul is a substance (*ousia*) without even being in a position to state its essence-specifying definition, or even to offer demonstrations involving it. Indeed, even if we have grasped the basic categorial facts about the soul, we may yet not be in a position to determine whether its study belongs to first philosophy or to natural philosophy. Here too the dual effect of Aristotle's observation is to highlight the extreme difficulty of the investigation at hand even while pointing out how some initial progress can be made.

**402a23–b8: Initial Questions Concerning the Soul:** The first question concerning the soul, as concerning any other sort of entity, is a question rooted in Aristotle's category theory: what sort of thing is it? At this early stage in the investigation, Aristotle leaves open the possibility that the soul is not a substance. This is in part because of his determination not to prejudge so fundamental a question about the nature of soul, but it also presumably reflects the fact—a fact which structures a good deal of the first book of *De Anima*—that Aristotle's predecessors had placed the soul into a variety of different categories (according to Plato it was a substance, to Xenocrates a quantity, and to still others a quality). In this sense, the categorial question mooted by Aristotle is motivated by his deep methodological conviction that philosophical inquiry begins by collecting and considering the credible opinions (*endoxa*) of those who have already assayed the same territory. Aristotle considers each of these proposals in the course of *De Anima* I.

Aristotle's second question concerning the soul is equally fundamental, but not categorial: is the soul something which exists in potentiality (*en dunamei*; 402a25–6) or is it rather some sort of actuality (*entelecheia tis*; 402a26)? Unlike the categorial question, this is a question which can be formulated only in terms of Aristotle's own dedicated technical terminology and as such finds itself at home only within the confines of his mature metaphysical system. (On the term 'actuality' (*entelecheia*) and its significance for dating *De Anima*, see the General Introduction, n.2.) This question is also non-categorial in the sense that an item in any one of the categories might be either something potential or something actual (cf. *Met.* 1046b30, 1047a23).

The question of whether the soul exists potentially or actually may sound initially peculiar: should one not assume that whatever exists is actual? Note, however, that Aristotle's is not a contrast between what *possibly* and what actually exists, but between what exists *potentially* (*en dunamei*) and what exists as an actuality. In general, something which is potentially $\phi$ is already actually $\psi$, and indeed has the capacity for being a $\phi$ only in virtue of its being actually a $\psi$. A human is potentially a general, whereas a beech tree is not. Humans have capacities for generalship precisely in virtue of being human. If there are no generals at present, so long as there are humans, generals exist in potentiality. By contrast, if there are no humans, generals do not exist in potentiality, even though it certainly remains possible, in a broad sense, for there to be generals. Thus, being potentially $\phi$ is not coextensive with being possibly $\phi$. When Aristotle asks the question of whether the soul exists in potentiality or as an actuality, he is asking whether it is more like a quantity of clay, which is potentially a statue of Hermes, or rather more like the Hermes structure of the statue, which makes that quantity of clay the statue it is. In his terms, then, he is asking inter alia whether the soul is merely a capacity of something else, some other actual something, or whether it is itself something actual.

In *De Anima* II 1 Aristotle answers his first two questions simultaneously by claiming that the soul is a substance as the form and actuality of a body which is potentially alive. This answer relies upon Aristotle's developed and technical hylomorphism, a framework he is not inclined to deploy at this juncture of his investigation. (For a general treatment of hylomorphism, see the General Introduction §§ II and III.A; for a more detailed treatment of Aristotle's answer to the questions here posed, see note to 412a16–21.)

To look further ahead, it should be borne in mind that in *De Anima* III 4–5 Aristotle introduces a conception of reason (*nous*) which challenges the suggestion just made, that if $x$ is potentially $\phi$, $x$ is already actually $\psi$. (For a discussion of these issues, see the General Introduction § II and the commentary to 429a23–5.)

The subsequent questions are less fundamental, but equally set the agenda for the work's following chapters and books. The question of whether the soul has parts or not turns out to be complicated, not least because different conceptions of parts yield different answers. On the one hand, if the soul is not a quantity or a magnitude (407a2, 410a21) (and here is one way answers to Aristotle's earlier categorial question will have immediate ramifications), then it will lack spatial parts. It may, nevertheless, have parts in a more attenuated sense by being analysable into species and genus, or by having parts which can only be distinguished in thought, in the way in which Plato introduces the axis and circumference of a top as counting among its parts (cf. *Republic* 436d–e). Further, there is a question whether one should regard the soul's capacities as parts, and if so, how so. (This question became highly prominent and also highly nuanced in later Aristotelianism; for a discussion of one highly developed treatment, see Shields (2014).) Aristotle himself takes up this question several times in *De Anima*: 411b5–30, 413b11–414a1, 432a22–b7. At least this much turns on it: if every body is a magnitude, and every magnitude has parts into which it may be divided, then if the soul lacks parts of this sort, it will not be identifiable with any body.

When approaching this question, it is important to bear in mind that Aristotle is keen to distinguish different senses of being a 'part' (*meros*), as well as different senses in which one thing may be 'in' (*en*) another (*Phys.* 210a14–24; *Met.* Δ 23 and 25; cf. *Cat.* 1a24–5). In its broadest, perhaps most natural sense, 'We call a part, in one way, the result of any kind of division of a quantity; for what is subtracted from a quantity qua quantity is always a part of that quantity' (*Met.* 1023b12–14). Other, broader, non-quantitative notions of part are, however, equally available, says Aristotle. A genus can, for instance, be part of its form or species (*Met.* 1023b22–4). So, when considering these sorts of questions, it is necessary at a minimum to bear in mind Aristotle's distinction between quantitative and non-quantitative parts. On the question and nature of psychic parts in Aristotle, see Corcilius and Gregoric (2010). On the relevant academic background regarding the terminology of 'parts' (*moria and merê*), see Shields (2011).

In asking whether there is one account of the soul or many, Aristotle foreshadows some complications which arise from his view that souls form a kind of hierarchy (434a22–b18; cf. *Part. An.* 687a24–690a10; *Met.* 1075a16–25; cf. also note to 414b19–415a13). In this connection, when he upbraids some of his predecessors for focusing too narrowly on the human soul (402b3–4), Aristotle makes clear that he regards *being alive* and *being ensouled* as coextensive (cf. 415a24–5). Still, perhaps not everything which is alive is alive in precisely the same way; if not, then we should not expect a simple definition which captures what is common to all living or to all ensouled beings, at least not insofar as they are living beings.

The comparison with animal (*zô(i)on*) is especially instructive: is soul, like animal, a genus, so that it admits of a single essence-specifying definition? Or is the soul unlike animal in not admitting of a single, univocal definition? It should be clear at once that the answers to these questions have immediate methodological repercussions. Are we in fact trying to define something which admits of a single non-disjunctive definition? Or are we rather considering a range of related cases, with only partial overlap, or even no overlap at all? Fairly clearly, different assumptions about our quarry will incline us to seek different sorts of accounts. If, by contrast, we do not know how unified we should regard the item whose definition we seek, then neither do we know the sort of definition for which we should be aiming—or indeed whether we should be aiming for a single definition at all. That Aristotle asks but does not answer this sort of question bespeaks an appropriate modesty for this stage of his inquiry. A contemporary analogue might be *consciousness*: a philosopher at the beginning of an inquiry into its nature would do well to leave open the question of whether it in fact has a single determinate essence, or indeed any essence at all.

**402b9–16: Some Subordinate Questions:** Aristotle revisits the question of whether the soul has parts or not (see note to 402a23–b8), but now connects this to two further, related questions: (i) should we seek a very general definition of soul, one abstracting from individual types of soul, and (ii) on the assumption that the soul does have parts, should we investigate them before considering the whole, and, again, if so, should we begin by considering their activities and characteristic objects?

Aristotle speaks of 'parts' (*merê*) loosely in posing these sorts of questions. The first seems a primarily taxonomical sense (one might ask: when thinking about animal populations, should a biologist focus first on a genus of animals or on its parts, the species which constitute it?). The second is more familiar, thinking of the faculties of the soul as in some sense or other as its parts. The questions relate, however, because one may think of the faculties as determining kinds of souls, so that 'the perceptual soul' is a distinct kind of soul from 'the nutritive soul' (see note to 414b19–415a11), both of which would then fall under the genus of soul. This explains why Aristotle frames his question by wondering whether soul is like the case of animal, where 'the universal animal is either nothing or is posterior to these' (402b7–8). His concern is that as nothing is an animal without being some kind of animal, so nothing will be a soul without being some kind of soul. Consequently, if the comparison holds, just as no definition of animal will define any actual individual animal fully and completely, so no generic definition of soul will fully define any individual soul at all. In effect, then, Aristotle is again raising the question of whether any general definition of soul would be contentful, registering as a concern that no such definition would fully describe any actually existing soul or even any individual kind of soul or 'part' of the soul (see *Met.* 999a6–10 and *Pol.* 1275a34–8; cf. *EN* 1096a19–35; *EE* 1218a1–8).

This same notion of 'part' recurs in Aristotle's contention that one must determine 'if there are not many souls but rather the soul has parts' (402b9). At first this distinction may seem ill-coordinated, since one might well suppose that there are many souls, all of which have parts. Aristotle's contrast, however, is to be understood as taxonomically cast: his distinction between there being many souls and one soul with parts is a contrast between there being a single genus of soul shared by all living beings or there being distinct kinds of soul, which might or might not prove to be species of a single genus. The contrast, then, evidently is one dealing not with different species of animals, but rather with kinds of souls typed by their capacities.

To illustrate the taxonomical character of this worry, one might in the same way ask whether we should say that there is just some one genus of *body*, of which living human bodies, bodies of water, bodies politic, and dead bodies are all species, or whether we are really talking about several different kinds of things, however related, all of which happen to be called 'bodies'. Perhaps, that is, it is a mere accident of a language that all these different kinds of bodies are called 'bodies'. Or perhaps this not accidental, even though bodies do not form a single kind. For instance, they might be related in the way in which Wittgensteineans think that games are related: although there is no one feature or set of features that all and only bodies have in common, still, there may be overlapping criss-crossing sets of features which explain how they form a loosely related group displaying a series of similarities to one another. Or, then again, bodies may exhibit still more structure, while still failing to constitute a single genus, such that they are Aristotelian core-dependent homonyms, that is, roughly, kinds of entities all of which bear close dependency relations to a core instance, in the way that healthy cheeks, healthy diets, and healthy exercise regimens qualify as healthy because of their being suitably related to health. (For a detailed treatment of core-dependent homonymy, see Shields (1999); for a more introductory treatment, see Shields (2014, § 3.6).) In this case, bodies would not form a single genus, but would, nonetheless, constitute a closely connected set of entities. Still, if it were uncovered that there really is some one genus here, then we would want to know how the 'parts'—that is the species of that genus—differ from one another.

So, much depends on whether we think we are dealing with one kind of thing, several kinds of only accidentally related things, or rather distinct but non-accidentally related kinds of things. If we were to form the view that there is no one genus *body* common to all the cases mentioned (as presumably we think there is not), then there is no point in our seeking a single essence-specifying definition of body, even if we think that the kinds of bodies mentioned are otherwise importantly related. To return to the case of the soul, then, Aristotle is raising the question of whether the various ensouled beings we recognize, all living beings, have something in common, the soul—which in turn prompts him to ask whether there is a univocal definition of soul capturing the single genus covering all souls, whatever their type.

Looked at from this perspective, Aristotle at first wanted to know whether one should think of the soul on the model of body or rather on the model of animal. He now asks, on the assumption that it is more like animal than body, how the various kinds of souls—nutritive souls, perceptual souls, reasoning souls—are to be distinguished from one another, and how, once distinguished, their definitions relate to one another.

He also asks in this connection, nodding to one of his own methodological precepts, whether we should not first inquire into the activities distinctive of the various types of souls, and if so,

into their various objects. The idea here is that two types of soul—
or two faculties of one soul—are distinct if they have distinct
activities ranging over discrete objects. Thus, nutrition and perception are distinct from one another because their activities,
digesting and perceiving, are distinct; and if we had any doubt
as to whether their activities were distinct, we could see straight-
away that they must be, since they range over different objects,
food and perceptible objects, since what it is to be perceptible is
not the same as what it is to provide nutrition, even though food is
perceptible. Of course, in these cases, we will not have doubted
that the activities ranging over these objects are distinct. In other
cases, for example in perceiving and understanding, or in remembering and imagining, we might not be initially so sure. At any
rate, Aristotle repeatedly accuses some of his predecessors of
failing to distinguish perception (*aisthêsis*) from understanding
(*phronêsis*) and of thereby reaping intolerable epistemic consequences (*Met.* 1009b12–1010a1; cf. note to 404a25–b7).

On the general character of Aristotle's principle of object-
driven capacity individuation, see the Introduction to II 4, and
notes to 418a11–17 and 429b10–21.

The difficult questions posed in this passage find an important,
if equally difficult, response in *De Anima* II 3, which in turn
should be explicated with a view towards the sort of answer it
offers to the problems posed here. See note to 414b19–415a11.

**402b16–403a2: Relations between Essences and Properties in
Definition:** After setting out most of the questions to be asked
concerning the soul, Aristotle interjects an observation regarding
definition and method, one which goes some way toward addressing the methodological worries introduced so far. If definition
requires essence specification, and essence specification presupposes knowledge of a thing's nature, which in turn requires
understanding whether the thing defined is separate, then demonstrations regarding the soul cannot proceed without knowing
whether it is separate. That knowledge, however, is precisely
what we lack at the beginning of our study.

Aristotle now suggests a way forward. Given that a thing's
properties, in the technical sense introduced at 412a7–10, as
what follows from a thing's essence of necessity without being
part of that essence, are related in stable ways to a thing's essence,

we can focus on them first, in the order of discovery, since they are more manifest than the essence upon which they follow. Here Aristotle implicitly appeals to his distinction between what is 'better known to us' and what is 'better known by nature' (*APo.* 71b9–16, 71b32–72a5; *Top.* 105a16; *EN* 1095a2–4), and to his contention that 'the road to first principles and causes proceeds naturally from what is better known and clearer to us to what is clearer and better known by nature' (*Phys.* 184a16–18). So, if we determine more or less by experience *that being able to process novel syntax* is a property of human beings, then we should have some clue as to the essence of humans, because we suppose that some essentially human capacity or other must underwrite this ability, a capacity such as rationality, which equally underwrites other properties (again in the technical sense of *sumbebêkota*) such as being able to make detailed plans for the future or to identify patterns in complex data sets. If, as we collect such properties, we discover repeatedly the same underlying explanation for their occurrences, we find ourselves on a road towards discovering the essence of their bearer and so closer to being able to formulate the scientific definitions we seek. Of course, as Aristotle cautions, if we misidentify a thing's properties, our eventual definitions will be false or simply vacuous.

These observations encapsulate a good deal of detailed Aristotelian philosophical methodology, some of it controversial and much of it fraught with interpretative difficulty. Needless to say, if that methodology proves untenable, the proposed way forward will lose much of its attraction. (For some of Aristotle's discussions of relevant scientific method, see *APo.* I 6, I 31, and II 19.) Still, at this point in a special inquiry, Aristotle will reasonably appeal to his developed methodology without pausing to conduct an investigation into its justification or even to recount his settled procedural principles.

**403a3–27: A Crucial Difficulty about the Soul's Affections and their Relation to the Body:**   Aristotle's reflection on method gives way to a final problem confronting the study of soul, a problem which he rightly regards as both central and extraordinarily difficult. It is a problem regarding the affections (*pathê*) of the soul: whether all are common to body and soul together, or whether some are peculiar to the soul alone. Two questions about his concern are immediately apposite. First, what is involved in something's being common (*koinon*) to soul and body? Second, which affections (*pathē*) are common, and which not, if any?

As his examples make clear, Aristotle here uses the term 'affections' generically, so that it includes a variety of mental states, from being angry to perceiving to reasoning (403a6–7). The first question seems straightforward on its surface, but its complexities emerge upon deeper reflection, and this is presumably why Aristotle observes, 'This it is necessary to grasp, but not easy' (403a4–5). The initial formulation of the question is just this: are there some psychological states which are states of the soul alone, or are all psychological states also states of 'what has the soul' (403a4)? Or should we conclude that it is also the case that some states are 'peculiar to the soul itself' (*esti ti kai tês psuchês idion autês*; 403a4–5)? Thus posed, the question evidently presupposes that being peculiar (*idion*) and being common (*koinon*) are exhaustive and exclusive options, and then also, as at 402a7–10, that at least some, or indeed most, of such states are common to the soul and its possessor.

The complexity of this question begins to emerge when conditions on commonality are queried; and its importance surfaces when Aristotle connects it to questions about the soul's separability. On the first point, Aristotle will elsewhere maintain that 'perception comes about *through* the body *in* the soul' (*De Sensu* 436b6). Is this sufficient to make perception 'common' (*koinon*) to soul and body? If so, will it also be sufficient to make reasoning common to soul and body, if it is assumed that all reasoning has its origin in sense perception (see note to 432a7–8)?

We can usefully, if non-exhaustively, distinguish weak from strong commonality:

Strong Commonality: $\phi$ is common to x and y *iff*: (i) x and y are distinct; (ii) $\phi$ is predicated of both x and y in a non-derivative way; and (iii) $\phi$ is predicated of x and y jointly if at all.

Weak Commonality: $\phi$ is common to x and y *iff*: (i) x and y are distinct; and (ii) $\phi$ cannot be predicated of one without its being the case that the other is ineliminably involved in the process of its coming to be so predicated.

According to weak, but not strong, commonality, if we assume that reasoning (or thinking, *noêsis*) requires perception (*aisthêsis*) or appearance (*phantasia*), as Aristotle later suggests (431a16–17, 432a7–14, with note to 432a10–15), then even reasoning will be common to soul and body, despite the fact that, as Aristotle will equally contend, there is no bodily organ for it (429a24–6, with note to 429a18–27). By contrast, according to Strong Commonality, this will not suffice, since reasoning could be a non-derived intrinsic property of the soul even if it required perception in the broad empiricist sense that *nihil est in intellectu quod non prius in sensu*. As stated, Strong Commonality ranges over many distinct sorts of cases. It is a bit harder to produce uncontroversial cases of Strong Commonality, though the notion does seemed tailored to hylomorphism. Two trees might have greenness in common, but being green is not jointly predicated of them, since it might well continue to be predicated of one when the other is felled; so they fail Strong Commonality by failing to satisfy (iii). By contrast— to use one of Aristotle's own illustrations—*weaving* is predicated of the body and soul together, though, let us suppose, the body is not identical to the soul. The weaver seems to be an ensouled body, not merely a soul and not merely a body.

In some places Aristotle seems to rely only on a version of Weak Commonality, as at 403a9, where he allows as a sufficient condition of reasoning's being common to the body and soul that it be 'not without imagination' (*mê aneu phantasias*). In this sense, the mere fact that it is tethered to the body by virtue of the fact that imagination is necessarily bodily makes reasoning common to body and soul. Yet, as stated, Weak Commonality seems unsatisfactorily profligate. According to it, *being French* is predicated in common of *les galettes des Rois* and the *pâtissier* who made them—the cakes are 'not without' a confectioner. Of course, it may be open to Aristotle to tighten up this principle, by restricting the ways in which the body must be involved in the production of thought; or it may be that on reflection his considered view will be a form of Strong Commonality. He does not here advance any determinate attitude towards these alternatives.

Another layer of complexity is added when we come to see what turns on this question of the conditions of commonality. For Aristotle connects it immediately with questions of separability, by making peculiarity (being *idion*) necessary and sufficient for separation (403a10–12). Here too we have different claims, depending upon the type of separation at issue (see the Introduction to this chapter). If it is mere definitional separation, then we have a less consequential claim than if ontological separation is in view. Ontological separation entails a capacity for independent existence, with the result that, if met, it allows Aristotle to envisage a form of post-mortem existence, provided that Strong Commonality fails. This seems to be the sort of separation envisaged by Plato in the *Phaedo* and elsewhere, where plainly Strong Commonality does fail.

In the current, aporetic context, it is difficult to decide which notion of separation Aristotle has in view. He seems mainly concerned with definition in this chapter, which may suggest that his primary consideration is definitional separation. At the same time, his earlier individuation of the sciences in terms of the form of separation of their objects, a topic to which he returns at the end of the chapter, suggests that he may be concerned with ontological separation as well (see notes to 402a1–4 and 403a27–b16).

Given the striking character of Aristotle's contention, it may be stressed that his Greek makes clear that he is talking about the separation of the *soul*, as opposed to a part of the soul, when connecting peculiarity and separation (at 403a12, the antecedent of the word 'separate' (*choristê*) is clearly 'soul' (*psuchê*), so that he is characterizing the whole soul and not one of its parts as separate). So, however separation is to be understood, it is held that a sufficient condition of the soul's being separate is its having some affection peculiar to it. This seems a surprising contention, since, as we have seen, Aristotle clearly thinks that most psychic affections are common to body and soul: his very way of posing his question at 403a3–5 presupposes that this is so. It is hard to see immediately how the soul could be separate either in definition or in fact if some of its operations are also operations of the body. At the same time, with independently defensible mereological principles, Aristotle could justifiably assert either ontological or definitional separation. These issues are further explored in II 3.

Those difficulties acknowledged, the alternatives proposed in this plainly aporetic passage seem clear. On the one hand, Aristotle is evidently tempted by the position that all of the soul's affections are common to the body (403a16), thus yielding a simple argument: (i) the soul is separable if and only if there is some affection peculiar to it, in the sense of not being common to it and the body; (ii) every property of the soul is common to the body; hence (iii) the soul is not separable from the body. Heading in the other direction, he hardly thinks commonality is obvious or unquestionably correct (403a5), yielding the opposite argument: (i) the soul is separable if and only if there is some affection peculiar to it, in the sense of not being common to it and the body; (ii) there is some affection peculiar to the soul; hence, (iii) the soul is separable from the body. Again, of course, the direction of the argument to be taken, as well as the final purport of that argument, will depend upon whether we understand ontological or definitional separation as in view. (For a development of this topic, see note to 413a2–10; for other passages where Aristotle is more sensitive to questions about the soul's parts, see *Part. An.* 641a14–b10 and *De Sensu* 436a17–b6).

However that may be, we should not attempt to infer too much positive doctrine from the current passage. Although the connection between peculiarity and separation figures prominently in Aristotle's considered thinking about the relation between soul and body, here he is merely intending to raise the issue, not to offer a determinate view.

Pursuant to these broader, more consequential issues in this important passage are several more local points, equally important for our understanding of Aristotle's way of thinking about the study of soul.

First, after adducing some commonplace data in support of the thought that all psychological affections are common to soul and body, all of which point to an intimate connection between psychic and bodily states, Aristotle advances the thought that such affections are 'accounts in matter' (*logoi en hulê(i)*; 403a25). The phrase thus translated relies on only one possible construction of the text. Reading an alternative text which many contemporary editors prefer, though it derives from inferior manuscripts and commentaries from late antiquity, we have instead 'enmattered accounts' (*logoi enuloi*). The difference is more than mere nuance, if the latter (*logoi enuloi*) is understood to carry the suggestion that psychic states are themselves *essentially* material, while the former (*logoi en hulê(i)*) stops short of that claim, asserting only that psychic states are merely *realized* in matter. If the difference between the texts is understood this way, the second, but not the first, version leaves open the question of whether the psychic states are essentially themselves material states. Probably Aristotle only intends the weaker claim, that psychic affections are accounts *in* matter, since: (i) he regards this issue as an open question much later in *De Anima*, at II 1 413a5–7, when he is offering his own positive view of the matter; and (ii) the word 'enmattered' (*enuloi*) is not otherwise attested in Aristotle or his contemporaries and seems to be a much later coinage, coming into currency only with the Greek commentators writing some centuries after Aristotle.

Second, whichever text one prefers, the notion of 'account' (*logos*) here requires explication, since, taken one way, neither 'enmattered accounts' nor 'accounts in matter' makes ready sense in English. I have preferred 'account' as a rendering of *logos* for consistency's sake, but it should be made clear that *logos* here corresponds to what is defined, as opposed to what does the defining. (English distinguishes analogously between the *definition* of man as some manner of linguistic formula characterizing the essence of man and as the *defining feature* of man, that is, the feature captured in that essence-specifying definition.) Similar uses are found at *Phys.* 209a21, *Met.* 1044b12, and especially 1058b19, where Kallias is said to be '*logos* with matter'; and elsewhere Aristotle contrasts a thing's *logos* with its name or names (*Met.* 1006b1, 1030a7). In all of these contexts *logos* is used in a manner closely connected to form (*eidos*). It is, therefore, reasonable to understand Aristotle—depending on the text preferred—as contending either that the psychological states mentioned are 'enmattered forms' or 'forms in realized in matter' or perhaps even, somewhat more loosely, 'enmattered structures' or 'structures realized in matter'. Consequently, our final understanding of all of these renderings will need to rely upon some prior understanding of form (*eidos*) in Aristotle's hylomorphism. For more on the notion of form in this framework, see the General Introduction § II; for a more developed overview of the notion of form in Aristotle's hylomorphism, see Shields (2007, §§ 2.4 and 2.5).

**403a27–b16: Dialectical, Physical, and Philosophical Definitions:** Given the connection Aristotle has forged between commonality and non-separability, and between peculiarity and separability, questions about the science appropriate to soul turn crucially on the prior question (prior to us, that is; cf. note to 402b16–403a2) of whether there are affections peculiar to the soul alone. Clearly, the science of psychology will be theoretical, rather than practical or productive. The difficult question concerns whether it is most akin to natural philosophy, mathematics, or first philosophy. (See the headnote to this chapter on the divisions among and within the sciences.)

Aristotle begins to answer this question by positing different forms of definition, some of which apparently cite material realizations (anger is blood boiling around the heart), while others cite formal features (anger is the desire for retaliation), and still others cite the form in matter and specify final causes (a house is a form in stone for the purpose of providing shelter). He then wants to know which form of definition falls within the province of the student of nature (the *phusikos*). This question in turn suggests a further question about which, if any, of the definitions of psychological states introduced qualifies as a privileged sort of definition. Which, that is, states the essence? This is, after all, what we seek (402a7–8).

Given the suggestion that all psychological states are accounts in matter (*logoi en hulê(i)*) or enmattered accounts (*logoi enuloi*), it is tempting to understand Aristotle as arguing very directly: (i) psychological affections are accounts in matter; hence, (ii) their definitions will need to make reference to the appropriate sort of bodily states; but if (ii), then (iii) the study of soul falls to the student of nature. Hence, (iv) the study of soul falls to the student of nature. From there it is a small step to the conclusion that psychology belongs to natural philosophy, rather than first philosophy. And so Aristotle is commonly read.

This is mistaken, especially if it is to be understood as Aristotle's final determination on this matter. First, it is worth re-emphasizing the preliminary, aporetic character of this first chapter: it sets an agenda for study, but does not execute that study. Second, and more to the point, Aristotle is much more circumspect than this argument would indicate. He does not embrace (iv) as stated. Instead, he says, 'A consideration of the soul, *either all souls or this sort of soul*, is already in the province of the student of nature' (403a27–8). The qualification is echoed and made still more prominent in a corresponding passage of the *Metaphysics:* 'it is clear how it is necessary in the natural sciences to investigate and define what something is, and also why it belongs to the student of nature to investigate concerning some part of the soul, however much is not without matter' (1026a4–6). So it would be wrong to understand Aristotle as now asserting, with any definiteness or finality, that the whole of psychology is a branch of natural philosophy. In fact this is a matter about which Aristotle exhibits a good deal of ambivalence, the root of which is his perplexity about the separability of soul.

It is noteworthy that despite the near universal agreement on this topic today, even the innocuous-sounding question of the branch of science (*epistêmê*) to which the study of soul belongs sparked lively controversies in earlier periods of Aristotelian scholarship. For a salutary discussion of how this general controversy played out in the Renaissance, see Bakker (2007). For a highly nuanced reading of the passage from a contemporary point of view, see Wedin (1996).

Finally, given the richly suggestive character of this passage, one should pause to decouple questions about the proper home of psychology as a science from the crucially related question of whether Aristotle here commits himself to the claim that forms are in any essential or even intrinsic sense matter-involving. One reason for thinking so, following Charles (2008) and Peramatizis (2011: 106), would be as follows. Aristotle here treats the affections (*pathê*; 403a25) as themselves matter-involving, because they are themselves hylomorphic compounds. He then contends that formulae (*horoi*, 403a25, sometimes rendered as *definitions* or as *defining formulae*) of such affections will consequently be matter-involving. Since, however, definitions are always definitions of forms, forms themselves are here presumed to involve matter not only intrinsically, but essentially, since definitions state essences. So, here forms, souls, are understood to be not only intrinsically but essentially material.

Against this argument two points should be noted. First, Aristotle may not be speaking of definition (*horismos*) in the strictest sense of the term; second, even if he were, it would not follow that a mention of matter would be a way of indicating that forms themselves are intrinsically material. As for the first point, Frede (1990) has plausibly argued that the notion of a formula, or defining formula (*horos*), here is likely not to be understood as definition in Aristotle's most strict and technical sense, where definitions in the strict sense are essence-specifying accounts of form alone. In some other, more relaxed cases, definitions are rather definitions of the compound, and in these instances they are not formal and will trivially mention matter (cf. *Met.* 1026a23, *Phys.* 193b35–194a7).

Further, second, even if we were to waive that response, it would not follow that a definition of form would require mention of matter in such a way as to treat it as intrinsic, let alone essential, to the form itself. A form might merely be matter-involving hypothetically, so that, for instance, if there is to be anger in a human being, then there must be some suitable material basis for the realization of anger, where that basis is understood as something functionally suitable, with blood boiling around the heart offered as a typical example. The upshot would then be that definitions of (some but not therefore all) affections of the soul would appropriately allude to the fact that in humans anger has some hypothetically necessary material basis. This seems, in any event, all that Aristotle overtly concludes in the present passage: 'For this is the account of the thing, but it is necessary that it be in matter of this sort *if it is to exist*' (*ei estai*, 403b2–3).

**403b16–19: A Return to Topic:**     The close of the chapter signals a return to its main topic and sums up some of its preliminary results. Though he clearly inclines toward the conclusion that the psychological affections of animals are inseparable from their natural matter, Aristotle does not finally embrace it for all attributes of the soul.

Psychological affections, at least those like anger and fear, suggests Aristotle, are unlike lines and surfaces as regards their separability. As mathematical objects, lines and surfaces are definitionally but not ontologically separate. So, in distinguishing psychological affections from mathematical objects, the chapter's final thought is that the affections of the soul are not even separable in definition. This does not, however, settle the question, raised at several points, whether *all* psychic affections are like anger and fear in this respect. This is a point worth recalling, since later Aristotle will assert directly that reason *is* separate, in some sense or other (see note to 429b5). If we think that the final conclusion of this chapter is that all psychological affections are inseparable even in definition, then we will have to understand Aristotle as later changing his mind, or as contradicting himself. It is probably, therefore, better to regard him as offering a partial judgement about some of the soul's affections rather than as issuing a fully comprehensive one about all psychic affections. This would, at any rate, be in keeping with his qualified finding about the proper domain for the study of soul.

The text of this passage is also extremely difficult and plainly corrupt. In particular, the phrase 'in this way inseparable from the natural matter of animals' (403b17–18) is very uncertain and has been subjected to several different proposed emendations. The translation accepts a highly conjectural proposal of Ross, the purport of which is that 'all those affections that are like fear and anger are not separate . . . in the manner in which lines and planes are separate—though they are, all the same, not separate.' Other possibilities include: (i) 'are not somehow separate'; or simply (iii) 'are not separate'. The latter possibilities, which result in ungrammatical syntax, omit any direct comparison with the manner in which lines and planes may or may not be regarded as separate. Bostock (2012: Appendix) offers an incisive discussion, along with a proposed restructuring of the text.

CHAPTER 2

**Introduction to I 2**

Aristotle follows his own regularly given advice in this chapter by beginning his study with a survey of the *endoxa*, or credible opinions, concerning the soul (cf. *Top.* 100a29–30, *Phys.* 189a31–32, *EN* 1097b8, 1145b2–7; *Met.* 995b24, *DC* 294b6–13). Although he does not respect this prescription in every work, Aristotle often prefaces his inquiries with a consideration of extant views on his topic of inquiry (e.g. *Metaphysics* A and *Politics* II), presumably because he regards such a practice as in one way or another salutary. Precisely why he should do so has, however, been a matter of some dispute, as has the nature of his attitude towards the methodological constraints, if any, imposed by this procedure. In some passages, Aristotle has been understood to suggest rather extremely that his philosophy proceeds solely by untying the conceptual knots bequeathed to him by those who had approached its questions with insufficiently developed explanatory frameworks (on the basis, e.g., of *Met.* 995a27–33); rarely, or never, though, does his actual practice provide any reason to suppose that he regards himself as bound by any such restrictive and indefensible methodology. On the contrary, Aristotle is willing to introduce the views of others only to reject them.

Indeed, in the present chapter, although he mainly recounts the views of those whose opinions he regards as worthy of record, Aristotle is primarily interested in eliciting agreement about at first two, and then, later, three features held to be central to the soul. Initially he notes that the soul is characterized predominantly by its role in *motion* (or *change*) and *perceiving* (*kinêsei te kai tô(i) aisthanesthai*; 403b25–7); towards the end of the chapter, in offering a summary, he adds *incorporeality* as another noteworthy psychic feature (*tô(i) asômatô(i)*); 405b12). When recounting these *endoxa*, Aristotle for the most part concentrates on the views of recognized natural philosophers. Some figures are introduced mainly only to be set aside (certain Pythagoreans, Thales, Diogenes, Heracleitus, Alcmaeon, Hippo, and Critias, the last three of whom have little standing in his mind, as does the unnamed author of the view that the soul is a self-moving number, whose contention receives an arch rebuke from Aristotle); others are accorded fuller treatment (Democritus, Empedocles, Anaxagoras, and Plato). For an account of Aristotle's methods of discussing the natural philosophers, see Hussey (2012).

A doxographer would want to investigate each of Aristotle's ascriptions in some detail. Our interest, by contrast, resides primarily with the purport of Aristotle's discussions for his own constructive account of the soul. Importantly, Aristotle accepts into his own positive theory, with certain refinements, the two dominant characteristics of the soul, perception and motion, while his attitudes towards the third, incorporeality, are more complicated and more difficult to gauge, not least because it is not entirely clear what is meant by this characterization (see note to 404b30–405b10). Indeed, the issue of incorporeality introduces significant difficulties into our understanding of Aristotle's approach to the soul in general, and in particular to his conception of reason (*nous*).

However that may be, the endoxic tone of the present chapter is primarily descriptive (one significant exception is the criticism of

Anaxagoras at 405b19–23). Subsequent chapters of *De Anima* I become increasingly critical, and so commensurately more consequential for our understanding of Aristotle's hylomorphism. Aristotle makes some effort to classify the theories of his predecessors by treating them as emphasizing either motion or perception. He does not adhere to this categorization at all strictly; rather, when he turns his attention to theories with a primary emphasis on perception at 404b7, he introduces and concentrates on the issue of which first principles (*archai*) or basic elements (*stoicheia*) the thinker under consideration employed to explain perception: earth, air, fire, water, or some combination of these.

**403b20–4: The Importance of Considering Earlier Views:** As suggested in the chapter's introduction, Aristotle places special importance on the consideration of the views advanced by his predecessors. Here he offers the humble, if sensible, justification that his doing so will afford him the opportunity to embrace what was correct in the views of those who came before him while guarding against what was wrong-headed in their approaches. This latter justification is noteworthy insofar as it makes plain that Aristotle does not regard himself as in any way bound by the views handed down to him. (Similar attitudes find expression at *Met.* 983 b1, 987a2, 993a25–b4; and *Pol.* 1260b32.)

**403b24–31: Primary Differentiating Features of the Soul:** The two features most distinctive of the soul seem to be motion and perception. Aristotle identifies as one of the soul's principal features not the *initiation of motion* but rather, simply, *motion*. He recognizes, of course, that lifeless entities can perfectly well be in motion. His speaking more generally of motion, as opposed, more narrowly, to the initiation of motion, probably results from his wanting to use this occasion to set up a criticism of his predecessors, to the effect that they wrongly inferred that souls must be in motion if they are to initiate motion. This is an important criticism which undergirds a good many of Aristotle's censures throughout the first book of *De Anima*.

Aristotle shows a bit of circumspection in his initial attitude towards the *endoxa* he recounts: 'These are also very nearly the two features of the soul which we have taken over from our predecessors' (403b27–8). The word 'nearly' (*schedon*) reflects

Aristotle's contention that entities capable of initiating motion need not themselves be in motion; he thinks that his predecessors were right to seize upon motion as a differentiating feature of the soul, but wrong, then, to infer that in order to be a source of motion the soul must itself be in motion. In the next chapter, he will also maintain that the soul is not even, in its own right, capable of being moved. So, in this restricted sense, it cannot be in motion, though it is a source of motion in ensouled beings and can be itself in motion in an attenuated sense by being appropriately related to what is in motion in its own right. On Aristotle's view of co-incidental motion, see the Introduction to I 3, together with the note to 405b31–406a12.

Here, though, Aristotle intends only to reject the inference, ascribed at first to some unnamed predecessors but then held to include Democritus at 403b31, that, necessarily, if x initiates y's motion, x must itself be in motion. See also 427a17 and 432a15.

**403b31–404a16: Democritus and Leucippus:**   Aristotle suggests that Democritus settles on fire as the stuff of the soul because: (i) without being in motion, the soul could not initiate motion; and (ii) the soul is most easily thought of as being in motion if it is understood to be made of the tiny spherical atoms which make up fire. These atoms are also compared to the tiny motes seen darting ceaselessly about in shafts of light. Aristotle thus treats Democritus' conjecture as an inference from some observed phenomenon, as he very often does when reconstructing the snippets of reasoning ascribed to the Presocratic naturalists. It seems safe to assume that Aristotle's reconstruction here, as elsewhere, is probably his own conjecture rather than a report of Democritus' actual pattern of inference.

A good example of his procedure is his observation that 'It is for this reason that they also say that the mark of life is breathing' (404a9–10). The philosophers discussed have not themselves overtly offered the ground in question, but Aristotle, rightly understanding it to be a reasonable basis for their view, offers it to them in his reconstruction.

The remaining remarks concerning breath and life are related to Aristotle's main point, but only tangentially. Democritus is represented as holding that the ceaseless motion of the tiny spherical atoms which make up the soul leads them to be expelled as the body contracts when exhaling. Aristotle offers a fuller account of Democritus on breathing at *De Resp.* 471b30–472a25.

**404a16–20: The Pythagoreans:** According to Aristotle, the same presupposition, that only what is already in motion can initiate motion, drives the view ascribed to certain unnamed Pythagoreans. They too contend that the soul is—or is made of—the tiny motes seen darting about ceaselessly in shafts of light even when the air is itself perfectly calm. Still others, Aristotle reports, identify the soul not with the motes themselves, but with whatever it is that moves the motes.

**404a20–5: Those Who Suppose the Soul Moves Itself:** There is some question concerning the authors of the view here recounted and criticized, though Plato and Xenocrates were evidently proponents of this view. Plato held that the soul moves itself, both in the *Phaedrus* 245c–e and, at the end of his career, in the *Laws* (894c–896e). The situation with Xenocrates, who succeeded Speusippus as head of Plato's Academy, is a bit less clear. Ancient testimony (Plutarch, *De Animae Procreatione* 1012D), ascribes to Xenocrates a view, discussed by Aristotle rather caustically at 404b28 and 408b32–409b18, which has the consequence that the soul moves itself.

Aristotle does not address this theory in detail, but mainly restricts himself to the suggestion that the position of those who regard the soul as self-moving results from a failure of imagination. He implies that it is only because they never see anything initiating motion without itself being in motion that such theorists assume that the soul moves itself. If that is so, he effectively represents them as relying on the simple inductive argument that since all the motion initiators experienced are in themselves in motion, the soul too, as an initiator of motion, must also be itself in motion. Cf. *APo.* 91a35–b1 and *Met.* 1072a1.

**404a25–b7: Anaxagoras:** Aristotle treats Anaxagoras alongside those who ascribe motion to the soul on the grounds that he: (i) identified reason (*nous*) and the whole soul, and (ii) thought of reason as the primary mover in the cosmos (cf. DK 59 B 12–13). He implies that his view is somehow unstable, because Anaxagoras suggests both that the soul and reason are the same (in (i)), but then also that reason is distinct from the rest of the cosmos (in (ii)).

Aristotle's first criticism, left undeveloped, may seem surprising: 'But reason—at any rate what is called reason in the sense of intelligence—does not appear to belong similarly to all animals, nor even to all humans' (404b5–6). He himself thinks that reason (*nous*) is a defining feature of the human soul (see the Introduction to II 3). In fact, though, he makes clear that he is speaking here of *nous* in normative terms, just as we may say that someone endowed with reason is not being at all reasonable just now. Still, if that is so, Anaxagoras evidently has a ready rejoinder, along the same lines.

Aristotle introduces Democritus in this connection mainly by way of background, in order to highlight the seeming instability in Anaxagoras' treatment of reason. Even so, Aristotle does take the occasion to rebuke Democritus, as he sometimes does, for implicitly identifying reason with perception, which Aristotle regards as a near consequence of his overtly identifying what appears with what is true (*Met.* 1009b1–17, 1010b1; *Gen. et Corr.* 315b9; and *DA* 427b3, where the doctrine re-emerges, though without being ascribed to Democritus; cf. Plato, *Theaet.* 153–7). Anaxagoras, at least, does not make this mistake.

Aristotle's quotation of Homer, that 'Hector lay with his thoughts elsewhere' (*allophroneôn*; 404a30), does not correspond to anything precise in the text of the *Iliad* as we have it. It may be a kind of amalgam of 22.330 and 23.698, where it is used of Euryalus; or it may be that Aristotle was operating with a different text or textual tradition. Aristotle's probable meaning may be inferred from *Met.* 1009b9–1110a1, where he associates Homer, and this passage in particular, with those of his predecessors who conflated perception (*aisthêsis*) and understanding (*phronêsis*). There he explains that some people cite this passage as evidence that even Homer accepted that perception and understanding are the same: 'they take him to mean that even those with a deranged understanding have understanding, though not about the same things'. A fuller context is also supplied by Theoc. *Idyl.* 22 128–30, where Amycus, savagely beaten senseless by Polydeuces, is so described. The phrase in that context evidently means that he 'lay unconscious' or that he 'lay with his thoughts elsewhere'. If the former, the point of Aristotle's reporting that Democritus approved of Homer's locution would be clear: on this reading, it implicitly equates sense perception (*aisthêsis*) with understanding (*phronêsis*), on the grounds that a lack of perception is tantamount to a lack of conscious awareness. If it means instead, as it may, 'lay with his thoughts elsewhere', the point would be rather that the delirium occasioned by a serious blow to the head scrambles the patterns of thought. That too would provide a reason for identifying perception and understanding, though via a less direct route: Hector, on this reading, has a kind of understanding, his own understanding, other than the understanding of those around him. They understand him to be unconscious; he understands himself, let us say, to be fighting in battle. What seems to be to him *is* what he understands.

**404b8–11: The Second Dominant Characteristic of Soul:** Aristotle's discussion of Anaxagoras and Democritus provides a segue to his treatment of the second dominant characteristic of soul identified at the outset of the chapter (403b25–7), perception, though he immediately rolls into his discussion another kind of cognition, knowledge (*to ginôskein kai to aisthanesthai*; 404b9). Presumably it is to be understood that perception had been introduced as a synecdoche for all of cognition. Aristotle's discussion of this second characteristic is framed in terms of the first principles (*archai*) or primary elements in terms of which cognition had been explained by his predecessors. He organizes them in terms of whether they understood the soul to be composed of only one or of more than one of the elements, and then in terms of which of the elements they favoured. For a parallel discussion, see *Gen. et Corr.* 334a9–12; cf. also *DA* 410b2–10.

**404b11–b27: Empedocles and Plato:** Aristotle first suggests that Empedocles treats the four common elements (*stoicheia*) as the principles constituting the soul: earth, fire, water, and air (or, rather, for Empedocles, air-like aether, an element which Aristotle himself describes as existing exclusively in the superlunary realm; *Meteor.* 339b18–27). He then adds, rather oddly, that Empedocles also treats the soul as being, or as being constituted by, each of the four elements considered individually. Taken one way, this may seem a simple fallacy of division on Aristotle's part and unfair to Empedocles, if the idea is supposed to be that the soul can be regarded as being composed exclusively of any single element which is a constituent of it, or even that it must have actually present in it every one of its constituents in an unmixed form. Though it contains water, we cannot say that there must be water in liquid form somewhere in the finished cake; it would thus be utterly unwarranted of Aristotle to attach any such inference to Empedocles.

It may accordingly be preferable to follow those among Aristotle's ancient commentators who understood him instead to be relying not on any such reasoning, but rather on the principle to the effect that anything individually capable of cognition must itself be a soul (so, e.g., ps.-Simplicius *in de An.* 27, 36). On this understanding of Aristotle's point, since according to Empedocles earth is known by earth, earth must itself be a soul—and so for each of the remaining three elements. If this is correct, then we have no grounds for ascribing a fallacy of division to Aristotle. That said, his mode of ascription would on this interpretation remain roughly the same: here too we would find him ascribing a view to one of his predecessors on the basis of an inference employing a conditional premise nowhere explicitly embraced by the thinker in question. Cf. *Met.* 1000b6, where Aristotle discusses the same fragment of Empedocles (DK B 17 109), and *Gen. et Corr.* 334a9, where Aristotle makes analogous claims about the absurdity of treating the soul as elemental.

The claim that like is known by like also figures in Plato's *Timaeus* (37a–c), a passage which thus provides Aristotle occasion to connect Plato's conception of the soul to the Empedoclean doctrine. Aristotle also seems to refer to an otherwise unattested work of Plato's, *On Philosophy*, though the matter is disputed; he may be referring to his own lost work, *On Philosophy*. (In the *Physics*, at 194a36, Aristotle uses the same title to refer to a dialogue of his own.) The suggestion that like is known by like is again cast in elemental terms, but there is a twist, in that the 'elements' (*stoicheia*) in question are no longer the familiar four, or even aether, but are rather more attenuated items, numbers. The basic idea behind the suggestion that numbers are the elements of the universe is easy enough to grasp. From a sufficiently abstract vantage point, the physical universe can be viewed as made up out of points, lines, planes, and solids, each of which correlates to a number: a point corresponds to one (though, properly, in Greek mathematics, one is typically not a number, but rather a starting point (*archê*) of numbers; see, e.g., *Met.* 1088a4–8, along with *Met.* 992a21, where it is reported that Plato made a correlative observation about points, preferring to speak not of the point as such, but rather of the starting point (*archê*) of a line); a line may be considered as two points at either end of an indefinite length; a plane may be conceived as three points on an indefinite breadth; and finally a solid is four points, the three of the plane, taken together with a fourth, marking out some indefinite depth.

With just this much background, it becomes possible to unpack Aristotle's obscure-sounding ascription that 'the animal itself is from the idea of the one itself and the primary length, breadth, and depth, and that the others come about in a similar way' (404b18–21). Presumably, Aristotle is characterizing a version of Plato's suggestion in the *Timaeus* (30b inter alia) that the whole sensible world is a living creature, an animal with a soul and reason: the 'animal itself' is the Idea or Form of Animal which serves as the paradigm for the creation of the physical universe which is modelled upon it. This Idea is here held to be itself complex, as constituted out of more basic elements, the Ideas or Forms of numbers and the geometrical figures to which they give rise. In a similar way, some today who believe in the existence of universals distinguish complex universals, e.g. *being a bachelor*, from simple universals, e.g. *being male*, in such a way that the simple universals figure into the complex as components or elements. In a broadly analogous sense, then, the view ascribed to Plato is held to accept numbers and geometrical figures as 'elements'.

Onto this already complicated picture, Aristotle grafts yet another layer: various doxastic and epistemic states are correlated to numbers considered as elements, so that, e.g., knowledge is correlated with two, insofar as it relates two discrete things, a knower and a known. It is difficult to develop Aristotle's observation in this regard systematically, but perhaps it is only offered *en passant*.

Those seeking a fuller understanding of the passage should consult in addition to those passages already cited: *Met.* 992a10–b13, 1078b9–12, 1080a12–14, 1085a7, 1090b20–24; and Plato, *Timaeus* 35a–b, 37a–c, together with Cornford, *Plato's Cosmology*, esp. 59–66.

**404b27–30: The Soul as a Self-Moving Number:** The view of the soul as a self-moving number, assumed since antiquity to derive from Xenocrates, successor to Speusippus in Plato's Academy, is treated more fully below in *De Anima* I 4, in connection with questions pertaining to the soul's motion. There Aristotle lets it be known that he regards this view as doubly ridiculous. See note to 408b32.

**404b30–405b10: The Various Elements and their Champions:** This long section recapitulates the views of a host of Aristotle's predecessors, recounted primarily in terms of the elements, or combinations of elements, held to be constitutive of the soul by the thinker under review. In most cases it is difficult or impossible to judge Aristotle's ascriptions for accuracy, since he is himself very often our first or only doxographical source for the position under review. While it is sometimes profitable to speculate about Aristotle's own sources and his degree of fidelity to them, we will largely restrict ourselves to the more modest task of understanding Aristotle's contentions in their own terms, in part because this offers greater insight into his own conception of soul.

To Aristotle's mind, the thinkers reviewed are to be categorized primarily by: (i) the number of elements they count as building blocks of soul; and (ii) the question of whether they regard these elements, whatever their number, as corporeal or incorporeal (404b30–405a2). Some thinkers have favoured only one element, others some combination of them; some thinkers have regarded the elements of soul as incorporeal, others as corporeal, and still others as some admixture of both.

The accounts of soul founded in these various alternatives are, understandably, distinct. For instance, because most have rightly seen that the soul is in some way a source of motion (cf. 403b20–4), some, presumably those who favoured there being just one basic element, often preferred fire, since fire is the most incorporeal among elements and also the one element most obviously capable of moving and initiating movement. It is worth noting that when speaking of fire as 'the most incorporeal' (*malista ... asômaton*; 405a7) among the elements, Aristotle evidently means only that it is the least solid. Cf. a similar non-standard use at 405a27 in connection with Heracleitus's contention that the soul is vapour, as well as 405b12 and 409b21. When he says that it is the '*most* incorporeal' among elements, Aristotle means not that fire is incorporeal in some exceedingly high degree, but that it exhibits more than any other element the features normally associated with the incorporeal. There is no confusion or linguistic impropriety here: one speaks, in an analogous vein in English, of 'the most heavenly chocolate on earth'.

In terms of their content, the views of Aristotle's predecessors, as represented by him, require only brief comment:

- **Democritus** receives praise from Aristotle because he, in his view, tries to ground two principal features of the soul, its incorporeality and its ability to initiate motion. The first follows from its being identified as reason (*nous*), which is held to be the subtlest of elements, and the second follows from the fact that the soul, like fire, is composed of the most mobile of all indivisible bodies, tiny spherical atoms.
- **Anaxagoras** holds a position which tends in incompatible directions. While he identifies soul and reason (*nous*) as having the same nature, he also at the same time implicitly differentiates them by elevating reason to the role of first principle (*archê*) of all things. Yet if both have the same nature, it seems odd to offer a status to one, reason, but not the other, the soul. Anaxagoras also ascribes knowing and motion to this first principle, because he believes that reason, a knower, initiates motion in the whole of the universe. In some respects, as regards the primary characteristics of reason, there seems to be a direct line of influence from Anaxagoras to Aristotle. At any rate, when he comes to characterize reason in his own terms at 429a18–20 and at 429b22, Aristotle appropriates some of the same language used here to describe Anaxagoras' view. See the notes to those passages.
- **Thales** is said to have regarded the magnet as imbued with soul. In an especially clear instance of conjectural reconstruction, Aristotle on this basis ascribes to him the belief that souls are productive of motion. Presumably Aristotle, upon hearing the report that Thales ascribed souls to magnets, reasoned thus: (1) the magnet is productive of motion; (2) whatever is productive of motion has a soul; so, (3) the magnet has a soul. Although we have no independent

confirmation that Thales held either (1) or (3), (1) seems easy to fathom on the basis of casual observation. If he was recorded as holding (3), then (2), as Aristotle suggests, would serve as a bridge premise and on this basis be reasonably ascribed to Thales. However accurate this bit of rational reconstruction may be, it is easy to imagine countless other patterns of inference in which Thales might have indulged; for that matter, perhaps his belief about the souls of magnets was not derived on the basis of any deduction whatsoever. Interestingly, in this passage at least, Aristotle omits mention of Thales's preferred element, water. Cf. *Met.* 983b20–8.

- **Diogenes**, presumably Diogenes of Apollonia, who is mainly lost to the history of philosophy, posited air as the stuff of soul. He is represented as reasoning on a par with those who accepted fire, on the grounds that air is fine-grained and highly ductile. Cf. *Met.* 984a5 and *Gen. et Corr.* 322b14–15. The 'others' mentioned as sharing this point of view presumably include Anaximenes, who accepted air as the primary element of the universe.

- **Heracleitus** is by contrast well remembered by the history of philosophy. Here he is represented as maintaining that the soul is itself a first principle (*archê*), though this is evidently again on the basis of an inference owing to Aristotle, not to Heracleitus himself. In order to frame this inference, it is first of all to be understood that Heracleitus regarded fire as a first principle and that the 'rising vapour' (*anathumiasis*, a word first attested in Heracleitus and perhaps coined by him) in question is not a cold, moist mist, but rather the dry heat arising from moisture; in addition, Heracleitus may have identified this vaporous heat with 'fire' (*pur*, the Greek word for fire, sometimes extends beyond fire proper, for example to the *heat* or *haze* of the sun). So, since fire is for him a first principle, and is not distinguished from vapour, vapour too is for him a first principle, that from which all else is derived. Accordingly, if soul is identified with this vapour, then by the same reasoning, the soul will itself be a first principle. This is the force of Aristotle's remarking that for Heracleitus 'the soul is the first principle, *if indeed* (*eiper*) it is the rising vapour from which other things are constituted' (405a25–6). Thus, when Aristotle reports that Heracleitus *claims* that the soul is a first principle, he is not purporting to quote him directly. In any case, the soul vapour, like the fire mentioned at 405a6–7, is thought by Heracleitus to be the most incorporeal sort of stuff, where, again, this presumably means little more than that it is the least dense or solid among the elements. Finally, the claim that what is in motion is known by what is in motion seems simply a special case of the more general principle, enunciated at 404b17, that like is known by like.

- **Alcmaeon** was a physician from Croton, in Sicily. Aristotle focuses again primarily on the soul's motion, this time, though, with an added twist: if the soul is always in motion, then it is likely it will be immortal, in virtue of its resembling immortal beings, who are equally perpetually in motion. In this respect, Alcmaeon's approach bears striking similarities to a view considered in the *Phaedo* at 96b, and may even have inspired Plato's discussion there.

- **Hippo**, derided by Aristotle as an especially crude thinker (cf. also *Met.* 984a3, where he receives comparably harsh treatment), was probably also a physician. He favoured water as the primary element of the soul. Aristotle conjectures that he was moved to this view because all seed (or perhaps every *newborn*, or conceivably every *womb*, all possible renderings of *gonê*) is moist.

- **Critias**, probably the Athenian oligarch who led the Thirty Tyrants, preferred blood, because of a conjectured connection between perception and blood. Perhaps the connection turned on the fact that bloodless bits of the body, like hair, bone, and teeth, lack sensation. Cf. 410a30–b1.

**405b11–30: Summary:** Whereas he had begun the chapter by noting that his predecessors had relied on two defining features of soul, motion and perception, in summation Aristotle adds a third, incorporeality (cf. note to 403b24–31, along with 409b20). It is not clear whether incorporeality is to be understood in the attenuated sense it received at 405a6–7 and 405a27, where what was fine-grained and ethereal qualified as the most incorporeal among the elements, or whether it has here its contrastive sense, with an implication of immateriality, so that it is meant to capture Plato's view. Aristotle does not distinguish these two senses overtly.

In the summary to the chapter Anaxagoras again merits special treatment for his contention that reason is unaffected, lacking any form of commonality with other things. This, as we have seen, is an approach so congenial to Aristotle that he appropriates some of its terms and incorporates them into his own account of reason. See note to 404b30–405b10, as well as 429a18–20 and 429b22. For some suggestions regarding the relation of this chapter to Aristotle's positive account of reason (*nous*) in III 4, see Lowe (1983).

Aristotle's remark that his predecessors sometimes 'take a cue from words' (405b26–7) does not mean that in his view they theorized on the basis of etymologies, but rather that they sometimes etymologized in simple-minded ways to suit their theories, as a kind of confirming evidence. Thus, those who say that the soul is the hot say that living (*to zên*) gets its name from boiling (*to zein*), while those who say that the soul is the cold suggest that the word 'soul' (*psuchê*) is derived from the cooling (*psuxis*) of the body which occurs in respiration. Aristotle would have been familiar with similarly fanciful etymologizing in Greek from Plato's *Cratylus* (see especially 436a, for a linguistic parallel to Aristotle's remarks here).

## CHAPTER 3

### Introduction to I 3

In this chapter Aristotle delves further into the views of his predecessors, primarily by focusing on the question of the soul's ability to move and initiate motion. He has already been critical of a view which, he alleges, is held in common by many of his predecessors, namely that the soul initiates motion only by being itself in motion (403b28–31). He does not, however, fault his predecessors for holding that the soul in fact initiates motion, nor even for holding that it is capable of being in motion. On the contrary, he himself agrees both that the soul initiates motion and that it can be in motion; he will, however, impose a severe regimentation on the correct understanding of these claims, one bound up with the question of whether the soul is itself a magnitude (*megethos*).

Ultimately, he will insist that the soul can be moved only co-incidentally (*kata sumbebêkos*), and that it cannot in its own nature be in motion, because it is not a proper subject of motion. According to Aristotle, only a magnitude can be in motion in its own right (*kath' hauto*), and the soul is not a magnitude. Some features of his own view are difficult and disputed, though as a first approximation it is probably best to reflect on the sorts of illustrations Aristotle himself finds it natural to employ: if a lonely man is pushed off the deck of a ship, it is true, perhaps, that his loneliness goes with him into the sea; but it would be more than linguistically perverse to say that someone pushed loneliness overboard. Aristotle will say that while it can be moved co-incidentally, loneliness is not the sort of thing which in its own nature is susceptible of being moved. (On this topic, see further the notes to 406b5–11 and 408a30–4.)

In a similar way, according to Aristotle, the soul's nature renders it incapable of being moved in its own right; so, if it is to be moved at all, the soul must be moved by being suitably related to something else: a body, which can be moved in its own right. One question regarding Aristotle's view will concern his reasons for denying that the soul is a magnitude (407a3, a16); this question will in turn give way to another, prior question pertaining to his understanding of magnitudes (on which, see note to 407a2–10).

In the present chapter, Aristotle does not assay the question of the nature of magnitudes, preferring instead to rely on a conception he has articulated elsewhere, most notably in the *Physics* and *De Caelo*. Here his focus is narrow. He first considers and finds wanting a series of arguments purporting to show that the soul can move (405b31–406b25). He then offers a brief recapitulation of a famous passage from Plato's *Timaeus*, followed by a succinct and trenchant series of criticisms of the doctrines it is represented as advancing (406b26–407b11). Aristotle ends the chapter with some importantly programmatic remarks concerning whether it is feasible or otherwise desirable to attempt a definition of the soul without making reference to the body whose soul it is (407b12–26).

**405b31–406a12: Being Moved in Virtue of Oneself and in Virtue of Another:**    Aristotle begins with the bold-sounding claim that 'it is presumably not merely false to say that its essence (*ousia*) is of the sort claimed by those who say that the soul moves itself, or is able to move itself, but it is, rather, impossible that motion belong to the soul' (405b31–406a2). He then spends much of the rest of the chapter qualifying and moderating this claim, though not to the point where it loses all significance. On the contrary, Aristotle's final insistence that the soul is not such as to be moved in itself offers some of the most important evidence in *De Anima* I regarding his own positive conception of the soul's nature.

That said, the distinction drawn here between being moved in virtue of oneself (or in its own right, *kath' hauto*) and in virtue of another (*kath' heteron*) (406a4–5) is also the first and most important step in his eventual qualification of the claim that the soul cannot be moved, since Aristotle concludes this introductory paragraph by limiting his inquiry into the soul's ability to be moved *in virtue of itself*—where the clear implication is, then, that his contention regarding the impossibility of the soul's motion is restricted to its being moved in virtue of its own nature.

Given the example used here, it is probable that Aristotle's distinction between these ways of being moved is equivalent to a linguistically parallel distinction used later in the chapter (406b3) between being moved in virtue of oneself (or in its own right, *kath' hauto*) and being moved co-incidentally (*kata sumbebêkos*; cf. *Phys.* 211a17, 224a23, 254b7–12; *DA* 406b31). He illustrates this latter distinction in the *Physics* in two different ways. First, using the same illustration he uses here (406a5–6), he speaks of sailors standing upon the deck of a ship as being moved when the ship is moved, though they are not in this instance moved in virtue of being themselves moved, as one sailor would be if he were thrown to the deck by another in the course of a brawl (*Phys.* 211a21–2). This sort of case he seems to conceptualize as one object co-inciding with a part of a larger whole which moves. In this sense, if a man is thrown off a bridge in Paris into the Seine by his enemies, then so too are the laces on his shoes, by co-inciding with a part of the object thrown; so, one can truly say that his enemies threw his shoelaces off the bridge. In such a case, of course, his enemies might have removed his shoelaces as an illustration and have thrown them into the Seine alone, as a warning to the man. They can be moved in their own right. In the second sort of illustration, we have cases more like loneliness mentioned in the introduction to this chapter, namely knowledge and whiteness. Knowledge and whiteness, like shoelaces, can be moved by co-inciding with something moved in its own right, but, unlike shoelaces, according to Aristotle, can only be so moved.

So, if the soul is moved in virtue of something other than itself, or is moved co-incidentally, then it may or may not also be the sort of thing which *cannot* be moved in itself. As we approach this claim, then, some circumspection is required, since we do not know to which class of things moved co-incidentally the soul belongs: (i) those which can, and (ii) those which cannot also be moved in their own right. Subsequent arguments in this chapter will contend that the soul is in the second class and so *cannot* be moved in itself. The significance of this determination for Aristotle's positive doctrine resides in his further view that *x* is a magnitude (*megethos*) *iff* *x* can be moved in itself (*DC* 268b14–16). It will follow, then, from Aristotle's conception of the soul's not being able to be moved in itself that it is not a magnitude at all. In this chapter, however, he mainly concentrates on one half of this bi-conditional: he simply asserts that the soul is not a magnitude and infers that it cannot be moved in its own right (e.g. 407a3).

**406a12–16: Types of Motion and Some Conceptual Entailments:** If the soul is to move in itself, then it must do so in terms of one of four types of motion: alteration (*alloiôsis*), growth (*auxêsis*), decay (*phthisis*), or locomotion (*phora*). Aristotle's assertion that there are 'four types of motion—locomotion, alteration, decay, and growth' (406a12–13) draws on his account of motion elsewhere. Aristotle sometimes offers longer or shorter lists of types of motion: three, often in the *Physics* (e.g. 243a32–5), and six in *Categories* (15a13–14). These are, though, mainly verbal differences. Sometimes he treats growth and decay as but two types of quantitative change (*kata ton poson*), so that there are three types. Sometimes he mentions generation (*genesis*) and destruction (*phthora*) as types of motion and sometimes not. This explains the difference between the current list of four and the list of six at *Cat.* 15a13–14, where generation and destruction are listed as discrete kinds (*eidê*) of motion. A more substantive question relevant to the current passages concerns whether all these types of motion are in some sense dependent upon locomotion (*phora*). Here Aristotle presumes they are in some sense dependent, presumably relying on *Physics* vii 2, where it is described as the 'primary' (*prôtê*) sort of motion (*Phys.* 243a10–11).

The four types of motion listed show that Aristotle is here thinking of 'motion' in broad terms, at least relative to our contemporary tendency to think of movement in space as the exemplary or exclusive kind of motion. This conception of motion corresponds to the first item on Aristotle's list, spatial motion (or movement in place, *kata topon*; cf. 414b17, 415a7). Context usually makes clear whether Aristotle has the broader or narrower notion of *kinêsis* in view.

Aristotle's broader approach recognizes as types of motion the ways in which things may change more generally, for instance by altering, or by being one of two correlative processes, growth and decay. On this basis, some prefer to render the word here translated as 'motion' (*kinêsis*) with the word 'change'. There are advantages and disadvantages to both translations, but we may bear in mind that we too are prepared to speak of there being movement in numerical averages, in political sentiments, in percentages of body fat, in bargaining positions, and so forth. What matters in the present context is that we recognize that Aristotle is not here speaking only of spatial movement, or locomotion. (Here it is also worth noting that 'change' is elsewhere used to translate another term, *metabolê*, as at 406b2. While Aristotle sometimes uses *kinêsis* in the narrow sense of 'locomotion', he does not do so with *metabolê*. For more on the types of motion or change, see *Phys.* 192b14, 218b19, 225a26–32; cf. *Met.* 1068a10.)

Importantly for our purposes, Aristotle contends that all these sorts of motion occur in place (*topos*); hence, if the soul is to move in its own nature, and in one of these ways, then it will move in place. Otherwise, it will move the way the white or three-cubits-long move (his examples at 406b18–19), by being suitably related to something which is a magnitude and capable of being moved in itself. Aristotle does not mean to speak, in these examples, of the motion of *something* white or *something* three cubits long, but rather, as may initially sound a bit odd, simply of *white* or of *three-cubits-long*. In so speaking, he means, for example, that if Ana learns Italian, her knowledge of Italian moves about with her, but only because she herself, the woman, can move around in space; if Ana weighs 51.5 kilos, then similarly, though the woman who weighs 51.5 kilos is moved, *weighing 51.5 kilos* is itself not a subject of motion in its own right. If the soul moves in only some analogous way, then it, unlike the animal or plant whose soul it is, is not a magnitude. These comparisons suggest that, according to Aristotle, it would be some manner of category mistake to treat the soul as a being capable of moving in place in its own right. Cf. *Phys.* 211a21–2.

Aristotle does not in this passage overtly draw the conclusion that the soul does *not* move in place or by its own nature, though his language strongly suggests that this is his view. Indeed, this is just the conclusion for which he proceeds to argue.

**406a16–b25: Arguments Against the Soul's Being Moved In Itself:** There follows a series of arguments all intended to show that the soul is not the sort of thing capable of being moved in its own right. Most of the arguments are brief but suggestive and would require amplification and ancillary defence if intended to persuade someone not already sympathetic to their shared conclusion.

The arguments run together a bit. The principal among them are these:

(A) 406a22–7
   (1) The soul is moved in itself if and only if it can be moved and brought to rest by force.
   (2) The soul cannot be moved by force or brought to rest by force.
   (3) Hence, the soul cannot be moved in itself.

Aristotle regularly aligns being moved by force with being moved against one's nature (*para phusin*), often, though not always, in connection with the simple elements, as indeed he proceeds to do in the next argument at 406a27–30. (Cf. *DC* 269a7, 274b30, 276a22, 300a23; *Gen. et Corr.* 333b26; and esp. *Phys.* 215a1.) Here Aristotle concludes that since even those willing to indulge in myth-making and other fanciful fabrications cannot make ready sense of the soul's being moved by force, it certainly cannot be understood to be moved in itself as things actually are.

(B) 406a30–b5:
   (1) The soul moves the body.
   (2) If (1), then if the soul moves in its own right (*kath' hauto*), it is subject to the same sorts of motions to which the body is subject.

(3) So, if the soul moves in its own right (*kath' hauto*), it is subject to the same sorts of motions to which the body is subject.

(4) The body is the subject of spatial motion (*phora*).

(5) Hence, if the soul moves in its own right (*kath' hauto*), it is subject to spatial motion.

(6) If the soul is subject to spatial motion, then it should be able to quit the body and subsequently return.

(7) If it can quit the body and subsequently return, then resurrection of the dead should be possible.

(8) [Resurrection of the dead is not possible.]

(9) Hence, the soul does not move in its own right (*kath' hauto*).

In fact, the argument is compressed in its execution and relies on still more logical structure than is exhibited here. Even so, this expansion captures the main flow of the argument. Importantly, since Aristotle eventually wants to accept some version of (1), he must ultimately deny (2) or (3). He endeavours to do so by insisting the soul can initiate motion in the body without being movable in its own right (cf. 408a31–b1), which might be taken in different ways, as a rejection of either (2) or (3), or indeed of both (2) and (3). Aristotle does not state (7), although it is suggested at 406b4–5. There is perhaps a weaker, non-modal version of the argument according to which both (6) and (7) simply assert that on the hypothesis under consideration we could easily encounter instances of resurrection of the dead among all animals, a state of affairs which, even if possible, is in fact never observed.

This understanding may be compared with that of de Ley (1970), who argues against the sort of interpretation embodied in (2), by favouring an approach earlier advanced by Shorey (1901). De Ley retains the key phrase 'in respect of body' (*kata sôma*) of the manuscripts at 406b2, which he renders, somewhat problematically, as 'throughout the body', and offers the following translation of 406b1–3: 'Now, the body moves by locomotion; so the soul as well must be able to change its place throughout the body, whether in moving as a whole or in its parts' (1970: 94). The current translation accepts an emendation proposed by Bonitz (1873), 'in respect of place' (*kata topon*), which yields: 'The body, however, is moved by locomotion, with the result that the soul would change in place.'

(C) 406b15–24

(1) If, as Democritus contends, the soul moves the body by being itself in motion, and so by being something subject to motion in its own right (*kath' hauto*), then it should cause the body to be at rest by the same means.

(2) The soul cannot cause the body to be at rest by being itself in motion.

(3) So, the soul does not move the body by being itself in motion.

Aristotle partly revisits ground already covered in *DA* I 2 (see esp. 403b29–404a9; cf. 409a32–b4) by again pointing out that the soul need not convey motion by being itself in motion. Here, though, he sets his sights not on the question of whether *x* can cause *y* to be in motion only if *x* is itself in motion. Rather, he now notes that on the picture advanced by Democritus, according to which indivisible magnitudes communicate motion by being themselves in motion, in which case they are movable in themselves, their activity should equally halt the body when it is brought to rest.

To generalize, as Aristotle seems inclined to do in this argument: if the soul is the sort of thing which communicates motion by being itself in motion in its own right, then it ought also to be able to communicate rest in the same way; but, Aristotle contends, it makes no ready sense to suggest that the soul could bring the body to rest by being itself in motion. Better, then, simply to deny that the soul is the sort of thing which is itself in motion in its own right. Cf. *Phys.* 258b23.

The comparison of Democritus to the comic playwright Philippus seems mainly ornamental, and rather derogatory. Philippus was the son of the comic playwright Aristophanes and has attested to him a play on the theme of Daedalus, the sculptor who brought to life a wooden statue of Aphrodite by filling it with mercury. Aristotle implies that tiny atoms would be about as likely to impart motion to the body as mercury would be to animate a statue.

(D) 406b24–5:
  (1) Generally, if the soul imparts motion in any of the ways mentioned, then it moves the animal by drawing it along with its own motion.
  (2) Evidently, however, the soul initiates motion through decision and thought.
  (3) [Decision and thought do not initiate motion by drawing bodies along with their own motions.]
  (4) Hence, the soul does not initiate motion in any of the ways mentioned.

This final argument is actually a compressed observation, acting as a kind of summary to the entire discussion of 406a12–b25. It is, however, highly significant in terms of revealing Aristotle's preferred approach to the question of the soul's role in initiating motion.

First, there is a point of method: Aristotle takes it as evident, and so as a reasonable starting point, that reasoning (or thinking, *noêsis*) and decision (*proairesis*) figure in the aetiology of action. He suggests that we know from our own experience that our reflections and decision-making processes eventuate in our acting. If someone deliberates about whether to take a walk for the sake of health or recreation, and decides that doing so at present is both possible and desirable, then when she commences to walk she does so *because* she has thought about the matter and has decided to do so. If someone now contends that she walks solely because the atoms of her soul are flittering about in this or that way, then a crucial component of the causal antecedents of her action is simply ignored. In Aristotle's terms, intentional action requires ineliminably teleological explanation. (On teleological explanation, see the General Introduction § IV.)

If that much captures Aristotle's posture, then much of the foregoing discussion is motivated by a demand for teleological explanation in human action. There is, though, a second point of significance. All of the individual arguments deployed in this section depend in one way or another upon the thought that explanations of motion as imparted by pulling or pushing are, in the psychological domain, at best incomplete. For a similar observation, see *Gen. et Corr.* 334a10–16, where Aristotle concludes a protracted assault on Empedocles with the contention that such manifest psychic alterations as remembering or forgetting cannot be explained solely in terms of the elements and their corporeal combinations and modifications. (He refers in that discussion to the current chapter of *De Anima* for elaboration.) In so speaking, Aristotle means to assail any austerely reductive or eliminative form of materialist explanation, in favour of a view according to which the psychic properties of complex living systems are causally efficacious and not readily explicated by the motions of the elements of which bodies are ultimately composed. Here he stresses the role of reason and decision, both themes that underscore the criticisms of Plato to follow. On Aristotle's preferred approach, see note to 407b32. Cf. also *Met.* 988b21–989a18.

**406b26–407a1: Recapitulation of the *Psuchogonia* in Plato's *Timaeus*:** A difficult passage from Plato's *Timaeus* (the '*Psuchogonia*,' or '*Soul Generation*,' 34b–36d) recounts the generation of the soul of the entire cosmos. It has been disputed since antiquity whether the passage is intended as figurative or as literal. Aristotle here somewhat remorselessly treats the characters of the dialogue as offering an account in the style of the Presocratic naturalists. (He mainly reserves the verb *phusiologein* ('to offer a physical account'), used at 406b26, for the earliest Ionians, who were materialist monists; cf. *Met.* 986b14 and 988b27; for an instructive discussion, see Hussey (2012)). He does so presumably because the account of the world soul's creation in the *Psuchogonia* proceeds in two stages: (i) the Demiurge, or Creator, first blends visible and invisible forms of Being, Sameness, and Difference into a dough-like soul stuff (cf. *Tim.* 41d); and then (ii) kneads, shapes, cuts, and forms the stuff into a harmonious series of seven embedded spheres, corresponding to the orbits of the sun, the moon, Venus, Mercury, Mars, Jupiter, and Saturn. The effect of Aristotle's diction is to align the speaker with Democritus and the other naturalists as someone who is offering an approach to the soul's motion which, in its unidimensional materialism, can be criticized from the standpoint of someone—like Plato in the *Phaedo* (95a–100a) and like Aristotle himself—who insists that material explanations be accompanied by formal and teleological explanations as well.

The astronomical details of Plato's world soul recounted here cannot be understood without careful reference to Plato's *Timaeus*, where they are already compressed and obscure. That said, it appears that Aristotle's presentation does not distort the basic account offered in the *Psuchogonia* in any obvious way. (For accounts of Plato's mathematical astronomy in the *Psuchogonia*, see Heath, *Greek Mathematics* vol. i, 310–15. For an illuminating discussion of the way in which Aristotle relates the *Timaeus* to Presocratic naturalism, see Hussey (2012).)

Aristotle claims that 'Timaeus offers a physical account of how the soul moves the body' (406b26–7). The translation ascribes the view to Timaeus, the character in Plato's dialogue, the *Timaeus*, rather than to Timaeus himself or to the author of the dialogue bearing his name. If this is correct, then Aristotle may be drawing particular attention to what is said in the dialogue, as opposed to what its author may or may not believe. Although there is room for doubt on this score, the translation offered is likely to be correct, since: (i) Aristotle is not in the habit of ascribing views to dialogues of Plato or any other writer by title (as we might say, 'The *Phaedo* maintains that the soul is simple, whereas the *Republic* holds that it is tripartite.'); and (ii) the particular linguistic formulation used here (*ho Timaios*; 406b26) reflects Aristotle's dominant practice, captured in Fitzgerald's Canon, of referring to characters in dialogues with the definite article (*ho*) and actual persons without. Ross provides a useful summary and endorsement of Fitzgerald's Canon (1924: vol i, xxxix–xli).

**407a2–b13: Objections to the Account of the *Timaeus*:** As with the previous sections concerning the soul's ability to move in its own right, in undermining the (allegedly) physiological conception of the soul from the *Psuchogonia* of Plato's *Timaeus*, Aristotle advances a whole series of arguments. Some of them are reasonably well developed, while others are brief to the point of obscurity; and some of them are directed against idiosyncratic features of Plato's account, while others have a more consequential cast.

In terms of their significance for understanding Aristotle's own approach to soul and reason (*nous*), the most important are these:

(A) 407a2–10:
  (1) When Plato speaks of soul (*psuchê*), he intends to refer to reason (*nous*).

(2) Hence, what he says of the soul should be true of reason.

(3) He says, or implies, that the soul is a magnitude.

(4) Reason is not a magnitude

(5) Hence, Plato's account of soul is incorrect.

Aristotle first states baldly that the soul is not a magnitude (407a2–3). Importantly, however, he makes clear immediately that he understands Plato to be speaking of reason (*nous*) alone, since the sort of world soul envisaged in the *Psuchogonia* has neither desire nor perception. So, when he denies that the soul is a magnitude, Aristotle should evidently be understood as speaking exclusively of *reason*, which, on his own theory, will be but one capacity of the soul—the defining capacity of the rational soul.

Why should Plato be understood to be treating the soul (or reason) as a magnitude? Presumably Aristotle is taking literally the suggestion from the *Timaeus* that the soul is a circle, and so a line of a determinate sort. Although he sometimes treats magnitudes as bodies and so as perceptible (as at 432a4), Aristotle is also fully prepared to call lines, planes, and solids magnitudes (*DC* 268a7; *Met.* 1020a11). So, if the soul is a circle, it is a magnitude and continuous in the way of all magnitudes.

What, ultimately, though, shows reason to be something other than a magnitude, as (4) contends? Aristotle relies here on his conviction that every magnitude is continuous, and so potentially divisible infinitely into smaller magnitudes (*Phys.* 219a11, 233a11), which view is paired with the view of Timaeus, as here represented, that reasoning consists in a succession of thoughts, which thus makes it roughly analogous to a discrete quantity. Having already introduced as a question for consideration whether the soul has parts or is without parts (402b1), he now contends (407a9–10; cf. 430b15) that reason is either without parts or is at best continuous in some way other than the way in which magnitudes are continuous. He thus leaves open the possibility that the soul, or reason, is continuous in the manner that discrete quantities, like number series, are. This possibility would presumably offer Plato a way of responding to at least some of the arguments launched against his view in this section. (On discrete versus continuous quantities, see *Cat.* 6, esp. 4b20–31.) This current argument is usefully read in conjunction with *Phys.* 266a10, where Aristotle contends that the prime mover is without parts (*amerês*), and so is not a magnitude. The main point of Aristotle's present contention is also better appreciated after having read *DA* III 4–6, whose main conclusions the current passage seems to accept as established.

(B) 407a10–22:

This argument is especially compressed and obscure in the text; its reconstruction here is thus perforce a bit speculative.

Reasoning takes place in virtue of there being some contact between what thinks and what is thought.

(1) If the soul is a magnitude, then, it will have parts and it will think (a) in virtue of the whole soul coming into contact with the objects of thought, or (b) in virtue of its parts coming into contact with the objects of thought.

(2) If (1a), then its parts make no contribution to its reasoning and so play no role.

(3) If (1b), then reason will come into contact with its objects in virtue of: either (i) some of its parts, or (ii) all of them.

(4) If (3-i), then the other parts make no contribution and play no role.

(5) If (3-ii), then reason thinks in virtue of its parts, which are (α) themselves points, or (β) themselves magnitudes.

(6) If (5α), then reason will need to make an infinite number of contacts in order to think, since lines are infinitely divisible into points, and reasoning will be impossible.

(7) If (5β), then reason will perforce think the same thing over and over, when it is in fact possible to think some things but once.

(8) Hence, the soul (=reason) is not a magnitude.

Although difficult, the argument provides important data regarding Aristotle's contention that no magnitude can think, assuming, as seems probable, that the soul (*psuchê*) is to be understood as reason (*nous*) throughout (see note to 407a2–10). This same contention plainly colours Aristotle's own approach to reasoning in *DA* III 4–5.

As reconstructed, the argument is predicated upon the assumption that reasoning involves some kind of contact with the objects of thought. The argument need not be in this respect ad hominem, since Aristotle is himself perfectly willing to speak of thought as involving a kind of touch (*Met.* 1072b21; cf. 1051b24), though, given the view espoused here, he must understand touch as akin to intellectual grasping rather than as contact between discrete magnitudes. That said, the current argument seems to foist upon Plato a quite literal notion of touch, perhaps, again, because Aristotle is treating the view of Timaeus as akin to Presocratic naturalism. Presumably Plato could respond to this argument by availing himself of the non-literal notion of touch Aristotle himself accepts.

On the assumption that literal contact is required for thought, however, one may ask whether the presumed magnitude, the world soul which is a circle, touches its objects as a whole or in part, and if in part, whether it does so with parts that are themselves line segments or parts that are points (though here already Aristotle is arguing *ex hypothesi*, since he regards it as mistaken to think of points as proper parts of magnitudes (*Phys.* 231a21–b18)). In any event, Aristotle traces out what he takes to be the unacceptable consequences of all of these alternatives. Thus the rhetorical questions at 407a10 and a18, the joint purport of which is that the very suggestion that the reason (or mind, *nous*) is extended and makes contact by some kind of literal touch is patently absurd.

Each of the alleged absurd consequences invites scrutiny, though only one requires explication as crucially obscure. Why should Plato be saddled with the consequence, asserted in (8), that if the soul comes into contact with its objects in virtue of some of its parts, conceived as magnitudes, it will of necessity think those objects over and over, when we can plainly think some things only once? Presumably Aristotle falls back on the earlier thought that every magnitude is infinitely divisible into smaller magnitudes (*Phys.* 219a11, 233a11). So, the subparts of the magnitude which are themselves magnitudes and not points will come into contact either serially, or all at once. If all at once, then the reasoning standing behind (3) will come back into play; if serially, then contact will be made over and over again as the magnitude cycles through its points of contact, yielding many thoughts of the same object instead of just one. This is why Aristotle suggests that on this hypothesis reason (or mind, *nous*) will very often or *endlessly* think the same thing (407a14): the alternatives correspond to construing the parts of the sub-magnitudes either as discrete and exhaustive quantities, line segments of the line segments, which are equally magnitudes, or as points, which are infinite in number.

The next few arguments, from 407a22–407b12 are briefer, dealing primarily with idiosyncratic features of Plato's contention that the world soul, or reason, is a circle and in motion. They do, however, show again, as at 406b24–5, that Aristotle expects from Plato a teleological cause of the soul's circular motion, a cause he finds lacking in the *Psuchogonia*.

The translation in the text is somewhat less direct than it might be, in order to capture the semantic connection between 'reason' (*nous*) and 'to reason' (*noein*): 'it will very often or endlessly reason about the same thing. But it is evidently possible to reason about something only once' (407a14–15). Another, more direct translation, though one which loses this connection, would be: 'it will very often or endlessly think about the same thing. But it is evidently possible to think something only once.' The more direct translation has the advantage of capturing the immediacy of Aristotle's suggestion that on the hypothesis under consideration reason (*nous*) will perforce repeatedly think the same thing (*noêsei to auto*). In Aristotle's Greek, the verb *noein*, unlike 'to reason' but like 'to think' in English, can take a pure accusative, that is, a direct object.

The text of 407b1 is disputed. The translation has 'If motion is not essential to it ... ' This reflects the manuscript reading of *not* (*mê*), which has seemed hard to understand, since motion could presumably be natural to the soul without being essential to it. (Humans are naturally hirsute, but being hairy is no part of the human essence.) Shorey (1901) tried to read the text as given by suggesting that it might mean 'If motion is the negation of its essence ... ', but that is not what is said in Greek, and such a view is neither prepared by what has come before nor explained by what follows. Torstrik (1862), followed by Ross (1961: 191), argues in addition to the difficult sense of the passage that the word order of the manuscripts as we have them is odd. On his proposed emendation *(hê(i)* for *mê* in 407b1), the passage reads: 'If the movement of the soul is a movement in so far as it is a substance...' The point would then be that if motion belongs to it in its own right, and not merely co-incidentally, then the soul would be moved contrary to its nature. I have retained the manuscript reading, supposing instead that Aristotle is characterizing a view he does not endorse, namely the view adumbrated in the *Timaeus*. If this is correct, his point, put periphrastically, will be that if the motion of the soul could start and stop, as per that account, then because it is not essential to it, the motion being thus characterized—that is, reasoning—would be toilsome and so less than a delight. That eventuality would offend Aristotle's own conception of thought as pleasurable (see, e.g., *Met.* 1072b24, and more fully *EN* vii 11–14 and x 8). That understanding, though only partly satisfactory, seems the best one can do without emending the text.

**407b14–26: The Connection Between Body and Soul:** The last argument of this chapter contains something consequential for our understanding of Aristotle's own positive doctrine. After indicating that further discussion of Plato's views would best be conducted elsewhere (407b12), Aristotle launches a final criticism of him by complaining that his account, in common with those of many others, leaves obscure the connection between the soul and body. His reference to other writings is indeterminate. He may intend *De Caelo* or the books of the *Physics* dedicated to motion (v–viii), from whose accounts he has been drawing in this chapter; or, if he is referring more narrowly to discussion of the soul's ability to move and initiate motion, he may intend *Metaphysics* Λ 10.

Here he argues that all of the views considered in this chapter fail in common to address a crucial question regarding the connection between soul and body. In schematic outline, his argument is:

(1) Soul and body causally affect one another only if there is some commonality *(koinônia)* between them.

(2) On the theories adumbrated, there is no commonality between soul and body.

(3) So, on these theories, there is no chance of there being mutual causal action between soul and body.

More weakly, Aristotle might be understood as inferring from

(1) and
(2′) The theories adumbrated fail to explain how there might be commonality between soul and body.

to

(3′) These theories leave obscure how bodies and souls are to be understood as causally interacting.

On the weaker reading (3′), the theories are rejected as at best incomplete; on the stronger reading (3), they are refuted on the grounds that they *cannot* account for the observed fact that souls and bodies interact, as when, e.g., thought and deliberation initiate bodily motion (on which, see note to 406b24–5). It is possible that Aristotle intends only (3′), though the general tenor of his remarks suggests that he has in view the stronger (3).

In either case, his complaint is rooted in an alleged failure on the part of his targets to take notice of the intimate connection between soul and body, a failure ultimately explained in Aristotle's terms by appeal to his contention that the soul is the form of the body (407b23–4, a central feature of his own hylomorphism, developed in *DA* II 1 and 2; see also the General Introduction § IV.A.)

Aristotle insists that there must be some commonality (*koinô-nia*) between body and soul if the one is to act upon the other and the other is to be affected by the one (407b17–19). At its most general level, his point is that *x* can affect *y* along some dimension $\phi$ only if *x* and *y* share what is commonly required for the transmission of $\phi$-ness into *y* by the agency of *x*. Though an acclaimed vocal coach, Professor Sabatini cannot teach his rose bushes to sing the role of the composer in *Ariadne auf Naxos*; nor can his rose bushes cause a passing bicycle to perceive red. This is because entities which causally interact must be categorially and dispositionally suited to one another. Cf. *Phys.* 201a11, 29, b5, 202a7, 251a9; *Met.* 1065b16–33.

If we fail to attend to the kinds of commonality required for soul-body causation, we will be apt, according to Aristotle, to accept the sort of view ascribed to the Pythagoreans by Xenophanes (DK 7D 18K), a metempsychosis according to which the soul of a human being might take up residence in a puppy. Or, more extremely, we might think that an old leather-bound edition of Machiavelli's *The Prince* could come to bear the departed soul of Richard Nixon. Aristotle regards this sort of view as worthy of ridicule. Whether or not ridicule is the right attitude, he does seem right to insist that soul-body causal interaction must respect the normal constraints of hylomorphic causation—if, at any rate, his general hylomorphic framework is to be adopted. Thus, his criticisms are at least as forceful as those constraints, as they are imposed by that overarching framework of explanation.

More particularly, Aristotle enters a complaint about the failure of his predecessors to respect an unexplicated constraint of commonality (*koinônia*), and he does so in somewhat colourful language: 'what they say is almost the same as if someone were to say that carpentry could clothe itself in flutes' or perhaps 'be outfitted in flutes' (407b24–6). The same language of a soul 'clothing itself in' (*enduesthai*) a body is also found in Plato's *Republic* (620c), where in the Myth of Er the soul of Thersites is said to clothe itself in the body of an ape. Supposing that the soul and body have no essential connection to one another, contends Aristotle, makes about as much sense as supposing that a carpenter's art could be manifested in flutes rather than in saws, hammers, and awls. Of course, the carpenter's art could express itself in the creation of wooden flutes; but Aristotle is thinking of 'clothing itself' as, effectively, its being manifested in and through the use of. More prosaically, he means that the craft of carpentry requires suitable tools in order to be implemented as the craft that it is. Carpentry can no more be practised by those wielding flutes than flute music can be performed by blowing onto awls or saws.

More generally, then, Aristotle clearly wants to call attention to the fact, as he sees it, that the bodies of living beings must be suitable for the realization of life functions, indeed for the life functions characteristic of the kind of beings in question. That is, if cows are to perceive colours, then their bodies must be outfitted with the appropriate sensory apparatus, eyes. It is wrong to think, then, that a cow's soul might be realized by just any chance body—and still less by just any chance parcel of matter. Cf. *Met.* 1045a7–b23, 1075b34.

In a general way, then, Aristotle's criticisms of Pythagorean-style conceptions of soul-body relations rely on his own commitment to material causation in explanation. (On the material cause, see the General Introduction § III.) More narrowly, his criticisms reflect three important substantive commitments of his own hylomorphism. The first is that as the proximate matter of the soul, the body must be suitably sophisticated, by being equipped with suitable organs, because it must be the right sort of tool for the soul (it must be an *organikon* body, in Aristotle's language; see 412a29–b1, with note to 412a28). That is, not just any chance body will suffice for the realization of life activity, just as Aristotle here contends at 407b19. The second commitment follows upon the first: the soul uses its body as an instrument for its own ends (415b18–20; cf. *Part. An.* 642a9–11, 635b14; *Pol.* 1254a34). This suggests a definitional priority of soul over body, a commitment which in turn leads to the third and most intriguing feature of hylomorphism reflected in Aristotle's current criticism: an unensouled body is a body only homonymously, where this entails, among other things, that a body's identity conditions are parasitic upon the soul whose body it is. (On the homonymy of the body, see note to 412b14 and the General Introduction § IV.A.2. On the priority of the soul over the body, see Shields (2009).)

In this regard, Aristotle's criticism in this passage draws upon his judgement that we are not at liberty when characterizing soul-body relations to assume that souls and bodies come ready-made and complete, only to be fitted together by a contingent connection of some sort. On the contrary, any such view leads to the absurdities recounted, because of its failing to take account of a living being's intrinsic unity; this is why Aristotle will want to maintain that a living being is a single entity compounded of form and matter, neither of which is present as an actually pre-existing ingredient simply to be conjoined with the other in the production of a living substance. Altogether, then, the current criticism draws more heavily upon Aristotle's own positive doctrine of the soul and body than is common in this first, primarily endoxic and aporetic book.

## CHAPTER 4

### Introduction to I 4

Aristotle criticizes two conceptions of soul in this chapter: (i) the doctrine that the soul is an attunement (*harmonia*; 407b32–408a28); and (ii) the doctrine that the soul is a self-moving number (408b30–409a30, with a brief recapitulation spilling over into what is in most texts the next chapter (409a31–b18), but is here made part of the current chapter, which is its natural home). Between these discussions, he revisits the question of whether it is appropriate to say that the soul can be moved in any way at all (408a29–b29). Although covering ground already traversed in *DA* I 2 and 3, this interlude, evidently intended to orient the discussion towards the question of whether the soul can be a self-moving number, takes on an independent interest of its own, since in it Aristotle reflects in a general way on the appropriate subject of psychological ascription.

The doctrine that the soul is an attunement had a reasonably broad appeal in Plato's Academy and before. It was introduced, for example, into the conversation of the *Phaedo* by Simmias (85e) and then discussed in some detail by Socrates in that same dialogue (92b–95b). Aristotle had himself considered it in his lost dialogue *Eudemus*, fragments of which suggest a significant argument against this view not recorded in the present work (on which, see note to 407b32–408a5). Although admitting of importantly different formulations, the general doctrine is clear enough at least in its rudimentary form: it is the view that the soul is neither more nor less than an order or structure of the body, in much the way the attunement of a violin is an order or structure of its strings, fingerboard, and bouts. (Aristotle specifies different and comparatively sophisticated ways of developing the view; see note to 408a5–18 below.)

Of all the positions considered in the first book of *De Anima*, the attunement theory most closely resembles Aristotle's own account; for this reason his criticisms of it should reveal a good deal about his own thinking about the soul.

To appreciate these criticisms, it is important to appreciate the misleading implications associated with the customary practice of rendering the word *harmonia*, here rendered as 'attunement', with the English word 'harmony'. In English, 'harmony' has inescapable

135

musical connotations. In fact, *harmonia* in Greek derives from *harmonizein*, a word with its home in carpentry, though it has musical applications as well. In its root sense, it means 'to join' or 'to fit', in the sense in which a carpenter joins two planks when fitting a drawer. For this reason, in musical contexts, *harmonia* is typically used to describe a tuned instrument, or the attunement of a tuned instrument, rather than the chords or the ratios of the sounds produced by a tuned instrument (for which the Greek word is *sumphônia*).

**407b27–31: The Attunement Theory Introduced:** The argument given on behalf of the attunement theory is brief and direct: (i) an attunement is a blending and compounding of opposites; and (ii) body is itself composed of opposites; so (iii) the soul is itself an attunement. The argument thus stated is obviously unsuccessful: (i) and (ii) do not entail that the soul is an attunement. Perhaps the gist is rather that given these premises, we can conclude that *something* qualifies as an attunement of the body, and then proceed to offer the soul as the only or best candidate for identification with this attunement.

Why, though, suppose that this identification obtains? If Aristotle has in mind the sort of reason Simmias had relied upon in the *Phaedo*, then the identification might be motivated by the thought that since it is not a primitive fact that the body is a unified whole, we are right to seek an explanation of its unity. Since what unifies the body is evidently something other than any of its own material elements taken individually or in combination (they might exist when the body does not, as Aristotle himself insists in *Metaphysics* Z 17), something else must play the role of unifier. The soul is then introduced as a principle capable of playing this role. With no more than this motivation in mind, one might reasonably be inclined to look for a theory of the soul with only minimal ontological commitments: this is just the sort of advantage the attunement theory offers over its more extravagant rival, Platonic dualism.

More specifically, we might characterize the body as constituted by various elements conceived of as contraries (ultimately, the hot, the cold, the wet, the dry); but, if we do, we must also concede that there are countless elements and countless oppositions in the region of any given living body. What makes any given subset of these contraries just those that constitute a living body, one might say, is that they stand in some *appropriate* ratio to one another, that they manifest the sort of structured organization which gives rise to the characteristics of life. We may then wish to call this ratio or structured organization the soul, since we are really conceiving of the source of unity, the soul, as just this ratio. If we proceed along these lines, then, we end up identifying the soul with an attunement of the elements.

This is part of the reason why even in its first, minimal formulation, the attunement theory of the soul raises some important questions about Aristotle's own eventual positive doctrine. It seems clear that he regards the attunement as superior to the more reductive elemental theories canvassed thus far in the aporetic and endoxic first book of *De Anima*. To begin, the attunement theory at least makes some effort to explain two central *phainomenon*a regarded by Aristotle as worthy of preserving and explaining. First, every living body exhibits both synchronic and diachronic unity even while sustaining material replenishment. To say that some elements are attuned is to say that they exhibit a discernible structure; if the presence of this structure suffices to allow for sameness through material replenishment, then that counts on behalf of the attunement theory, and against the simple materialist theories, which at least in their rudimentary formulations offer no ready explanation of this *phainomenon*. Second, and more simply, the soul, like an attunement, seems to cease precisely when the object whose attunement it is ceases. If this also counts as a *phainomenon* to be explained, then this too counts on behalf of the attunement theory. In general, like Aristotle's own preferred hylomorphism, the attunement theory seems to seek a middle way between the extremes of austere materialism and Platonic dualism.

Precisely what sort of middle way this may be depends partly on the precise form of attunement theory we have in view. Aristotle proceeds to consider two formulations in this chapter: (a) that an attunement is the structure of some object, where this might be thought of as comparatively abstract; or (b) that it is the object itself so structured, where this appears to be something comparatively concrete. For a fuller discussion of these alternatives, see the note to 408a5–18.

**407b32–408a5: Initial Criticisms of the Attunement Theory:** Indulging in just the kinds of puns we find in the *Phaedo* (e.g. 92c), Aristotle laments that the attunement theory is 'out of tune' with the facts. Indeed, Aristotle's initial criticisms are themselves immediately reminiscent of the objections to the theory advanced by Plato in that dialogue. (The puns are a bit better in Greek, but not much.) Aristotle's complaints are these. First, an attunement must be either a proportion of things mixed or a compounding of some sort; the soul is neither of these. Second, whatever it is, the soul originates motion, or so everyone agrees (see 403b25–7, 427a17–18), while no attunement does so. In a more general way, Aristotle complains, third, that no attunement can reasonably be regarded as discharging the functions of the soul. Although he does not elaborate on any of these points here, Aristotle evidently regards an attunement as a mere feature, an inert supervenient feature, of some structured body, whereas the soul, he supposes, is something more, something with a causal priority and autonomy. Indeed, on Aristotle's approach the soul is itself a substance (*ousia*; 412a19), while no attunement, he supposes, qualifies as a substance. A bit of Aristotle's *Eudemus* preserved by Damascius makes this point more explicit than it is in *De Anima*: 'lack of attunement is contrary to attunement, but the soul has no contrary; for it is a substance' (*Commentaria in Phaedonem* 383 = F 45 R$^3$). See also *Topics* 123b30 for the sort of dialectical procedure upon which this sort of reasoning relies.

**408a5–18: Two Senses of Attunement Distinguished and Rejected:** It seems at first as if Aristotle means to proceed by focusing on two main formulations of the *harmonia* theory known to him: 'if we may speak of attunement by focusing on its two main varieties' (408a5–6). As the argument proceeds, however, it emerges that he is speaking instead of the two main uses of the term '*harmonia*', one of which he says, using language he often uses in marking out the fundamental or core sense of the term, is the 'most proper' (*kuriôtata*; 408a6). That said, we should not infer that he is indulging in lexicography or ordinary language philosophy here. Rather, he is relying on the term's use as a guide to setting out some alternatives for consideration.

That said, it is clearly the case that various versions of the theory were in the air and discussed within the Academy. Simmias and

Echecrates, who moved in Pythagorean circles, both express affinity to the theory in the *Phaedo* (at 88b6–7 Simmias says that 'we' hold it, though he does not say who 'we' are; Echecrates also reports that he is favourably disposed to the theory at 88d3–4). The Aristotelian Aristoxenus was also a proponent; some late reports also ascribe it to Philolaus, reportedly the teacher of Simmias and Echrecrates, but it is plainly inconsistent with other things he is reported to have maintained (DL viii 46; cf. DK 44 A 23). For the provenance of the theory, see Gottschalk (1971). Taylor (1983) also reviews the question of its likely adherents before formulating in detail various possible versions of the theory as it appears in the *Phaedo*. Different aspects of the theory and its development are also well discussed by Hicken (1954) and Caston (1997).

Aristotle immediately renders the two senses of '*harmonia*' he introduces more precise in order to launch his criticisms of the theory, his strategy evidently being one of divide and conquer. The two versions he articulates are these:

- Attunement as compounded magnitude: $x$ is an attunement of $y$ just in case $x$ is a compounding (*sunthesis*), an exact combination, of (y) things that have magnitude.
- Attunement as proportion: $x$ is an attunement of $y$ just in case $x$ is a proportion or ratio (*logos*) in terms of which the elements of $y$ are mixed (*mixis*).

The difference between these interpretations is more than a matter of emphasis: on the first interpretation, an attunement is something concrete, a magnitude—a measurable quantity—which is attuned, while on the second it is something more abstract, the ratio or proportion of the thing mixed. As a rough analogy, when we speak of *recipes* in English, we normally have in mind the abstract instructions for the production of some dish or other, though we sometimes intend instead to refer to the dish produced in accordance with the set of abstract specifications ('Taste my new recipe and see if it meets with your approval.'). The two approaches to attunement thus differ in consequential ways.

Moreover, on the assumption that Aristotle is adhering to his usual terminology, the first notion, where an attunement is a compounded magnitude, is a case of compounding (*sunthesis*) and the second notion, where an attunement is a proportion, is a case of mixture (*mixis*). A *sunthesis* is a process of blending whereby the elements mixed remain once blended. For instance, if we distribute white and black marbles in a jar, the individual marbles remain actual individual marbles, and also actually white and black. By contrast, if we blend eggs, flour, sugar, and water in a process of *mixis*, each ingredient undergoes a change such that it no longer actually persists with its original features in the mixture. (In one sense a cake contains eggs and in another sense not—one cannot borrow two eggs from someone whose only eggs have been mixed into cake batter.) On mixture, see *Gen. et Corr.* I 10, together with Fine (1995). In sum, then, the first notion of attunement treats parts attuned as persisting through the process of attunement, whereas the second does not.

Aristotle deploys distinct but related arguments against these two views. Directed against the first, attunement as a compounded magnitude, is a somewhat obscure argument to the effect that there are many different kinds of compounding in a body. To understand this argument, it is first of all important to stress that in speaking of a magnitude (*megethos*), Aristotle has in mind not a measurement of any kind, but rather a thing measured. He in fact has two notions of *megethos* in his writings, either as a body extended in three dimensions, so that, e.g., a line would not count as a *megethos*, and another, more encompassing notion, such that anything measurable in extension is a magnitude, so that lines but not points qualify (*Met.* 1020a, *DC* 268a7–12; see Lear (1982) for a useful presentation of narrower and broader notions of *megethos* in both Aristotle and Euclid). Here Aristotle has the first, more restricted view in mind. So, when thinking of an attunement as a magnitude in this sense, he is focusing on bodies compounded out of the elements which make up all material beings.

More exactly, Aristotle is relying here on his view that bodies are composed from three distinct kinds of compounds: (i) basic elements (earth, air, fire, and water), (ii) homoeomerous compounds (parts which are continuously the same, so that any given portion of the part has the property of the whole, e.g. blood and bone); and (iii) anhomoeomerous parts (parts for which this fails, e.g. the hand, since a finger is not itself a hand). (Aristotle refers to these three types of parts as three types of compounding at *De Partibus Animalium* 646a12–22, 647a1–3.) If all of these forms of compounding qualify as attunements, then, suggests Aristotle, there must be one part of soul for each kind of compound—on the assumption, that is, that being an attunement of some compound is sufficient for being a soul. These types of compounds cannot, however, be mapped directly onto the individual faculties of soul. Hence, we can say neither that the individual faculties nor the whole soul itself is any kind of attunement. This worry finds an especially clear motivation in the case of reason (*nous*), which Aristotle denies has a bodily organ (see note to 429a26.)

Developing a similar point against the second, comparatively abstract interpretation of the attunement theory, attunement as proportion, Aristotle notes that even within homoeomerous types such as flesh and bone, there are different ratios or proportions present. Consequently, if we think of the soul as identical to a ratio or proportion, there will be as many souls associated with each individual body as it has ratios or proportions. Indeed, even within each part of the body, whether homoeomerous or anhomoeomerous, we will encounter as many souls as ratios or proportions. So, each body will have very many souls, not one, something Aristotle understands to be patently absurd.

An attunement theorist might plausibly seek to block this inference by rejoining that not just any ratio of elements is an attunement; but that would force a third articulation of the theory not considered here, one which would, of course, then face the task of sorting in some non-arbitrary manner those attunements (or ratios) which are sufficient for being souls from those which are not.

**408a18–23: A Moral for Empedocles:**    Aristotle observes that his reflections on the relations of mixtures and the soul have ramifications for Empedocles, who had held that bodily parts are themselves ratios of mixtures of the basic elements, and may be understood on the basis of a passage in the *Part. An.* (642a.18–24) to be a representative of the second notion of attunement theory. Aristotle wonders how Empedocles conceived the relationship between such ratios and the soul. If he thought they were identical with one another, Empedocles would presumably be liable to the criticisms mounted against the second version of the attunement theory. Otherwise, Aristotle mainly complains that the Empedoclean account is incomplete, insofar as it explains unity by positing a primitive notion of attraction, personified as Love, among the elements. (Empedocles comes in for fuller criticism in the next chapter, at 410a2–b15. Cf. also *Met.* 988a33 and esp. 1001a13–16, where Aristotle also amplifies his criticism of Empedocles.)

**408a23–8: What is Right about the Attunement Theory:**  Before leaving it behind, Aristotle gamely observes that the attunement theory does offer several advantages, insofar as it explains some of the things any theory of the soul ought to explain. He mentions two: (i) when the flesh and other parts of the body are destroyed, so too is the soul; and (ii) in some sense of the term, at death the soul leaves the body. The attunement theory, Aristotle concedes, neatly explains both of these facts. As for (i), since it supervenes on the flesh and other parts of the body, an attunement perishes when precisely they are destroyed. If a bourgeois rock star smashes his guitar on stage during a concert, then such attunement as the guitar might have had perishes along with the guitar. As for (ii), it is clear that the soul comes to an end when the body dies. As dependent upon the body, again, an attunement behaves as expected.

In connection with (ii), some care is needed regarding Aristotle's unanswered question: 'what is it that perishes when the soul departs (*tês psuchês apolipousês*)?' (408a28). When he says that the soul 'departs' or 'leaves behind' the body (*apolipousês*), Aristotle does not mean that it 'takes its leave and goes somewhere else,' but speaks of leaving rather in the way that love leaves a relationship after too many transgressions. Love simply ends. Indeed, Aristotle is at present acknowledging as a virtue of the rejected theory that an attunement precisely does not go anywhere, but rather ceases, at the moment of death.

In both these ways, then, the attunement theory gives the right results; and in each case the results flow from an attunement's being supervenient upon the body. It will accordingly be reasonable to determine how—and how well—Aristotle's preferred hylomorphism fares in these regards.

**408a29–b18: A More Difficult Question Regarding the Soul's Motion:**  On the basis of what has been said so far, Aristotle concludes that the soul neither is an attunement nor moves in a circle. The second conclusion implicitly reintroduces the question of the soul's ability to move and be moved, which in turn induces Aristotle to pose a more consequential question regarding psychic motion than we have so far encountered. He has agreed that the soul can initiate and be in motion co-incidentally (see the Introduction to *DA* I 3 and note to 405b31–406a12). Aristotle now envisages someone reasonably objecting that the soul seems to be in motion in a more intimate way, not merely co-incidentally by being moved when its body is moved in its own right, but rather in its own nature, in virtue of its own intrinsic alterations.

Whatever its provenance, the objection is close to home: '*we* say' (408b1; cf. 403b17, 406a5, 408a5). We are inclined to say, more specifically, that the soul feels pain and joy, that it is at times angry, and generally that it perceives and thinks. Since these are all motions (they are changes (*kinêseis*); see note to 406a12–16), and intrinsic to the soul, it seems to follow directly that the soul itself is the subject of motion, and not co-incidentally.

So, the opponent is imagined as arguing, as against the thesis that the soul cannot move in its own right (*kath' hauto*): (1) episodes of pity, perception, reasoning and other mental states are motions; (2) the soul is the subject of these states; hence, (3) the soul moves in its own right.

Aristotle's response to this argument has occasioned considerable discussion. He says: 'For it is perhaps better not to say that the soul pities or learns or thinks, but that the human being does these things with the soul' (408b13–14). On its surface, Aristotle's response to the challenge about motion he is currently considering seems to involve him in some deep reflection on the suitability of predicating psychological states to the soul as opposed to the ensouled being, that is, the human being. This in turn has resonated with those among Aristotle's modern readers inclined to think of psychological states in primarily dispositional terms. (Thus, Barnes (1971–2) refers to this section of *DA* I 4 as the 'celebrated Rylean passage.') This understanding gains some support from another possible rendering of the sentence at 408b13: 'For it is *probably* (*isôs*) better to say not that the soul pities or learns or thinks, but that the human being does these things *by means of* his soul.' The main differences between the two renderings, each of which is perfectly acceptable, concern the beginning and the end of this sentence. At the beginning, the word *isôs* is sometimes used by Aristotle and other authors to express caution ('perhaps') but other times to express cautious endorsement ('probably' or 'presumably'). At the end of the sentence is a second and more consequential difference involving the phrase *tê(i) psuchê(i)* at 408b15, rendered in the text neutrally as (i) 'with the soul'. It might be taken to mean (ii) 'in virtue of his having a soul' or 'by means of having a soul', where the purport would be that it is the living human being, the composite substance, which is the proper subject of these motions, not the soul. Barnes (1972) spiritedly approves of (ii). Shields (1988b) and (2009) rejects (ii) in favour of (i).

In support of (ii) is the thought that, taken this way, Aristotle's response straightforwardly denies a key premise in his opponent's argument, namely premise (2) that the soul is the subject of the sorts of psychological states. Against (ii) is the thought that, however congenial to modern sensibilities it may prove, this retort is not easily ascribed to Aristotle, since he elsewhere freely treats the soul as a substance (*ousia*; 412a19–20; *Met.* 1037a5), and so as a subject (*hupokeimenon*; *Met.* 1029a1–2), and indeed also elsewhere introduces the soul as the proper and non-derivative subject to a variety of mental states (e.g. 429a10–11). So, if he denies here that the soul is a subject, then he threatens to contradict himself twice over by treating it as a substance elsewhere and then again as something to which mental states are immediately ascribed.

In support of (i), then, is the thought that Aristotle is offering an appropriately nuanced response to the argument about motion he is currently considering. He is challenged by the suggestion that the soul moves in itself, since his own hylomorphic analysis represents perception and thought—and, presumably, psychological states generally—in terms of form acquisition and so as involving alteration. (On the hylomorphic analysis of perception and thought, see the General Introduction § IV.B.2 and IV.B.4.) So, he is right to be concerned about this objection. Still, it is noteworthy, according to this alternative, that Aristotle explains himself by allowing that motion 'sometimes reaches as far as the soul, and sometimes proceeds from it' (408b16; cf. 408b7), where the implication seems to be that the soul is not in motion in its own right, but in virtue of its standing in relation to the body, which is in motion in this way. This would comport with

Aristotle's general denial of the soul's ability to move in its own right (*kath' hauto*), as well as with his contention that it can, nevertheless, move in virtue of another (*kath' heteron*) or co-incidentally (*kata sumbebêkos*). This he had been at pains to establish in the last chapter. See note to 405b31–406a12.

On either interpretation, Aristotle intends to reject the unwanted conclusion (3), that the soul moves in its own right (*kath' hauto*).


**408b18–29: The Case of Reason:** Aristotle regularly treats reason (*nous*) as somehow exceptional relative to the other faculties of the soul. Here he begins somewhat curiously by suggesting that reason may itself be a substance (*ousia*), or a sort of substance, whereas he elsewhere characterizes it as a capacity (*dunamis*; 413b24, 428a5); one would normally expect a capacity to be a capacity *of* a substance. The current passage is anomalous in other ways as well. For example, the argument that reason is somehow indestructible relies on an analogy with the sense organs (408b21), to a rather odd effect. Aristotle seems to argue that reason does not itself deteriorate with the enfeeblements of old age, on the grounds that the sensory faculties would remain strong if their organs were replenished or replaced periodically. This in the first instance ignores the alleged disanalogy between reason and perception upon which Aristotle elsewhere insists: reason, alone among the faculties of soul, lacks an organ (see 429a26–7, with note). Moreover, the argument evidently proves more than it should, if it proves anything at all, since it seems to have the consequence that reason is imperishable if and only if perception is—in which case it is hard to understand how reason is exceptional. The note to 429a18–27 revisits this matter briefly.

Conceivably the passage is better understood less directly, such that Aristotle is not speaking *in propria persona* but is rather making a further ad hominem point against those who suppose that the soul moves in its own right. Here it can be observed that the characterization of reason as a substance is introduced at 408b18–19 only rather gingerly, as what *would seem* to be the case, *scilicet* to Aristotle's opponents, and that its final characterization as unaffected and somehow divine at 408b29 remains noncommittal on a point about which Aristotle is himself firm (cf. *Gen An.* 736b27; *Met.* 1074b16; *EN* 1177b30; *DA* 429a15, b23, 430a18–24).

On this approach, the oddness of the passage dissolves, since its purport will be that even those who think that the soul moves in itself agree that *reason* does not move in itself, and further that since reason moves as the other faculties do, they all move in virtue of something else, co-incidentally, and not in themselves. This much would also cohere with Aristotle's own considered view, since although he thinks that reason is in various ways exceptional, he also thinks that it behaves as the other capacities of soul do with respect to motion. All move only co-incidentally.

The matter is somewhat complicated by a difficulty of translation. The sentence at 408b27–8, rendered 'Accordingly, when this is destroyed, one neither remembers nor loves,' tries to remain neutral between distinct interpretative traditions. The first tradition, suggested but not strictly entailed by the translation in the text, takes the 'one' in question to be (i) the entire human (*anthrô-pos*); (ii) a second approach takes it instead to be the soul (*psuchê*); and (iii) a third supposes that the one in question is reason (*nous*) itself. Aquinas favours the second (*De an.* I, lec. 10, n.20), while Themistius develops a version of the third, by looking forward to the vexed discussion of active reason in *De Anima* III 5 (*in de Anima*, 101.18–102.23).

**408b30–409a31: That the Soul is not a Self-Moving Number:**    On the basis of what has preceded, Aristotle concludes that the soul does not move, from which it follows trivially that it does not set itself in motion. In both the conclusion and the further inference Aristotle means that the soul does not move *in itself*, for it can move only co-incidentally.

If it does not move itself, then whatever else it is, the soul is not a self-moving number. Aristotle seems to regard any suggestion to the contrary with particular derision. The view perhaps owes to Xenocrates, Plato's eventual successor as head of the Academy. Aristotle does not in fact name him, though Plutarch does (*De Animae Procreatione* 1012D; cf. 404b28–30; *APo.* 91a35–b1). In any case, whatever its provenance, the view is, Aristotle contends, doubly perverse. It not only succumbs to the problems following upon its claim that the soul moves itself, but faces a whole set of distinct objections owing to its characterization of the soul as a number. From Aristotle's perspective, the view combines two false views into one absurd view.

That said, Aristotle does not summarily dismiss the view out of hand. Instead, he develops a series of arguments against it, directed mainly against the proposal that the soul is a number of some sort. His interest in the view derives in part from its kinship to the second of the two interpretations of the attunement theory distinguished earlier in the chapter (see note 408a5–18), according to which the soul is a ratio, or mathematical structure of the elements or parts of the body. On the current proposal, the soul is similarly a kind of mathematical entity, though now it is not a complex ratio, but a simple number. In the ensuing discussion, Aristotle implicitly reviews different ways of conceiving of numbers and their features: as without parts (408b32–409a3); as entities capable of entering into arithmetic relations (409a7–10); as akin to Democritean atoms in their simplicity (409a10–20); and as numbers identifiable or not with points in the body (409a16–30).

Armed with these features of numbers and simple units characterizable by numbers and analogous to numbers in their noncompositeness, Aristotle launches a series of attacks, the most consequential of which include:

(A) 406b32–409a2:
    (1) A number is a unit, without parts.
    (2) Something can move itself only if it has parts.
    (3) Hence, numbers cannot move themselves.

Aristotle regards a number variously as a synthesis or plurality of units (*Met.* 1039a12, 1053a30, 1057a3), as a plurality of indivisibles (*Met.* 1001a26, 1085b22), or as either the measure of plurality or a measured plurality (*Met.* 1088a5; cf. *Phys.* 207b7). This last bifurcation helps explain how Aristotle can move so readily from thinking of numbers to other forms of simples, including Democritean atoms and points (409a10–30). In the present argument, however, he is focusing on the simplicity and indivisibility of numbers, however construed, and relying on his view that nothing simple can set itself in motion (*Phys.* 254b27–33). More generally, Aristotle holds that nothing simple can be in motion in its own right, but only co-incidentally (*Phys.* 240b8, 241a6).

(B) 409a7–10:
(1) If one number is subtracted from another, then what remains is something differing in species.
(2) When an animal or plant is bisected, the souls in the bisected parts remain in one and the same species.
(3) So, a soul is not a number.

Aristotle's argument proceeds by a simple appeal to Leibniz's Law: souls have features which numbers lack and consequently cannot be identified with them. The feature in question is that numbers can enter into arithmetic functions to yield other numbers. Thus, when one is subtracted from an even number, an odd number results, something differing in kind from the original number. As he says, 'even when one takes away or adds the smallest thing, the definition and essence [of the original number] will no longer be the same' (*Met.* 1043b36–1044a2). Yet if an earthworm is severed, the two halves, which continue to live, do not change in kind: each is still an earthworm and so the definition and essence will remain unchanged. Aristotle is impressed by the phenomenon of bisection in connection with the soul and cites it several times in the service of a variety of claims (411b19, 413b16; cf. *Meta* 1040b10–13; *Parva Nat.* 467a18, 468a25, 479a3; *Part. An.* 682a5, b30; *Gen. An.* 731a21). Here, though, he mentions the easier case of plants as well. His point is that the soul as a whole admits of division without forcing a change in species, whereas no number has this ability. Hence, the soul is not a number.

(C) 409a16–30:
Although not stated with maximal clarity, the last major argument of the chapter appears to be a sort of dilemma. It is predicated upon two exhaustive alternatives, whether the soul, conceived as a point, is or is not coextensive with the points of the body, which, as a magnitude, is infinitely divisible. Aristotle first seems to reason that if the soul is a unit, and if there are a plurality of souls, then the soul must be a point, since a point is a unit having position (cf. 409a6). At any rate, he treats units (*monades*) and points (*stigmai*) interchangeably in this argument:
(1) Suppose the soul is a unit or a point.
(2) The body, as a magnitude, can be divided into an infinite number of points.

(3) Given (1), either each individual point of the body is to be identified with a soul, conceived as a point, or it is not.

(4) If not, then there are conceivably an infinite number of souls in the same place as each point in the body—which is absurd.

(5) If so, then each point is a soul, which entails that (a) every body will be alive, and (b) there will be an infinite number of souls associated with each composite body.

(6) (4) is absurd, and (5a) is manifestly false, since some things are alive and others not, while (5b) too is is absurd.

(7) So, (1), the hypothesis that the soul is a unit, or point, must be rejected.

The argument thus stated retains some obscurities, including especially the source of the absurdities associated with (4) and (5). To begin, though, (2) simply follows from Aristotle's conception of being a magnitude (*megethos*), on which, see note to 407a2–10. Every magnitude, he maintains, is infinitely divisible; since the body is a magnitude, it too is so divisible. Given that, and on the assumption that the soul should be conceived as a unit or point, the question arises as to whether one should suppose that each individual point in the magnitude of the body is to be identified with the soul so conceived.

(4) entertains the suggestion that we should identify souls and bodily points. In that case, there will be two points in one place (*topos*), namely the body point and the soul point. But if there may be two points in the same place, then there may also be more, uncountably many more, with the result that there might be an infinite number of souls co-located with each point of the body. It is noteworthy that the absurdity does not seem to arise with the possibility of there being an infinite number of souls in the same place as each point of the body, but emerges already with the possibility of there being two discrete entities in the same place, since Aristotle thinks that each thing exhausts the place in which it is; that there could be an infinite number of co-located entities simply draws out the consequence of allowing that there could be two. On Aristotle's conception of place as the inner limit of that which contains a thing, see *Phys.* 212a20, along with *Met.* 1067a8–31, 1092a17–21.

Having shown the presumed absurdity of denying that soul points are to be identified with body points, Aristotle turns, in (5), to the other horn of the dilemma, by sketching what follows from such an identification. Presumably, he is assuming something articulated only later in the work, that it is the presence of a soul which differentiates the living from the non-living (413a22; cf. 413b1–2, 415a25, 434a23). On this assumption, if points of the body are taken to be identical with soul points, then all bodies will be animate, which is absurd. Furthermore, for each composite body, such as the human body, there will be an infinite number of souls, because, again, the body is a magnitude and infinitely divisible.

**409a31–b18: Summary and Recapitulation:** In most modern texts these lines appear at the beginning of the next chapter. As late as the fourteenth century, manuscripts of *De Anima* evidently had the text divided differently, with these lines concluding the present chapter. Since they clearly belong here, and not in the next chapter, I have followed the pre-Renaissance practice by including them in the translation of *DA* I 4. Nothing much turns on their placement, beyond continuity of expression.

Aristotle adds no new arguments in this section, though he does offer several additional observations. He adds, for instance, the idea that if the soul is a body, as Democritus claims, there will be two bodies in the same place, which he regards as an additional absurdity. Further, he introduces the observation that anyone wishing to define the soul as a number or any such thing would be well advised to reflect upon the actual functions of the soul, including perception, feeling, and calculating. It seems a bizarre and twisted contortion, suggests Aristotle, to try to find any basis for these activities in the nature of number.

CHAPTER 5

**Introduction to I 5**

Aristotle understands himself thus far to have considered two of the three prominent conceptions of soul bequeathed to him by his predecessors, that it is an entity capable of initiating motion by moving itself and that it is something composed of the finest, least corporeal of material bodies (cf. 405b11).

He has in the preceding two chapters discussed both of these views, together with a variety of issues sometimes only tangentially related to them. In the present chapter, he turns to the third traditional account of the soul, the view that it is something constituted out of the elements. In fact Aristotle mainly speaks simply in terms of the soul's being 'from the elements' (*ek stoicheiôn*), and the translation reflects this terse way of speaking. In the commentary, however, this is often expanded to reflect Aristotle's fuller meaning (made clear at 410b19–20: 'from which the soul is to be constituted'; *ex hôn tên psuchên sunestanai*), that on the hypothesis under consideration the soul is 'made up of elements' or 'constituted from elements' or simply 'constituted of elements'.

As in earlier chapters, Aristotle once again explores not only the announced topic, but a host of allied matters surrounding it. In the current chapter these include: (i) the principle of unity needed to explain the aggregation of elements into single souls; (ii) the sense in which like is known by like; (iii) the relation of the various capacities of the soul to distinct parts of the body; and (iv) the divisibility of the soul. Although plainly distinct from one another, discussion of each of these matters is prompted by some question pertaining to the thesis that the soul is composed of elements.

**409b19–24: A Return to the Central Topic:** Having already dispatched two of the three traditional accounts of soul (on which, see the Introduction to this chapter), Aristotle turns his attention to those who contend that the soul is constituted out of the elements (*stoicheia*). In this chapter Aristotle sometimes treats the elements narrowly, as encompassing only the traditional four basic elements, namely earth, air, fire, and water; but he sometimes also adverts to a broader conception of elements continuous with the root meaning of the word (*stoicheia* were initially *letters*, as the elements in a syllable, a meaning which subsequently generalized to cover elements of all sorts), as the constituents of compounds, whatever their own natures might be (cf. *Gen. et Corr.* 314a15; *Met.* 992b18, 1034b26–1035a14, 1041b11–33). It is in this broader sense that Plato is able to speak of the soul as compounded out of the 'elements' of Being, Sameness, and Other (*Tim.* 35a–b). In this chapter Aristotle moves back and forth without warning between the more restricted and the more liberal uses of the term. Thus, for example, the argument at 409b26–410a13 trades on the narrow conception, while the argument immediately following at 410a13–22 entertains the more inclusive notion.

**409b24–5: Motivation for the View under Consideration:** Aristotle begins by ascribing a distinctive motivation to proponents of the elemental view of soul: 'They say this [*sc.* that the soul is constituted out of the elements] so that the soul may perceive and come to know each of the things which exist' (409b24–5). It is important for understanding the direction of the chapter that Aristotle represents those who maintain that the soul is compounded out of the elements as doing so on the basis of a sort of inference to the best explanation, or perhaps more strongly as an inference to the only possible explanation. To be sure, Aristotle does not put the matter in these terms, but his treatments of his predecessors follows some such pattern of reconstruction. On this reconstruction, for example, it is taken as given by the proponents of this theory that 'like is known by like' (which I will call the 'like-like theory'); it is then inferred by them that since various elements are known, the soul must itself be elemental. The elemental theory of the soul is thus advanced on behalf of Aristotle's predecessors as a sort of required grounding explanation for the like-like theory. In its simplest form, the inference pattern is: (1) like is known by like; (2) elements are known; (3) if (1) and (2), then the soul is itself elemental; so (4) the soul is elemental.

Aristotle immediately notes that if *all things* are composed of the elements, and like is known only by like, then since the soul can in principle know all things, it must be composed of all the elements. Having represented his opponents in this way, Aristotle has paved the way to attack not only their inferences but the putative grounds for their inferences, that like is known by like. In this chapter, he proceeds to attack on both fronts.

Aristotle does not here consider the provenance of the like-like theory in any systematic way: 'For they maintain that one comes to know like by like' (409b26–7): Who are 'they' whose view is under scrutiny? Aristotle has already mentioned Empedocles (404b13–15), who commands the most attention in this chapter, Plato (404b17; cf. *Phaedo* 79c2–e7), Diogenes of

Apollonia (405a23), Heracleitus (405a27), and has noted that many others were attracted to this same thesis (405b13–19). He does not, however, characterize their view in any substantive way; nor does he offer any motivation for this sort of way of thinking. For an illuminating, somewhat critical discussion of Aristotle's treatment of the like-like theory as it emerges in Empedocles, see Kamtekar (2009).

**409b25–410b15 Objections to the View:**   Aristotle offers a series of arguments against the view that the soul is compounded from the elements, the most important of which are these:

(A) 409b26–410a13:
   (1) Suppose that like is known by like.
   (2) If (1), the soul must be or have within it the items it knows, since $x$ is like $y$ in being $F$ only if $x$ and $y$ exemplify *F-ness*.
   (3) The soul knows the elements.
   (4) So, by (1) and (2), the soul must be made of elements.
   (5) Still, in addition to the elements, there exist compounds of elements (including such things as flesh, bones, humans, stones, god, and the good, to name but a few).
   (6) The soul knows, in addition to the elements, the things compounded from the elements.
   (7) So, the soul must be like the compounds.
   (8) So, the soul must have in it such things as flesh, bones, humans, stones, god, and the good.
   (9) That is too absurd even to entertain (410b10–11; cf. note to 431b24–432a1).
   (10) So, either (1) or (2), or both, must be rejected.

Expressing it in this way, Aristotle in (2) remorselessly ascribes to his opponents a literal way of understanding the like-like theory. This seems fair in the dialectical context, since at least as represented, his opponents wish to infer the literal presence of the elements in the soul from the like-like theory, and so seem constrained to assume the restriction on likeness set in (2). Note, however, that because it restricts likeness to shared property exemplification, (2) places a severe constraint on the proponents of the theory, one precluding representational forms

of likeness. This is significant, since on one interpretation of
Aristotle's own theory of perception, he will avail himself of a
more relaxed conception of likeness (see the General Introduction § IV.B).

In any event, the purport of Aristotle's objection is that if his
opponents prove anything with their argument, they prove much
more than they can want to prove.

(B) 410a13–22:

The second argument draws upon features of Aristotle's
own categorial scheme, according to which there are
(canonically ten) irreducibly distinct kinds of beings (v.
402a23–b1, 412a6–11, where Aristotle raises and answers
questions about the soul's proper ontological category; cf.
*Cat.* 1b25–2a11 for a statement of the theory; Ackrill
(1963) offers a succinct and illuminating presentation of
Aristotle's doctrine of categories).

(1) Suppose the soul is constituted from the elements.

(2) Being is spoken of in many ways: there are irreducibly
distinct categories of being, including substance, quantity, and quality.

(3) If (1), then the elements from which the soul is constituted will belong either (a) to the category of substance
or (b) to several of the categories.

(4) If (3a), then the soul will be a substance and (according
to the like-like theory) know only other substances.

(5) The soul knows things other than substances.

(6) So, not (3a): the soul is not constituted of elements
belonging exclusively to the category of substance.

(7) If (3b), the soul will be made of elements belonging to
several of the categories, including the elements of
substance, quantity, and quality.

(8) If (7), the soul will be at once a substance, a quantity,
and a quality.

(9) Nothing is both a substance and a quantity and a
· quality (since, indeed, nothing is essentially in any
two categories).

(10) So, not (3b): the soul is not constituted of elements
belonging to various categories at once.

(11) So, not (1): the soul is not constituted of the elements.

The first point to note about this argument is that it relies upon the more liberal notion of 'element' (*stoicheion*), which we have not seen so far, according to which elements are regarded as basic constituents of any kind (on the broader rather than the narrower notions of elements, see note to 409b19–24). The second point is that it relies upon Aristotle's own theory of categories, a theory to which his opponents may not subscribe. (2) simply asserts that theory. Of course, if that theory is cogent, Aristotle is, nonetheless, entitled to rely upon it without setting out its defence in the present context.

One question pertains to the correct understanding and ultimate defensibility of (3b), the suggestion that perhaps the soul is constituted of elements drawn from more than one category. On one interpretation of this alternative, it is to be understood exclusively, so that a given soul is drawn entirely from elements of one category other than substance. This interpretation seems incorrect, since then the alternative would immediately succumb to the objection launched against (3a), namely, that the soul is made of elements exclusively in the category of substance: no one soul could then, according to the like-like theory, know anything not in its own category. This is not, however, the objection Aristotle offers. Rather, he complains, in (8) and (9), that if (3b), the soul will be at once a substance, a quantity, and a quality, it being assumed evidently that a sufficient condition for $x$'s being a member of category C is that $x$ be made of elements belonging to C. So, the correct understanding of (3b) is rather that the soul is made simultaneously of elements belonging to several distinct categories of being.

It is interesting to note that the argument holds force only for those motivated to endorse the thesis that the soul is constituted of the elements on the basis of the like-like theory. For it is the like-like theory which permits Aristotle to tease out the unacceptable consequence of (3a), in (4), that the soul, if constituted from elements in the category of substance, will be confined to knowing other substances only. Presumably, it remains open to someone not motivated by the like-like theory to maintain on other grounds that the soul is constituted out of elements. Again, however, Aristotle is treating all of his opponents in this chapter as motivated, ultimately, by some version of the like-like theory (see note to 409b24–5).

Finally, the argument raises interesting but unanswered questions regarding the mereology of souls, as Aristotle conceives it. According to (9) nothing is both a substance and a quantity and a quality. If that is true, it is true only in the sense that nothing is a quality *insofar* as it is a substance. (Marcus, the slave, is both a substance and a relative, but presumably he is not a relative insofar as he is a substance.) The question thus arises as to why Aristotle's opponents, having ceded (9), need to accept (10), the claim that the soul is not constituted of elements belonging to various categories at once. An individual soul can in some sense be 'made up' out of elements from different categories—it may be a substance and accidental qualities, for example—and not yet violate (9) as Aristotle understands it. Presumably it is open to his opponents to respond in a similar vein, especially given that the argument is working with the broader rather than the more restricted notion of 'element' (*stoicheion*). For more on psychic mereology and the question of whether capacities are 'parts' of the soul, see note to 411a26–b14 below.

(C) 410a27–b7:
The next series of arguments are ad hominem, directed against Empedocles, though some of them could presumably be generalized. The arguments are:
(1) 410a30–b2: (i) If $x$'s being like $y$ in being $F$ is sufficient for $x$'s knowing $y$, then the earthen parts of the body (the hair, sinews, and bones) will know earth; but (ii) these know nothing; (iii) hence, Empedocles' claim to the contrary (410b2) is unsustainable.
(2) 410b2–4: (i) If a necessary condition of $x$'s knowing $y$ is that $x$ be like $y$ in being $F$, then the individual elements will know only other elements and will be ignorant of most things; (ii) Empedocles' like-like theory requires that elements know only things they are like; (iii) hence, on this theory, much ignorance will result. In this argument, Aristotle evidently understands the like-like theory to require that like knows what it is *essentially* or *compositionally* like, thus restricting the range of suitable substitution instances for '$F$'. This is reasonable enough, since without some such restriction, the theory becomes trivial inasmuch

as everything is like everything else in some respect or other. Even so, this restriction has the effect of making the like-like theory more demanding than at least some of its opponents have supposed it to be. The question then becomes whether any given individual proponent can plausibly be thought to subscribe to the like-like theory in its more demanding formulation. Here Aristotle makes Empedocles accept a fairly strong version of the theory and thus also allows further room for response by Empedocles or someone disposed to respond on his behalf. Aristotle launches a similar complaint against Empedocles in *Metaphysics* 1000b3.

(3) 410b4–7: Again reverting to the more encompassing notion of elements, Aristotle argues: (i) A necessary condition of knowing element $x$ is being made at least in part of $x$; (ii) god, according to Empedocles, has no strife in him, though mortals do; (iii) hence, god will not know strife; (iv) hence, god will know less than mortals in this respect. Presumably Aristotle is drawing on the sort of Empedoclean view contained in frags. 17, 18, and 20, according to which the Sphere, Empedocles' divinity, is said to be free of strife, a basic constituent of things he adds, along with friendship, to the traditional four elements of earth, air, fire, and water.

(D) 410b7–15:
Aristotle now generalizes beyond Empedocles, by contending that the like-like thesis as applied to elements generates the wrong extension for the soul, because everything material is made of elements. Consequently, anyone inferring upon the basis of the like-like theory that the soul is this or that element, or any combination of elements, will run up against obvious counter-examples: there are plainly entities made of elements which lack souls and so neither perceive nor think, e.g. pencils, rubbish bins, or mounds of dirt. Significantly, in this section, Aristotle raises in passing a serious and consequential objection involving the soul's function in providing unity to the body. He returns to this important objection more fully later. See note to 411a26–b14.

When assessing this argument, it is again necessary to realize that Aristotle is implicitly ascribing a particular understanding of the like-like theory to his opponents. In this case, the argument requires that the theory holds that a sufficient condition for knowing something—and hence for being a soul or at least for being ensouled—is that something be like something else. This seems an extremely strong and implausible version of the theory. That said, it will at least fall to the proponents of the theory to restrict it in ways such that it avoids this obviously bad result; it will then become a further question as to whether the restricted versions of the theory will be strong enough to yield any version of the elemental theory of the soul. Hence, Aristotle's argument has at least that modest clarificatory value.

**410b16–411a7: The Narrowness in Elemental and Other Views:** Those advancing elemental views of the soul on the basis of the like-like theory share a defect with other early thinkers: they focus too narrowly on some of the soul's functions to the indefensible exclusion of others. Those who try to characterize the soul in elemental terms because of its perceiving or knowing ignore plants, which are alive but do neither; and those who focus on the production of motion ignore not only plants but stationary animals. In mentioning stationary animals elsewhere, including shellfish and sea nettles, Aristotle draws upon his expertise in marine biology. He thinks, in fact, that there are no stationary land animals (*Hist. An.* 487b6–8). Be that as it may, Aristotle shows in this section again that he himself makes life co-extensive with being ensouled (412a13, 413a21, 423a20–6; cf. *Gen. An.* 736b13; *Part. An.* 681a12). Since plants no less than animals are ensouled (413a25–31, 434a25–30), and since they too are made of elements, the elemental theory of soul, as motivated by the like-like theory, yields perverse results.

In closing, Aristotle faults the authors of some Orphic poems (which his language suggests he regards as possibly spurious) on similar grounds, noting that they fancifully introduce soul as breath borne upon the winds to the bodies of the living. Yet neither plants nor, he thought, fish breathe (421a3; cf. *De Resp.* 480b12–20; *Hist. An.* viii 2).

**411a7–23: Against Treating the Soul as Inherent in the Elements:** Aristotle has rejected as extensionally inadequate any view which treats the elements as themselves ensouled on the grounds that a kind of panzoism would result: everything would be alive (see note to 410b7–15). Aristotle now revisits the question, again considering those willing to affirm *modus ponens* to his *modus tollens*: perhaps everything *is* alive. Aristotle notes, though only tentatively, that Thales may be credited with such a view, along with anyone who builds the soul into the elemental fabric of the universe. (Aristotle's treatment of Thales suggests that he may be wondering whether some earlier thinkers had only unwittingly committed themselves to the view that the soul, the animating principle of life, was present in the elements.) Aristotle's response comes in two discrete phases, the first direct (411a8–16) and the second indirect, involving the deployment of some technical features of his own theory of mixture (411a16–23).

The first phase pushes a dilemma with repugnant consequences for panzoists: either the air and every other element is alive or such elements, though ensouled, fail to be animals. Although strictly Aristotle's point should concern not animals but all living things, including plants, for the reason he has himself insisted upon (see note to 410b16–411a2), his observation easily generalizes. If, e.g., the air is ensouled, then either it is alive or some ensouled things are not living. Aristotle's way of setting the dilemma involves him in asking why the soul should emerge only in elemental mixtures of the sort we find in animals, perhaps because he once again understands panzoism to be a non-starter: some things are alive and others are not. Importantly, his way of structuring the dilemma suggests that he wants his opponents to appreciate that it is not open to them to look to life as an emergent property of some sort, since, as characterized, they have treated the soul as inherent in the elements of the universe from the outset.

The second phase of Aristotle's argument is more complicated than the first. He imagines his opponents arguing to the conclusion that the soul is inherent in the elements from the premise that the whole universe is one in kind with its parts. Aristotle thus treats them as arguing: (i) the universe is homoeomerous; (ii) the animal draws the soul in from the universe; hence, (iii) the soul is either (a) *homoeomerous* (because altogether drawn in) or (b) *anhomoeomerous* (because only partly drawn in).

In this passage, Aristotle is relying on his own theory of mixture. He believes that some things are homoeomerous, that is, that there are stuffs whose every part is an instance of the stuff, mixtures in which the mixed elements surrender their individual properties to the features of the whole. An example of a homoeomerous mixture for Aristotle is bronze: when mixing copper and tin into bronze, every part of the resulting mixture, the bronze, is itself bronze. The tin and copper are no longer discernible as tin or as copper in the bronze. A more contemporary example of this sort of surrendering might be sodium chloride: although we do not suppose that every part of salt is salt, we do think that chloride surrenders some of its features, e.g. its toxicity, when combined with sodium. In contrast to the homoeomerous is the *anhomoeomerous*: these are entities whose parts are not instances of the whole. A hand is anhomoeomerous, because a knuckle is not itself a hand. Aristotle thinks that animals are made of both the homoeomerous (blood, bone) and the anhomoeomerous (hands, gills). (See note to 408a5–18; cf. *Gen. et Cor.* 314a18–20, 321b16–19, 328a10–12, b22; *Metr.* 389b23–8.)

In the present context, if the elements are to be regarded as living on the basis of an inference from a premise treating the universe as homoeomerous, then one of two possibilities accrues. Either (a) what comes in from the universe does not exhaust the soul, in which case it is either anhomoeomerous and so not composed strictly of an element (air) presumed to have life built into it, or (b) what comes in does exhaust the soul and it is homoeomerous. Aristotle does not explain what is wrong with the second alternative, but he is probably assuming that not every part of the soul exhibits the same features as the whole, as every part of bronze does. The nutritive soul, for instance, is not rational. That this is Aristotle's concern gains some credence from the fact that the chapter now gives way to more speculative questions pertaining to the mereology of the soul.

**411a24–b14: The Unity of the Soul; the Soul's Role in Unifying the Body:** Aristotle has now finished his criticisms of the two main theories of soul handed down to him (411a24–6 serves to punctuate the discussion thus far). Although he has been critical of his predecessors, sometimes harshly, Aristotle nonetheless agrees with them regarding many of the general features they have wanted to ascribe to the soul. Although it does not know or perceive because of the presence of the elements, the soul does, nonetheless, know and perceive; and although it cannot be moved in itself (see note to 408a29–b18), changes and motions of all kinds come about in an animal because of the soul.

Evidently because his various criticisms of elemental theories conclude with some considerations of the soul's own internal nature, including the question of whether it is to be regarded as homoeomerous or not (see note to 411a7–23), Aristotle turns in the last sections of the chapter to some worries about: (i) the soul's internal unity; and (ii) the soul's role in unifying the body.

Although provoked to ask a series of questions pertaining to the soul's internal unity at 411a26–b7 by a consideration of the views of his predecessors, it seems plain that the questions apply equally to Aristotle himself and that he recognizes that this is so. Thus, for example, he remains tentative on the question of whether the soul has parts even at 413a5, when advancing his own contention that the soul is inseparable from the body.

Aristotle notes that his predecessors have been inclined to partition the soul: 'To be sure, some say that the soul has parts and that reasoning is by means of one part and desiring by means of another' (411b5–7). Here again, though, he contents himself with an anonymous ascription. Aristotle's targets presumably include Plato (*Rep.* 434a–444b; *Tim.* 69c), though he may also simply have popular opinion in mind. In the present passage, he mentions just two parts of the soul, one for thinking and one for desiring, whereas Plato argues for three in *Republic* iv. (For Aristotle's own bipartite division of the soul, one evidently rooted in some common conceptions, see *EN* 1102a26–1103a10).

When assaying the unity of the soul, Aristotle asks two related questions, each with significant consequences for his own view. First, if the soul naturally has parts, what unifies it? Second, if the soul has parts, are the parts such that each of them unifies a different part of the body?

Regarding the first question, Aristotle contends immediately that the soul cannot be unified by the body. It is rather the case, he claims, that it is the soul which unifies the body (411b7–8). Further, if we are to look to something beyond the soul itself for its principle of unity, then either we arrive at an external principle of unification up to the task, which, being other than the body, will probably be itself a soul, in which case we may as well have stopped at the soul itself, or we move, unsatisfactorily, into an infinite hierarchy of souls. Thus, his argument:

(1) If the soul has parts, then it is unified either by: (a) the body; (b) a principle external to it which causes it to be unified; or (c) in virtue of itself.

(2) Not (1a): it is not possible for the body to unify the soul, since it is rather the soul which unifies the body.

(3) If (1b), then that external principle will presumably be itself a soul, soul$_2$, which is: (i) multi-parted or (ii) without parts.

(4) If it is without parts, then it seems otiose to posit a second soul, soul$_2$, and we should simply accept the original soul, soul$_1$, as without parts.

(5) If it is multi-parted, then there will need to be yet another principle, soul$_3$, which unifies soul$_2$.

(6) Either this process goes on into infinity, which is impossible, or we assume that some soul along the way is unified by being partless, in which case (as contended in premise (4)), we should simply accept the original soul as the one without parts.

(7) So, not (1b).

(8) Hence, (1c): if the soul has parts, then it is nonetheless unified in virtue of its own nature.

This is a rich and important argument, one which evidently draws upon the discussion of form and unity in *Metaphysics* Z 17 and H 6, or at any rate upon the sorts of considerations standing behind those discussions. (See especially *Met.* 1041a33–b33 and 1045a22–b17).

One key premise is (2), the claim that it is not possible for the body to unify the soul. Aristotle does not argue for this claim. Presumably he is relying on the sort of argument he advances at *Metaphysics* Z 17 1041b11–28: (i) the existence of the parts of the body is compatible with the non-existence of the soul; (ii) hence, the body, considered as an aggregate of its parts, cannot explain the unity of the soul. When my bodily parts are scattered across an expanse of space, they no longer form a body. What makes them a single body in the first instance, thinks Aristotle, is rather that they subserve a single end in common. He may also have in view a point made elsewhere *in De Anima*, at 416a6–9, to the effect that the elements earth and fire have naturally opposing motions, with the result that when they form a unified body, something must hold them together.

In any event, the conclusion of the argument as stated leaves unresolved the question of how the soul might have distinct capacities and yet be unified in its own nature, such that it can unify the elements of the body. Aristotle proposes a solution at 414b28–415a14, which should be read in conjunction with the present primarily aporetic passage, as should 416a6–9.

**411b14–19: The Parts of the Soul and the Parts of the Body; Reason:** Suppose it is granted that the soul unifies the body. A question then arises as to whether the individual parts of the soul (where parts are now broadly taken to include capacities) unify individual parts of the body. Does the perceptual faculty unify just those parts of the body associated with perception, while the nutritive unifies the organs employed in nutrition and generation? Precisely which organs are those? In *Generation and Corruption* I 5, Aristotle argues that the whole body grows simultaneously when it absorbs nutrition; so, in that sense, the entire body is in any case immediately implicated in the activities of the nutritive soul. The body thus considered, however, is already conceived as enformed, so that judgements about growth implicitly appeal to the formal cause of an organism (*Gen. et Cor.* 321b18–28). Thus, even the most basic life capacity involves the entire body, as individuated by the entire form or soul.

Further, Aristotle claims, it is difficult to fathom what bit of the body reason (*nous*) might be thought to hold together. The stridency of his language suggests that he thinks that reason *cannot* have an organ, not merely that it happens not to have one, that he has arrived at this judgement on the basis of an impoverished empirical judgement of some sort. In fact, Aristotle has already introduced reason as exceptional among the faculties of soul (see note to 408b18–29), and will produce an argument for its exceptional status in *De Anima* III 4. See especially 429a6–7, with note.

**411b19–30: The Divisibility of Some Plants and Animals:** Aristotle has already appealed to the phenomena of simple animal bisection (409a9), as he in fact often does for a variety of allied purposes (411b19, 413b16; cf. *Met.* 1040b10–13; *Parva Nat.* 467a18, 468a25, 479a3; *Part. An.* 682a5, b30; *Gen. An.* 731a21).

Here the discussion is motivated by the question of whether distinct parts of the soul unify distinct bits of the body. The fact of bisection provides evidence that the whole soul, with all of its capacities, is present in each part of the body. An earthworm when divided continues not only to take on nutrition but to perceive as well. This suggests that each of the faculties is present in each of the divided parts.

The interpretation of this section is complicated by some difficulties in the text, the transmission of which is at this juncture inconsistent and garbled. Of special difficulty is the phrase: 'and with the entire soul inasmuch as it is not divisible' (411b27). One crucial difficulty pertains to the 'not' (*ou*; 411b27), which is present in none of our best manuscripts. The alternative translation would be, then: 'and with the entire soul inasmuch as it is divisible'. The translation preferred reflects a textual reconstruction which has Aristotle arguing that each of the two souls present in bisected insects or other simple animals is the same in form as the other (each is, for example, an earthworm soul) and with the whole soul, of which each is an instance. Each individual soul is a complete and indivisible soul, as a complete instance of the kind of soul in question: there is no half earthworm soul. Further, each individual earthworm soul carries with it all the capacities of its kind, since the faculties cannot be detached from one another (cf. 413b1–10, 12–b19). This way of understanding Aristotle's point makes sense in the current context, because he is wondering both about the internal unity of the soul and the whole soul's role in unifying the body.

This interpretation, if correct, makes the argument at 411a26–b14 still more consequential. Given that the body, considered as an aggregate of parts, is not a unity, some non-aggregative principle must serve to unify it; unless that principle is itself an intrinsic unity, any question of unity, either synchronic or diachronic, is merely postponed to yet another principle capable of doing the job of unifying. So, the eventual principle must itself be a unity capable, ultimately, of unifying the body. For living beings, contends Aristotle, that principle is simply the soul, and not some principle external to the soul. This contention, he now suggests, finds some modest confirmation in the observed phenomena of bisection.

# BOOK II

## CHAPTER 1

### Introduction to II 1

Aristotle now offers his own positive account of the soul. In view both of the richness of the hylomorphic theory it presupposes and the problems immediately attendant upon Aristotle's deployment of that theory in the arena of soul-body relations, this first chapter has generated much discussion. For the primary commitments of Aristotle's psychological hylomorphism, see the General Introduction § III.A.

*De Anima* II 1 highlights primarily two implications of hylomorphism, that (i) it is not necessary to ask whether the soul and the body are one (412b6–9); and (ii) the soul is not separable from the body (413a4–6). The final meaning of these implications has been disputed. To begin with, the second claim admits of non-equivalent interpretations in line with Aristotle's varying characterizations of separation (*chôriston*; see Introduction to *DA* I 1 for a brief orientation to these types). Moreover, the arguments immediately leading up to these claims, which might be expected to help explicate Aristotle's intended meaning in the current context, are not always perfectly perspicuous.

A second dominant source of interest in the chapter has derived from a controversy surrounding Aristotle's contention that a body which has lost its soul is only homonymously (*homônumôs*) a body. As Ackrill (1972) has noted quite forcefully, this claim evidently entails that a body is a body only when ensouled. Briefly, this consequence seems to upset the very terms of the hylomorphism within which Aristotle's entire theory is adumbrated: if the wax is the matter of a candle, and the shape its form, then the wax is only contingently the matter of a candle, precisely because the same wax could sustain a different form and so serve as the matter of something other than a candle, for instance a figurine. If, by contrast, a body is a body only when ensouled, then the body is necessarily, and not contingently, ensouled. Consequently, it appears that the body, as the matter of the form, both is and is not necessarily enformed by the soul. This appears a straightforward contradiction at the heart of Aristotle's theory, one generated by his application of the metaphysical apparatus of hylomorphism to the special case of soul-body relations. (For a fuller statement of this problem, together with some lines of response, see the General Introduction § III.B).

**412a1–6: Making a Fresh Start:** After recounting and considering the relevant phenomena (*phainomena*) and credible opinions (*endoxa*), Aristotle occasionally announces the need for a fresh start to the inquiry at hand (cf. *Met.* 1041a6–7; *EN* 1117a13–14; *EE* 1218b31–2). When he does so, he does not mean that he will now ignore the discussions which have come before, but rather signals that he will proceed to his preferred account, having derived such value as there may be in the approaches of his predecessors (cf. 403b20–5). Nor does he mean to set aside his own preliminary reflections, as they have emerged in his presentation of the *phainomena* and *endoxa*. In this connection, it is worth revisiting the notes to 402a7–10 and 402a23–b8 in order to recall the sorts of questions about the soul Aristotle had said he would like to see answered.

When he now says that he wishes to determine what the soul is by way of specifying its most common account (412a4–6), Aristotle attends fairly closely to the problems as he posed them in 402a23–b8.

See also note to 413a11–20, where Aristotle makes a different sort of fresh start, concerning the soul as a principle of life.

**412a6–11: Answering the Categorial Question about Soul:** When setting out the dominant issues to be addressed regarding the soul, Aristotle had contended that the first order of business would be to determine the soul's appropriate ontological category (402a23–b1). Here he follows the course he recommends by offering the judgement that the soul is a substance (*ousia*). Although he only now articulates this conclusion, it seems already to have undergirded his rejection of the attunement theory in *DA* I 4 (see esp. note to 407b32–408a5). An attunement of the body seems to be a quality or attribute of the body; the soul is, by contrast, not a mere attribute of the body, but a substance in its own right. This is an especially significant result, since one might be tempted to think of the soul as a form of the body falling into the category of quality (*poion*), just as, in Aristotle's terms, the proponents of the attunement were inclined to do.

The sentence running from 412a6–9 finds Aristotle drawing crucially on his general metaphysical hylomorphism, but is expressed in extremely compact terms: 'We say that among the things that exist one kind is substance, and that one sort is substance as matter, which is not in its own right some this; another is shape and form, in accordance with which it is already called some this; and the third is what comes from these.' This translation is necessarily a bit expansive, and reflects two unavoidable interpretive decisions. First, Aristotle does not say that matter is a 'sort' of substance, but only that matter, along with form and compound, in some sense 'belongs to substance' or 'belongs [to the category of] substance' (literally 'to this' or 'of this', *tautês* in 402a7, the antecedent of which is *ousia*, or substance in 402a6). Other possible expansions would be that matter is: 'one aspect of substance' or 'one type of substance' or even 'one part of [of the category of] substance'. The translation reflects the thought that Aristotle's hylomorphism recognizes three sorts or grades of substance. (On Aristotle's metaphysical hylomorphism, see the General Introduction § II.)

The second point of translation pertains to the phrase 'in accordance with which it is already called some this' (*kath' hên êdê legetai tode ti*, 412a8–9). A parallelism in Greek is obscured in this rendering, since Aristotle has just said that matter is not 'in its own right some this' (*kath' hauto*; 412a6), and now says that form is that 'in accordance with which' (*kath' hên*) 'it' is called some this. Nothing in the Greek corresponds to 'it'. Aristotle thus might be making the point that *matter* is called some this (*tode ti*) because of the presence of form, or rather, more generally, that form is that 'in accordance with which *something* is already called some this'. The translation may tend to favour the first of these alternatives, but is meant to be as neutral as possible, and in any event not to exclude the second possibility. Taken in this second way, Aristotle is saying that matter is not some this, and that form is that whose presence makes anything at all some this—some particular thing. The second alternative is compatible with matter's never qualifying as a particular thing.

Abstracting from those finer points slightly, Aristotle here distinguishes three ways of thinking about substance: as matter (*hulê*), which is not some this (*tode ti*); as form (*eidos* or *morphê*), in terms of which something qualifies as some this; and as the compound (*to ex toutôn*) of form and matter (412a6–9; cf. 'of both', *ex amphoin* at 414a16).

Given the confidence of his assertion a few lines later that 'It is necessary, then, that the soul is a substance as the form of a natural body which has life in potentiality' (412a19–20), Aristotle seems already at the start of the chapter completely settled about his determination of the soul's ontological category: it is a substance (*ousia*). His categorial question in this passage thus becomes effectively a disjunctive syllogism whose conclusion will identify the preferred alternative among the three ways of thinking about substance specified: is the soul a substance (*ousia*) as matter, form, or compound? There is, to emphasize the point, no argument in this passage for the general conclusion that the soul is a substance—which is precisely what one might like to see in view of Aristotle's rejection of the theory that the soul is an attunement (see notes to 407b32–408a5 and 408a23–8).

In posing the question effectively as a disjunctive syllogism, Aristotle accepts as settled doctrine the account of substance developed in *Metaphysics* Z–Θ. Unfortunately, since the final purport of that account is heavily disputed, it is not possible simply to recapitulate its principal findings. Nonetheless, in the present context, it appears that Aristotle approves of just these three different candidates for the title of substance—matter, form, and compound—and wishes to know which sort of substance among these the soul is. In his comprehensive treatment of substance (*ousia*) in the *Metaphysics*, Aristotle canvasses all manner of candidates, many promulgated by his predecessors but some proposed by Aristotle himself: the substratum (*hupokeimenon*), the essence (*to ti ên einai*), the four elements of earth, air, fire and water, numbers, points, inter alia (for one preliminary list of candidates, see *Met.* Z 2).

The further question of whether the soul is a potentiality (*dunamis*), as matter is, or an actuality (*entelecheia*), as form is, will weigh heavily in his final determination. For the two senses of actuality to which Aristotle alludes here, see note to 412a21–7.

**412a11–21: Soul is Substance as Form:**     These lines provide the core statement of Aristotle's soul-body hylomorphism: soul and body are related as form and matter.

The passage contains two mutually supporting arguments for a preliminary conclusion, stated at 412a17, that the soul is not *a* (or perhaps is not *the*) body. Although neither argument is completely clear, because each is compressed, each makes some progress towards Aristotle's contention that the soul and body are not the same. He notes first that natural bodies top the list of candidates for substance, especially those having life. His implied contrast is not between the living and the dead, but between the living and the inanimate, not, that is, between a living body and a corpse, but rather between a living being and an element or an artefact. Cf. *Met.* 1028b8, 1042a3–31.

Despite its intimate connection to a living body, the soul is not to be identified with either an animate or an inanimate body. The first argument is direct and simple:

(1) Every natural substance having life is a composite.
(2) The soul is not a composite.
(3) Hence, the soul is not a substance as a natural body having life.

Further, Aristotle immediately adds a second argument:

(1) A body is not among those things belonging to a subject, but is rather itself a subject, as matter.
(2) The soul, by contrast, belongs to a subject.
(3) Hence, the soul is not a body.

Stating the arguments thus is controversial, since in the first instance, many commentators find only one argument in these lines. If read in that way, however, Aristotle's reasoning will fall short of establishing what he next concludes, that soul is substance *as form* (412a19–20). In order to reach that conclusion, he must understand himself to have eliminated two of the three candidates for substance listed at 412a6–9 (namely matter, compound, and form). The first argument eliminates the compound, and the second, the matter.

That allowed, there is, of course, a further question as to why one must accept the second premise of either of these arguments (that the soul is not a compound; that the soul belongs to a subject). At a minimum, in the second argument, Aristotle needs to show why the soul belongs to a subject in a manner in which the body does not. Further, in at least one sense of 'belonging' both the soul and body belong to the compound, which is surely a subject; so, one would further need to specify the sense in which the one does and the other does not belong, and indeed to specify which subjects we have in view in making this appeal. A similar train of reasoning emerges in the next chapter at 414a13–27, with which this present passage is usefully compared.

An alternative interpretation understands Aristotle to be denying that the soul is a compound by denying that it is any sort of body at all, with the result that it has no intrinsic material properties in its own right, as the compound of form and matter does. Here one may usefully consult *Met.* 1001b29, 1029a10–27, 1088a17–21.

Whatever his route, however, Aristotle concludes that the soul is a substance (*ousia*) as the form (*eidos*) of a natural body having life in potentiality (*dunamis*) (412a19–21). What, though, does it add to Aristotle's account that the soul be the form of a body which has life *in potentiality*? This might seem trivially the case, since the soul, as a principle of life, will not be the form of a body which cannot support life. Presumably, Aristotle's contention is more than just that the soul is the form of a body which is *possibly* alive. Rather—if by 'possibly' we are meaning abstract metaphysical possibility in a broad sense—he means a good deal more. Instead, he means that not every body is appropriately arrayed to be a living body—a point which not everyone has found trivial or even true. This was after all the reason Aristotle had found wanting in the Pythagorean view of metempsychosis; that view pretends that just any old body can sustain just any old form of life, without reference to the particular physical structures required to realize particular life activities (on Aristotle's attitude towards the shortcomings of such views, see note to 407b14–26). The presence of a soul will not turn a paper clip into a perceiver; or, looked at from the other side, no paper clip will have a soul, because paper clips lack the organs requisite for life, and so are not potentially alive, or alive in *dunamei*. This is a consequence Aristotle reaffirms at 412b15–17. Cf. *De Interp.* 23a3; *Met.* 1045a7–b23, 1075b34.

**412a21–27: Types of Actuality:**   Since soul is substance (*ousia*) as form, and form is substance as actuality (*entelecheia*), the soul is the actuality of an appropriate sort of body. Aristotle notes, however, that actuality is spoken of in two ways, or as his illustration suggests, as coming in two grades. Although humans, as rational beings, have the ability to learn set theory, only some do. Someone who has learnt and mastered elementary set theory knows the paradox generated by the Russell set, and so has actualized her capacity to know in that respect. We mark a further difference, however, when we say that the one who knows the paradox is now actually contemplating it. Even while sleeping, the student of set theory is one of the people who know the paradox, even though she is not just then actually contemplating it. Aristotle suggests, though does not state explicitly, that mere knowing is a *first actuality*, whereas actively contemplating is a *second actuality*. Cf. 417a22–9, *Phys.* 255a33, *Met.* 1050a21–3.

Having marked that distinction, Aristotle contends that the soul is a *first actuality* of a body of an appropriate sort. This may seem initially to have the odd consequence that someone could have a soul without actually living, as one can have knowledge without actually using it. Indeed, there has long been a controversy about the best way to interpret and apply Aristotle's contention here (see, e.g., Ackrill (1972–3), Whiting (1992), Hübner (1999), Burnyeat (2002)). Minimally, of course, it must be allowed that necessarily if $x$ has a soul, then $x$ is alive. It does not follow immediately, however, that if $x$ is alive at time $t$ that at $t$ $x$ is currently actually (= second actuality) engaging in some one of life's characteristic functions, i.e. digesting, or reproducing, or perceiving, or knowing (cf. 412a14–15, 415b28). To insist that whatever is actually ensouled is actually (= second actuality) living, is simply to insist without argument that the distinction introduced here collapses or is otherwise incoherent. Aristotle is not constrained to accept either of these conclusions. (For a sustained, sophisticated treatment of these issues, see Hübner (1999).)

**412a28–412b4: The Relevant Body is Organic:** The word organic (*organikon*), formed as an adjective from the noun *organon* (organ, or tool) is used by Aristotle in a technical sense. Many commentators understand him to mean that the sort of body appropriately arrayed for life is one which is equipped with organs capable of implementing life functions. On this approach, nothing will see, for example, unless it has the requisite organs, that is, unless it has equipment dedicated to the task of light detection. From this perspective, Aristotle's contention derives ultimately from his overarching teleology, reflecting his judgement that 'every organ is for the sake of something' (*Part. An.* 645b14), and further coheres with the observation made in *DA* I 3 that bodies and souls must be suited to one another (see note to 407b14–26). This understanding seems correct, as far as it goes. Probably, however, Aristotle's intended meaning is more technical and still more enmeshed in his teleology. As Everson (1997: 64) observed, Aristotle probably means that the body itself, as a whole, is an organ of the soul, as a whole. Thus, something qualifies as an organic body just in case it is such as to be used by the soul for its ends. This extension of our understanding of what is involved in being *organikon* has two advantages. First, it coheres with—and helps to explain—Aristotle's straightforward contention that every natural body is the organ of a soul (412b15; cf. *Part. An.* 642a11; *Pol.* 1254a34; *EN* 1161a35–b6). Second, it also moves some way towards helping to explicate Aristotle's contention that a body which has lost, or cast off (*apobeblêkos*), its soul is not a body except homonymously, on which, see note to 412b10–413a3.

It should be noted that these two interpretations of '*organikon*' need not be taken as competitors, although they are sometimes presented that way. If Aristotle speaks of the whole body as '*organikon*' because it is a tool of the soul, he might reasonably also mean that organic bodies, like tools suited to performing various tasks, will have parts suited to performing those tasks. (A kitchen blender comprises tools for chopping and mixing.) In the case of living bodies, those parts will include what we ourselves, quite reasonably from an Aristotelian perspective, call 'organs'.

This compatibility explains why Aristotle is able to move directly to talking about the parts of plants as suitable organs analogous to the organs of animal bodies. Aristotle's point about plants serves to remind the reader that all living things have souls (cf. 413b5–7, 415a23–5, 416a19) and that in all ensouled beings we find parts suited to the tasks associated with life. (Aristotle elsewhere calls such parts or features 'life-supporting' or 'fit for life' (*zôtikos*), *Gen. An.* 761a27.) Where the tasks of plants are the same as they are in humans, as in the case of nutrition, we find it easy to speak of the appropriate plant parts as analogous to the parts of animals because of sameness of the functional role played. This is the sense in which plants have 'mouths'. Cf. *Part. An.* 655b37–656a3, 686b32–687a1.

**412b4–9: The Common Account of Soul and its First Significant Implication:** The common account of soul requested at 402a23–b8 and promised at 412a4–6 is now stated, using the terms articulated to this point in the chapter: the soul is *the first actuality of a natural organic body*. This provides a compact formula of what has so far been established, but adds nothing new.

What is new, and surprising, is Aristotle's immediate inference from the common account of soul. He concludes directly that given such an analysis, it is not necessary to inquire into the matter of whether the soul and body are one (412b6–9). In an alternative translation, often preferred, but less well grounded in Aristotle's Greek, the inference is turned into an admonition: '*it is necessary not to ask* whether soul and body are one', as though doing so already betrayed a confusion on the part of the one asking. (Various translations are collected and compared in Shields (1999: 156 n.1).) Aristotle might, in principle, offer such an admonition if he thought it obvious on hylomorphic grounds that the soul and body are identical. Yet he has in this very chapter argued that the soul and body are not identical (see note to 412a11–21). More generally, the wax and its shape are not identical with one another, since, as Aristotle himself rightly notes in *Metaphysics* Z 17 (1041b11–25; cf. *Gen. et. Cor.* 322a4–16), a form can sustain a change in the matter, and, at least in non-organic bodies, the matter can outlast the form (see note to 412b10–413a3). So, he evidently cannot be thinking that it is necessary not to ask this question (or indeed even that it is not necessary to ask it) because its answer is so blindingly obvious, viz. that soul and body are identical.

On the translation preferred in the text ('For this reason it is also unnecessary to ask whether the soul and body are one'; 412b6), what Aristotle actually says is less strident and more complicated than the alternative translation suggests. Given this translation, the question of the soul's oneness with the body simply becomes less pressing than it might otherwise have been, because hylomorphism removes one motivation for wishing to pose this question in the first place. One can begin to see why by examining the rather truncated argument offered for this conclusion.

The argument of the passage, however, drawing as it does upon features of Aristotle's metaphysics, is more complicated than sometimes assumed. This becomes clear when we reflect upon the reason Aristotle actually supplies for his contention that it is not necessary to ask whether the soul and body are one: 'For while one and being are spoken of in several ways, what is properly so spoken of is the actuality (*entelecheia*)' (412b8–9). This grounding appeals to Aristotle's apparatus of mulitvocity or homonymy, and in particular to his suggestion that when a concept is multiplicitous, it may have a 'most proper' (*to kuriôs*) or 'controlling' core sense or core concept. (For an introduction to multiplicity and homonymy, see Shields (2007: Ch. 3 § 6); for a fuller treatment, see Shields (1999).

As this technical machinery is deployed in the current passage, we find Aristotle explicitly stating only a single premise on behalf of his ultimate conclusion:

P-1: Actuality (*entelecheia*) is the controlling sense of unity.
C: It is not necessary to ask whether the soul and body are one.

The challenge for interpreters of the passage is thus to determine what bridge premise or premises Aristotle may be presuming. One natural thought, adopted by, among others, Guthrie (1981: 284 n.3: 'The entelechy is here the concrete object at its highest stage.') is:

P-2*: The concrete object (viz. the form-matter compound) is an actuality (*entelecheia*); and, if so, (C).

This would yield a valid argument, but fails to come to terms with the plain fact that in the present chapter Aristotle refers to the *soul* as the actuality *four times* (412a9–11, a19–22, a27–9, b4–5). Presumably, then, the better alternative reconstruction will be:

P-2**: The soul is an actuality (*entelecheia*); and, if so, (C).

On this approach, equally valid, of course, the soul is prior to the body, and indeed makes it the case that the body qualifies as a unified entity in the first instance. He is claiming, that is, that the soul unifies the body, a point he had already emphasized in *De*

*Anima* I (411b6–10; see note to 411a26–b14). If that is correct, then in the present passage, he is offering the judgement that such unity as the body has is already parasitic on the presence of its soul—in which case asking whether they are one is rendered unnecessary. The question in fact will have a false presupposition, namely that there are two independently specifiable entities about whose associations with one another we might wonder. Aristotle's point is not, then, that they are the same. He offers, rather, a much more nuanced view, namely that the identity conditions of the one, the body, are parasitic on the identity conditions of the other, the soul. See Shields (2009) for an analysis of Aristotle's inference in this passage, together with discussions of several alternative approaches.

If this is correct, then, Aristotle appears to be suggesting that one might have wanted to pose a question of soul-body unity for a specific reason: to determine, for instance, whether the soul can exist without the body, as Plato had argued at length that it could in the *Phaedo*—and as perhaps did the youthful Aristotle himself in the dialogue, *Eudemus* (Them. *Comm. in DA* 106a29–107.4, Elias, *Comm. in Cat.* 114.25–115.3). Once it is seen that hylomorphism distinguishes the soul from the body, even while requiring that the soul be realized by a body of an appropriate sort, which body is in turn parasitic for its identity conditions on that soul, then the question of oneness becomes largely idle—at least relative to its Platonic motive. Looked at this way, Aristotle's point is that on hylomorphic principles, one has no more reason to inquire into the question of whether soul and body are one than one has to inquire into the question of whether the wax and its shape are one. No one is motivated to ask the latter question, because no one supposes that hylomophism provides any impetus to wonder whether the shape of a candle is capable of existing separately from the wax whose shape it is.

If something along these lines is correct, then the two main implications of hylomorphism drawn by Aristotle in this chapter are importantly connected. On the second implication, that the soul is not separable from the body, and its connection to this first inference, see note to 413a3–7 below.

**412b10–413a3: Soul Functions, Activities, and Homonymy:** Aristotle repeats that the soul is a substance (*ousia*), where the sort of substance is the one 'corresponding to the account (*kata logon*, 412b10–11)', viz. the form. Aristotle has not used just this formulation of the sort of substance the soul has been understood to be, though his meaning is clear. Below he says more directly that the soul *is* a *logos*, translated as: 'For the soul is not the essence and organization (*logos*) of this sort of body' Here, as elsewhere, it is not easy to capture Aristotle's use of the word *logos* with a single word in English. As discussed in the note to 403a3–27, sometimes it is semantic, having to do with meaning or sense, and other times, as here, it is rather ontological, and is interchangeable with *eidos*, or form. Cf. 414a9, 424a24; *Met.* 1006b1, 1030a7, 1044b12, 1058b19; *Phys.* 209a21; see also the glossary entry *logos*.

Aristotle's reliance on artefacts in this passage to illustrate his broadly functional conception of soul is in some ways illuminating, but in other ways puzzling. The comparison is initially helpful, given the threefold schema upon which he relies. The being of an axe (*to pelekei einai*), its essence (*to ti ên einai*), is cutting—an axe, that is, is essentially a tool for cutting. Aristotle reasonably infers on this basis that if an axe lost its ability to cut, it would not be an axe at all, or, rather, would be an axe only homonymously. In introducing this point about homonymy, Aristotle means at a minimum that if an instrument *x* of kind *F* were incapable of performing the defining function of *Fs*, *x* would cease to be an *F*—except, as the illustration in 412b20–1 contends, in the sense that an eye in a painting or a statue is an eye. Since they do not see, we may reasonably say that such 'eyes' are not *real* eyes at all.

In relying on this sort of illustration, Aristotle takes it for granted that eyes and axes admit of functional specifications. One reason for his doing so is that he is relying on his general approach to kind individuation, which involves a *functional determination thesis*. He states directly, for example, that 'all things are defined by their function' (*Meteor.* 390a10–15; cf. *Gen. An.* 734b24–31; *Pol.* 1253a19–25); and strikingly, when he offers this general thesis of functional determination (on which, see Shields (1999: 31–5), Aristotle regularly draws out its implications regarding the homonymy of entities which have the outward appearance of *Fs* without being, in fact, *Fs*. This is why, without having the functional capacities of human beings, or of eyes, something which has the outward appearance of a human being, or of an eye, is not really a human being, or an eye—except homonymously. Cf. also *Part. An.* 641a18, 645b14.

It is to be observed that Aristotle offers a stark statement of his view, which he presumably expects to be initially jarring, namely: 'The body which has cast off its soul is not a being which is potentially such as to be alive; this is rather the one which has a soul' (412b25–7). Given the regimented parallel advanced in this section, such a body is held to be the same as an 'axe' which cannot cut or an 'eye' which cannot see, for example, the eye in a statue made of stone (412b21–2). Aristotle is not disputing that we will call such an 'eye' an 'eye'; he is claiming that whatever we may call them such 'eyes' are in fact not eyes—except homonymously. By parallel, if we call a human body which has lost its soul a 'body' or a 'human body', we are doing so, according to Aristotle, only by habit and only incorrectly; strictly speaking, any such is not a human body—again, except homonymously.

If this is correct, however, an initially unattractive result accrues: it seems that bodies cannot be the matter of souls in a compound, since according to the homonymy principle, a human body which has lost its soul is no longer a human body, as Aristotle affirms at 412b20–1. If that is right, then the body, unlike the matter of a bronze statue, is necessarily, and not contingently enformed. This seems to upset the very hylomorphic scheme which Aristotle is attempting to apply to soul-body relations in this chapter. For more on this problem, see the Introduction to this chapter; for a fuller discussion, along with possible solutions, see the General Introduction § III.B. Fuller discussions can also be found in Ackrill (1972), Shields (1993), and Frey (2007).

**413a3–7: Second Significant Implication of Hylomorphism:** If the soul and organic body come together to yield the compound animal in just the way a pupil together with sight make up an eye, then the soul as a whole will not be separable from the body any more than sight is separable from an appropriately configured pupil. In making this determination, Aristotle answers a question posed in 403a3–27. There he had argued, rather strongly it now seems, that if there were affections peculiar (*idion*) to the soul, they would be separable, but otherwise not (see note to 403a3–27 on questions about separation of the whole soul as distinct from the separation of its parts). Here he concludes, in a way evidently incompatible with that earlier contention, that the soul is not separable, even though, he hastens to add, some parts of it may well yet be. He clearly has reason (*nous*) in view in adding this important rider. Eventually, in fact, he decides that reason is separable, though it is disputed in what way (see notes to 429a10–14 and 429b5; cf. also 430a17 and the parallel claims of *Gen. An.* 736b21–9).

Aristotle offers as grounds for the possible separability of some soul parts that they may not be the actualities of any bodily parts: 'For the actuality of some parts belongs to the parts [*sc.* of the body] themselves' (413a5–6). In so speaking, he implies that since other parts are the actualities of bodily parts, they are not separable. He thus makes it necessary and sufficient for a psychic part's being inseparable that it be the actuality of a part of the body, or, conversely, that a soul part *x* is separable *iff x* is not the actuality of any part of the body.

Where Aristotle speaks of *parts* in this connection, he presumably means *faculties*. Thus:

(1) A psychic faculty *x* is separable from the body *iff* the actuality of *x* is not the actuality of some part of the body.

(2) The actuality of some psychic faculties (presumably including nutrition and perception) is the actualities of parts of the body.

(3) So, these faculties are not separable from the body (413a3–5).

Then again:

(1) The actuality of some psychic faculties (presumably including reason) is not, or may not be, the actualities of any parts of the body.

(2) Hence, 'nothing hinders' (*outhen kôluei*; 413a7) their being separable (413a6–7).

Since Aristotle believes that it is possible that there exist actual beings which are the actualities of no body (*Met.* 1072b26–9), he cannot (consistently) be reasoning that a necessary condition of being an actuality is being the actuality of some body or other. Rather, he is arguing that *if* the actuality of some psychic capacity is also the actuality of some body, then that capacity is not separable from the body. By contrast, if some psychic capacity does not have as its actuality the actuality of some body, then nothing stands in the way of its being separable. On the question of why Aristotle supposes that some psychic capacity might not have the actuality of any body as its own actuality, see note to 419a25.

Finally, while it is claimed here that the soul is not separable from the body, it is *not* claimed the body *is* separable from the soul; but that suggestion, given the direction of Aristotle's contention, may nonetheless seem to lie near. Given Aristotle's contention that a body without a soul is but homonymously a body (see note to 412b10–413a3), however, no such implication can obtain—at least not where the organic body, the body which is the matter of the soul, is concerned. Accordingly, for a full appreciation of Aristotle's soul-body hylomorphism, it is important to resist the tendency to read any such purport into the present passage: the soul cannot be separated from the body, but neither can the body be separated from the soul.

**413a8–10: A Surprising Coda:**    Given this mutual inseparability of soul and body, the seemingly random sentence that closes the chapter has occasioned a good deal of consternation among Aristotle's commentators, both ancient and modern. Aristotle wonders aloud whether the soul bears the relation to the body that a sailor bears to a ship, when one might have supposed that a sailor at liberty, unlike the soul, can and does leave his ship.

Among the ancient commentators, we find some unsatisfactory approaches to this problem. Themistius, for instance, suggests that the soul is both an actualization of the body *and* something separable (*Paraph. de an.* 43.27). Is it not the case, however, that Aristotle has just denied that the soul is separable from the body, and so has concluded that the relationship between soul and body is precisely *not* the relationship which a sailor bears to a ship?

To Ross (1961: 214) the answer is clear: the text as we have it 'flatly contradicts' all that has preceded and so requires emendation. He proposes to add 'or' (*ê*) in 413a8, which would yield 'It is still unclear, however, whether the soul is the actuality of the body *or* [is related to the body] in the way that a sailor is of a ship.' I have not followed his emendation, translating the text as we have it: 'It is still unclear, however, whether the soul is the actuality of the body in the way that a sailor is of a ship.' One reason for favouring the text over Ross's proposal is that his emendation seems merely to postpone the problem he identifies—if it really is a problem. That is, if there is a flat contradiction between saying (i) that the soul is the actuality of the body and (ii) that the soul is related to the body as a sailor is to a ship, then nothing at all is gained by saying that 'it is still unclear' whether (i) or (ii). For (i) has been asserted in the chapter (412a27), and if it 'flatly contradicts' (ii), then it is anything but unclear whether (i) *or* (ii).

In fact, although there clearly is some tension generated by some ways of understanding Aristotle's comparison, we do not really have a flat contradiction here. A soul might be related to a body as a sailor is to a ship in several different ways, all of which are at least compatible with the dominant claims of the chapter. One fairly unlikely possibility for avoiding a contradiction would be that Aristotle has abruptly and without notice changed the topic from the separability of the soul to some other consideration, by suggesting, e.g., that it is still an open question whether the soul directs and steers the body as a sailor directs and steers a ship (cf. *Phys.* 254b30). This possibility, however remote, may be given some mild credence by a discussion below, in II 4. See note to 416b11–28.

Another, more radical possibility would have it that Aristotle had not after all meant to foreclose on the question of the separability of the soul, that he is suggesting that just as no sailor sails without sailing a ship, still, a sailor may leave the ship when not sailing. See, e.g., Bos (2003) for this more radical kind of proposal.

More modest, and more probably correct, is the suggestion of Siwek (1965) and Lefèvre (1972 and 1978) that Aristotle is thinking here in causal terms and, having determined that the soul is the formal cause of the body, now reports that he has not yet taken a stand on the question of whether it is also its efficient cause.

It must be said, however, that though each is possible, nothing in the text actually commends any one of these suggestions. In fact, we have only the analogy itself to guide us; and despite its sounding as if Aristotle were using it to allude to an earlier or well-known trope, the analogy has no obvious precedent in Aristotle or in any other earlier author. So, although there are ways of avoiding the imputation of a contradiction to Aristotle, and thus of obviating the move to emend, no one of them seems uniquely to be preferred over its competitors.

## CHAPTER 2

### Introduction to II 2

Aristotle makes another fresh start in his inquiry concerning the soul by emphasizing his contention that the soul is a principle of life, the presence of which differentiates the living from the non-living. Although this has been his contention since the very beginning of the work (see 402a4–7, with note; cf. 413b11–13), only now does Aristotle begin to give some content to the claim. Importantly, he claims that *life* is 'spoken of in several ways' (*pleonachôs legomenon*). In so contending, he means at least that there is no single, univocal definition of *life*, no unified, non-disjunctive essence-specifying analysis capturing all the varieties of life manifested in the universe. Two points pertinent to this claim should be borne in mind: (i) although issued without argument in this chapter, the claim is evidently intended to have some anti-Platonic purport, insofar as it rejects univocity; and (ii) it does not entail that Aristotle denies that any analysis of life is possible, or that life should be understood on the model of family resemblances. It is consistent with Aristotle's contention in this chapter that he regards life as a core-dependent homonym. On Aristotle's treatment of life, see Matthews (1992), Shields (1999: ch. 7, and 2011), and Katayama (2008), as well as the papers collected in Mouracade (2008) and Föllinger (2010).

**413a11–20: Scientific Framework for Making a Fresh Start:** We have seen Aristotle announcing the need for a fresh start once already, at the beginning of the last chapter (see note to 412a1–6). Here he begins anew once more, now adverting, however, to the highly technical framework for scientific discovery and expression articulated in the *Posterior Analytics*. In the present context, he speaks of what is better known in conformity with reason (*kata logon*) as a kind of knowledge more secure than what is known initially, in sense experience; such knowledge conforms to the *logos* of an entity, in the sense where this means its form or essential nature (see meaning (iii) of *logos* in the glossary) (cf. *Part. An.* 653b22–30; *Pol.* 1328a20).

Although drawn along a different axis, this distinction is consonant with Aristotle's contention that in the order of discovery, we begin with what is better known to us (*gnorimôteron hêmin*) and proceed to what is better known by nature or *simpliciter* (*gnorimôteron phusei* or *haplôs*) (*APo.* 71b33–72a5; *Top.* 141b3–142a4; *Phys.* 184a16–b14, *Met.* 1029b3–12). In coming to know what is better known by nature, we uncover the essential features of things, which we discover only posterior to our knowing *'the that'*, which is to say that we know *that something exists*. Aristotle maintains that only when we know *that* something exists ('the *that*') can we discover the causes of its existence ('the *why*'). (For Aristotle's way of introducing this claim, see *APo.* II 1, 8–10; for an exploration of its correct understanding, see Barnes (1994) and Charles (2000: 23–57).) In the present context, he means to suggest that we have already ascertained that the soul exists; now we need to fix its extension and to discover more about its nature.

Aristotle's example overlaps with Euclid, *Elements* II 14 and esp. VI 13 (cf. *Met.* 996b14). Definitions are like conclusions because they state the *that*; the proofs arriving at those conclusions state the *why*. In the illustration employed, Aristotle has in mind the following Figures 1 and 2:

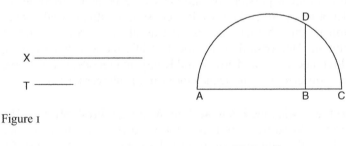

Figure 1

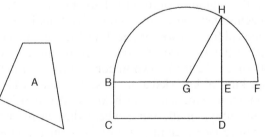

Figure 2

A square equal in area to a rectangle with sides equal to lines AB and BC will have a side equal to line BD (identifying this square is known as 'squaring'); and it will also be the case that AB: BD : : BD : BC, so that BD will be the proportional mean—a fact explanatory of the conclusion that AB and BC will have a side equal to BD. Thus, on the sort of deductive model which Aristotle envisages, it is appropriate to seek a syllogism, or series of syllogisms, explaining the facts about the soul thus far adduced. Nowhere in *De Anima* does he in in fact produce these sorts of syllogisms pertaining to the soul.

**413a20–31: The Multivocity of Life:** Aristotle claims that life is spoken of in several ways (*pleonachôs legomenon*), a locution commonly used by him when he means to assail a univocity assumption (*Top.* 129b31–130a28; *EN* 1129a23–5). He provides some reason for thinking that those who seek univocal definitions of life are misguided in the *Topics* (148a26–31), where he criticizes Dionysius for failing to appreciate that 'life seems not to be spoken of according to one form, but belongs in one way to animals and in another way to plants.'

Aristotle does not pursue the question of life's non-univocal definition further here (cf. 412a14, 415a22–b2), except insofar as he proceeds to list a set of individually sufficient conditions for *x*'s being alive: *x* is alive if *x* (i) thinks, or (ii) perceives, or (iii) moves (itself) in space, or (iv) moves by way of taking on nourishment, or by growing or decaying. As regards (iii) and (iv), Aristotle allows growth and decay to qualify as kinds of 'motion' in the broad sense, where these are distinct from spatial motion (*kinêsis kata topon*), which is motion in the most familiar sense of the term (the types of motion, discussed in note to 406a12–16 above, are four, namely 'locomotion, alteration, decay, and growth' (406a12–13); cf. *Phys.* 225a5–9, 226a23–b8). With the exception of (iii), this list corresponds to the hierarchy of souls discussed later in this chapter (and also at 434a22–b18; cf. *Part. An.* 687a24–690a10; *Met.* 1075a16–25). For (iii), see *Phys*ics 255b20–256a2, where Aristotle makes clear that it is not just anything capable of moving in space which is alive, but only those beings with an internal principle (*archê*) of motion. Though moving in space in a natural direction, rocks are not alive.

Plants are alive, however, because they plainly fulfil condition (iv). Moreover, because what is alive is coextensive with what has a soul, we may appropriately say that plants have souls (cf. 415a24–5, and note to 402a23–b8). It is noteworthy that Aristotle indicates that even the lowliest living beings, those which merely take on nutrition and neither perceive nor think, not only grow and decline, but are subject to *limited* and *patterned* growth. That is, plants do not merely grow ceaselessly without end while they live, but grow only into specifiable magnitudes and in determinate ways. Their doing so is symptomatic of their being ensouled; living things do not merely get bigger haphazardly, as forest fires do, but in structured ways, in accordance with their own internal principles, following predictable patterns subordinate to their ends, which include their own mature states and, typically, their ability to generate others of their own kind. On the patterned growth of living beings, see *Gen. et Corr.* I 5. For more on the multivocity of life, see Shields (1999: ch. 7).

**413a31–b10: The Inseparability of Lower Faculties:** Plants show that the capacity for nutrition can and does exist separately from the higher faculties of perception and reason; by contrast, among mortals, the higher faculties cannot exist without the lower. The qualification 'among mortal beings' (or 'in the case of mortals'; *en tois thnêtois*, 413a33) is required, since Aristotle elsewhere commits himself to the existence of immortal living beings who think without perceiving or eating (*Met.* 991a10, 1050b16–29, 1069a30–3, 1071b3–5). This possibility by itself already shows that the form of necessity obtaining between the higher and lower orders of psychic faculties must be somehow hypothetical and not absolute. There is, thus, no contradiction in saying that a rational soul exists without a perceptual soul or a perceptual soul without a nutritive soul. Rather, Aristotle will argue on exclusively teleological grounds that the kind of necessity which obtains here will take the following general form: *if* in the sublunar realm a being $x$ has a perceptual soul, *then it is necessary* that $x$ also have a nutritive soul—or else $x$ would not be in a position to secure its ends as the perceptual being it is, and nature would have acted in vain in so equipping it (see note to 434b9–25).

Further, just as the lower faculties of soul can exist without the higher, so within the single capacity of perception, touch alone can exist without the other sensory modalities. Aristotle often notes that some animals have only touch and no other sense (434b9–23, 435a12, 435b5–7; *De Sensu* 436b15; *Hist. An.* 489a17). For the explanation of why the nutritive soul can exist without the perceptual or intellectual souls, see 434a22–30; and on the matter of why touch can exist without the other sensory modalities within perception, see 434b9–25. In each case, again, the explanation is given in teleological terms.

**413b11–414a3: Soul Parts and their Internal Relations:**   While Aristotle sometimes speaks freely of the soul as having parts (for instance just above at 413b7), his dominant tendency is to express doubt regarding whether the soul should be deemed to be the sort of thing which has parts at all (413a5; cf. 403b1, where he mentions this very question as one among those to be investigated in *De Anima*). This need not reflect any tension in his thinking, since he evidently conceives of parts differently in different contexts, much as we do. In some contexts one might fairly assert that 'Part of her problem is her tendency towards excessive optimism,' even while insisting in other contexts that a *tendency* is not really the sort of thing which qualifies as a part. To put it in modern terms, one might say that Aristotle sometimes thinks of parts as akin to the notion of parts employed in extensional mereology, and in other contexts uses a comparatively relaxed or loose notion. In this passage, Aristotle seems to be speaking of parts loosely, as roughly equivalent to capacities.

His usage in this connection may be usefully compared first with Plato's similarly loose diction, and then also with his own occasionally relaxed tendency to speak of 'parts' (*merê*) as features which are hardly separable from the entities whose parts they are.

As for Plato, we may compare the ease in the *Republic* and *Timaeus* with which he moves between different vocabularies for both the parts of the soul and the soul as whole. The *Republic* moves indifferently between the parts (*merê*) of the soul 442b11, c5; 444b3; 577d3; kinds (*eidê*) belonging to the soul: 435b9–c1, c5, e2, 439e2), and the types or sorts (*genê*) belonging to the soul: 441c6; 443d3. The *Timaeus* speaks of the whole soul in similar terms: as a part (*meros*): 91e5; as a type or sort (*genos*):

69d5, e4, 73c4; as a kind (*eidos*): 69c7. For a review of Plato's language regarding parts more generally, with a special focus on the partition of the soul in *Republic* iv and x, see Shields (2010). As for Aristotle's own diction, we must note his willingness to call the soul itself a part (*meros*) of a human being (e.g. *Met.* 1022a31), even though it is clearly not the case that he regards the human being as assembled from one part soul and one part body. Again, no harm accrues from his speaking in these loose ways; it is clear that 'part' (*meros*) admits of a range of meanings, and may be restricted in various technical contexts. These are distinguished by Aristotle in several passages, including especially *Phys.* 210a14–24 and *Met.* Δ 23 and 25. In these passages, Aristotle draws multiple distinctions, including a crucial one between quantitative and non-quantitative parts (on which, see note to 402a23–b8). For a rigorous attempt to take Aristotle's talk of the soul and the form more generally as part of the compound literally and strictly, see Koslicki (2006).

Once one allows that the soul may have parts in this more relaxed sense, the question arises as to whether these are parts 'in such a way as to be separate in account alone or also in place' (413b14–15). Aristotle is concerned here with whether various psychic parts or capacities are the sorts of things which can exist separately in place (*topos*) or only in account (*logos*). On the kinds of separation (*chôriston*) in general, see the introduction to I 1, as well as the entry in the glossary. His way of posing this question implies that he already agrees that perception and nutrition are separable in account (*en logô(i)*), presumably because the essence of perception is not the same as the essence of nutrition, and sameness in essence-specifying definition is necessary and sufficient for sameness in account (*APr.* 67b12; *Top.* 133b33). But are they also separable in place?

Aristotle approaches this question indirectly. As often elsewhere, he introduces the phenomenon of bisected plants and certain insects and other small animals, those capable of living after having been bisected, as illustrating various facts about the relations of psychic capacities to one another. If a plant or insect yields two living beings when divided, then, suggests Aristotle, the original entity had only one soul in actuality, but two in potentiality. Observation confirms that the entire nutritive soul is present in each of the divided plants, and that nutrition and perception travel together in the divided insects (cf. 409a7–10, 411b19; *Met.* 1040b10–13; *Parva Nat.* 467a18, 468a25, 479a3; *Part. An.* 682a5, b30; *Gen. An.* 731a21). So, each of the new actual souls replicates the original. Indeed, we find a more fine-grained sort of connection: since each of the severed insects has perception, each also has imagination (*phantasia*) and desire (*orexis*), since anything which perceives also has a capacity for pleasure and pain. Having an awareness of pleasure and pain, however, implicates the subject of perception (*aisthêsis*) in desire (*orexis*).

Elsewhere Aristotle denies that all animals have imagination (415a6–11, 428a9–11), which seems to contradict the chain of inference here. The probable resolution turns on the two forms of imagination distinguished at 433b31–434a10, perceptual and deliberative, coupled with Aristotle's suggestion that determinateness of image may be scalar. (For the scalarity of imagination and its relevance in resolving the seeming contradiction in the present passage, see the note to 433b31–434a5).

In the present context, his main point is that separation in account does not entail separation in place. One question regarding the force of Aristotle's reasoning pertains to whether the grounds offered are simply factive, that as a matter of fact we never find creatures with perception lacking desire, or something more, some nomological connection stronger than mere contingent concomitance but weaker than metaphysical necessity of the sort required by sameness in account. Though the observations adduced here would not by themselves warrant the stronger inference, the teleological arguments of *De Anima* III 12 push for the stronger connection.

As usual, reason (*nous*) is singled out as requiring special consideration. The question regarding its status was raised early on, at 403a3–16; 408b18–29, and 413a2–7. These questions recur; and they also introduce *De Anima* III 4, the first chapter devoted to reason (429a11). Here the phrase translated as 'reason... seems to be a different genus of soul' (*psuchês genos heteron* at 413b25–6) might also be rendered, improbably, as 'reason... seems to be a different kind of thing from soul'. One might prefer the second rendering insofar as the translation offerred in the text may seem to suggest that reason, a capacity of soul, is itself also a soul, with the result that Aristotle has implicated himself in some kind of category mistake by confusing a capacity belonging to a substance with a substance proper. Since, however, he is willing to speak of the *reasoning soul* (*noêtikê psuchê*; 429a28), it is probably safe to understand him as speaking elliptically here: 'When it comes to reason, we confront a different sort of soul.' Cf. also the tentative suggestion that 'reason would seem to come about in us being a certain substance (*ousia*) and not to be destroyed' (408b1–19, with note), and also Aristotle's remark at *Met.* I 10, 1058b36–1059a10, where he claims that the perishable (*to phtharton*) and the imperishable (*to aphtharton*) cannot belong to a common genus (*genos*), which is continuous with the sort of point he is making about reason in this passage.

**414a4–19: An Ambiguity Resolved:** The soul has been broadly characterized in functional terms as 'that in virtue of which we are alive and perceive' (414a12–13), with the result that the presence of soul distinguishes the living from the non-living. Now Aristotle returns to this topic by noting that the phrase 'that in virtue of which *x* is φ' is crucially ambiguous, between: (i) the form whose presence makes *x* φ, and (ii) the substrate capable of realizing the form, that is, the substrate capable of becoming φ. One may say, e.g., that Socrates is healthy in virtue of health, or in virtue of his body being such as to realize health.

The illustration regarding knowledge is a bit trickier, since the soul is potentially such as to know, and is thus, in the illustration, what plays the role of the body relative to health. To see the point of Aristotle's example, it is necessary to bear in mind that the soul can be both the actuality of some body and also itself potentially such as to be φ. Here Aristotle is thinking of the soul as potentially such as to know. Taken together, his examples suggest that when we say that the soul is that in virtue of which one is alive, we might mean that: (i) the soul is the form whose presence makes someone alive, or (ii) the soul is a body of an appropriately disposed sort. According to (ii), but not (i), the soul is itself a composite entity, in whose own account formal and material features must be mentioned. Conversely, according to (i), but not (ii), the soul is a purely formal entity. It is consequently important to disambiguate what is meant by saying that the soul is that in virtue of which we live.

Although this section is fraught with textual difficulties, the progress of Aristotle's argument is clear enough. Indeed, we know where we are heading ultimately, since the soul has already been distinguished from the body (the matter) and the compound of matter and form (see 412a11–21, with note). Here he adduces several additional considerations favouring this conclusion. First, the body is a capacity or potentiality (*dunamis*) and not an actualization; but the soul is what actualizes the body. Indeed, says Aristotle, the soul is that by which we live and perceive *primarily* (*prôtôs*) (414a13), where the implication is that what is capable of receiving the form is alive in a secondary or derivative sense. Aristotle often treats 'primarily' in this sort of context as interchangeable with 'properly or 'centrally' (*kuriôs*), or 'simply' in the sense of 'unqualifiedly' (*haplôs*) (cf. 403b29; *Met.* 1015b11, 1016b8, 1030b5, 1031a13, 1052a18; *EN* 1157a30). The effect, then, is to treat the soul as what explains the presence of life in a primary and non-derivative way. This in turn explains Aristotle's parenthetical suggestion that 'the actuality of productive things seems to reside in what is affected and is disposed to receive it' (414a11–12). He means that the body's being actualized as a living being resides in the body, in virtue of the soul, in much the same way that learning occurs within a pupil by means of the agency of a teacher teaching (cf. *Phys.* 202a13).

Aristotle once again relies on the actuality (*entelecheia*) of the soul as form in arguing that the soul is that primarily in virtue of which we live (414a12–19). His argument runs:

(1) If *x* accounts for something's being actually *F*, then *x* is non-derivatively that in virtue of which *x* is *F*.

(2) The soul, as form and so as something actual, rather than the body, which as matter is something potential, accounts for a body's being actually alive.

(3) Hence the soul is non-derivatively that in virtue of which the compound of soul and body is alive.

(3) specifies Aristotle's reason for treating the soul as form, and so as resolving his initial ambiguity in favour of (i), that the soul is a form whose presence makes a body a living being.

**414a19–28: Summary and Conclusions:** The summary restates and reinforces conclusions established, though now from a slightly different angle. Aristotle takes the occasion of summarizing his conclusions to reach back and add a parting criticism of those among his predecessors who had attempted to yoke random bodies and souls together without understanding the need for them to be suitably fitted to one another. Although he does not mention his targets by name, the criticism here is immediately reminiscent of the objections of *De Anima* I 3, launched principally against the Pythagoreans, though generalized to include others as well. (See note to 407b14–26.) In the current context, Aristotle regards himself as further justified in those criticisms because it has now been shown that soul and body are related as actuality to potentiality. Since $y$ can make $x$ actually $\phi$ only if $x$ is potentially $\phi$ and suited to be made actually $\phi$ by $y$, while $y$ is actually and in a primary way such as to make $x$ actually $\phi$, it follows that those who pay no attention to the commonalities required for soul-body connections have gone astray.

In saying that the soul is an 'organization' (*logos;* 414b27) of a suitably potential sort of body, Aristotle uses the word *logos* in its non-linguistic sense, according to which a *logos* is a structuring principle of matter, equivalent to form (*eidos*) (as earlier in this chapter at 414a9 and 414a13; cf. 403a25, with note; *Phys.* 209a21; *Met.* 1006b1, 1030a7, 1044b12, 1058b19).

CHAPTER 3

### Introduction to II 3

Among mortal living beings, the faculties of soul are nested, so that, of necessity, what has reason also has perception, and anything with perception also has nutrition. An immediate question concerns the force of the necessity Aristotle intends when advancing this hierarchy. Plainly, in view of the qualifier regarding mortals (on which, see note to 413a31–b10), the necessity cannot be broadly logical or metaphysical: Aristotle himself thinks that there are imperishable rational beings which lack any psychic capacity beyond reason. On the form of necessity in play, see note to 414a29–b16.

A second question concerns a difficult, highly suggestive comparison Aristotle offers between psychic capacities and the series of geometric figures (414b19–415a3). This comparison grounds two important theses, both with significant consequences for the proper understanding of the soul and its capacities. The first concerns the soul's general definability, a result which colours the various accounts of the soul advanced in the last two chapters. The second concerns how we are to conceive the intrinsic relations of the various faculties. Aristotle takes care to reject a natural, basically extensional picture, according to which the capacities of the soul are regarded as discrete components, related to one another more or less in the manner of a layer cake. On that view, each capacity is a sort of discrete, self-contained layer, and if the higher layers depend upon the lower, it is only because they rest upon them. They do not interpenetrate in any significant way. Importantly, Aristotle rejects this position by insisting that lower souls are present only in potentiality (*dunamei*; 414b28) in higher souls: 'for in the case of both figures and ensouled things, what is prior is always present potentially in what follows in a series—for example, the triangle in the square, and nutritive faculty in the perceptual faculty' (414b29–32).

Aristotle's rejection of this picture has immediate and negative consequences for those who maintain that on his account the soul is a set of capacities, where this is understood to mean inter alia that each capacity is a discrete element, detatchable from the whole. His rejection thus has equally immediate and significant consequences for our understanding of his approach to the soul's unity.

For an introduction to Aristotle's treatment of the capacities of the soul, see the General Introduction § IV.

**414a29–b16: From Perception to Desire:** Every soul has at least one of the capacities determinative of life, and among those with more than one there is an asymmetry in terms of possession implications. The capacities enumerated here as determinative of life are: nutrition (*threptikon*), perception (*aisthêtikon*), desire (*orektikon*), motion with respect to place (*kinêtikon kata topon*), and understanding (*dianoêtikon*) (414a31–2). As Aristotle notes, he had already mentioned these matters in the last chapter, at 413a30–b10 and 413b11–13; he will return to them again late in the work at 434a22–30 and 434b9–25.

In this section of the text, Aristotle argues twice over for the first of the chapter's two main contentions, that there is a kind of implication relation between the higher and lower faculties of soul— 'higher' and 'lower' at least in so far as their asymmetric dependency relations suggest. Here he argues that any creature with a perceptual faculty also has desire. His first argument is accessible and clear, though his second is truncated and obscure. Both arguments contend that perception (*aisthêsis*) implies desire (*orexis*), the first via a connection of perception to the pleasurable and the second via the role of touch in the acquisition of nutrition.

When arguing that perception implies desire, Aristotle draws upon his not perfectly consistent terminology pertaining to the desiderative and motivational faculties of animals, rational or otherwise. For the progress of the argument, it is important to appreciate that here he treats desire (*orexis*) and the desiderative faculty (the *orektikon*) as generic terms, covering appetite (*epithumia*), spirit (*thumos*), and wish (*boulêsis*), all of which are here regarded as species of desire. In the present context, it is important to appreciate that Aristotle tends to connect the last species of desire mentioned, wish (*boulêsis*), primarily to the rational part of the soul and the first two, appetite (*epithumia*) and spirit (*thumos*), primarily to the non-rational, as at 432b5; further, he equally supposes that animals with rational desires also have non-rational desires. Hence, when he contends that perception implies appetite (*epithumia*), he likewise contends the faculty of perception present in rational animals implies desire (*orexis*). (Cf. Plato, *Republic* iv, 434d–445e), where appetite and spirit are extended to non-rational animals; and also *Rhet.* 1369a3, where Aristotle makes the good the object of wish (*boulêsis*), and *EN* 1116b23–1117a9, where he approaches the complex notion of spirit (*thumos*).)

Aristotle's first argument for the thesis that the perceptual faculty of the soul implies desire exploits this connection between non-rational desire and pleasure:

(1) If *x* has perception, then *x* has perception of the pleasurable and the painful.
(2) If *x* has perception of the pleasurable, then *x* has appetite (*epithumia*).
(3) Appetite (*epithumia*) is a kind of desire (*orexis*), namely desire for the pleasurable.
(4) Hence if *x* has perception, then *x* has desire.

Evidently, as Aristotle conceives it, if (2) is to be given a true reading, then (1) requires not just that *x* perceive what is in fact pleasurable, but that *x* perceive the pleasurable *as pleasurable*. This probably explains some of Aristotle's language in stating this argument, which is at first a bit cumbersome: 'that to which perception belongs, to this belongs also both pleasure and pain, as well as both the pleasurable and the painful' (414b4–5). His point, when unpacked, is so far perfectly reasonable, even pedestrian: all animals in fact experience pleasure and pain, and they track the pleasurable and the painful—i.e. track objects in the environment capable of providing pleasure or pain. If, though, animals track the pleasurable as pleasurable, then they attend to what *appears* pleasurable to them. If an animal seeks the pleasurable insofar as it appears pleasurable, then its doing so is a function of its having appetite, which is a species of desire.

The argument does not, then, posit a conceptual necessity between perceiving and desiring, but nor does it therefore trade on a mere accidental concomitance. Presumably, Aristotle will appeal to teleological considerations to defend (1) (see notes to 413a30–b10 and 434b9–25); otherwise, if a stronger connection is to be asserted, his claim will fail, since it is plainly metaphysically possible for an animal to have perception without therefore having perception of the pleasurable. He will need at least this much in favour of (1), however, since otherwise it might just be an accidental concomitance that (1) is true, which in turn would result in its being the case that it might also then be an accidental concomitance that beings with perception (*aisthêsis*) also have a faculty of desire (*orexis*). Presumably Aristotle is after a stronger conclusion than just that.

The argument is open to other queries as well. We might allow (3) as somehow analytic, or as harmlessly stipulated: appetite is a desire for the pleasurable; so, in line with the final conclusion (4), whatever has appetite, has desire. Yet such a stipulation would not show, in any but the most trivial of senses, that whatever has appetites has a *faculty* (*dunamis*) of desire—unless this just collapses into the claim that whatever desires anything is able to desire things. In that case, however, Aristotle's argument would be otiose: Alicibiades has the ability to love and be loved, as well as the ability to act with vanity, but Aristotle nowhere suggests that he therefore has a love faculty, an *erôtikon,* or a vanity faculty, a *kenodoxikon.* If this is all that were at stake, there would for every ability to φ be a trivial transformation to the existence of a φ-*tikon*, a φ-capacity, and no argument of the sort being offered would be necessary. Aristotle is thus presupposing a stronger notion of capacity (*dunamis*), but he does not characterize it in any general or abstract way here.

The second argument tying perception to desire, which runs from 414b6–16, is less clear and a good deal more complex. It trades on the fact that in Aristotle's view any creature with perception has at least the sense of touch (cf. 434a30–b8). Only the outline of the argument is reasonably clear:

(1) If $x$ has a faculty of perception, then $x$ has at least the sense of touch.
(2) Touch is employed in the identification of food (in part because taste turns out to be a kind of touch; cf. 422a8, 423a17–20).
(3) If $x$ identifies food, then $x$ identifies an object of appetite.
(4) Hence, if $x$ has perception, $x$ has appetite.

If this is the argument's main thrust, then it adds little to the first argument; it is, rather, a specification of something already given: food is an object of appetite.

That said, there are some obscurities in the details of the argument worth mentioning, because of their being likely to cause confusion. As translated, the point about touch having other objects co-incidentally is not strictly relevant to the argument, though it is not altogether irrelevant either: 'Touch is perception of other sensibles co-incidentally' (414b9–10). Presumably, Aristotle is anticipating an objection to the effect that touch is not restricted to food, since we can also touch objects with colours, sounds, and scents. His response is that we do not touch colours, sounds, or scents as exclusive (*idia*) objects of touch. Even so, we do touch flavours, since taste will prove to be a kind of touch (cf. 422a8, 423a17–20). Aristotle will return to the issue of exclusive versus co-incidental objects of perception in II 6.

**414b16–19 Motion, Imagination, and Understanding:** Aristotle opened the chapter by listing not only the faculties he has dwelt upon thus far, perception, desire, and the nutritive faculty, but also motion with respect to place and understanding (414a31–2). He now mentions the two previously ignored capacities and observes that imagination (*phantasia*) has an unclear status. Presumably its unclarity derives first from the question of whether it is a fully fledged capacity, on par with the others listed and having its own distinctive individuating objects; but it is equally problematic because of its complicated relations to the other faculties of soul. For Aristotle's treatment of imagination, see III 3. On the relation of imagination to reason (*nous*), see 403a8; on its relation to perception (*aisthêsis*), see 433b31–434a2. There Aristotle will quite reasonably puzzle over whether animals which have only the sense of touch should be supposed to have imagination, that is, whether perception as such, in its most rudimentary form, implies imagination.

In the current passage, Aristotle seems oddly tentative about the existence of rational creatures distinct from and superior to humans. He affirms their existence quite clearly at *Met.* 1073a23–34 and again at *EN* 1141a34–b1. Perhaps he means to suggest in the present context only that such beings are not in the purview of the current discussion regarding the implication relations between psychic faculties. This is, in any event, a point he makes clear towards the end of the chapter, at 415a9 (cf. 413a32).

**414b19–415a11: Souls and Figures: Consequences for Unity and Definition:** In his agenda-setting I 1, Aristotle had set down as a central question for investigation whether there is but one definition of the soul, or rather several, each corresponding to a distinct class of beings, one for dogs, another for humans, and still another for god (402b5–9). He now addresses this question by comparing the hierarchy of souls to the succession of figures, contending that the nutritive faculty of soul is present *in potentiality* in the perceptual soul, and the perceptual in the rational, in the way that a triangle is present in a square (414b30–1). He maintains further that there will be a general account of the soul taken as a whole in much the same way that there is a general account of figure spanning triangles, squares and on up in a series—an account which is not also an account of any given kind of figure. From this comparison Aristotle has often been understood to deny that a general account of soul as such is possible (Rodier (1900), Siwek (1965), Ward (1996)). Bolton (1978) offers a more nuanced assessment.

Such an understanding of the comparison of souls and figures overstates the case. To begin, any such contention would be jarring immediately after Aristotle has just himself provided not one but several general accounts of the soul (412a27–b1), if at times with a tinge of reluctance, as at 412b4–6. Further, so strong a reading in any case misrepresents what is asserted here. Aristotle does not in fact conclude that it is impossible to forge a general account of soul; on the contrary, he maintains that a common account *is* possible for souls, as for figures, but insists that it would be ludicrous (*geloion*; 414b25) to seek such an account 'while neglecting what is of this sort' (*aphentas ton toiouton*; 414b27–8)—namely what is distinctive of the diverse kinds of souls corresponding to the variegated living beings we encounter, beings whose distinction from one another turns precisely upon the level of and kind of psychic capacity they manifest.

In addition to the language of this passage, an instructive parallel may be found in the *Politics*, where Aristotle draws an analogous inference about citizens and governments (1275a33–b1), which he holds in a similar way to be arranged in a series (cf. *EN* 1096a19–35; *EE* 1218a1–8; *Met.* 999a6–10 for analogous claims in other arenas, usually advanced with an anti-Platonic purport). One can offer a general definition of 'government' or 'citizen', but the common account is thin, and scarcely (*glischrôs*; 1275a38) captures anything about, say, democracy or tyranny or monarchy. There is a sense in which a feudal serf of tsarist Russia and a capitalist entrepreneur living in Tokyo in the twenty-first century are both citizens—but we will not learn much about the political life of either without going on to provide content to the sort of citizen each is. So too with the soul: without specifying what kind of soul we are considering, implies Aristotle, our common account, however correct, will not yield much information about the life of a given ensouled being.

For these sorts of reasons, Aristotle focuses attention in his psychology on the capacity-driven approach he prefers. An account of the perceptual soul is more informative, because more contentful, than an account of the soul in the abstract, something common to all levels of soul but not a complete account of a nutritive or a perceptual or a rational soul. In comparing souls to figures, Aristotle shows himself to have a primary interest in questions pertaining to the nature of the soul's faculties, but then also, in a less pronounced way, to the relation of the faculties to one another.

Here, on the question of the relation of the faculties to one another, Aristotle contends only briefly that among perishable beings souls form a kind of hierarchy, given in terms of asymmetries of implication of existence. He offers a fuller justification for this contention, given in teleological terms, in III 12–13 (see the chapter Introduction to III 12, along with note to 434a22–434b8). The comparison of souls and figures also has important consequences pertaining to the unity of the soul. It has been tempting for some among Aristotle's interpreters to regard the hierarchy of souls extensionally, so that a rational soul is conceived as a set of capacities stacked one upon the other in the manner of a layer cake (see the General Introduction § IV, n.9). He insists, however, that just as a square is not an actual triangle with a spare leg, or, going up the hierarchy of figures, that any given n-sided figure has an actual n-1 figure inscribed within it, a perceptual soul is not merely a nutritive soul with a perceptual faculty stacked on top. Rather, the lower-soul capacities are present in the higher souls only in potentiality (414b28–32). The exact purport of this claim, and of the comparison with figures in general, turns, of course, on the sense in which prior figures are in posterior figures in potentiality.

Two interpretations have seemed attractive: (i) a square has two triangles discernible in it, sharing the diagonal as a side, a pentagon a square inscribable within it, and so on; and (ii) an n-1-sided figure is prior in an n-sided figure in that an n-1-sided figure requires fewer angles for its construction, namely n-1 rather than n (triangles have three angles, squares four, and so on up the series). In this respect, the priority is akin to the series of numbers discussed at *Met.* 999a1–16, where numbers are explicitly compared to figures in terms of priority and posteriority.

Of these interpretations, (ii) seems preferable. The point thus understood suggests that souls of any number of capacities are unities, with any lower-order souls discernible in higher-order souls only potentially in the sense that a removal of a higher capacity will generate a lower-order soul which is itself an actuality and a complete psychic unity. By contrast, a higher-order soul is not discernible in a lower-order soul. Looked at another way, Aristotle's point is simply that higher-order souls actually manifest lower-order capacities, whereas lower-order souls trivially do not manifest higher-order capacities. Yet he claims, crucially, that these lower capacities are present only in potentiality (*dunamei*; 414b29) in the higher. He thus wants to insist on an asymmetry between higher- and lower-order souls, but to do so without endorsing an extensional or aggregative account of souls; such approaches are inconsistent with the sort of unity he envisages for souls as forms. This feature of Aristotle's conception of the soul generated a good deal of discussion in later, medieval Aristotelianism, where it was often assessed with a particular emphasis on the question of unity. Of course, the question of unity will be conditioned in the first instance by the conception of 'parts' (*merê*) we may have in view when posing the question. For Aristotle's distinction between quantitative and non-quantitative parts, see note to 402a23–b8. For a treatment of how soul capacities came to be treated as present only in potentiality, or only 'virtually', see Shields (2014); for an instructive discussion of souls and soul faculties in general, see Perler (2015).

Perhaps if we connect the two main consequences of the chapter we can better appreciate why one faculty, the faculty of desire (*orektikon*), will manifest itself differently in rational and non-rational animals: a rational soul will, as rational, have a richly articulated conceptualization of the objects of its pursuit unavailable to a non-rational animal. This is, then, another important way in which the hierarchy of souls is not merely extensional: higher-order faculties bleed into lower-order faculties, with the result that lower-order faculties will be altered by their subordination to the higher. A near implication seems to be that John Stuart Mill and his pig will have, or will have available to them, distinct perceptual experiences when sharing a bottle of St. Emilion. Later in *De Anima*, Aristotle will also distinguish two ways in which the imagination (*phantasia*) is present in rational and non-rational animals (see note to 433b19–30), and then will even proceed to offer more fine-grained accounts of the way in which imagination is to be understood in connection with the deliberative faculty, on which, see note to 434a5–10.

**415a12–13: Final Conclusion:**　　The last sentence of the chapter looks forward to the accounts of the capacities of the soul which begin in earnest in the next chapter, starting with the nutritive soul. Importantly, the final purport of the chapter ties the investigations of the sundry capacities of the soul to the study of the soul itself: to learn what is substantive about the soul is to learn about the nutritive soul, or the perceptual soul, or the rational soul; and to learn about these souls is to learn about the faculties which dominate and define them.

## CHAPTER 4

### Introduction to II 4

Aristotle embraces the procedure articulated at the end of the last chapter by conducting his substantive inquiry into the soul by focusing first on its most fundamental and common capacity: the nutritive and generative capacity. Despite its having these two distinct functions, Aristotle speaks of it as a single capacity of soul. This is the capacity which, among mortals, denotes the presence of life; it thus serves to differentiate the living from the non-living.

In this chapter, Aristotle settles a question of method raised in the agenda-setting I 1, concerning how best to approach the faculties of soul, there called 'parts' (*moria*): are we to consider first the part, its activity, or its object (402b10–14; cf. notes to 402a23–b8, 402b9–16, 418a11–17, and 429b10–21)? He now answers that we consider the objects first, then the activity, and finally the part or capacity. This order of inquiry derives from the individuation conditions assumed by Aristotle for psychic capacities (on which, see Everson (1995)). What makes hearing one sensory modality and seeing another is their having exclusive objects which are necessarily discrete: no colour is in its nature a sound. Extrapolating from the sensory modalities, the same principle of individuation will pertain to the distinct capacities of soul: what makes perception distinct from thought is that perception detects perceptible objects and reason detects intelligible objects. This method then raises a question as to the appropriate objects of the nutritive soul: in this chapter, Aristotle contends that it is food, or nutriment (*trophê*—a word, like 'nourishment' in English, which can be used to denote either food or the process of being nourished). Interestingly, for something to be counted as food, it must already be characterized in terms of its ability to provide nourishment, that is, with reference to its use relative to a living system outside itself (see note to 416b9–11). To some extent both Greek and English diction reflect this fact: for carnivores, the flesh of other animals is *meat*; and plants cultivated for food are *crops* (cf. *Phys.* II 218b17–32).

**415a14–22: Some Methodological Precepts:** This section answers some of the questions posed in I 1, at 402b10–14, regarding how best to approach an analysis of the capacities of the soul. Aristotle contends that we begin first by identifying the objects correlative to a capacity, turn next to the activity determinative of the capacity, and then finally advance an account of the capacity itself. This order of explication is not recommended as a matter of convenience. Rather, a capacity is essentially a functionally defined entity individuated by its correlative objects (see the Introduction to this chapter).

This understanding assumes that the 'priority' mentioned in 415a18–22 of activities to capacities and of correlative objects to activities is definitional and not merely epistemic, that is, that Aristotle is here relying on a general functional determination thesis rather than on a priority in the order of our understanding alone. This understanding is reflected in the translation of the phrase *kata ton logon* at 415a19–20, as priority 'in account'. An alternative, acceptable translation, favoured by many of Aristotle's commentators treats *kata ton logon* as priority 'in thought'. This may (but perhaps need not) be because there is a more narrowly epistemic understanding of his procedure for individuating capacities, to the effect that we tend, when thinking about the soul's faculties, to begin by thinking of its objects first. While this approach is possible linguistically, it obscures Aristotle's motivation for grounding activities in the priority of their objects, which is given here in terms of the priority of actuality to potentiality, on which, see *Met.* 1049b10–17 and 1071b12–1072a18.

It is difficult to avoid circularities, whether vicious or not, in Aristotle's procedure of faculty individuation, if, that is, the objects in terms of which they are individuated are to be understood as both necessary and sufficient for that task but then are also characterized in terms of those very tasks. If we accept, e.g., colour as the object of sight, and so as individuating sight from smell and hearing, we run into difficulty if we then proceed to define or even characterize colour in terms of its being the sort of quality detected by sight. For an instance of this threatening circularity in the case of the nutritive soul, see note to 416b9–11.

A second sort of worry concerns Aristotle's willingness to treat the nutritive and generative soul as effectively rooted in the same capacity. If discrete objects are sufficient for distinct activities, which are in turn sufficient for distinct faculties, then we should expect the nutritive and generative faculties to be distinct. Yet Aristotle does not conceive of them as distinct. On this worry, see the following note, to 415a22–b7.

**415a22–b7: The Functions of the Nutritive Soul:** The nutritive soul, the most natural and common soul whose defining capacity is shared by all living things, has a dual function: it not only processes food but generates others like itself. (Elsewhere Aristotle goes so far as to say that the nutritive soul *is* also the generative soul, at *Gen. An.* 740b29–741a2; he also explores this same theme in more detail below at 416b11–28.) This may be thought to violate a reasonable definitional stricture laid down elsewhere to the effect that each functional kind has but one essential function (*Pol.* 1252b1–5), and indeed, it seems to run foul of the suggestion that faculties of the soul are individuated by their objects—if, that is, discreteness of object is thought to be necessary and sufficient for distinctness of faculty. Here, however, Aristotle seems to be thinking of nutrition and generation as twin aspects of the same overarching function, one serving the drive for self-preservation.

This would explain why he moves immediately to suggest that living beings seek immortality by their participation in the eternal species via generation, a point akin to one given voice by Plato (*Symp.* 207a–d, *Laws* 721b–c) and repeated by Aristotle at *Gen. An.* 731b24–732a1. The generic function of self-preservation manifests itself in the individual qua individual by its eating, and in the individual qua member of an everlasting species by its reproductive activities. This propensity towards self-propagation or preservation is common to all living beings.

Still, Aristotle notes, there are mutants of various kinds and immature members of every species whose drive towards reproduction is inoperative. He also at the same time seeks to set aside beings which are 'spontaneously generated' (415a27–8), which reflects his false but empirically motivated belief that various animals, including insects, generated out of putrefying matter (*Hist. An.* 539a22–5, 569a13–19, 25–6, 570a2–10; *Gen. An.* 763a24–b5). These sorts of cases seem to show that beings who take on nutrition are not extensionally equivalent with beings capable of engaging in generation. So, these capacities cannot be even extensionally equivalent, let alone identical.

Aristotle's response to this worry is not completely clear. In the case of monstrosities and the maimed, he tends to blame deficient matter; immature members of the species are not yet completely actual, and need to become so before engaging in reproduction (cf. *Gen. An.* iv 4). Perhaps, then, he takes himself to be treating only the faculties of fully normal or fully functioning members of a species. That there is a normative dimension to his approach seems confirmed by Aristotle's elsewhere characterizing the deformed as 'contrary to nature' (*para phusin*) (*Gen. An.* 770b9). Here, Aristotle uses correlative language when introducing the everlasting and divine as what 'everything desires, and for the sake of that everything does whatever it does in accordance with nature (*kata phusin*)' (415b1–2).

The parenthetical remark about two senses of 'that for the sake of which' (*hou heneka*; 415b2) is repeated just below at 415b20–1; it may be an interpolation in one or both of the passages; in neither is it required for good sense, though it is perfectly relevant to both. In any event, the point is that we might specify one of two different states of affairs when citing a final cause: the subject who benefits or the benefit which is being sought. (He who writes music 'only for the sake of entertainment' might, but need not, find his own music entertaining.) This distinction took on an important life of its own in later Aristotelianism, and this passage was routinely cited as its first expression (see, e.g., Suárez, *Disp. Met.* XXIII 2.1); it was commonplace in medieval philosophy to distinguish an end considered as *finis cuius*, the end sought, e.g. health, and *finis cui*, the beneficiary for whom the end is sought, e.g. a patient whose health is to be restored.

Aristotle would reasonably be prompted in the current context to apprise his readers of the distinction, since it makes sense of his suggestion that each living thing seeks to 'partake of the everlasting and the divine', but only 'insofar as it is able' (415a30–b1). The activity of reproduction leads to a state whose attainment is sought (= *finis cuius*), though it is not a state from which the actor is a personal beneficiary (in this case the actor is not the *finis cui*).

**415b8–27: Soul as Cause and Substance:**   This section digresses from the main thread of the chapter, though as a self-contained excursus it is especially rich in its characterizations of the causal character of the soul. The soul is a cause (*aitia*) and principle or source (*archê*) of the living body. Importantly, the soul is in these respects prior to the body, a consequence sometimes underappreciated by those interpretations of Aristotle's hylomorphic approach to soul-body relations which assimilate the soul to a quality or feature of the body, as the form of a bronze statue might be thought of as a quality or feature of some quantity of bronze. (On the priority of the soul to the body, see Shields (2009).).

The treatment of the soul as a cause and source is in keeping with Aristotle's general hylomorphism; the soul has the features which Aristotle imputes to all substantial forms. Here, Aristotle makes clear that the soul is a cause of the living body in three of the four ways in which things can be causes: it is the formal, final, and efficient cause. That it is not the material cause is plain enough, since it is rather the body itself which is the material cause of a compound. Aristotle groups the formal, final, and efficient causes together in distinguishing them from the material cause, elsewhere suggesting, as here, that one and the same entity can be the formal, final, and efficient cause of another (*Phys.* 194b16–35, 198a14; *Met.* 983a26, 1013a24–b3).

The current passage is usefully read in conjunction with *Generation and Corruption* I 5, where Aristotle makes clear that form as essence is identified with the final cause (*Gen. et Corr.* 335b5–7), just as the soul is in this passage. More generally, the account of growth in that chapter is continuous with the present discussion, and shows in greater depth why substantial forms cannot be identified with qualities. A growing organism has numerically one and the same form even while its qualities alter (*Gen. et Cor.* 321b28–34). (For more on Aristotle's general soul-body hylomorphism, see the General Introduction § III.A.)

Aristotle introduces the soul as the formal, final, and efficient causes as follows:

*Soul as Formal Cause* (415b12–15): Aristotle does not in fact assert in this passage that the soul is the form of the living body, but says rather that it is its substance (*ousia*). Even so, he regularly identifies form as the substance of that whose being it provides (*Met.* 1041a27–b10) and has already in any case identified the soul as the substance *as form* at 412a20. He also refers to it as organization (*logos*) of the body, a locution sometimes used interchangeably with *form* (*eidos*; cf. 403a25, 403b2; *Phys.* 209a21; *Met.* 1044b22, 1058b19). The argument in this section provides much more content than was given in the bald assertion of 412a20. Aristotle argues:

(1) The substance (*ousia*) of x is the cause of x's being (or essence, *aition tou einai*; 415b12–13).
(2) In a living system, being (or essence) is the same as being alive (415b13).
(3) Hence, the *ousia* of a living system is the cause of its being alive.
(4) The soul is the cause of being alive (cf. 414a12).
(5) Hence, the soul is the *ousia* of a living system (415b13).

While each of the premises invites scrutiny, only (2) is a novel and substantive claim, one which helps ground the assertion made at 412a20 regarding the soul as form. Aristotle says, with an arresting concision that 'and living is being for living things' (*to de zên tois zôsi to einai esti*; 415b13). One immediate consequence is that every living being is essentially alive: its being or essence (*to einai*) *is* its being alive.

Otherwise, it should be appreciated regarding (1), the claim that the substance (*ousia*) of x is the cause of x's being is to be taken predicatively, so that what is being said, more fully, is that the substance (*ousia*) of x is the cause of x's being φ, where φ is any substantial predicate. So, to expand, the substance of a human is the cause of that human's being human. This cause is the formal cause. In arguing this way, Aristotle draws directly on the conclusion he offers regarding substance as form in *Metaphysics* Z 17, especially 1041b27–8: 'this is the substance of each thing, for this is the primary cause of its being <φ>' (cf. also *Met.* 1017b14–16).

*Soul as Final Cause* (415b15–21): Aristotle's language here is confident and striking. He treats the soul as an end in a very strong sense: the body is an *organ* of the soul, that is, an instrument used to bring the soul's activities to fruition. Further, the view here is once again continuous with the difficult discussion of

*Metaphysics* Z 17, and seems to draw upon it (especially 1041a27–32, where the formal cause being sought is said also to be the final cause of the substantial being whose form it is). The fuller discussion in *Metaphysics* Z 17 makes clear that the presence of an individual soul explains what makes so much matter a synchronic and diachronic unity. In and around a living body there are countless discrete material interactions and causal processes. What selects the relevant subset of those interactions and processes as *bodily* processes is, Aristotle contends, their subordination to the singular end provided by the soul. It is for this reason and in this sense that he maintains that the body is an organ of the soul. The body is posterior to the soul in that its identity conditions are parasitic upon it. For similar remarks about the soul's relation to the body, see 407b25 and *Part. An.* 642a9–11, with 645b14. For an account of the posteriority of the body to the soul, see Shields (2009) and for the broader background of the relation between *Metaphysics* Z 17 and the substantiality of the soul, see Shields (2008).

*Soul as Efficient Cause* (415b21–6): The presence of the soul equally accounts for a full range of motions and alterations, ranging from locomotion, growth, decay, and even perception (*aisthêsis*), which is introduced here as a sort of alteration: 'perception seems to be a sort of alteration' (*aisthêsis alloiôsis tis einai dokei*; 415b24). Perhaps Aristotle means only that perception is an alteration—sort of; his Greek is ambiguous on this point, since the word '*tis*' here translated as 'a sort' might also be rendered as 'sort of'—the so-called *alienans tis*. In any event, Aristotle eventually will deny that perception is properly thought of as a kind of alteration (416b33–4, 431a5, with note to 416b32–417a2; see also the General Introduction § IV.B).

Whatever type of alteration perception may be, 'nothing perceives which does not partake of the soul' (*aisthanetai d' outhen ho mê metechei psuchês*; 415b24–5). As above at 415b29, Aristotle uses a verb with Platonic resonances in this passage: 'to participate in' (*metechein*). He elsewhere criticizes Plato for using this word as a way of describing the connection between sensibles and Forms (*Met.* 990b31, 1037b19), though he finds it useful himself in other contexts, as when speaking of the logical relations between definitions (*Top.* 121a12). Here the word seems to be used in a fairly non-technical sense (cf. 406a12, 22, 410b23,

412a5, 416b9, 433b30). One might also render it as 'has a share in', but that has been reserved for the similar verb *koinônein* ('to have a share of' or 'to have in common with') used just below at 415b27.

However that may be, Aristotle here introduces little argument for his claim that the soul is an efficient cause, mainly relying instead on the observation that all and only living things engage in a full range of activities. Since soul is coextensive with life, it is plausible to regard the soul as the relevant causally sufficient factor. Earlier, in I 3 he had introduced as a datum that the soul moves the body by means of decision (*proairesis*) and reasoning (*noêsis*) (406b24–5; with note to 406a16–b25).

**415b28–416a18: Against Empedocles; Against Heracleitus (?)**
Aristotle's criticism of Empedocles has several related well-springs. First, and foremost, an account of the body's unity given only in terms of the elements is insufficient. If, as Aristotle supposes, the various elements have natural directionalities (fire up and earth down), then something in addition to the mere presence of the elements is required to explain unity. If left to their own devices, earth and fire would head off in their naturally opposite directions. What principle holds them together? According to Aristotle, this principle is the soul (416a8). What is more, he maintains, any attempt to explain perceived directionality in terms of the basic tendencies of the elements is unduly anthropomorphic: the top of a plant is not its head, nor its blossom its mouth. Organs are functionally individuated, with the result that the roots of a plant, through which nutrition enters the plant, are analogous to the mouth (cf. 412b3; cf. *Part. An.* 686b18).

Another sort of elemental account challenges Aristotle's preferred efficient cause of nutrition and growth, which is, again, the soul. Aristotle does not name the proponent of this account, but likely has Heracleitus in mind as his target (cf. *Met.* 984a7–8). Perhaps, because alone among the elements, fire is seen to spread and thus is said to 'grow' and also to 'consume' what it finds in its path, one should identify fire as the cause of nutrition and growth in living beings. Aristotle will himself implicitly deny that this way of speaking of fire can be both literal and correct at 416b9. Here, though, he is more concerned to resist any suggestion that fire could be a sufficient explanation of nutrition and growth, because fire spreads in an unpatterned and unconstrained way, flowing towards the combustible without end, whereas living systems nourish themselves in patterned, limited ways, reaching maturity and then ceasing to grow. Instead, fire is at best a kind of co-cause (*sunaition*), a term Aristotle elsewhere identifies as a necessary condition, a mere *sine qua non* (e.g. *Met.* 1015a20). His rejoinder is, then, partly conciliatory: perhaps fire, or heat, is required for processing food in nutrition; but the presence of fire cannot alone suffice to explain the life process of nutrition. Aristotle himself allows near the end of the chapter that the soul, as final cause, employs heat in the digestion of food (416b27–8). Typically, then, Aristotle's complaint is not that the Heracleitean-style account is positively wrong-headed, but only that it is woefully incomplete. This sort of sentiment is equally the purport of the final sentences of his criticism: Aristotle closes by making clear that he understands the suggestion being rejected to be a species of simple materialism, and therefore as incomplete in view of its failure to specify the formal cause (416a15–18).

**416a19–b9: A Return to Topic: A Difficulty about Food:** Though differently related to the chapter's main topic, the nutritive soul, both the criticisms of materialism (415b28–416a18) and the excursus concerning the soul's status as a cause of the living body (415b8–27) have been somewhat digressive. Aristotle now returns solidly to the topic of the nutritive faculty by raising a difficulty about nutrition. Though obscure in some particulars, the dominant thrust of this section is clear enough.

Since the same capacity of the soul is responsible for nutrition and generation (see notes to 415a22–b7 and 416b11–28), it is necessary to be clear in the first instance about nutrition, because it is in virtue of this feature in particular that the function in question is distinguished from other capacities of the soul (perhaps, because, as we have seen at 415a27–8, not everything living is in fact capable of reproducing). Aristotle notes that some (including, presumably, Empedocles; frs. 62 and 90) think that nutrition, like growth, occurs by like affecting like, while others think the opposite, that nutrition is a case of what is unlike affecting what is unlike (cf. *Phys.* 260a26–b4). Aristotle adjudicates this dispute in a somewhat prosaic way, by pointing out that both sides have a point: food at the beginning of its journey is unlike flesh, though once it has been digested to the point where it can be affixed to flesh, what was food has become like flesh. Cf. *Gen. et Cor.* 322a3.

### 416b9–11: Eaters and the Eaten: A Methodological Circularity?

This passage presents a potential problem of circularity for Aristotle, and it is one which affects his general methodological principle of individuating capacities by their activities and activities by their objects. The methodological precept endorsed in 415a14–22 (see the note as well as the Introduction to this chapter) as applied here has it that the nutritive capacity of the soul is individuated by its activity, namely the nourishing of the ensouled body, which activity is in its turn to be individuated by its object, namely food (*trophê*). Now it turns out that food can be characterized only with reference to (or relative to, *pros*; 416b11) an ensouled body—that is, a body with at least a nutritive soul. The problem cannot be immediately set aside by saying that food is only co-incidentally related to the nutritive soul, in the way that a man is only co-incidentally a slave (see *Cat.* 8a13–28); for Aristotle insists that food is not only co-incidentally related to the nutritive soul: food is itself a functional kind and is essentially such as to provide nourishment to living beings.

Aristotle could either embrace or attempt to elude the circularity. Eluding it would involve noting that capacities of the soul are *individuated* by their objects and not therefore *defined* in terms of them. Perhaps there is no circularity in claiming that the *x*s are individuated by the *y*s, even though the *y*s are essentially defined in terms of the *x*s. Embracing the circularity would be to allow that capacities and objects are after all interdefinable, but then to aver that such circularities are benign: possibility is defined only in terms of necessity and vice versa, as are the positive and negative charges of particles. Indeed, given the commitment to the irreducibility of life reflected in Aristotle's rejection of Empedocleanism, it is to be expected that for him psychic capacities cannot be defined in terms of predicates not drawn from life's own domain.

That leaves a question, however, of how the objects could yet be *prior* to the activities and faculties, as they must be if they are to individuate them. Aristotle does not face this problem in *De Anima*, though he does address it squarely in *Categories* 7, his chapter on relatives (*pros ti*). There he appeals to two related considerations in arguing for the priority of objects of perception (*aisthêta*) over perception (*aisthêsis*): (i) destruction of the objects of perception leads to destruction of perception; and (ii) possibly, objects of perception could exist without perception (*Cat.* 7b35–8a12). Thus, he concludes: 'hence, the object of perception (*aisthêton*) would seem to be prior (*proteron*) to perception (*aisthêsis*) (*Cat.* 8a10–12). This suggests an attempt to elude the circularity which exploits the fact that 'object of perception' (*aisthêton*) might be taken factively (= something perceived) or modally (= something perceptible). To apply this sort of response to the current problem would involve Aristotle in allowing that *food* (*trophê*) might exist even though no living systems capable of existing in fact exist.

**416b11–28: The Nutritive Soul as Active and as Generative:** An ensouled body is both an essentially living being and a quantity. Insofar as it is a quantity, it can be augmented in bulk; but its bare augmentation is not growth, since growth differs from getting bigger in being patterned and structured (cf. the criticisms of Empedocles at 415b28–416a18). Growth, unlike mere getting bigger, involves the active appropriation and subordination of nourishment for the preservation of a living substance. A pile of rocks alongside a garden gets bigger with the addition of each new rock, but is not fed in the process. In this passage, Aristotle relies heavily on his metaphysics of growth, a topic more fully explored in *Generation and Corruption* I 5, 322a16–33.

According to that broader account, nutrition is a phenomenon of life, belonging to all and only (mortal) living systems. Living systems are, crucially, *active* in the procurement of their own nourishment. Aristotle ascribes the activity of nourishment primarily to the nutritive soul. This sort of ascription helps explain the difficult metaphor intended to distinguish two senses of 'that by which it is nourished' (*hô(i) trephetai*; 416b25–6). Aristotle contends that three factors must be present in a process of nourishing: (i) that which effects the nourishing (*to trephon*), that is, the primary or nutritive soul (*hê prôtê psuchê*); (ii) that which is nourished (*to trephomenon*), that is, the body which has the soul (*to echon tauten sôma*); and (iii) that by which it is nourished (*hô(i) trephatai*), the food (*hê trophê*). He then notes that (iii) might rather be understood still more broadly: the expression 'that by which it is nourished' *(hô(i) trephetai)* might also mean the instrument employed in procuring nourishment. What is it by which the helmsman steers? Aristotle suggests that one might with equal correctness point to either of two different candidates: the helmsman's own hand or the ship's rudder. Similarly, he now suggests, in subordinating food to its own ends, the nutritive soul employs heat for the purposes of digestion. So, 'that by which it is nourished' *(hô(i) trephetai)* might be the food, or it might be the heat used in effecting digestion of the food.

In offering this sort of analogy, Aristotle understands himself to be justified in relying on two theses advanced earlier in the chapter, that the soul is the efficient and final cause of the ensouled body (see note to 415b8–27). It is just barely possible that Aristotle's analogy here also sheds some light on the otherwise perplexing question which closes II 1. Looked at through the lens of this passage, his question there concerned the issue of whether the soul was an actuality of the body in the sense of being its efficient cause. His answer here, if it is any sort of answer to that question, is that it is.

In any event, Aristotle points out that nutrition finds its ultimate end not just in the organized growth of the organism, but ultimately in generating another like itself. Because it is appropriate to name things after their functions (it is appropriate to call a tin opener a 'tin opener'), the nutritive soul is also appropriately called the generative soul (416b25). In calling the nutritive/generative soul 'primary' *(prôtê;* 416b25), Aristotle evidently means to call attention to his contention that the nutritive soul is the most basic kind of soul in two senses: it is shared by every living mortal (415a24–5) and it is presupposed by the higher capacities of soul (413a30–b10, 413b11–13, 414a29–b16, 434a22–30, and 434b9–25).

**416b28–31: The Appropriate Treatise:** Aristotle closes the chapter by promising a fuller treatment of the sketch of nourishment advanced here. No treatise on that topic survives, though Aristotle elsewhere refers to the existence of one even more definitely than he does here (*De Somno* 456b6; *Meteor.* 381b13, with more tentative references also found in *Part. An.* 650b10, 653b14, 674a20, 678a19; *Gen. An.* 784b2).

That said, as regards the metaphysics of growth (as opposed to the physiology one might expect in the *Parva Naturalia*), it is clear that this entire chapter draws heavily on *Generation and Corruption*

I 5; and as for the metaphysics of substantial unity, this chapter is importantly continuous with the conclusions reached in *Metaphyics Z* 17. Both of these chapters are usefully consulted as background for the current chapter.

CHAPTER 5

**Introduction to II 5**

Following his treatment of the most fundamental kind of soul, the nutritive soul, Aristotle turns to a full and rich explication of perception (*aisthêsis*) and the perceptual soul (*aisthêtikê psuchê*). Considered in terms of the total number of chapters devoted to the topic in *De Anima*, perception dominates the work: the present chapter introduces the entire faculty; the next is given over to the nature of perceptible objects; the following five discuss the canonical five senses; and the second book closes with a return to a consideration of the entire faculty. Thereafter, Aristotle devotes another two further chapters, III 1 and 2, to issues pertaining to perception before turning to imagination (*phantasia*) for a single chapter, and thence to reason (*nous*) for three.

Aristotle's discussion of perception in *De Anima* is rich and nuanced, conducted for the most part in a less materially enmeshed way than the many comparable discussions found in the *Parva Naturalia* and his biological writings. We find Aristotle referring the reader to those more detailed discussions several times in the course of his treatments of the individual faculties here, more regularly to passages in *De Sensu* 3–5, which should be read in tandem with *De Anima* II 7–11. In general, in *De Anima* Aristotle is concerned to characterize the faculty of perception relatively abstractly, endeavouring to capture its essence and nature, together with the features crucial to the activity of perceiving, though he occasionally dips into the mechanics of the matter in order to make a given claim crisp and concrete.

In approaching perception at this level of generality, Aristotle relies upon his hylomorphic explanatory framework, even while extending its analysis of change in order to take into account features of perception which do not fit comfortably or readily into that framework. (For a general characterization of Aristotle's extension of hylomorphic change to perceptual activity, see the General Introduction § IV.B).

The current chapter begins by introducing perception as a species of being moved and affected, indeed, as a kind of alteration (*alloiôsis*) and so as ripe for hylomorphic treatment given in terms of form reception (416b32–417a2). He does not, however, apply such a treatment immediately, preferring instead to raise some puzzles about perception which need immediate attention. First among these puzzles is why the senses do not perceive themselves in the absence of external objects (417a2). In approaching this puzzle, Aristotle finds it opportune to distinguish between kinds of potentialities and actualities, which distinction in turn provides an impetus for reflecting upon the ways in which we can and cannot treat perception as a straightforward instance of alteration liable to treatment in unadapted hylomorphic terms.

Aristotle will ultimately avail himself of an extension of the base case of hylomorphic change understood as form reception: in the basic kind of change, the reception of a form displaces its contrary, as when a non-musical man becomes musical by studying the piano; in the extended kind, a change involves not a destruction of a contrary by a contrary, but of a perfection or actualization of something already present, as when a schooled pianist moves from potentially playing to actually playing.

**416b32–417a2: Perception and Alteration:** Aristotle begins his account of perception by appealing to some general features of his hylomorphic approach to change. If a fence is made white by the application of white paint to it, then, contends Aristotle, the fence was suited to the reception of colour (because it has a surface), and the process of its becoming white was a process of form acquisition. As he himself notes, Aristotle had already contended that perception is a kind of alteration at 415b24— or an alternation, *kind of* (see note to 415b8–27). (This latter relies on the so-called *alienans tis*, the use of the Greek indefinite championed in this chapter by Burnyeat (2002: 74): 'a perception is an *alloiôsis tis* in the *alienans* sense, "alteration of a sort": an alteration from which you cannot expect everything you would normally expect from alteration'.). Thus, one way of taking Aristotle's language in that earlier passage, as here, is to treat it as qualified or tentative, roughly akin to the distinction in colloquial English between 'Unitarianism is a sort of religion' and 'Unitarianism is a religion—sort of.' Aristotle may be tempted by the looser, more tentative understanding, because he also insists, later in this same chapter, that the sort of transition involved in perceiving and reasoning is either not a species of alteration or else a different kind of alteration, one which must be carefully distinguished for the kind of alteration countenanced in the base case of hylomorphism. See note to 417b2–16 for a discussion of his motivation. The question of whether in perception like is affected by like is also discussed in *Generation and Corruption* I 7. It is worth recalling in this connection Aristotle's view that a commitment to the like-like theory created difficulties for those of his predecessors, discussed in I 1 and especially in I 5. Aristotle's own approach to this matter, as is typical for him, divides the question, deciding that 'it is affected while being unlike what affects it, but when it has been affected, it has been made like it and is such as what affected it is' (418a5–6). When he does so, however, he raises a serious question regarding the manner in which what is affected is made like what affects it. See note to 418b3–5 (cf. 417a18–20 and note to 431a4–6).

**417a2–14: A Puzzle about Perception:**    Aristotle's first puzzle about perception (*aisthêsis*) is, like some others among his puzzles, puzzling in its own right. Initially, the puzzle seems clear: given that a sufficient condition for perception is the presence of a sensible object to a properly functioning sensory faculty, why is it there is 'no perception of the senses themselves' (*tôn aisthêseôn autôn ou ginetai aisthêsis*; 417a3)? The eyes are, after all, themselves coloured, the nose has odour, and so forth. (It is sometimes remarked in this connection that one *can* in fact taste one's tongue.) As formulated, the puzzle speaks only of 'perception' (*aisthêsis*), which sometimes refers to the faculty, sometimes the activity, and sometimes to the sense organs (more regularly called the *aisthêtêria*). In this case, it is clear that Aristotle is speaking of the activity of perception and not of the faculty or organs. His puzzle is thus why, given that the sense organs themselves have perceptible features, their presence is not immediately sufficient for their being perceived. Yet, unless we are looking in a mirror, we do not see our eyes. We might put his question in English by wondering why the senses do not sense the senses.

The puzzle about this puzzle arises not in its statement, which seems reasonably clear, at least initially, but in its proffered resolution, which seems not to address the puzzle introduced in any direct or obvious way, leaving the impression that the puzzle set by Aristotle was understood by him in some way other than has just been suggested. In his response to his puzzle, Aristotle adverts to a view he is on the brink of articulating, namely that the sensory faculty is in potentiality, and that just as the combustible requires an actual spark to ignite into fire, so perception requires an actual external object as its object.

Again, this is puzzling insofar as it seems not to address the puzzle just articulated. For, according to that articulation, the sensory faculties are already assumed to be in potentiality: an eye is potentially seeing when no object of sight (*horaton*) is present to it; it is actually perceiving when, in suitable conditions, such an object is present to it. The organs themselves have features in virtue of which they are such objects; because made ultimately of the material elements, they should have the properties whose presence is sufficient for perception (417a5–6), and yet they are not perceived. If, by contrast, stress is to be laid on the fact that *external* objects (*tôn exô*; 417a4) are required, then the appeal to potentiality and actuality seems idle. For then the answer is simply that the senses do not perceive themselves because they are not external to themselves. Looked at from this perspective, the puzzle is either not as it seemed, or its answer seems to miss its point.

Aristotle's language in setting the puzzle suggests that it is one he himself finds at least initially puzzling ('There is a puzzle as to why...; *echei d' aporian dia ti*...; 417a2). This suggests, then, that the initial puzzle is more than it seemed. One possibility is that the assumption made in the original explication of the puzzle is false, namely that the question pertains to why the senses do not perceive the 'sense organs themselves'. This assumption is reflected in the rendering of the phrase *tôn aisthêseôn autôn* preferred in the text; (417a3; cf. *De Sensu* 440a19). Aristotle might in principle also mean the sensory faculty (*aisthêtikon*) or the activity of perception (as *aisthêsis* most often means), but then it would be odd for him to proceed by characterizing the potential objects of perception by saying that 'present in them are fire, earth, and the other elements of which there is perception either in themselves or in respect of their co-incidental properties (417a4–6). This sounds very much as if he has the sensory organs in mind. That assumption then seems reasonable, and it is perhaps confirmatory that it is made in common with most (though not all) of Aristotle's ancient commentators (Them. *in DA* 54. 23; Phil. *in DA* 291.3; Alex. *Aporiai kai Luseis* 82. 35; cf. ps.-Simplicius *in de An.* 118.3).

**417a14–20: Types of Potentiality and Actuality; Acting and Being Affected:** However Aristotle's solution to his puzzle about perception is to be understood, its appeal to a potentiality/actuality distinction occasions a discussion of that topic which, with some interruptions and asides, extends through the rest of the chapter.

Aristotle has already introduced a distinction into grades of actuality and potentiality in *De Anima* in II 1 pertaining to the soul and illustrated by knowledge (see note to 412a21–2; cf. *Phys.* 255a33, *Met.* 1050a21–3). Here he applies this same distinction to perception, and, though the text is uncertain, evidently to the object of perception as well (*aisthêton*; 417a13). Aristotle's point about grades of potentiality pertaining to perception is just that we can speak of someone as 'having perception,' i.e. as having a faculty of perception, or as 'having *a* perception', i.e. as exercising that faculty, that is, as perceiving something right now. Even a sleeping person has an actual faculty of perception, but is at that moment—and for that reason—merely in potentiality with respect to perception. The distinction finds an English analogue when we speak of a blind person as someone who does not see, where we mean that she lacks the faculty of sight; a sighted person who does not see, by contrast, can see, but is not exercising the faculty at present.

Aristotle's probable contention that the object of perception no less than perception itself admits of degrees of potentiality naturally gives rise to the suggestion which follows, that there is a sense in which what is moved, what is affected, and what is actualizing are the same. An actual capacity to perceive is yet in potentiality until it is moved by an object of perception, in which case its being moved and affected is the same process as something's actualizing it. A surface which is potentially white is, while being painted, being altered just when what alters it is actual, namely the actual process of a painter painting (cf. 416b33, with note). For a useful

215

discussion of the framework provided by Aristotle's account of change and its application in this chapter, see Kosman (1969). Although the matter is complicated by some discussions elsewhere (especially *Met.* 1048b18–35, where a critical distinction between actuality (*energeia*) and motion (*kinêsis*) is introduced), Aristotle's stated reason in the present context for arriving at this conclusion helps show why he believes that *being moved, being affected,* and *actualizing* are the same. A motion or a change, when moving towards its resolution, is at that time potential because perforce incomplete (else it would no longer be changing or moving), but at the same time an actualization (else it would not be changing or moving in the first place). The exact textual reference intended at 417a17 is unclear. Some likely candidates are: *Phys.* 201a10–b31; *Met.* 1048b28; *EN* 1174a19.

On the way in which like is and is not affected by like in the process of perception, see note to 418b3–5.

**417a21–b2: Further Concerning Potentiality and Actuality:** Although it at first appears that Aristotle is merely reiterating the distinction between grades of actuality made above at 417a10–14, in fact the discussion in this passage incorporates the earlier distinction and adds further content. In the earlier passage we learned that someone might be in potentiality with respect to knowledge in one of two ways, by being ignorant or by being enlightened while not actually making use of that enlightenment at the moment, only the first of which potentialities is destroyed as it is left behind in the process of actualization. Now Aristotle adds the further content: someone is in potentiality of the sort which is destroyed by its opposite when learning occurs merely by being a member of a genus with the right sort of matter, while someone who already knows but is not contemplating at present can do so at will. The first person cannot contemplate at will, since he lacks the conceptual wherewithal; he needs to be taught before he is in potentiality in the higher degree which permits contemplation at will. The second person can, by contrast, contemplate at will, because she already has, in actuality, all of the wherewithal she needs to do so. Significantly, in the next section (417b2–16), Aristotle will contend that as regards degrees of potentiality, perception and reasoning are not perfectly parallel.

It is striking that in the present passage Aristotle evidently allows, as he does in *Metaphysics* M 10, at 1087a19–20, that contemplation (*theôrein*) may be understood as having an individual object. The translation seeks to leave this open by rendering '*tode to A*' as 'this A', though it might also be more strongly translated as 'this particular A'. Although it has a clear parallel in the passage from *Metaphysics* M 10, this passage does not comport with Aristotle's more standard contention that perception is of the particular, while thought is of the universal (see note to 417b16–27; cf. *APo.* 87b28–88a2, 100a6–b1; *Met.* 1039b28–1040a7, 1087a19–20). In *Metaphysics* M, unlike the current passage, Aristotle suggests that contemplation of the particular requires: (i) an appeal, whose precise contours are disputed, to an actuality-potentiality distinction; (ii) a background knowledge of the universal; and (iii) some sense in which the particular co-incides with the universal (*Met.* 1087a19); see the glossary entry on co-incidence (*kata sumbebêkos*). If we accept the stronger translation (viz. 'this particular A), then we have, on the basis of this parallel, some conception of how contemplation can after all be of an individual. In this respect, see Heinaman (1981), who also renders precise some of the larger themes associated with Aristotle's contention that contemplation can be of the particular.

### 417b2–16: Complexities Concerning Being Affected and Alteration:
The text of this passage is a bit uncertain, with the result that Aristotle's intended meaning is difficult and disputed. There are two contrasts at play: (i) one between two ways of something's being affected: 'Nor is being affected unqualified' (417b2); and (ii) another between two ways of regarding alteration as it occurs in various psychological processes, where, in some cases, one: 'either should not be said to be affected or there are two types of alteration' (417b6–7). It is only the second contrast which creates difficulties, and then only in some instances.

In the simplest case, (i) and (ii) cohere easily. Aristotle has already maintained that only the standard kind of hylomorphic alteration involves the destruction of a contrary by a contrary, whereas something which is already φ (e.g. someone who already knows the Pythagorean theorem), but is now not making its φ-ness fully actual (someone who is not attending to the Pythagorean theorem), preserves the φ-ness in the transition to its full actualization (see notes to

412a21–7 and, in this chapter, to 417a14–20). Now Aristotle points out that the latter sort of transition is either not an instance of alteration at all or is of a discrete sort, which needs to be distinguished from destructive alteration.

The second main claim (ii) is more difficult, especially in its application to teaching and learning. It is initially confusing to find Aristotle denying (or seeming to deny) at 417b10–11 that teaching occurs when someone leads someone from potentially knowing to actually knowing. Is this not precisely teaching? What is more, Aristotle goes on to contend that when actual teaching does occur, either the student is not affected or there are two types of alteration (417b12–14). Again, though, one will want to know how a student fails to be affected or altered in the process of learning.

Some have thought to remove the oddness of Aristotle's first remark about the impropriety of calling a leader a teacher by regarding the one leading someone from potentiality to actuality as not teaching her, e.g. the Pythagorean theorem, but rather as inducing her move from the second stage of potentiality (i.e. from knowing but not attending) to the complete state of actuality (i.e. to knowing and attending). A day-care provider on an outing to the beach with her charges might divide the children into the swimmers and non-swimmers and then instruct the swimmers to swim and lead them into the lake; but she is not then their swimming teacher.

If that is so, however, why does genuine teaching not involve the destruction of a contrary by a contrary? Teaching, when successful, evidently involves the destruction of ignorance by the learning which supplants it; and this seems a straightforward form of alteration, one not easily assimilated to the kind of non-destructive development we have seen in the case of one moving from one degree of actuality to another, higher degree. Moreover, this seems to be Aristotle's own contention just above at 417a30–1, where he speaks of one 'being altered through learning, with frequent changes from an opposite state'.

This need not be a contradiction, if Aristotle now intends to suggest that there are two ways states might be contrary to one another: (a) broadly, so that the change from ignorance to knowledge is the destruction of a contrary by a contrary; or (b) narrowly, so that only two positive states stand in contrariety to one another, where the acquisition of a positive state (*hexis*) inherent

218

to a kind of thing is rather a development into that thing's own nature. The broad notion fails to distinguish the kind of change which occurs in development and maturation from change in general. When a grey wall is painted white, the greyness is destroyed by the encroaching whiteness. It is not so easy to specify in any non-artificial way what positive attribute is destroyed when a child learns to walk. (Cf. *Phys.* 255a30–b5; *Met.* 1019b6–9, 1022b22, 1069b10–12; *EN* 1174a13–b13.)

If that is correct, then, Aristotle offers in this passage two distinct ways in which psychic changes are not alterations: (i) when something already actually φ transitions into its fullest state of actuality with respect to φ-ness; and (ii) when something not already actually φ becomes actually φ by developing into a positive state (*hexis*) natural and characteristic to its kind of thing. This would implicitly divide the second half of Aristotle's general contrast into two. He says: 'either should not be said to be affected or there are two types of alteration, (i) one a change towards conditions of privation and (ii) the other towards positive states and a thing's nature' (417b14–16). Looked at this way, the second half of the contrast would then itself be twofold: (ii. a) a change into a positive state consonant with a thing's nature (*epi tas hexeis*), and (ii. b) a change into that thing's nature (*tên phusin*). One might say in case (ii. a) that a teacher does not alter a pupil, because she does not make her other than she already is essentially, namely the kind of being capable of knowing, that is, a being with a rational soul. To teach is to develop a pupil into a positive state consonant with her nature.

**417b16–27: The Potentiality of the Perceptual Faculty; Some Consequences:** In learning, the acquisition of settled knowledge is equally the acquisition of a positive state (*hexis*). Aristotle has just suggested that the acquisition of knowledge is natural for beings capable of knowing. Learning is then the 'first change' (*prôtê metabolê*; 417b17) in the direction of actual knowing, whereas in the case of perception, the first change is complete at birth, having been effected by the parents. This is to say, then, that animals have their matter already enformed so as to be born with an ability to perceive which does not have to be developed further: infants can see, though they must learn in order to know.

This, at any rate, is Aristotle's probable meaning. The text here is compressed and perhaps corrupt. The sentence translated as 'In what is capable of perceiving, the first change is brought about by the parent; what is born is also already able to perceive, just as we have knowledge' (417b16–18) reflects both an editorial decision and an interpretive expansion. As for the expansion, one might possibly render the last section as 'when it is born it has perceiving too just as it has knowledge' (*echei êdê hôsper epistêmên kai to aisthanesthai*; 417b18). This is, however, unlikely to be his meaning, since Aristotle has just said that acquiring knowledge and the ability to contemplate at will requires in the learner a change from one contrary to another, presumably, then, from ignorance to knowledge (*epistêmê*). The translation offered agrees with the one offered by Alexander (*Ap. kai Lu.* III 3. 85), though it must be said that the linguistic parallels used to justify it by, e.g., Hicks (1907: 358) are rather strained.

This interpretation is perhaps strengthened by the thought that Aristotle has allowed above that someone capable of perceiving may yet not be perceiving, as when sleeping (417a10–12). (If it is doubted that sleepers fail to perceive, it will yet be possible to think of humans in sensory deprivation tanks.) So, someone fully equipped to perceive may not, in the absence of an external object, which is made by Aristotle a necessary condition of perceiving (417b28), actually perceive. The consequences, assuming this interpretation, are (i) that animals do not need training or habituation to perceive, because they arrive fully equipped for the task (cf. *Met.* 1047b31–1048a1); and (ii) they are at a level of actuality akin to someone on the cognitive side who has already learnt; and (iii) that actual perceiving is akin to active contemplation and not mere knowing. Aristotle embraces the second consequence plainly at *De Sensu* 441b22.

Given that one who knows but is not contemplating can do so at will (417a27), one might expect the same ability for someone equipped with sense perception, since by (ii) they are at the same level of actuality. As we have seen, however, Aristotle denies this consequence, since a necessary condition of actual perceiving is the presence of an external object of perception, the presence of which is not immediately subject to will. By contrast, someone who has actual knowledge has, in some sense, the universals already present in the soul. The precise sense in which the wherewithal to contemplate is in the soul of one who knows is a matter for investigation (cf. 429a22–31, 431b26–432a3), though the contrast upon which Aristotle depends is so far unproblematic. The woman in the sensory deprivation tank cannot will herself to see its surfaces, though she can think that those surfaces, like all surfaces, are limits of a three-dimensional body.

Aristotle explains the need for external objects in perception by appealing to his dominant practice of understanding perception to range over particulars and thought over universals (*APo*. 81b6, 87b28–37, 87b39–88a7; cf. note to 417a21–b2; *Met.* 1039b28–1040a7, 1087a15–20). The basic idea is simply that perception is activated by the presence of a particular perceptible to a functioning faculty of perception, while thought requires greater activity on the part of the thinker. That Aristotle deviates from this doctrine in its simple form, even in the present chapter, does not impugn his ability to appeal to it in explaining why conditions differ for the transitions from grades of actuality in the cases of perception and knowledge. At any rate, if the (slightly) fuller picture of *Metaphysics* M 10 (see note to 417a21–b2) requires prior association with a universal before 'contemplating' a particular falling under it, in the sense of co-inciding with it, then he may continue to insist that perception requires activation by the presence of a particular object of perception (*aisthêton*) in a way in which reasoning (*noêsis*) or contemplation (*theôrein*) does not.

**417b27–418a3: Summary; the Inadequacy of Ordinary Language:** Tracking the distinctions drawn in this chapter between various degrees of potentiality and actuality and their sundry relations to Aristotle's hylomorphic analysis of change and alteration is a delicate matter. The general illustration he now employs by way of summary is coarse, though serviceable: we say that a boy is potentially a general and that a grown man is potentially a general, though we do not ascribe the same states of readiness to them; nor do we think their transitions into generalship traverse the same paths, since one is a proper part of the other. Aristotle notes, fairly, that we do not have words to mark the distinctions we have observed between the ways our psychic faculties need to be affected and altered in order for actual perception and contemplation to occur. So, he suggests, we shall have to make do with our ordinary language, while being alert to the fine-grained distinctions such language obscures. (There are similar remarks made at 426a12–14; cf. *EN* 1107a34–b2, 1115b31–3). It would not be fair, however, for Aristotle to fault the inadequacies of ordinary language alone. Rather, he has seen the need to deviate from his own standard model of hylomorphic change in order to account for the variety of transitions he has himself thought necessary to identify in his general account of perception.

**418a3–6: Assimilation and Being Made Like:**     These final sentences are given as summary, though they do not serve to recapitulate the main claims in the chapter. A crucially important claim, that the perceptual faculty (*aisthêtikon*) is in potentiality such as its objects are in actuality, is introduced as having already been made. This claim has not, however, been made in these terms in this chapter or earlier—though what Aristotle now concludes can be gleaned from 417a12–20 in a general sense; and 418a4–5 does seem to be a clear echo of 417a18–20. What is *not* settled by the language of this summary is how the sense faculty is in potentiality *such as* (*hoion*; 418a4) its objects are already in actuality; nor does the account thus far decide precisely how the perceptual faculty is *made like* (*hômoiôtai*; 418a5) its objects once it has been affected. For some competing approaches to the proper understanding of these matters, see the General Introduction § IV.B.

Interestingly, the final resolution of the like-like controversy in one respect directly parallels the resolution Aristotle had offered in the case of nutrition (on which, see note to 416a19–b9). There Aristotle had equally settled the matter by splitting the difference: before it is altered by the digestive process, food—the object of the nutritive soul—was unlike what it eventually nourished; once captured and altered by the nutritive soul, it was like the ensouled body. So too, evidently, with the objects of perception: at the beginning of the process, perceptual faculty and perceptual object are not, in the relevant sense, alike; but the complex alterations in perception bring faculty and object into likeness with one another. The causal directionalities seem opposite, however: food is made like the ensouled body, whereas the perceptual faculty is made like its objects. It is in any case important to understand this general conclusion in connection with 424a1–5, where it is significantly qualified, and 424a17–24, where it is appreciably augmented. Cf. also *Generation and Corruption* 324b13–31.

## CHAPTER 6

### Introduction to II 6

In response to a procedural question posted in II 1 (402b10–14; cf. note to 402b9–16), Aristotle had determined that discussion of the senses properly begins with their objects (see the Introduction to II 4, together with notes to 402a23–b8, 402b9–16, 418a11–17, and 429b10–21). In this chapter, he follows the precepts laid down there by considering the kinds of perceptible objects there are. He claims that 'perceptible object is spoken of in three ways: in two cases we say perceptible objects are perceived in their own right, and in one co-incidentally' (418a8–9). Of these three, the first two are perceived in their own right (or per se; *kath' hauto*; 418a8–9), and the third only co-incidentally (*kata sumbebêkos*; 418a9). Finally, of those which are perceived in their own rights, one sort is exclusive to each sense (or peculiar or proper to that sense, *idion*; 418a10), and another is common (*koinon*; 418a11). Aristotle does not argue that these categories are exhaustive, though this seems to be his working assumption. In general, this brief chapter for the most part prefers description to argumentation. Still, Aristotle's treatment of the sensible objects distinguished here does provide grounds for agreeing that the distinctions he draws do capture natural and defensible categories.

It is noteworthy that Aristotle's distinction between two kinds of perceptible objects into the exclusive and common objects runs partially parallel, extensionally speaking, to later entrenched distinctions, differently motivated, between primary and secondary qualities. The common perceptibles listed in this chapter are 'motion, rest, number, shape, and magnitude' (418a17–18). Compare Locke: 'These I call original or primary qualities of body, which I think we may observe to produce simple ideas in us, viz. solidity, extension, figure, motion or rest, and number' (*Essay Concerning Human Understanding* II 8. 9). On the parallel, see Block (1965), and Ganson (1997), who investigates in an instructive manner the more general question of the relation between Aristotelian sensible qualities and a primary-secondary quality distinction.

**418a7–11: Taxonomy of Sensible Objects:** Aristotle's contention that a perceptible object (*aisthêton*) is 'spoken of (*legetai*) in three ways' (418a8) reproduces in his standard language his oft-repeated *non-univocity judgement*, a judgement to the effect that φ-ness does not have a single meaning, or that the φs do not form a single natural class. In many cases, Aristotle's contention is best taken intensionally, where it is most readily understood as a claim about non-extensional semantic value (for instance, that *love* is spoken of in several ways, as between, e.g., 'Manfred loves his son' and 'The newly reunited couple made love into the small hours'; cf. *Topics* I 15). In other cases, Aristotle's judgement is more naturally taken extensionally (for instance, that friendship is spoken of in three ways, that there are friendships of advantage or business friendships, friendships of affection, and true friendships; *EE* 1235a17–20, 1236a7–19). Here Aristotle is making an extensional judgement, that there is not just one kind of perceptual object.

We accept Aristotle's non-univocity contention if we agree that 'perceives' differs at least in some measure in these applications: (i) my eyes perceived blue; (ii) the trail guide perceived motion in the bushes; and (iii) she perceived that her daughter was a bit peaky. Framed in terms of the objects of perception, (i) corresponds roughly to *exclusive* objects, those objects in terms of which the individual sensory modalities are individuated (see note to 418a11–17), (ii) picks out common objects, those not perceived by any one sense alone (note to 418a17–20), and (iii) identifies objects which are neither exclusive nor common, but instead involve the identification of objects co-inciding with special or common objects (see note to 41a20–4).

Whether taken extensionally or intensionally, Aristotle's non-univocity judgements are regularly accompanied with a positive judgement to the effect that one sense is core or controlling (*kurion*) relative to the others, because most primary or basic. In this case, he contends that exclusive objects form the base case (see note to 417a24–5).

**418a11–17: Exclusive Objects of Sense:** Aristotle introduces two distinct conditions for an object's qualifying as exclusive: (i) it cannot be perceived by another sense; and (ii) it presents as somehow deception-proof. Although he does not say so, he presumably regards these conditions as individually necessary and jointly sufficient. With respect to (i), it is clear that Aristotle supposes that the natures of the various discrete exclusive objects render them detectable each by one sense only: it is not an accident that colours cannot be heard or odours touched, except perhaps incidentally (cf. 425a30–b3). This fact, if it is a fact, underwrites Aristotle's contention that the objects of sense provide the individuation conditions for the individual sensory modalities. In this connection, as Aristotle himself later observes (422b17–34), touch presents some difficulties. Touch detects the hot, the smooth, the rough, and the wet, among others. So, it is hard to see what the exclusive object of touch might be, unless we are to stitch these together under the rubric of *the tangible*; if we go that route, however, we seem to identify the object of touch by the sense itself and so are left without a non-circular way to individuate the sense by its objects. Such potential circularity has equally threatened in other contexts in which Aristotle has sought to individuate psychic faculties by their correlative objects (see especially notes to 415a14–22 and 416b9–11).

Aristotle's contention that we are not deceived with respect to the special objects of sensation sounds a common, if not perfectly consistent, theme for him. He often suggests that the senses (or that *we*, when using the senses) cannot be deceived with respect to exclusive objects (427b12, 428a11, 430b29; *De Sensu* 442b8; *Met.* 1010b2–26). This claim appears importantly qualified, however, at 428b18 (regarding which, see note to 428b10–429b30).

To assess Aristotle's thesis it will be necessary to determine both its strength and its extent. Some questions relevant to these determinations include: Are the (nearly) incorrigible objects in any sense private? Does Aristotle mean that the senses cannot be deceived or that *we*, using the senses, cannot be deceived? What is the role of judgement in the constitution of these claims? About what precisely can we not be deceived? Something propositional or non-propositional? That we perceive colour? That colour is present? That a colour is not an odour? This last question is not motivated by the current passage, though it is strongly suggested by *Metaphysics* 1010b2–26. If Aristotle means only that we will never mistake a sound for an odour, then his point is rather more limited than it would otherwise first appear. Further, when he later qualifies this contention at 428b18, Aristotle says that we might be deceived to some small extent about white, not about colour as such, the more coarse-grained object specified in the present passage. Is this difference significant? Aristotle provides at least some direction with respect to these questions in the present passage when, by way of contrast, he allows that we are not incorrigible with respect to what or where the coloured or sounding thing is (418a16).

**418a17–20: Common Objects:** Common objects are not exclusive to any one sense. Hence, since we perceive common objects in their own right, if a necessary condition of perceiving an object non-co-incidentally is its being perceived by a single sensory faculty, then there is, of necessity, a kind of common sense (or common perception; *koinê aisthêsis*) in addition to the five sensory modalities. Aristotle evidently accepts a faculty of common perception, though he does not motivate it by just this argument. Indeed, one might well doubt whether there are grounds for ascribing any such argument to Aristotle, since his stated view here is not that a necessary condition of perceiving an object in its own right is being perceived by a single sensory faculty, but rather that *some* objects perceived in their own right are exclusive (*idion*), because they are perceived by one sense alone. He does not say, conversely, that each sensory modality can perceive *only* its exclusive objects. On the contrary, he identifies one common object, motion (*kinêsis*) as 'in some cases . . . an object of perception for both touch and sight' (418a19–20). See also note to 425a14–b3.

Aristotle displays some variation on two matters pertaining to common sensibles. First, his list shifts from work to work: here he includes motion, rest, number, shape, and magnitude, though in *De Sensu* (442b5–7) he adds the rough and smooth, and the sharp and the blunt as well, objects introduced as exclusive to touch in *De Anima* 422b25–7. This first variation may be partly generated by a second. In the present passage, Aristotle suggests that common objects are perceptible by all senses (418a19), though in *De Sensu* (437a 8–10) he suggests that some are perceptible only by sight and touch (Cf. also *De Insomn.* 458b4; *De Mem.* 450a9; *EN* 1142a27).

If a sufficient condition for being common is being per se (or in its own right, *kath' hauto*) perceptible without being exclusive (*idion*), then the suggestion that common sensibles can as such be perceived by all senses cannot be sustained. Further, and at any rate, it is difficult to see how some of the items listed even in this passage could be perceived by each and every one of the sensory modalities. Thus, for example, it is not easy to appreciate how shape is perceived by smell. A more relaxed condition would hold only that common perceptibles are detectable by more than one sense; the contrast with exclusive objects of perception would remain sustainable, since they are perceptible by one and only one sensory modality. For a fuller discussion of common perception, see III 1, with note to 425a14–b3.

**418a20–24: Co-inciding Objects:** A witness asked what he saw at a crime scene might reasonably respond that he saw a red Jaguar speeding away. Which sense has as its exclusive objects red Jaguars? Aristotle suggests that no sense, properly speaking, perceives any such object in its own right (or per se; *kath' hauto*). Rather, sight perceives red, and only insofar as the red object of sight co–incides with a car does Aristotle allow that one sees the Jaguar. In this case, he suggests, the red Jaguar is a co-incidental object of perception, that is, an object co-inciding with some proper or exclusive object of perception. In so speaking, Aristotle is not maintaining that it is improper linguistically or otherwise to talk of *perceiving a red Jaguar*. On the contrary, he is allowing that we perceive such objects, but not in the manner of exclusive objects or common objects. Nor does he maintain that one *constructs* co-incidental objects of perception from perceptual data derived from exclusive objects; still less does he imply that one somehow *infers* the existence of co-incidental objects from the several perceptions of exclusive objects.

Aristotle's concern in this passage is evidently in part to identify the features of perceptible objects in virtue of which they are perceptible (418a23–4), and so to highlight those qualities appropriately cited in connection with a hylomorphic theory of perception of the sort characterized in the last chapter. However the sensory faculty is to be made like a red Jaguar, this feat is accomplished by being made like the colour and shape of the car, not by its being made car-like (cf. note to 418b3–5). For the language of co-incidence (*kata sumbebêkos*) employed in this connection, see *APr*. 43a33; *APo*. 83a1–14; see also the glossary entry on co-incidence.

**418a24–25: The Core Notion of Sensible Objects:** The chapter has divided sensible objects into those perceived in their own right and those perceived co-incidentally, and has introduced exclusive and common objects as species of objects perceptible in their own right (418a9–11). One might expect Aristotle here, immediately after characterizing co-incidental objects of perception, to point to exclusive objects as the most proper or fundamental sort relative to both other kinds of objects. Strictly, however, he says only that exclusive objects are basic relative to things perceptible in their own right; perhaps, though, this is because he now takes it as established that as a category the per se is prior to the co-incidental (so much being the likely purport of 418a22–3).

In any event, unsurprisingly, exclusive objects are now characterized as the most proper or core case of per se sensible objects. Aristotle's characterization of them as proper (or controlling; *kurion*) is not intended to indicate that the other kinds of sensible objects are improper, but only that the non-exclusive are posterior to and somehow derivative upon the exclusive (cf. *Phys.* 191b7; *Gen. et Corr.* 314a10; *EN* 1144b4). While it is easy to see how co-incidental objects are derivative, it is less obvious why common objects are to be so regarded. Aristotle's conclusion in this regard may be connected to his earlier contention that exclusive objects afford the highest degree of immunity to error (on which, see note to 418a11–17).

CHAPTER 7

## Introduction to II 7

Chapters 7–11 characterize the individual senses, each in considerable detail. In some respects, these discussions have only antiquarian interest, insofar as they rely upon outmoded physiology and obsolete physical theory. In many other respects, however, these chapters shed considerable light on Aristotle's hylomorphic theory of perception and therefore lend considerably to the joint tasks of characterizing and assessing that theory.

Just as the commentary to *De Anima* I stressed the philosophical over the doxographical, so the commentary to II 6–11 emphasizes the theoretical over the mechanical.

The present chapter characterizes sight, though along the way Aristotle extends some of his remarks about the importance of the existence of a medium for perception to the other sensory modalities as well. It is noteworthy that Aristotle begins with sight, when his announced principles require him to begin from the bottom up, from the most widely diffused to the most rare. Following this principle would call for him to begin with touch, as the most basic and widespread form of perception (413b5–6, 414b3, 415a4, 435a13–b2; cf. 434b10–30). Aristotle's decision to begin as he does may reflect a conscious plan to treat sight as a paradigmatic perceptual modality (429a3), or it may simply betray the unreflective optocentricism characteristic of many philosophers. He does, however, connect the primacy of sight to its role in action and especially knowledge acquisition: 'sight, more than any other sense, provides knowledge and clarifies the differences among things' (*Met.* 980a24–17).

However that may be, the principal ingredients required for sight are: (i) distal objects; (ii) colour; and (iii) a medium affected by the visible object. Aristotle will go to some lengths to preserve the presence of a medium for the other modalities, though it is not always immediately clear what he takes to be at stake in this regard. On the one hand, when we perceive distal objects, there must be a medium affected by the object's qualities unless we are willing to countenance action at a distance; this, however, is perfectly consistent with the absence of a medium for other modalities, including most obviously touch (see note to 419a7–15).

For more detail on sight, see *De Sensu* 3.

**418a26–b26: Sight, Light, and the Visible:**  The object of sight is colour, as well as something 'which has no name,' says Aristotle, where he has in mind what is now generally referred to as *phosphorescence* (though may more properly be termed *luminescence*; 418a27–8, 419a1–6; *De Sensu* 418a26–8). Aristotle at first ignores the phosphorescent and focuses on colour. Colour sets the transparent (*diaphanes*) in motion, where the transparent is equally present in water and air. Colour is only briefly characterized as that inhering in the surface of what is seen, which is, in its nature, capable of setting an actual transparent in motion (cf. *De Sensu* 439a30–b13). The actual transparent is the *lighted* transparent, since light actualizes the transparent in the medium of sight but does not create it (cf. 419a7–9); the transparent is equally present in the dark, though evidently only in a state of potentiality.

When he calls colour the visible, or the object of sight (*horaton*; 418a29), Aristotle is presumably speaking in a somewhat restricted sense, since he elsewhere denies that the visible and colour are the same (*Phys.* 201b3–4, *Met.* 1065b32) and has just now held that the phosphorescent is also visible, though it is not a colour; so colour and the visible are not even coextensive. If this is not perfectly perspicuous, it is not really in this respect problematic either (though it again raises problems for the suggestion that faculties are individuated by their objects; see notes to 415a14–22, 416b9–11, and 418a11–17). Here he may fairly be understood as holding that colour is a primary and paradigmatic object of sight.

Since we have seen that Aristotle's list of sensible qualities marches in step with the secondary qualities of later traditions (see the Introduction to II 6), it is worth asking whether he assumes in this chapter that colour is always seen, or whether there is unperceived colour. To begin, one may ask whether Aristotle regards colours and other sensible qualities as intrinsic monadic features of external objects which exist whether perceived or not. The issue is complicated, and the present chapter does not decide the matter. One linguistic consideration to be borne in mind when approaching this issue pertains to an ambiguity in Greek: when Aristotle speaks of the visible, or the object of sight, the *horaton*, he uses a word which may be either factive or modal. He may mean, that is, *what is in fact seen* or *what can be seen*, that is, what is *visible*. The translation tries to capture the ambiguity to the degree that it is possible to do so. In any event, when he says, e.g, that light is a necessary condition of the visible and contends that every colour is seen in light (418b2–3), he may mean that there is no colour without light, or more trivially that though there is colour without light, it is not visible until the transparent in the medium through which it is perceived is illuminated (cf. 419a7–9; *De Sensu* 447a11).

That said, Aristotle complicates the question in a welcome way when he applies the potentiality/actuality distinction to the objects of perception at 431b24–6 (see note to which; cf. 417a4, 422a17).

**418b26–419a7: The Transparent and the Phosphorescent:** Something transparent may be illuminated or not. Fire, or something capable of illuminating the transparent, makes the medium actual, whether it be air, water, or the semi-translucent solids mentioned at 418b7 (presumably glass, crystals, and the like). This is the sense in which light is a sort of colour of the transparent (418b11; cf. *De Sensu* 439a18): although it is not itself a colour, because, not inhering in the surface of any body (cf. *Phys.* 210b4), light makes the transparent an actual medium of colour.

Aristotle never names the phosphorescent as such in this passage, suggesting instead that the items seen in the dark, glowing without an illuminated medium, lack a name but must be counted as visible (418a27). Aristotle mentions mushrooms, horns, and various fish bits (*De Sensu* 437a31 adds cuttlefish ink). An obvious question arises as to why glow-in-the-dark objects should not be counted as coloured. One quick answer is that, as we have seen (418b2–3), without light there is no colour. This mainly postpones the question, however: why, in that case, given that we can see glowing objects, should we accept that there is no colour without an illuminated medium? One more consequential response appeals to the *nature* of colour, which is twice defined causally or functionally in this chapter. At 418a31–b2 and again at 419a9–11 Aristotle uses strong language, the language of essence-specifying definition, when characterizing colour as that which is capable of setting the transparent in motion. If colour is essentially such as to cause motion in the transparent, and this is possible only with light, then what is seen glowing in the dark will not qualify as colour. In this sense, the issue will turn on a substantive discussion of the nature of colour, a discussion not undertaken in this chapter or elsewhere (though cf. *Topics* 103b32, 120b21; *De Sensu* 439b11). Unfortunately, the discussion to which Aristotle refers at 419a7 does not seem to exist.

**419a7–21: An Argument for the Necessity of a Medium:** After summarizing the main results thus far, that colour is what is seen in light (419a8), while light is the actuality of the transparent (419a11), Aristotle contends that a medium is not only typical for sight but necessary: (i) if someone places a coloured object on the eye itself, seeing does not accrue; (ii) the only or best explanation of (i) is that seeing requires a medium (no medium, no seeing); hence, (iii) seeing requires a medium, viz. the transparent. The argument thus structured expands a bit upon what Aristotle says in the text, though this seems to be the tenor of his thought; he does not state (ii), though seems to be relying on some such premise. The argument may seem to be of little moment if one is indifferent to the question of whether a medium is required for vision. Yet given Aristotle's tendency to treat sight as a paradigmatic sensory modality (see the Introduction to this chapter), it has some disturbing implications. If we suppose that a medium is required for sight, and accept sight as paradigmatic, then we will be tempted to infer that a medium is required for every sensory modality. This indeed seems to be Aristotle's actual conclusion, with the result that he will want to insist that even touch and taste (which will prove to be a species of touch) require a medium. These further conclusions then require special pleading. Indeed, there seems to be some tension in Aristotle's final position, inasmuch as we are to infer that sight requires a medium on the basis of the fact that we cannot see what touches the eye, even while touch itself requires a medium to operate. (See note to 419a22–b3; cf. 422b34–423a13, 431b1–26.)

**419a22–b3: The Account Extended to Other Modalities:** Aristotle closes the chapter by generalizing the result of 419a7–15 to the other sensory modalities. Just as sight requires a medium, so too do smell and hearing, and for the same reason. When an object with the relevant sensible quality is pressed against the organ, no perception results. Aristotle allows that the case is not so obvious with respect to touch and taste, but promises to provide a reason to extend the view to them as well. He delivers on his promise in II 10–11, offering an intriguing argument at 422b34–423a13 intended to show that the kind of contact we experience in touch only serves to show that flesh is itself the required medium.

It is noteworthy that Aristotle closes the chapter as he began it, compelled to introduce a nameless something into his account of perception. If a medium is necessary for perception, then just as the transparent, which is common to air, water, and certain bodies, serves as the medium for colour, so there is something, unnamed, common to air and water which plays the same role for odour. Since fish can, Aristotle supposes, smell (*Hist. An.*

533a31–b5), then there must be something common to air and water capable of conveying odour from the scented object to the sensory organ. The Greek commentators kindly named it the 'transodorous' (*diosmon*) for Aristotle (Alex. *in Sensu* 89.2).

## CHAPTER 8

### Introduction to II 8

In view of its pronounced physiological orientation, Aristotle's treatment of hearing and sound offers less insight into the character of the hylomorphic theory than some of his other chapters on perception. Indeed, although the chapter is meant to be dedicated to the sense of hearing, Aristotle veers into topics which, however interesting, may seem only peripherally related to his overarching hylomorphism. To the extent that this appearance is accurate, the chapter will add little to our understanding of his more theoretical orientation in much of the rest of the work. Still, one can glean interesting and consequential data from a close reading of Aristotle's primarily physiological focus.

Aristotle characterizes the nature of sound; he asks whether an object struck or an object striking is rightly deemed the cause of sound; he identifies and characterizes voice as an especially important kind of sound; and he determines the sort of physiology required for the production of vocal sound. On the last topic, he pauses to explain why fish do not have voices: they lack vocal chords.

In one way, then, this chapter (like the next, on smell) has a comparatively local interest. It is somewhat out of keeping with the general level of theorizing characteristic of much of the rest of *De Anima*, displaying a tone and interest more typical of the more empirically oriented *Parva Naturalia*. Indeed, in the relevant sections of *De Sensu* 6 and 7, Aristotle allows that he has little to add to the treatment of sound offered here (see, e.g., *De Sensu* 440b27).

That allowed, if one approaches the chapter armed with questions drawn from the general theories of perception (*aisthêsis*) in II 5 and II 12, some interesting, if controversial results accrue.

**419b4–33: Actual and Potential Sound:** It is natural to assume that the distinction between actual and potential sound drawn in the beginning of this chapter corresponds in some way to a distinction between perceived and unperceived sound. The subsequent discussion in this section makes clear, however, that Aristotle's initial distinction is less consequential than it first seems: it is really rather a distinction between the kinds of things which are capable of producing sound and the kinds which are not. Brass urns sound when struck by a metal mallet; a tuft of wool hit with a blade of grass does not. The question of actual and potential perception emerges in a more interesting guise at 425b26 (cf. 417a10, 431b24–5).

**419b33–420b4: Void and the Air:**    Some of Aristotle's remarks regarding void and the air are initially obscure; others are initially surprising. Surprising is the claim at 419b33–4 that the 'the void (*kenon*) is rightly said to be chiefly responsible for hearing.' This is surprising not least because Aristotle elsewhere vigorously combats the existence of the void as something impossible (*Phys.* 213b32–214a17). Aristotle is not, however, contradicting his own view of the void, but rather reporting that the void is rightly said (*legetai*, 419b33)—sc. by those who wrongly identify the air with the void—to be responsible for hearing, since air (= what they wrongly think of as the void) causes hearing when it moves as a continuous mass and reaches the tympanum. Although for consistency's sake *kenon* is rendered as 'the void', here it is also worth noting that the ordinary adjective *kenos* means simply 'empty' or 'devoid of'.

Less surprising but more obscure is Aristotle's contention that 'air is congenital (*sumphuês*) to the organ of hearing' (420a4). The text is understandably debated here, and various commentators have taken it variously. The translation follows a sensible if not strictly necessary suggestion of Ross, and also treats hearing (*akoê*) as the organ of hearing, which has evident parallels at 419b8 and 425a4. On these assumptions, Aristotle's meaning emerges with reasonable clarity: the organ of hearing has air *within* it as a natural or congenital feature. As Aristotle proceeds to explain (420a4–5), it is not just that air in general is required for hearing (it is), but that air must be enclosed within the ear itself, to receive the motion transmitted via the air without.

This same requirement helps to explain a further obscurity in this passage. Aristotle contends that the 'air inside the ears has been encased, in order to be unmoving, so that it can accurately perceive all the variations of motion' (419a9–11). In fact, the air within is not altogether unmoving, but relatively so, as is clear from 420a16–17. On the view advanced, the air within the ear is not accidentally encased as it is, but rather so as to detect sound-bearing motions optimally; were it already moving or easily dissipated, it would not be suited to be affected as it is by fine-grained motions in the air striking it. Here, then, Aristotle relies on the background teleology of this account of perception in general: we may, in this passage as elsewhere, better understand the structures of the sensory organs if we appreciate that they are suited by nature to perform their functions.

**420b5–421a6: Voice:** Although it is dedicated to sound and hearing, Aristotle pauses in this chapter to consider a special kind of sound, voice (*phônê*). He does not restrict voice to human, significant speech (see *Gen. An.* v 7; *Hist. An.* 535a27), though only living beings are capable of producing it. Nor, however, does he suppose that every sound produced by a living being qualifies as an instance of voice. Here (at 420b12), for instance, Aristotle remarks that fish in the river Achelous emit sounds without having voices. This is explained in *Hist. An.* iv 9: they, along with various other fishes, make unvoiced noises. Their sounds are not strictly instances of voice, because they lack the requisite organs; hence, even if one may speak of them as having voices in an extended sense, this will in fact be more closely akin to the perfectly understandable but non-literal way in which we describe instrumental parts in a polyphonic score as voices.

Sometimes Aristotle speaks of voice as the matter (*hulê*) of the bearer of semantic value, where the contrast evidently involves him in denying that voice is the immediate bearer of semantic properties (*Gen. An.* 786b21; *Met.* 1038a6). If that is so, then voice is wider than speech, though narrower than bare breath-induced sound (cf. *Pol.* 1253a14). Since he also requires voice to be produced along with a definite appearance, or perhaps more loosely with some kind of imaging (*meta tinos phantasias;* 420b32), Aristotle does seem to be thinking of voice as nonetheless related to representation of some sort. So, perhaps he is thinking of snarls, sighs, and groans of exasperation as voiced, as opposed, e.g., to hiccups and coughs (420b34). If so, then he means to suggest that nothing has voice without also having at least rudimentary capacities for mental representation. Cf. 433b29, with note, for a distinction between kinds of imagination. This explanation coheres with a point Aristotle makes about voice in *Politics* I 2, which in its turn serves to explicate his remarks about the role of voice in the attainment of well-being in the present chapter (420b19–22). In the *Politics* (1253a7–18), Aristotle notes that voice (*phônê*) pertains to pleasure and pain, which non-human animals experience, whereas discourse (*logos*; 1253a14), which among the animals humans alone manifest, has a role to play in articulating what is advantageous and what not, and so also what is just and unjust, and so finally what is good and what evil. Rational exchange regarding all of this is necessary for political life. As other gregarious animals, like bees, congregate in rudimentary societies, humans, the political animal, form together into societies which are political communities as well, and this they do first for the purpose of living but finally for the purpose of living well (*Pol.* 1252b29–30, 1253a31–7). Thus, one requisite for human flourishing is semantically laden voice, that is, speech. Voice, then, is in this way required for the attainment of living well (*to eu*; 420b22).

## CHAPTER 9

### Introduction to II 9
As with his treatment of hearing in the preceding chapter, Aristotle's discussion of smell is largely physiological in character (see the Introduction to II 8). It is augmented in several respects by *De Sensu* 4–5. Like the last chapter, however, it too contains some puzzling and opaque remarks, and has some interesting implications for Aristotle's broader perceptual hylomorphism as well.

Aristotle introduces smell as more difficult to characterize than the senses thus far considered, hearing and sight. He explains this difficulty by noting humans have a comparatively weak and imprecise faculty of smell, one far inferior to that capacity as it is manifested in some other, non-human animals. He does not say, however, precisely why this causes a difficulty in specifying what it is (though see note to 421a7–16).

Much of the chapter is devoted to a problem generated by a physiological difference between animals which breathe and those which do not: some animals smell, even though they do not breathe air. By contrast, humans cannot smell without inhaling. This particular problem and its resolution contribute little to our understanding of perception generally, though in the context of addressing it Aristotle does point out that any perception of scent, of any kind, is as such an instance of smelling (see note to 421b21–3). This suggests, then, one way in which his account of perception is functionally driven: to smell just is to perceive scent, irrespective of the particular organ deployed, in this instance perception.

Johansen (2005) offers a detailed account of this chapter, arguing plausibly that it is more consequential for our general understanding of Aristotle's approach to perception (*aisthêsis*) than is typically supposed.

**421a7–16: The Obscurity of the Sense of Smell:** Aristotle regards the human sense of smell as feeble in two respects: it is the weakest of the five human sensory modalities and it is plainly inferior in power and discrimination to many non-human animals (see *De Sensu* 440b31–441a3). This latter point might mean one or more of several different things, not necessarily in competition with one another: that some non-human animals can make finer-grained discriminations than humans; that they can detect fainter traces of odour; or, more consequentially, that non-human animals are better able to act on the basis of olfactory information.

In one respect, however, as the parallel discussion of *De Sensu* 5 makes clear (see esp. 443b21–444b7), Aristotle holds humans superior to all other animals. According to that discussion, odours divide into: (i) those co-varying with flavours, which prove to be only co-incidentally pleasant or unpleasant, altering with the dispositions of the perceiver's degree of appetite; and (ii) those which are appetite-independent, like the scents of flowers, which prove, according to Aristotle, to be agreeable in their own right (443b26–7). Only human beings, he somewhat surprisingly thinks, have perception of the second sort.

237

In the current chapter, Aristotle mainly focuses on the ways in which humans are inferior to the other animals, likening the way humans smell to the way that hard-eyed animals see. He thinks that insects, beetles, and lizards see only dimly, because it is as if their semi-transparent eyelids have adhered to their eyes, thus affording them the protection they need but resulting in vision much inferior to soft-eyed creatures (*De Sensu* 444b25; cf. *Part. An.* 657b29–658a1, 691a24). He does not here offer a parallel physiological reason for the deficiency of the olfactory organs in humans.

Even so, he does advance the judgement in passing that humans are more intelligent than other animals, which he derives from their having a much more precise sense of touch (421a20–2); he then proceeds to secure this latter judgement, rather unstably, by noting that humans with delicate flesh—presumably, then, to those with flesh more attuned to fine-grained gradations in the tactile—have a greater aptitude for intelligence than those with hard flesh do (421a23–6).

**421a16–b8: Smell as Analogous to Taste:**   The text of this passage is troubled. On the text as translated, Aristotle suggests that scents are analogous to flavours and are named after them: 'But just as we said, because smells, unlike flavours, are not especially clear, they have taken their names from things by way of likeness' (421a31–b1). An alternative text, preferred by Torstick (1862), Hicks (1907), and defended by Johansen (2005: n.8) might be translated: 'But just as we said, because smells, unlike flavours, are not especially clear, they have taken their names from them [i.e. flavours] because of a likeness in things.' Although both texts are possible, and both give some sense to the passage, Ross's emendation gives an overall better sense. Hence, since either translation requires some manner of emendation, Ross's is perhaps marginally to be preferred. If we accept that determination, then Aristotle's point pertains in the first instance to the first kind of odour distinguished in *De Sensu* 5 (see note to 421a7–16), and is reasonably clear at least in this connection: he is noting that we speak, e.g., of melon scent or lemon scent, by their relation to melons and lemons—even if we detect a melon scent in a glass of Chenin Blanc or a lemon scent in table wax. The text as translated then also allows him in principle to extend the same point to scents of the second sort, scents pleasant in their own right, as when we speak of lilac scent or patchouli scent, even though we are not in the habit of eating lilacs or patchouli plants. Be that as it may, Aristotle's main point in this stretch of text is that flavours are more determinate in humans than smells are, and because more discretely apprehended, they are also more naturally discriminated and named.

**421b9–21: The Medium for Smell:** Aristotle adduces several arguments for the contention that fish smell. If he is right, then air cannot be the medium of smell. Presumably, just as there was something common to air and water as a medium of colour (see note to 418a26–b21), namely the transparent, so there is something common to them as a medium for smell. Aristotle has already suggested that this medium lacks a name (see note to 419a22–b3).

**421b21–3: Sufficient Condition for Smelling:** Aristotle worries about the plain fact that humans smell only when inhaling, whereas other animals, the bloodless ones, cannot inhale and yet have a sense of smell. The source of his worry is at first a bit obscure, though it is noteworthy that he is keen to insist that its resolution cannot make recourse to a sixth sense in fish. On the one hand, he believes that it is in some sense impossible for there to be more than five senses (see the Introduction to III 1). More importantly, Aristotle here makes the perception of scent sufficient for smelling, going indeed so far as to say that smelling is just the perception of scent (421b22–3). This strengthens Aristotle's more typical contention that the modalities are individuated by their objects (see note to 418a11–17, and the Introduction to II 4).

Commentators have been concerned that he seems to suggest something false in this connection, namely that it is peculiar or exclusive (*idion*; 421b19) to humans to smell only when inhaling, when, as he knows, this is equally true of many other animals as well. Possibly he means only that it is peculiar to humans within the comparison class mentioned.

In any event, Aristotle's solution is physiological: inhaling opens a flap analogous to the eyelid, thus permitting a scent to be present to the organ of smell as colour is present to the eye only when the eyelid—in animals which have them—is pulled back.

## CHAPTER 10

### Introduction to II 10

Aristotle allies taste with touch insofar as neither requires an external medium, though in so speaking he does not deviate from his firm belief that every instance of perception requires some medium or other (see note to 422a8–17). His treatment of their connection carries over into the next chapter, which is dedicated to touch (see esp. 423b1–26). Like the preceding chapters, II 10 is primarily physiological in orientation. It does, however, contain the first hint of what will become an increasingly important theme in Aristotle's conception of perception, that overly powerful objects can damage or destroy their correlative sensory modalities (see note to 422a20–31). Equally significant is the deployment of the actuality/potentiality distinction at the end of the chapter. Already introduced at the end of II 5, this distinction plays an important role in Aristotle's general account of perception, though its precise contours are left undeveloped in this chapter (see note to 422b15–16).

Additional details regarding the physiology of taste can be found in *De Sensu* 4.

**422a8–19: The Objects of Taste as Tangible:**     Aristotle does not intend to suggest that the objects of taste are a subspecies of the objects of touch. For then, given his practice of individuating sensory modalities by their objects, taste would merely be a kind of touch, with the result that there would be four senses and not five (see notes to 418a11–17 and 421b21–3, together with the Introduction to II 4). Rather, he contends that what is tasted is also something tangible, a point of contact which helps explain why neither sense requires an external medium. Aristotle suggests, in fact, that flavour perforce resides in something moist as its matter (422a11). Presumably, although he does not say so, his view is that although what can be tasted is of necessity something tangible, what it is to be tasteable differs from what it is to be tangible. Cf. 414b11, where Aristotle subordinates the objects of taste to the tangible, and 423a17–21 (with note), where he makes clear that the senses of taste and touch are two, and not one, despite their close connection.

Aristotle also makes much the same point, still more emphatically, in a polemical passage of *De Sensu*, where he derides the Democritean account of perception on the grounds that it would treat all the senses as special cases of touch (442a28–b2).

That said, there remains a possibly consequential difficulty in Aristotle's treatment of the relation between taste and the tangible, which one might express in the form of a heuristic dilemma. Either taste and touch have overlapping objects or discrete sets of objects. If they overlap, then it is unclear how Aristotle can maintain his preferred practice of individuating sensory modalities by their respective objects; if they are discrete, then it remains unclear precisely how taste is subordinated to touch. It is tempting to approach the issue by distinguishing between broad and narrow conceptions of objects of perception (on which, see the General Introduction § III.B, and notes to 418a25, 424a29–b31, 426a23, 432a3–6), by suggesting that the objects of taste overlap with the objects of touch considered broadly construed, so that, e.g. a lemon may both be touched and tasted—but it may equally be seen, smelled, and even heard. If we say, by contrast, that he is thinking objects narrowly construed, so that the flavours are objects of taste qua tasteable and objects of touch qua tangible, then we preserve the discreteness of the objects, but evidently at the cost of making them suited to individuate the sensory modalities since any such appeal would be plainly circular. This is, however, a sort of circularity, or potential circularity, one sees threatening elsewhere in *De Anima*. See, e.g., notes to 415a14–22, 418a11–17, and especially 416b9–11, where the case of the nutritive soul and its objects is considered.

The matter is compounded by the fact that touch already seems to admit of a plurality of objects, on which, see note to 422b17–23.

**422a20–31: Objects of Taste and Sight: Ranges of Contraries:** In drawing a parallel between the objects of taste and sight, Aristotle contends that there are natural extremes in ranges of contraries beyond which the senses cannot operate. Beyond one extreme resides the non-perceptible, which might be so either contingently or necessarily. (Oscar Wilde deep in an unilluminated mineshaft cannot be seen, though, unlike the sound of a snigger, which cannot in Aristotle's view be an object of vision, Wilde can be seen when outside the shaft; cf. 421b6). Beyond the other extreme lie damage and destruction: when we perceive an excessively bright light or loud sound, the sense is temporarily rendered inoperative or, in extreme cases, permanently damaged. Aristotle adverts to this phenomenon several times in his treatment of perception (424a14, 29, 426a30, 429a31); because he uses this fact to ground a distinction between perception (*aisthêsis*) and reason (*nous*) (see 429a29–b5, with note), it is worth asking precisely what he understands to be damaged in sensory overload: the sensory organ (the *aisthêtêrion*) or the capacity (*dunamis*). (Aristotle will contend at 424a24–8 that the sensory organs and the sensory capacities are extensionally equivalent, though differing in their essential natures.) Here he does not specify which he means, though he seems to have the capacity in mind (422a31).

**422b15–16: Potentiality and Actuality in Perception:** Aristotle closed II 5 with a somewhat underdeveloped parting observation, glossing his general account of perception (*aisthêsis*) in terms of form reception and being made like (see note to 418b3–5). He closes the present chapter in a similar vein, though merely by treating taste as a special case of perception. After what he takes to be something approaching an exhaustive list of the kinds of flavours there are, all of which are ultimately some mixed ratio of the bitter (*pikron*) and the sweet (*gluku*) (the point is made more fully in *De Sensu* 442a13–25), Aristotle suggests, in keeping with his general account of perception, that what is capable of tasting is in potentiality what the object of taste is in actuality.

This passage accordingly presents data relevant to an interpretive worry (discussed in the General Introduction § IV.C) pertaining to what is meant by the contention that the faculty is *made like* its object. Two questions pertinent to this worry are: (i) what are the *relata* in the form assimilation and (ii) what are the conditions under which the altered organ is made like its objects? As for (i), Aristotle in this passage speaks simply of the faculty of taste or 'what is capable of tasting' (*geustikon*), just as at the end of II 5 he speaks of the general faculty of perception as 'what is capable of perceiving' (*aisthêtikon*; 418a3). Although no answer is given in the present section, his approach to (ii) in this chapter puts some strain on the suggestion that being made like involves literal form transference.

On that approach, what is capable of tasting will, when perceiving something with a chocolate flavour, come to be itself something chocolate-flavoured.

CHAPTER 11

Introduction to II 11

Aristotle struggles a bit with the sense of touch, primarily because its objects are not readily identifiable. When he wanted to name the exclusive (*idia*) objects of each sense in II 6, Aristotle hesitated when he came to touch: 'sight is of colour, hearing is of sound, and taste is of flavour, whereas touch has a number of different objects' (418a13–14; see note to 418a11–17 for the difficulties this presents). Given his practice of individuating senses by their correlative objects, the unavailability of an obvious unified object in the case of touch leads him to wonder whether touch is after all a single modality. This difficulty is particularly striking in view of the fact that touch is the only sense shared by all creatures with perceptual souls, and is thus the lowest demarcator of animality (see 413b5–6, 414a3, 414b3, 415a4, 434b24, and 435a13–b2).

In the present chapter Aristotle is primarily concerned with two issues pertaining to touch: (i) whether touch is a single modality (see note to 422b23–423a21); and (ii) whether, regarding the location of the sense of touch, one should regard the flesh itself as its organ or rather something internal, with the flesh serving as a sort of medium (see note to 423a22–b26). Subordinate to the second question, then, is a question pertaining to the medium of touch and its manner of conveying the tangible (see note to 423b27–424a10).

In the course of addressing these worries, Aristotle adverts to his overarching hylomorphic framework (423b30–424a6). To some extent, the peculiarities associated with touch stress that framework in ways which help bring into sharper relief Aristotle's understanding of its contours and its appropriate application.

For more on the physiology of touch, see *De Sensu* 4.

**422b17–23: Two Problems Pertaining to Touch:** Aristotle's principal preoccupations with touch concern: (i) its lack of a single object, and (ii) the obscurity of its organ. The first concern

243

yields a problem concerning whether it is appropriate to treat touch as a unified modality at all. If it has discrete ranges of objects, then why should it be a single sense any more than hearing and smell are? The second matter raises a difficulty for Aristotle's steady view that all perception occurs via some medium. If flesh is the organ of touch and its organ contacts its objects, then where is there room for (or need of) a medium?

**422b23–423a21: First Problem Addressed: Multiple Oppositions:**
Aristotle addresses the first problem immediately, though in a way which appears to skirt its real force. Sight sees colour; hearing hears sound; but touch has no single independently identifiable object (cf. 418a13–14). Consequently, there is no single range of contraries whose admixture exhausts the range of its objects. That is, since colour is the object of sight, sight has a determinate pair of contraries, black and white, mixtures of which yield the colour spectrum (*De Sensu* 439b16–440a6). Touch, by contrast, says Aristotle, admits of a series of distinct contraries: hot and cold, dry and wet, hard and soft, and even, he allows, 'whatever else is of this sort' (423a27).

His concern evidently centres on the following objection: (1) if *x* is a single sensory modality, *x* has a discrete, unified object; (2) if *x* has a discrete, unified object, then *x* ranges over a single determinate pair of opposites; (3) so, if *x* is a single sensory modality, *x* ranges over a single determinate pair of opposites; (4) touch ranges over several determinate pairs of opposites; hence (5) touch is not a single sensory modality.

Aristotle responds by denying (2), since he insists that sight and hearing have discrete, unified objects, namely colour and sound, even though it is possible to identify various pairs of contraries in their range. Thus, in sound, for instance, we speak of highness and lowness, loudness and softness, and so on (422b29–31).

The response does little to blunt the objection, since as Aristotle notes, it remains easy to treat the contraries specified as *sonic* contraries, or as contraries subordinate to colour. It is not clear, he allows, what the 'substratum' (*hupokeimenon*) of the various pairs of opposites identified by touch might be. In effect, Aristotle himself points out that a denial of (2) is a hollow victory, since (2) is easily rewritten as (2′): If modality *x* has a discrete, unified object, then *x* ranges over pairs of opposites specifiable only as determinants of that object. (2′) evidently holds true of all sensory modalities other than touch; and with the appropriate adjustments to the remaining premises, the damaging (5) remains intact. In implicitly making this concession, Aristotle does not, of course, positively insist that there is no appropriate substratum, or object, of touch; rather, he concedes that if there is such, it is difficult to identify.

**423a22–b26: Second Problem Addressed: The Medium of Touch:** It is plain that the eyes are the organs of sight, the ears of hearing, the nose of smelling, and the tongue of taste. What then is the organ of touch? One natural suggestion, now to be rejected by Aristotle, would be that the organ of touch is flesh. After all, as we see with the eyes, so, it would seem, we touch with the flesh: at any rate, just as Aristotle notes, perception occurs at the moment we handle tangible objects (423a1–2).

Aristotle disagrees with this easy suggestion and, by way of explaining his reasons for doing so deploys what Ross rightly calls 'a remarkable piece of imaginative thinking' (1961: 262). Suppose, says Aristotle, that a membrane were placed upon the skin (we can imagine it to be a piece of cellophane). One would nonetheless perceive tangible objects at the moment of contact with them; but no one would want to treat this membrane as in any way an organ. This shows, Aristotle concludes, not that flesh cannot be the organ of touch, but, more narrowly, that the fact of simultaneous perception is not sufficient to treat flesh as the organ of touch. He contends, then, that we would reach the same result even if the membrane so placed became naturally attached (*sumphues*; 423a5) to the skin.

Imagining, perhaps, that someone might counter that in such a case we might well be entitled to treat simultaneous perception as evidence for the unwanted conclusion on the grounds that a naturally affixed membrane would be living, and thus plausibly an organ after all, Aristotle adds a second argument. Suppose a thin layer of air completely surrounding us became naturally affixed. Then, if we were to treat simultaneous perception as sufficient for something's being an organ, we would be constrained to treat all sensory modalities as having the same organ, namely, the naturally affixed layer of air surrounding them. This result contravenes the plain facts: the various modalities have distinct organs.

245

Once again, then, we are not entitled to infer that flesh is the organ of touch from the fact that perception of tactile qualities occurs simultaneous with the moment of contact. Aristotle's preferred view holds that the organ of touch is internal (423b23; cf. *Part. An.* 656a27–30; *De Iuv.* 469a4–27). Even so, later in *De Anima*, he seems to suggest that flesh itself is the sensory organ. See note to 435a11–b3.

**423b27–424a10: Perceptual Objects, Discrimination, and the Mean:** Aristotle closes the chapter in a manner similar to his ending of II 10, by positioning touch within his broader hylomorphic theory of perception. Treating touch as a special case of perception, he infers that the organ in which it primarily resides is in potentiality what the object of touch is in actuality (see note to 417b16–27). He further appeals to his contention that perception is a sort of being affected (cf. 416b33, 424a1; see note to 416b32–417a2). So, touch, either the faculty or the organ in which the faculty resides, is potentially what its objects are actually, and is affected by them in being made actual. It is noteworthy that in this passage Aristotle seems to treat the sensory organ (*aisthêtêrion*; 423b30) as the subject which is made like. By contrast, in the conclusion to II 10, he spoke more generally of the *faculty of taste* or *what is capable of tasting* (*geustikon*), which was itself more in line with the end of II 5, where he spoke of the *faculty of perception* or *what is capable of perceiving* (*aisthêtikon*; 418a3) as the thing made like its object in perception (*aisthêsis*). See also 422a7 and 422b15.

In any event, Aristotle also applies the doctrine of the mean (*meson*) to touch. Just as what perceives black or white cannot be itself already actually so, so what perceives the hot or cold cannot already be hot or cold in a measure equal to what it is perceived. (Parents test the temperature of an infant's milk by testing it against their own skin; when its temperature is not perceived, it is neither too hot nor too cold.) Although he has not yet articulated the doctrine to which he appeals here, it is clear that Aristotle has in mind the view he introduces more fully in the next chapter at 424a25–b3 (see note to 424a28–b3 for an explication of his position). Here Aristotle introduces something of significance which is later omitted, that the mean is capable of discriminating (it is *kritikon*; 424a6). By this he does not intend to suggest that the mean is itself a faculty capable of judging or discriminating. Rather, he suggests that the presence of a calibrated structure in a sense organ or faculty is something capable of being altered, and so allows the detection of sensible qualities by the perceiver.

## CHAPTER 12

### Introduction to II 12

Having now completed his investigation of the various senses, Aristotle pulls back to offer a recapitulation of the general theory of perception in terms of which the individual accounts have been articulated. The present chapter, then, serves as a sort of bookend to II 5, which proceeds at a similarly general level. There are, however, some striking and consequential differences between the two chapters: (i) most significantly, Aristotle stresses here that perception involves the reception of the form *without the matter* (*aneu tês hulês*, 424a18–19; see note to 424a17–24), where no such stricture had been offered earlier; further (ii) Aristotle now distinguishes between the sensory organ (*aisthêtêrion*) and the faculty (*dunamis*), maintaining that the faculty is not a magnitude (*megethos*) at all (see note to 424a24–8): and finally, (iii) in the present chapter, he codifies two related themes which, though left unmentioned in II 5, have emerged intermittently in II 7–11, that (a) the faculty is a certain kind of proportion (or ratio, *logos*); and (b) it can consequently be impaired or destroyed by excessively strong objects of sense (see note to 424a28–b3).

Because the chapter is relatively brief, many of these themes are left undeveloped and have accordingly been subject to intense exegetical controversy.

### 424a17–24: Perception as Receiving the Form without the Matter:

The important formula introduced here comes as a bit of a surprise. Aristotle has spoken earlier of the media involved in perception as receptive (*dektikon*) (418b27–419a2), but he has not yet characterized the senses or the sensory organs in this way. Further, though he has said that the faculty is made like its objects, he has not earlier explained this contention in terms of receiving a sensible form without the matter (see note to

418b3–5). So, the important formula introduced here cannot be regarded as a generalizing summary so much as an attempt to encapsulate what has been advanced regarding the special senses in a new and theoretically enriched manner.

Given the importance of this formula in understanding Aristotle's general hylomorphic theory of perception, it is necessary to grasp each of its central terms precisely. Some pertinent questions towards this end: (1) what are the *relata* involved in form reception and (2) what does it mean to receive the form *without the matter?*

Unfortunately, if unsurprisingly, each of these questions has given rise to exegetical controversy. Some first approaches to each question are:

(1) Aristotle characterizes *perception* (*aisthêsis*) as receptive of perceptual forms, but then goes on to specify the faculty (*dunamis*; 423b25) as the relevant *relatum*. Note, however, that he elsewhere speaks freely of the sensory organ (*aisthêtêrion*) as what is receptive of the form (e.g. 425b23–4, 435a22–4); but the sensory organ and the capacity are not the same (see note to 424a24–8).

So, he might have one of two different views in mind, according to which either the sensory organ or the capacity comes to manifest the form in perception. If one focuses on the sensory organ (*aisthêtêrion*), then some literalist conception of form reception becomes at least initially viable, whereas if the capacity (*dunamis*) is the *relatum* in view, then a variety of intentionalism gains some initial traction. (On the distinction between these two approaches, see the General Introduction § II.B.) So, the distinction is consequential, though the matter will not turn exclusively on this difference. (See also note to 424a24–8 on the relation between the sensory organ and the capacity.)

As a further complication, when speaking of the objects of perception, Aristotle might be thinking of them as broadly or narrowly construed (thinking, e.g., of the rose as the object smelled rather than its scent, more narrowly; on this distinction, see the General Introduction § IV.B). Here he evidently has the broad notion of object in mind, since he suggests that a perceiver is affected by the things which have sensible qualities (424a21–3), but only insofar as they have sensible qualities. If that is correct, then there is a natural consequence for question (2), the question of what it means to receive the form without the matter.

There are two basic approaches to (2): (i) the perceiver receives the form without its matter, that is the matter of the broad object of perception which has the quality in question, i.e. the perceiver receives the rose's scent, but not the matter of the rose itself; or (ii) the perceiver receives the form without making it enmattered upon reception. (Importantly, these two views are not finally in competition, in the sense that even if Aristotle intends (i) rather than (ii) here, or (ii) rather than (i), he might still believe the other.

If we answer (1) by taking the objects of perception broadly, then it is a small step to understand the phrase 'without the matter' (*aneu tês hulês*, 424a18–19) as referring to the matter of the objects of perception. Thus, when Juliet smells a rose, her olfactory capacity receives the sensible form of the rose without receiving the matter underlying that form as it is realized in the rose. This approach is evidently supported by the illustration of the signet ring whose impression is left in wax: the gold in which the form is realized in the signet ring is not received into the wax. Whatever the causal process of transference in the case of perception, the matter in which the perceptible form is realized is not itself received into the capacity or organ. This passage is helpfully discussed by Ward (1988), Silverman (1989), Caston (1998), and Polansky (2007).

This is equally the purport of the obscure-sounding contention that the sense receives the qualities of the objects of perception, but 'not insofar as each of these is said to be something, but rather insofar as each is of a certain quality, and corresponding to its proportion' (424a23–4). Aristotle means that when smelling a rose, a perceiver is affected by the rose not *insofar as it is a rose*, but *insofar as it has a certain scent*. The gloss 'corresponding to its proportion (*kata logon;* 424a24) makes this still clearer: the proportion, sometimes rendered 'ratio' (*logos*) is the quality taken abstractly. Recall that *'logos'* is in some cases to be taken non-semantically, as it is here (cf. *Phys.* 209a2; *Met.* 1006b1, 1030a7, 1044b22; see notes to 403a3–27 and 418a7–11; see glossary entry *logos*). In the context of perception, this is especially so when it is intended to draw upon Aristotle's contention that sensible qualities are ratios (*logoi*) of contraries (see note to 422b23–423a21; cf. *De Sensu* 439b16–440a6). Form reception, on this approach, involves becoming made like by being made to come to receive a sensible form, considered as a ratio of contraries. Ward (1988) develops this sort of interpretation to good effect.

Again, however, this interpretation does not by itself settle the overarching dispute between literalism and intentionalism, even if it paves the way for a form of intentionalism; for it does not by itself rule out literalism.

**424a24–8: The Relation of the Faculty to the Sensory Organ:** This significant passage makes three important claims about the apparatus involved in perception. Although his terminology is not always perfectly consistent, Aristotle distinguishes here quite clearly between the sensory organ (*aisthêtêrion*) and the capacity (*dunamis*), and identifies the sensory organ as that in which the sort of capacity suited to receive perceptual forms without matter resides. In saying that the capacity and the organ are the same though differing in being (424a25), Aristotle means that they are extensionally equivalent but non-identical, because of their having distinct accounts. When thinking of particular extensional equivalence, Aristotle will say, e.g., that the musical man is the same as the white man, though they differ in being, because *what it is to be a white man* is not the same as *what it is to be a musical man* (*Met.* 1037b6; *Phys.* 202a18–20, b11–16). In the same way, though the capacity resides in an organ, what it is to be an organ is not the same as what it is to be a capacity. So, an account of the capacity of sight, e.g., will not be the same as an account of what it is to be an eye, even if, as Aristotle contends, the capacity is localized in the eye.

Aristotle's confidence on this point derives from his insistence that the capacity is not even a magnitude (*megethos*), while plainly the sensory organ is. Indeed, Aristotle extends this point to both the perceptual faculty (*aisthêtikon*) and perception (*aisthêsis*) generally: neither is a magnitude, but each is instead a proportion or ratio (*logos*) (424b26–8). Insofar as Aristotle thinks of the capacity (*dunamis*; 423b25) as the recipient of the sensible form, it follows that form reception cannot involve literal property exemplification; it would be a category mistake to think of a ratio as being blue, on a par with believing that squares snore. For more on the controversy regarding the proper understanding of form reception in perception, see the General Introduction § IV.B.

**424a28–b3: Two Explanatory Consequences:** Aristotle relies upon the results of the chapter thus far, including especially his contention that perception is not a magnitude, but a ratio (*logos*), to explain two further facts: (i) that an overly intense object destroys the sensory organ; and (ii) that plants do not perceive. His first contention, regarding intense objects of sense, has already been introduced in passing (see note to 422a20–31). Here Aristotle employs an analogy to explicate more fully his grounds for holding that, when overpowered, the senses are destroyed. Just as an instrument loses its pitch when its strings are stretched beyond their limits, so a sense, when jarred out of ratio, cannot perceive. Aristotle's explanation here should be understood in conjunction with his conception of a capacity (*dunamis*) as a certain kind of ratio involving a mean, to which he appeals in explaining his second fact, that plants do not perceive (cf. 424a4–6, 431a11, 435a21).

This second fact, that plants do not perceive, is taken as given, in need of no defence (cf. 414a32). There is a sense in which plants are affected by tangible objects; but their being affected in this way does not eventuate in perception. Aristotle mentions three reasons, at least the first two of which are closely connected: (i) they lack a mean (*mesotêta*); (ii) they lack the sort of principle (here *archê*, not *logos*) suited to receive sensible forms; and (iii) they are affected *with the matter* (*meta tês hulês*; 424b3). Evidently (i) explains (ii): since a perceptual capacity is not a magnitude, but rather a certain kind of ratio (see note to 424a24–8), and a plant does not manifest such ratio, it does not have the internal structure requisite for form reception. Most probably, (iii) is intended to explain further, in a concessive vein, how plants are affected by sensible objects only in ways irrelevant to perception.

If that is correct, Aristotle is actually guarding himself against an objection of the following form: (1) perception occurs when an ensouled being is affected by an object of perception; (2) plants, which are ensouled beings, are affected by tangible objects (tangible objects include the hot and the cold, 423a27); (3) so, on the hylomorphic theory adumbrated, plants should perceive; (4) plants do not perceive; hence, (5) the hylomorphic theory adumbrated is false. Aristotle denies both (1) and (2): (1) because something is capable of perceiving only if it has a suitably structured sensory faculty (which plants lack); and (2) because plants are affected by tangible objects, but not qua tangible. Taken this way, being *affected with the matter* need not be understood as sufficient for *not* being affected by the sensible form; rather, plants are affected *only* with the matter, and never by the sensible form qua sensible form alone.

To be precise, then, one can imagine three scenarios: (i) x's being affected with the matter alone; (ii) x's being affected with the matter as well as the sensible form; and (iii) x's being affected with the sensible form alone. Plants are affected in sense (i) only, since they lack the requisite faculties to receive sensible forms. Case (iii) occurs when animals, including humans, perceive. Case (ii) might in principle occur in animals, but perception will be indifferent to the matter received. This is the sense in which receiving a sensible form with its matter is not perception but is not sufficient for non-perception either. Drinking iced water will cool the tongue, but perceiving cold will consist not in the tongue's being cooled, but in the capacity's (*dunamis*) receiving the sensible form and being thereby appropriately altered.

**424b3–21: An Aporia about Smell and Soulless Affection:** The last section of the chapter explores further problems pursuant to being affected by sensible objects in the absence of perception. Unfortunately, there are some textual problems which render the task of extracting Aristotle's exact meaning difficult. The text reflected in the translation closes with a pregnant question which may or may not be intended as rhetorical. According to this reconstruction, Aristotle asks: 'What, then, is smelling beyond being affected by something? Or is smelling also perceiving, whereas the air which is affected quickly becomes something perceptible?' (424b20–31). This same text might be translated as: 'What, then, is smelling beyond being affected in a certain way?' The latter translation would then echo a point made in II 5 (see note to 417b2–16) that 'suffering something' might be variously understood, with the result that some forms of suffering something might not be regarded as alteration.

An alternate text, favoured by Burnyeat (1995a) omits the 'also' (*kai*) to give: 'Or is smelling perceiving, whereas...?' Taken this way, Aristotle's question may seem a bit ill-motivated, though he might be understood to be saying, roughly, 'Or is it simply a brute fact that smelling is perceiving, given that form reception in the case of those with the right sensory apparatus *simply is* perception, whereas no medium has the requisite apparatus?'

Taken as including the 'also', Aristotle's question is highly consequential: if form reception, suitably understood as being affected in a certain way (*paschein ti*, 424b20; cf. notes to 416b32–417a2 and 429a13–18), is *sufficient* for perception, then given that even the medium is, or seems to be, somehow itself affected, we might expect the medium itself to perceive. Since the medium manifestly does not perceive, then evidently either (i) being somehow affected (*paschein ti*) must be robustly, or technically, understood in the case of perception; or (ii) only specifiable subjects perceive when they are so affected—or perhaps both (i) and (ii). If (i), then more will need to be said about the kind of affection involved in perception. If (ii), then a kind of explanatory vacuity threatens: perception occurs when beings capable of perceiving are affected by sensible objects capable of affecting them in the way that occasions perception in such beings. (On the question of the ways in which the medium is or is not affected, see Johansen (1998), together with the review of Ganson (2000).)

The worry understood in this way extends beyond the medium and is thus consequential for our eventual appraisal of Aristotle's account of perception. On the text as reconstructed, Aristotle is exercised by a puzzle involving the transmission of sensible form in the absence of perception. Suppose, e.g., that a block of tofu sits in the refrigerator next to an onion. Eventually, the tofu will take on the odour of the onion. If odour is a sensible form, and if it is received by the tofu in being affected by it, then are we not constrained to say that the tofu perceives, that it smells the onion? Aristotle's first rejoinder hearkens back to a point already made (see note to 424a28–b3): only what is capable of perceiving, i.e. what is a suitably structured sensory capacity manifesting an appropriate mean, is capable of being affected by a sensible object qua sensible object. The tofu fails this condition. This is to insist in the first instance, then, that form reception in perception is more than merely being affected.

So construed, the concluding two sentences of this chapter ask a question which ought to be of concern to the author of the hylomorphic theory of perception, but do not undertake to answer it directly. If form reception is sufficient for perception, and various non-ensouled entities are in some sense affected by perceptual forms, then they ought to perceive—which is plainly contrary to what we observe. If we counter that their manner of being affected is not form *reception*, then that will simply refocus our attention on the question of what perceptual form reception consists in. If on the other hand we hold form reception to be insufficient for perception, on the grounds that the insensate beings receive sensible forms without perceiving, then we will need to know what more is required for perception to accrue.

It will be, as suggested, altogether unilluminating to counter that what is required in addition to form reception is *perception* of form reception. This is one reason, then, to resist another possible reconstruction of the text, one favoured by Ross (1961), which yields the following paraphrase: 'What, then, is smelling, over and above being affected? Smelling is also *perceiving*, and air when it has been thus affected becomes perceptible' (1961: 264). This would in effect represent Aristotle as posing a pertinent question only to answer it ineffectually: 'What more is needed beyond the reception of sensible form for perception to accrue? What more is needed is this: perception.'

For more on the general question of the role of form reception in perception, see the General Introduction § IV.B.

# BOOK III

## CHAPTER 1

### Introduction to III 1

The current division between *De Anima* books II and III is
inappropriate. As is reflected in some preferable book divisions
employed in medieval manuscripts, III 1 carries forward Aristotle's
treatment of perception, taking up a topic which, though of a
higher level of generality than the more detailed and intrinsic
characterizations of II 5–12, is nevertheless naturally continuous
with them. Still, the current translation follows the modern book
divisions for ease of reference. For a discussion of the book divisions of *De Anima*, see Hutchinson (1987).

Thus far we have received two general accounts of perception
(II 5 and II 12), a taxonomy of perceptual objects (II 6), and minute
treatments of each of the five senses taken individually (II 7–11).
A question thus naturally arises as to whether the account of the
faculty of perception is now complete: are there more than the
customary five senses? Aristotle takes up this question in the present chapter, arguing that there are not.

Aristotle's argument for this conclusion is initially obscure,
because it relies on some unclear contentions about the media of
perception and their relation to perceptual faculties (see
424b22–425a13 for an attempted reconstruction). Indeed, there
are some questions as to what Aristotle intends to accomplish in
this chapter. He announces as a thesis to be established that 'there
is no other sense beyond the five' (424b22), but this claim might
be taken more or less modestly. The modest thesis (supported, if
inconclusively, by 425b11–13; cf. *Hist. An.* 532b39, *De Sensu*
444b19) holds that humans and other animals *in fact* have five
and only five senses. A less modest thesis aims for a modal claim,
that human beings *could not* have more than five senses, or that it
is impossible that there should be more than five senses. The
modal thesis, though much more ambitious, need not be thought
extravagant; if (i) a necessary condition of there being a sense

255

faculty is its having an exclusive object (*idion*), and (ii) we have reason to believe that there could be no exclusive objects beyond the five already mentioned, then we would have at least that much reason to entertain the modal thesis. The modest thesis, though less ambitious, is not without interest. If the task before us is to provide a complete account of perception, then it behoves us to consider whether we have inadvertently overlooked any of its faculties.

It is common for contemporary researches in psychology and cognitive ethology to assert that theorists of Aristotle's ilk have overlooked any number of sensory modalities, that, e.g., bees have perception of magnetic fields in view of the magnetite organs in their abdomens, or that sharks and platypuses perceive voltage with electric sensors rightly regarded as sensory organs. Others hold that many other animals, including humans, have a sixth sense, proprioception.

One need not accept without reflection on the preconceptions involved in these contentions that the more common Aristotelian model has been superseded; in particular, it is not immediately obvious that just any information-supplying mechanism in fact qualifies as a perceptual capacity. It is not clear, for instance, that the often cited vestibular sense, or sense of balance, qualifies as a sensory modality. Fairly plainly, in all such disputes suppositions regarding the conditions under which a system qualifies as a sensory modality must be identified expressly and evaluated.

Accordingly, Aristotle's investigation of the number of sensory modalities proves worthwhile if for no other reason than that it enjoins us to reflect on what is meant when we claim that there are *n* number of senses. Should we agree that our sense of time, or our sense of balance, or our kinesthetic sense are senses on a par with the traditional five? Aristotle's discussion reminds us that it need not be ceded without further reflection that they are.

By the same token Aristotle's discussion gives us reason to believe that we are not constrained to agree without further discussion with those pragmatically inclined investigators who contend that we have only a decision and not a discovery to make in this area. At root, under review in this chapter, then, is the question of what is required for a psychic ability to qualify as a sensory modality. Interestingly, in this regard, if we can trust a late report, such questions and controversies had already arisen in Aristotle's own time. According to Stobaeus (*Ecl.* 1.51), for instance, Democritus had contended that irrational animals, sages, and gods have more than the canonical five senses. If that report is credible, and Aristotle had been aware of Democritus' claim, it would be typical of him to feel the need to offer a rejoinder (cf. the Introduction to I 1). It must be said, however, that Aristotle provides no reason to believe that he was aware of any such claim by Democritus or anyone else (indeed, *De Sensu* 442a29 may come close to implying that he was not aware of any such contention).

In any event, if Aristotle's thesis about the number of sensory modalities is false when taken modestly, as a mere descriptive claim, then so too is the stronger, modal version, though, of course, the modal thesis could fail while the modest thesis remains intact.

So much, though, proceeds on the assumption that the chapter is about what it seems to be about, viz. the question of how many senses there are or could be. Even this has been informatively challenged. For an alternative approach, see Maudlin (1986), who seeks to show that this traditional interpretation is wholly misguided.

The second half of the chapter gives way to a discussion of the common perception (*koinê aisthêsis*), more regularly, if misleadingly, rendered as 'common sense'. Assuming some version of the traditional interpretation, the discussion of the existence of the common sense follows naturally, since Aristotle has already allowed that there are common objects of perception (see note to 418a17–20). The question thus arises as to whether there is a common perception, or a common sense, and then if so whether it is to be regarded as a faculty in its own right, on a par with the five standard senses. Questions about the existence and nature of common perception are investigated exhaustively by Gregoric (2007), who offers an expansive interpretation but also provides a fair-minded survey of much of the extensive literature on this topic.

**424b22–425a13: There are Five and Only Five Faculties of Perception:** The difficulties in this section begin but do not end with the fact that after the first brief introductory sentence (422b22–4), there follows one long, ungainly sentence of dubious grammaticality containing the whole of the argument for the thesis that there are but five senses (424b24–425a13). (The translation breaks this complex construction into six sentences, some of which already individually tax English syntax.)

Aristotle's argument trades on the fact that there are a limited number of elements available, and attempts, rather obscurely, to show that this fact alone constrains the number of sense organs. In its schematic outline, Aristotle's argument is:

(1) We are missing a sense only if we are missing the sensory organ in which it resides (424b26–7).

(2) All sensible qualities are apprehended either by handling or via an external medium (424b27–31).

(3) If anything is apprehended by handling, it is tangible, for which there is an organ (424b28–9).

(4) If anything is apprehended indirectly, it is via an external medium, composed of either air or water (424b29–30).

(5) An organ is suited to perceive something via an external medium if and only if it is composed of the elements of that medium (viz. air or water) (424b31–425a4).

(6) Hence, any organs there may be for perceiving via an external medium are composed of air and water (425a7–8).

(7) Animals are in fact outfitted with organs composed of air and water (425a8–9).

(8) Hence, without an alien element, animals have all the organs there may be for perceiving via an external medium (425b11–13).

(9) Hence, by (1), (2), and (7), without an alien element, animals have all the organs there may be.

(10) There is no alien element

(11) Hence, by (9) and (10), animals have all the senses there may be (424b22, 425a13).

Although this reconstruction must be regarded as conjectural, in part because it sometimes relies on an interim conclusion to discern how a prior premise must be construed, it does capture the main movement of Aristotle text.

Some brief comments, mainly intended as explicative: The final conclusion (11) as stated is neutral between the modest and modal interpretations ('may be' meaning either: (i) may in fact be, or (ii) may possibly be). (1) relies upon the thought that every power of sense resides in some faculty or other, on which, see note to 424a24–8. (2) renders the Greek word *haptesthai* somewhat unnaturally as *to handle*, partly because Aristotle's considered view is that we do not touch the tangible directly, but via an internal medium; the same fact explains the 'external' in the premises which follow. See note to 423a22–423b26. The most difficult premise to appreciate is (5), though Aristotle does deploy a sub-argument on its behalf. It need not be assumed that he is relying upon a like-like theory (on which, see notes to 418b3–5 and 416b32–417a2). More probably, he is suggesting, evidently as an empirical hypothesis, that there is some natural affinity between the external medium of a sensible quality and the dedicated sensory organ in which its related faculty resides. Thus, the pupil is composed of water and the inner ear of air (424a4–5). Here one may usefully compare *De Sensu* 438b16, where the same point is made about the eye and ear, though a conflicting suggestion is made regarding smell.

One obvious trouble spot in the argument as structured would be the inference from (6) and (7) to (8), the interim conclusion that without an alien element, animals have all the organs there may be for perceiving via an external medium (425b11–13). There seems to be no reason why one must suppose that the bare presence in animals of organs composed of elements present in the media exhausts the possible range of organs with such material constituents. One possibility, made unlikely by Aristotle's concession that fire may also be present in all the organs (425a5–6) would be that he is thinking that an exclusive or dominant element is present in each non-tactile organ, such that each such organ finds a single counterpart in an external medium to which it is specifically suited. This is his avowed view in *De Sensu* 438b16–20. Still, the discrepancy about smell between that passage and 425a5 makes this suggestion hard to credit. In *De Sensu*, Aristotle is prepared to make fire the correlative element of the olfactory organ; here, he doubts that. If that is so, and if Aristotle's views on the physiology of perception are in transition, then the present argument should not rely on a one-to-one correspondence between organs and external elements for the non-tactile organs.

Finally, this reconstruction inserts premise (10), which is not stated in the text; it does, however, seem required for validity. Unfortunately, though, (10) raises the spectre of a question-begging argument, since there seems little reason to deny that there is an alien element present beyond the fact that we have never perceived one—which, presumably, we could do were we equipped with the appropriate sensory modality. In any event, in order to avoid this sort of difficulty, on the assumption that (10) plays an indispensable role, Aristotle would need some perception-independent reason for denying the existence of any element beyond air and water as a medium.

**425a14–b3: The Common Sense; Co-incidental Perception:** Aristotle has already allowed that there is a class of common objects of perception over and above the exclusive (*idion*) objects individuative of the five senses (see 418a7–11, 17–19, with note to 418a17–20). In the text adopted for the translation, Aristotle lists six common sensibles (*koina aisthêta*) (motion, rest, shape, magnitude, number, and unity; 425a16), thus adding unity to the list given at 418a17 (cf. also *De Sensu* 442b5–7). In the present context, the existence of this class gives rise to a worry about whether there must not be some additional faculty of perception responsible for them. If one thought, for instance, (1) that a sufficient condition for there being a discrete sense is the existence of a correlative object not exclusive to any other sense, and added to that the thought (2) that common objects are not exclusive to any sense, it might be thought to follow (3) that there is a discrete sense, common perception (*koinê aisthêsis*), existing in addition to the canonical five. The case for (1) in the case of common objects is sharpened by the hypothesis that we perceive each of the six listed common sensibles by perceiving motion. If motion is not an exclusive object of any of the five senses discussed thus far, perhaps it will be necessary to posit a sixth modality, common perception (*koinê aisthêsis*).

In responding to this sort of argument, Aristotle implicitly relies on the taxonomy of objects given in II 6 (see the Introduction to which), where exclusive (*idia*) and common (*koina*) objects are jointly contrasted with co-incidental (*kata sumbebêkota*) objects (418a8–11). Aristotle now suggests that there would be a special organ for common objects only were there also a special sense. But there cannot be a special sense, for if there were, then perception of the common objects would proceed in the manner of co-incidental perception, as when, for example, we *see* that the white thing is sweet. Insofar as we may be said to see this at all, this is due to our having correlated, e.g., the whiteness of sugar with its sweetness, just as we see the son of Cleon only by seeing something pale and grasping independently that the son of Cleon co-incides with the pale thing.

Note that Aristotle, taken this way, is envisaging two very different notions of co-incidental perception, (i) that of one object by a sense other than its dedicated sense (e.g. sweetness by sight), and (ii) that of a co-inciding complex object, the son of Cleon, with an exclusive or proper object, being pale. In II 6, we encounter instances only of kind (ii). This has led some commentators to represent the argument here alternatively, as follows. If there were a special sense of common objects, we would perceive common objects by the special senses only as we perceive sweetness by sight, that is, not really at all, but only by seeing, e.g., motion, presented with some colour or other. But we are able to perceive motion directly, and not merely by its being presented alongside the exclusive objects. Moreover, if there were a special sense, it would be akin to co-incidental perception. On this second interpretation, Aristotle is appealing to distinct phenomena, *indirect* perception and *co-incidental* perception. Probably it is better to understand him in the first way (on the basis of 425a30–1), as introducing a new form of co-incidental perception, but the second approach cannot be absolutely ruled out.

For detailed discussions of co-incidental perception, see Cashdollar (1973), Owens (1982), and Modrak (1987).

The sentence beginning at 425a14 ('Moreover, there cannot be some special sensory organ for the common objects, which we perceive co-incidentally by each sense...') has caused consternation. To some, it has seemed incompatible with Aristotle's clear contention at 418a8–11 that common objects are to be contrasted with co-incidental objects precisely because we do *not* perceive them co-incidentally. It may also seem to conflict with what comes just below at 425a27–8 ('We have common perception of the common objects, however, and a not co-incidental one.'). This has led some editors to emend the text by placing a negation in the sentence (yielding, then: '...which we do *not* perceive co-incidentally'). The emendation, though understandable, is unnecessary. Aristotle's probable meaning is the one adopted by the majority of the Greek commentators, according to whom he is in the midst of entertaining a counterfactual hypothesis whose dominant contention he does not himself accept.

Further, when he says that we have 'common perception' (often rendered as 'common sense) at 425a27, Aristotle is not suggesting that we have a dedicated, autonomous faculty; for this is indeed what he seeks to deny. Rather, we perceive such objects by more than one dedicated sense, in common. (See note to 418a17–20.)

The translation reflects these conclusions, though the flow of argument here has rightly been regarded as challenging by Aristotle's commentators.

For more on common perception and the common objects of sense, see *De Sensu* 437a9, 442b4–10, and *De Memoria* 450a9–12, 452b7–13.

**425b4–11: Why Do We Have More than One Sense?**  Aristotle concludes the chapter with a puzzle in whose resolution he is prepared to entertain engagingly speculative counterfactuals. Because certain objects can be ascertained conjointly, the question arises as to the reason for our having more than one sense— where this may mean for our having more than one sense *at all*, or, as ps.-Simplicius (186, 26) reasonably suggests, for our having more than one sense *of the common sensibles*. (ps.-Simplicius' suggestion is plausible insofar as we have independently given reasons for there being a plurality of senses, namely that each of the five senses is required for perception of its individuate exclusive object.) In any event, motion, for example, can be seen, touched, and perhaps heard. Is this not an unnecessary surfeit of detectors? (See note to 418a17–20 on Aristotle's vacillation regarding the number of senses capable of apprehending common objects.) Why do we need more than a single sense capable of detecting common (*koinon*) as well as exclusive (*idion*) objects, or, on ps.-Simplicius' approach, more than a single sense, e.g., sight, capable of detecting both its own exclusive object and all common objects?

Aristotle responds by envisaging a world in which animals have sight but no other faculty of sense. We would nonetheless perceive colour and the common sensibles, motion, magnitude, and number. Still, suppose further that we lived in a sight-only, all-white world. We would even then, Aristotle concedes, be able to detect, e.g., motion and magnitude, though we would be less well placed than we are now to discriminate between exclusive and common objects, or among the various common objects. All common objects would, in such a world, forever accompany one another, as well as the exclusive object of sight, colour, thus making it that much more likely that the real differences between them would escape our notice. (See *Met.* 1053b32–a5 for similar thought experiments.)

Aristotle's response is, then, unsurprisingly, at root teleological: for the purposes of discriminating between exclusive and common sensibles and among the common sensibles themselves it is better for us to have multiple senses.

## CHAPTER 2

### Introduction to III 2

Although lacking a single clear focus, this chapter contains some exceptionally intriguing data regarding Aristotle's general conception of perception (*aisthêsis*). It is, in this way at least, a fitting coda to his discussion of perception, which Aristotle leaves at the end of this chapter in order to turn to an investigation into imagination (*phantasia*) in the next. The present chapter begins and ends with puzzles about perception; as sometimes happens with Aristotelian puzzles, the puzzles have themselves proven puzzling to commentators. Aristotle takes it for granted in the beginning of the chapter that 'we perceive that we are seeing and hearing' (425b12). He then wonders how this occurs: is it by the very sense which perceives or by some other sense? Neither alternative strikes him as attractive. He immediately rules out the suggestion that a sense external to the modality engaged in perception perceives that we perceive, on the grounds that we would then be launched on an infinite regress. On the assumption that the initial disjunction was exhaustive, however, that leaves only the sense which does the perceiving to perceive that it perceives, a possibility which in turn invites unhappy consequences.

A general interpretative worry about this puzzle recommends caution in our approach to these matters. What precisely does Aristotle take for granted in suggesting that we perceive that we perceive? He does not say directly that 'we perceive that we are perceiving,' though he does assert that 'we perceive that we are seeing and hearing' (425b12), where the sensory modalities seem arbitrarily chosen, and then proceeds to identify seeing (*to horan*) and 'perceiving by sight' (*to tê(i) opsei aisthanesthai*; 425b18). Bearing that in mind, we may generalize for ease of exposition.

Two approaches to Aristotle's puzzle commend themselves, corresponding to different meanings of 'to perceive' (*aisthanesthai*), one assuming univocity and one not: (i) when we perceive (see) something white, we also perceive (perceive, in just the same sense: we *see*) that we see white; and (ii) when we perceive (see) something white, we are *aware* that we see white. Both approaches are linguistically admissible. Although the semantic fields of 'perceive' and '*aisthanesthai*' do not march completely in step, we find similarly broad ranges for both verbs. In addition to the narrow and broad sense of *objects* of perception already noted (see the General Introduction § IV.B; see also 418a25, 424a29–b31, 426a23, 432a3–6)—that is, smelling a rose or smelling the scent of a rose—we also have more or less cognitive or conscious connotations in each case, as between, e.g., 'She perceived a foul odour' and 'He was one of the first to perceive the impending downturn in the economy' or 'Although he was being scalded, his shock was such that he could barely perceive his own searing pain.'

Both the univocal and non-univocal approaches deserve a hearing, because each accounts for at least some features of the opening section of the chapter. While a univocal treatment of 'we perceive that we perceive' seems at least initially perverse (because we do not see that we see white, and still less do we see our seeing white), some features of the puzzle Aristotle produces may recommend such an approach. By contrast, while it seems perfectly natural to take for granted that we are aware that we see or hear when we see or hear, we might well wonder, unless he is somehow confused, why Aristotle supposes that the phenomenon of awareness might lead to an infinite regress, or indeed why he should think that the sense which perceives is a possible subject of awareness. See note to 425b12–25 for further detail on this matter.

Although its opening sentences have attracted the most scholarly attention, we find a good deal more of significant interest as we move further into the chapter. For instance, its middle section, 425b26–426b7 is also exceptionally fruitful, though also similarly challenging. In particular, Aristotle's resolution to the chapter's opening difficulty occasions the suggestion that the relationship between a sense and its object in an actual, occurrent perception is, if not identity, then some other suitably intimate sort of unity. He says, strikingly, that the 'actuality of the object of perception and of the senses are one and the same, though their being is different' (425b26–7). This formulation provides a framework for some criticism of earlier theorists, who had wanted to maintain that colours and other sensible qualities existed only when perceived (426a20–6). Aristotle urges in response that demanding a simple yes or no answer to the question of whether sensible qualities exist only when perceived yields a view which, if uncomplicated, is, therefore, also unsustainable. If he is right, then this simple-sounding question proves in fact to be complex in ways easily overlooked, even by philosophers working in the philosophy of perception.

The end of the chapter is similarly freighted. Aristotle tackles foundational questions about unity and diversity in perception, including, evidently, some perennially difficult questions about the unity of apperception: by which faculty do we judge, e.g., that a white thing is a sweet thing? White and sweet are two sensible qualities, ascertained by discrete sensory modalities, sometimes judged to be co-present in an object. It is difficult to see how this sort of judgement could eventuate from the senses taken individually; yet it does seem to be a judgement belonging broadly to the faculty of perception. The phenomenon will once again, then, invite Aristotle to reflect upon the need for a faculty of common perception (or common sense, *koinê aisthêsis*), if not explicitly, then at least implicitly, now though with an emphasis lacking in his earlier, related discussion in III 1 (on which, see note to 425a14–b3). See further note to 426b8–427a16 below.

**425b12–25: Perceiving That We Perceive:** Aristotle asserts that 'we perceive that we are seeing and hearing,' using (for him) an unusual combination of words, 'we perceive *that*' (*aisthanometha hoti*; 425b12), an exact phrase appearing in only two other passages in his corpus, one directly below in 426b14 and another at *EN* 1142a28. (There is also another extremely remote possible parallel in *DA* III 13, 435a25; there we very likely have an interpolation, which, if retained at all, must be punctuated in a way making the passage not parallel after all.) In the two attested parallel uses, Aristotle employs the construction in such a way as

to treat *perceive* as a so-called verb of intellectual perception—
that is, 'perceive' as it is used in 'She perceived that the coalition
would not hold.' Thus, below at 426b14, Aristotle is concerned to
know how it is that we perceive that white and sweet differ; and at
*EN* 1142a28, he actively contrasts perception *that* with perception
*of* a proper or exclusive (*idion*) object of perception, offering as an
example of perception *that* our perceiving that a triangle is the
simplest sort of mathematical figure (presumably in the series of
closed plane figures).

Relying on this slender evidence, we may tentatively conclude
that Aristotle's concern is closer to a question of how it is that we
come to be aware of perception than it is to any question concerning how we, e.g., see our episodes of seeing. That is, we may,
in the terms employed in the chapter introduction, assume that he
is using *perception* non-univocally when asking how we perceive
that we perceive, or, more precisely, that he is treating the kind of
perception involved in perceiving *that we see* as distinct from the
kind of perception which seeing is.

One advantage to this approach is that it renders Aristotle's
question perfectly intelligible: how is it that we are aware that we
see? Looked at in one way, this is simply the question required of
any full theory of perception, including, then, any hylomorphic
theory of perception. In the framework of hylomorphism, that
question queries precisely how it is that the form reception
involved in perceiving differs from the form reception involved
when tofu comes to adopt the odour of an onion simply by being
placed next to it in a refrigerator. (For more on this question, see
the General Introduction § IV.B and note to 424b3–21).

To follow this line further, Aristotle's problem is this. We see
and we are aware that we see. But by what sense is it that we are
aware that we see? If it is by some sense other than sight, then we
shall have to ask by what sense we are aware that the other sense
perceives and so on; if we nip the regress in the bud and allow that
it is by sight itself that we are aware that we see, then since sight is
of colours, the original sense, sight, will be coloured in a primary
way. This last would perhaps seem unproblematic if we were to
suppose that the sense is the sensory organ (*aisthêtêrion*), the eye;
but this is something Aristotle denies (see the General Introduction to II 12, together with note to 424a24–8). So, the worry is
then how the sense can be fully responsible for perception,

COMMENTARY

including perceptual awareness, without its also being the case that what sees itself is already the sense organ.

Aristotle's response, however inchoate, begins with the contention that 'perceiving by sight is not one thing' (425b20). Following further along the track thus far laid down, this too is reasonable. If we think that seeing involves awareness in addition to bare detection of light, then perceiving by sight is not one thing. That said, there are also some reasons for considering a more deflationary approach to Aristotle's worry. One is that if his real concern were with issues of perceptual awareness, it would be odd for him to infer, as he does, that sight must itself be coloured. At this stage in the argument, Aristotle seems to collapse 'perceive' in its intellectual sense into its more common non-intellectual sense. Further, it is in any case perplexing to find Aristotle structuring his worry about our perceiving that we see by supposing that what is aware that we see must be sight or some other sense. His proceeding this way also suggests a partial blurring of the intellectual and non-intellectual senses of 'perceive'.

Still, it is plain that Aristotle intends his remark that 'perceiving by sight is not one thing' (425b20) to provide some sort of resolution to the worry he entertains. To the extent that this resolution reflects a belief that perception is a complex enterprise, an approach heading in the direction of the non-univocal interpretation seems preferable.

For fuller discussion of this passage, see Kosman (1969), Caston (2002), Johansen (2005), and Corkum (2010).

**425b26–426a26: Actual Perceptions and Objects Actually Perceived:** Once he has cleared away his initial worry about perceiving that we see and hear, Aristotle moves on to an important consideration centrally relevant to any refined appreciation of his theory of perception. Aristotle makes two crucial points regarding the relationship between the exercise of a sensory capacity and the existence of a sensory object.

Let naïve realism be the view that objects of sense are intrinsic monadic properties of external objects, so that, e.g., a wall has the sensible property of being beige as an actual intrinsic feature to be apprehended by perceivers. Several theorists prior to Aristotle, including most notably Democritus, alive to the observation that sensible qualities vary from perceiver to perceiver, relative to context and to differences in perceptual faculties, rejected naïve realism. They supposed that if the wine tastes sweet to S′ and bitter to S″, then unless one is privileged relative to the other, neither could pronounce authoritatively as to which sensible quality, sweetness or bitterness, ought to be regarded as the genuine perceiver-independent intrinsic feature required by naïve realism; and unless at least one is, then neither is. Consequently, they concluded, naïve realism should be set aside. So Democritus: 'by convention sweet and by convention bitter, by convention hot, by convention cold, by convention colour; but in reality atoms and void' (DK 68 B9).

What should replace it? One thought associated by Aristotle with the natural philosophers who came before him is that objects of perception exist only when perceived (426a20–6). Although he does not mention them by name, Aristotle usually reserves the term 'natural philosophers' (*phusiologoi*) for the earliest Presocratic philosophers. (On this term and its use in Aristotle, see Hussey (2012).) The view he criticizes here, however, Aristotle also finds present, if in varying degrees of clarity, in the Sophist Protagoras, as well as Empedocles, Anaxagoras, and Democritus (cf. *Met.* 986b14, 1009b11–1011a2). Aristotle regards these philosophers as half right, but as, therefore, all the more misleading (426a22–3). They were half right when they rejected naïve realism, since they thought that there were no sensible qualities without perceivers. They share with Aristotle a rejection of naïve realism, then, but subsequently go wrong when they infer further that perceivers are themselves the subjects of sensible qualities, or that sensible qualities are in some sense wholly conventional, or wholly subjective, both views regarded by Aristotle as indefensible.

Aristotle will counter that the account needed is perforce much more complex. Although perception is a change *in* the perceiver (426a2, a11), this will in fact be a change occurring only in the presence of an actual object of perception. The suggestion that the change occurs in the perceiver follows from Aristotle's general hylomorphism about change: when a student is altered by the activity of teaching, although the learning and teaching are in a sense the same process, the change is effected in the student (see *Phys.* III 3 for a general defence of this claim, esp. 202a13; cf. *Gen. et. Corr.* 324b5). Part of the welcome complexity in Aristotle's approach stems from his initially difficult claim that the sensible quality whose presence is responsible for a change in a perceiver does not exist *in actuality* as a sensible quality before perception; for that would be to embrace a form of naïve realism. To avoid this consequence, Aristotle contends that 'the actuality of the object of perception and of the senses are one and the same, though their being is different' (425b26–7; cf. 426a15–16). When saying that $x$ and $y$ are the same, though differing in being, Aristotle means that though $x$ *and* y are extensionally equivalent, they have different accounts or analyses. Thus, even if the Chancellor of the Exchequer is by statute the same person as the Second Lord of the Treasury, what it is to be the Chancellor and what it is to be a Lord of the Treasury are distinct (see note to 424a24–8 for more on this point). In the current context, Aristotle means that whereas there is but one motion which is an actual object of perception being actually perceived, what it is to be an object being perceived is, nonetheless, not the same as what it is to be a subject actually perceiving an object. This is in part shown by dint of the fact that a potential object of perception, something perceptible but not now actually being perceived, is not at all the same thing as a merely potential subject of perception.

Although ordinary language typically fails to reflect the fine-grainedness required by a fully adequate account of actual perception, Aristotle thinks that linguistic discriminations made ordinarily for the modality of hearing come closest to marking the relevant distinctions (cf. note to 417b27–418a3 on the insufficiency of ordinary language). Consider a bell in a tower in a remote mission church with no one in its vicinity. We might say that the bell is capable of making a noise when still; if a mild earthquake shakes the tower, then the bell is making a noise, though not succeeding in making a sound, or an instance of hearing, or, less naturally, in making a *sound-being-heard*. The state of affairs obtaining when the bell is *making a noise* is clearly not the same as the state of affairs of there being a *sound-being-heard*. A noise may remain unheard. Further, a single noise may be implicated in non-equivalent episodes of sounds-being-heard, as when one person with keen hearing is receptive to the harmonic overtones of the bell, while another person with a diminished capacity hears only a dullish thud, and still another, with average abilities, hears a clapping clang but no harmonic overtones. There are thus facts about entities capable of making sound which are not also facts about other entities capable of hearing them, and vice versa; still, every case of actual sounding (i.e. of a sound-being-heard) is also a case of actual hearing.

Taking all that together, Aristotle concludes that the earlier natural philosophers were right to implicate perceivers in actual perceiving, but wrong to infer that perceptual qualities were properties of the perceivers themselves. They failed to mark a fine-grained distinction between (i) actual and potential sounding and (ii) hearing according to which while a sound-being-heard is necessarily coextensive with some instance of a perceiver hearing a sound. Still, insists Aristotle, what it is to be a sound-being-heard is not the same as what it is to hear a sound; so, he concludes, the earlier natural philosophers overlooked a necessary qualification to their views (426a26). They consequently held views which distorted the actual facts of perception, overreacting to the falsity of naïve realism by skewing perceptions inordinately towards the subjects whose perceptions they are.

Although we come close to marking the needed distinctions in ordinary language in the case of sounding and hearing, even then it is a bit of a strain to make Aristotle's point in English, or for that matter in Greek, without beginning to stilt common discourse somewhat. Still less is it possible to proceed without introducing quasi-technical terminology for the other sensory modalities (426a11–15).

Again, if ordinary language tends to give out in this domain, it may be worth explicating Aristotle's point by reiterating one of his preferred illustrations (*Phys.* 202a32–4, 210a15–19). While an actual instance of learning is coextensive with an actual instance of teaching, it being a change occurring in a student who learns, nonetheless, what it is for the change to qualify as an instance of teaching is not at all the same as what it is for it to qualify as an instance of learning. In Aristotle's terms, teaching and learning differ in being (*einai*), just as *x*'s actually sounding differs in being from *x*'s being actually heard (425b27, 426a16–17).

**426a27–b7: Perception, Proportions, and Destruction:** Although beset with textual difficulties, the dominant claims of this section are, nonetheless, reasonably clear. Perception is a proportion (or ratio, *logos*), with the result that if an excessive object of one sort or another succeeds in distorting the balance required for form receptivity, the power to perceive is temporarily damaged. Elsewhere Aristotle seems to draw the same inference on more or less phenomenological or experiential grounds: when overwhelmed by a bright light or crushing sound, we are temporarily deprived of sight and hearing (see notes to 422a20–31 and 424a28–b3; cf. also 429a31). Here, however, his argument is different and more difficult, in part because of the textual difficulties mentioned. As translated, the argument runs:

(1) Voice is a kind of concordance (*sumphônia*; 426a27).
(2) A concordance is a proportion (*logos*; cf. *Met.* 991b13, 1092b13).
(3) So, voice is a kind of proportion.
(4) Hence, if voice is the same as hearing (*akoê*), then hearing too will be a proportion.
(5) Voice is the same as hearing.
(6) Hence, hearing is a kind of proportion.

(4) and (5) provide the basis for Aristotle's suggesting at the beginning of the argument that the sameness of actual perception and actual object provide the basis for the further conclusion he now seeks to draw, that the senses are proportions (or ratios, *logoi*). (1) is somewhat obscure, since it is a bit unclear how voice is to be understood as a kind of concordance, or why, more generally, Aristotle restricts his observation to voice (*phônê*) as opposed to sound (*psophos*) in the first place. Voice is usually thought of as intentionally produced, significant sound (cf. 423b5–8, b30–2; cf. *De Interp.* 16a3; *Rhet.* 1404a21). That allowed, he may simply be thinking that voice is an especially clear case of a sound which is a concordance, since its being intentionally produced involves voices being delivered at a deliberate sonic level and so forth.

In any event, once we agree that we have extensional equivalence between actual sounding and actual hearing, we can infer, with due caution, that hearing (*akoê*) is equally a proportion (or ratio, *logos*), in which case the upset of a proportion would disable the faculty until such time as it is restored. If this captures his train of thought, there is a further question as to any inference backward from actual hearing, which might legitimately on the grounds given be inferred to be a proportion, to the faculty whose expression involves such a proportion. It may be conjectured that Aristotle is simply inferring on the basis of a presumed non-satisfaction of a necessary condition: if hearing is a proportion, and the faculty cannot be moved into such a state because of its being out of commission, then hearing cannot occur.

**426b8–29: Perceiving Unity and Diversity:** There is a bit of discontinuity between this discussion and the preceding. The first lines in this section have the air of a summary and recapitulation: each episode of actual sensing involves an external object but is a change occurring within the perceiver involving the discrimination of elements blended in a proportion (or ratio, *logos*). So much may be drawn from what has just been said. Presumably, the notion of discrimination (*krinei*; 426b10) now invoked occasions further reflection on the manner in which overlapping discrete objects of sense may in turn be discriminated from one another. Sugar is white and sweet, though we are able to discriminate the white in sugar from the sweet and are easily prepared to judge (another possible rendering of *krinein*) that the white is not sweet.

However Aristotle passes to the topic, his discussion here recalls his treatment of common perception (*koinê aisthêsis*) in the last chapter (on which, see note to 425a14–b3). Strikingly, Aristotle insists on what is later called the synthetic unity of apperception, demanding that one and the same judge or discriminator distinguish white from sweet in an object or judge that white is not sweet. Otherwise, as he observes, I might watch you, blindfolded, eating white powder; I judge that it is white while you judge silently that it is sweet. In such a case, neither of us is in a position to judge that it is both sweet and white and so neither of us can say non-inferentially, on the basis of an immediate perception, that its being sweet is not the same as its being white. Its being both sweet and white must 'both be manifest to some one thing' (426b18–19).

Aristotle demands further that this one thing to which co-instantiated sensible qualities be manifest must have certain additional determinate characteristics. One might say, perversely, but to illustrate Aristotle's point, that in the circumstance envisaged you and I are, after all, one thing, a pair, and that we can jointly judge that white is not sweet. Aristotle's additional strictures rule this out, by demanding that the one thing be non-separate (*achôriston*), and, indeed, that the time of the discrimination be non-extended. You and I, however fine a pair we form, are separate (*chôriston*) from one another. We will consequently fail a central condition required for the synthetic unity of apperception: grasping the concurrent distinctness of discrete sensory objects requires a discrimination made by a single judge at a single time. In sum, concludes Aristotle, a subject of discrimination is a non-separate thing in a non-separate time, that is, a single, unified judge exercising its synthesizing ability in a single moment. (This discussion may also be compared with a somewhat more leisurely treatment of the same topic at *De Sensu* 447b7–448b1, 448b17–449a30.)

**426b29–427a16: A Difficulty for this View and a Rejoinder; the Rejoinder Revised:** Grant that what judges is something strictly unified in the way demanded. Aristotle passes from its being non-separate (*achôriston*) to it its being indivisible (*adiaireton*), which would presumably be a sure way to satisfy his strictures on the sort of unity required for synthetic discrimination. How is it, though, that what is indivisible can sustain opposite, incompatible, or even numerically distinct motions—as discrete individual perceptions must be? If there are discrete motions occurring concurrently in a single subject, and each is coextensive with that subject, then must not the subject too be at least bipartite, and so divisible after all? If it is divisible in this way, however, the synthetic unity of apperception will be threatened; perhaps we will once again find ourselves with distinct perceivers in close proximity, lacking any hegemonic coordinating faculty to synthesize our sundry perceptions. Then we are only fractured internal committees, never able to offer the coordinated judgement that *this sweet* is not *this white*.

Aristotle's initial rejoinder is brief and partly conciliatory. (Here too caution is required owing to a troubled text.) What discriminates is in its being divisible (*tô(i)einai . . . diaireton*; 427a4–5), and may manifest itself severally in an indivisible time and place. It is tempting to think that 'in its being' here is covertly predicative, so that one faculty might differ in becoming ϕ or in becoming ψ, though that would involve an abrupt change of vocabulary in the chapter. If we do not follow that lead, then Aristotle is suggesting

273

that the faculty is essentially divisible, but that its exercise in offering coordinated discriminations is limited to an activity which is unified in time and place. Of course, one divisible being cannot become opposite sensibles simultaneously, and so cannot perceive black and white in the same respect at the same time, though it might yet become compatible objects at once, and so might yet perceive sweet and white.

Feeling some strain in this rejoinder, Aristotle further hazards the conjecture that the unified judge might be like a point (which *is* indivisible in its essence). On this approach, presumably what issues the unified judgement is like a point in being genuinely both divisible and indivisible, by being in one respect one and in another respect two. Considered intrinsically, a point is one and indivisible in both time and place, and is indeed a star instance of such unity and indivisibility. Even so, a point might be two relationally or two in account, e.g. by being the end of line segments AB and BC: in such a case the point B is a limit of two discrete, non-identical lines, and its being a limit to AB is not the same in account as its being a limit to BC (cf. *Phys.* 220a10–11).

If this is the purport of the comparison, the capacity responsible for making fine-grained discriminations in perception might in the same way be simple without thereby being incapable of registering a variety of features. Such would be the common capacity (the *koinê dunamis* not named in *De Anima*, but referred to at *De Somno* 455a16) required for coordinated synthetic discrimination.

If Aristotle does little to offer a developed treatment of the synthetic unity of apperception in this chapter, it is nonetheless noteworthy to find him contending with some incipient problems attendant to this vexed topic. We find ourselves grappling even today with binding problems of a variety of sorts, some interior to single sensory modalities and others pertaining to intermodal synthesis.


CHAPTER 3

**Introduction to III 3**

Aristotle contends that higher animals have a capacity, or semi-capacity, distinct from both perception (*aisthêsis*) and reason (*nous*): imagination (*phantasia*). When he speaks of imagination, Aristotle does not have in view a capacity for creative thought or fanciful construction. Rather, as a first approximation, he means to draw attention to the ability in humans and most animals to store and manipulate mental images. In view of the connection between *phantasia* and its root verb *phainesthai* (to appear), one sometimes finds 'appearance' preferred as a translation over 'imagination'. Although neither rendering is perfect (in English, 'appearance' is not normally associated with a mental faculty, while 'imagination' is regularly associated with too narrow a faculty), it seems best to employ 'imagination', which has in its favour at least the pedigree of philosophical appropriation, inter alia in Hobbes, Locke, Hume, and Mill. (See, e.g., Hobbes, *Leviathan* i.2.2 for an early quasi-technical use in English keeping with Aristotle's general meaning.) It is, however, necessary to bear in mind that misleading connotations will result if it is assumed that Aristotle is discussing nothing more than the narrow ability to engage in creative or artistic kinds of thinking.

To some extent, this concern about translation is mitigated by Aristotle's actual procedure in this chapter. He is mainly interested to isolate the faculty he has in mind by differentiating it from other more robust faculties, especially perception (*aisthêsis*) and reason (*nous*). In so doing, he does not begin with a clear idea of a determinate faculty whose existence requires no special pleading or whose boundary conditions should be plain to just anyone; on the contrary, he thinks he owes his readers some proof of our even having such a capacity or faculty, and he thinks that such a proof intimately involves distinguishing imagination from some other capacities to which some might be inclined to reduce it.

Impulses towards reduction are not altogether alien to Aristotle. Indeed, it is not evident that the imagination meets one of Aristotle's own preferred criteria for faculty individuation: faculties are individuated by their objects. (See the Introduction to II 4; 402b9–16 and 415a14–22, with their relevant notes; and also notes to 418a7–11 and 418a11–17.) If he adheres to this criterion, we should find Aristotle proposing a class of objects, imaginables (*phantasta*), alongside objects of reason (*noêta*), perception (*aisthêta*), and desire (*orekta*). He mentions no such class of objects in this chapter, and may never even use the relevant term (*phantaston*) at all. (There is one disputed passage, at *De Memoria*

450a23–5, where the word may make an appearance; the passage is judiciously discussed by Wedin (1988: 57–63, 255–259).) Of course, his not using that word is consistent with his accepting but never mentioning the relevant objects. Still, it would be odd, given his methodological precepts, not to find him appealing to such items if he intended the present chapter to contain his primary defence of the existence of such a full-blown faculty.

Be that as it may, Aristotle is keen in the current chapter to avoid any identification of imagination with one or more of the more familiar psychic faculties. Two possibilities thus present themselves: (i) he thinks it is a fullyfledged faculty alongside them; or (ii) he regards the imagination as something distinct from reason and perception, but not as a proper faculty in its own right—hence my opening suggestion that the imagination might be a faculty or a semi-faculty. Its being a *semi-faculty* would suggest that the imagination is akin to an algorithm deployed in a subprocessing loop of various related but non-equivalent computer programs, that is, as something with a definite and discrete functional role to play relative to the full faculties of perception and thought, without being itself a free-standing fully functional faculty. Cf. *Rhet.* 1370a28.

Whatever its status, imagination receives little by way of a positive analysis in this chapter. Aristotle offers only two positive characterizations, each truncated and general. First, he depicts imagination in broadly functional terms as 'that in virtue of which a particular image (*phantasma*) comes about for us' (428a1–2), but then only in an effort to set up a discussion of the ways in which it cannot be reduced to perception, belief, knowledge, or reason (428a4–5). Later in the chapter, after sketching its relation to perception, he characterizes it in broadly causal terms as 'a motion effected by actual perception' (429a1–2), without any further intrinsic specification.

The chapter is thus primarily negative, but that has not precluded speculation about Aristotle's positive conception of imagination (*phantasia*). It is, however, understandable that there should be controversy regarding its status, its function, and its relation to other faculties. First is the question, already mooted, as to whether it should be regarded as a faculty in its own right at all. (The fullest discussion of this topic, careful and fully informed, is Wedin (1998).) As for its function, in addition to Wedin, one prominent interpretation owes to Schofield (1978), who treats it as trading in 'non-paradigmatic sensory experiences' (192: 256), and another, critical of Schofield, to Caston (1996), who stresses its role in accounting for error and whose paper is alert to the range of roles for which imagination is pressed into service (1996: 41, n.46 and 42, n.47). Scheiter (2012) offers a good overview of some of the prominent problems and approaches to the chapter, investigating especially the relation between the role of imagination as a producer and manipulator of images and its evidently distinct, because more richly hermeneutical or explanatory, role in dealing with images, in desire, the interpretation of appearances, and animal action.

As for the structure of the chapter itself, it divides reasonably neatly into: (i) prefatory material on discrimination, and on the general relation between thought, perception, and conceiving (*hupolêpsis*) (427a17–b14); (ii) an argument that imagination is neither perception nor thought (427b14–24); (iii) an approach to a positive characterization of imagination (427b24–428a5); (iv) more detail on the distinction between imagination and perception (428a5–16); (v) more detail on the distinction between imagination and thought (428a16–b9); speculations on the relation between imagination and perception, culminating in a second brief positive characterization of imagination (428b10–429a2); and some closing remarks (429a2–9).

**427a17–29: Introductory Material: Reasoning and Perceiving:** The opening of the chapter marks a transition. Aristotle has completed his discussion of perception (*aisthêsis*); before passing to his next main topic, reason (*nous*), he pauses to reorient his discussion. He does so first by noting that when characterizing the soul his predecessors had tended to rely primarily upon two distinct sets of features, those pertaining to the soul's role in locomotion and those involved in cognition, broadly construed, namely reasoning (*noein*), judging (sometimes rendered as discriminating; *krinein*), and perceiving (*aisthêsis*) (427a17–19; the division recalls similar remarks in I 2, 403b25–7; cf. 405b11–12). Aristotle uses much the same transitional device when he turns his attention to desire (*orexis*) at the beginning of III 9 (432a15–17).

Aristotle first focuses on the broadly cognitive factors in terms of which people differentiate the soul from other sorts of things, noting that reasoning (*noein*) and understanding (*phronein*) seem (*sc.* to others) to be a kind of perception (*aisthêsis*). Indeed, some of the ancients go so far as to identify reasoning and perceiving. Aristotle cites Empedocles (frs. 106, 108) and Homer (*Od.* xviii 136–7) in this connection (cf. *Met.* 1009b12–28), though in neither instance does the passage cited provide any conclusive reason for ascribing so baldly stated a thesis to them. The truncated quotation from Homer is especially obscure. Expanded, it is: 'For such is the mind of earthly men as the father of gods and men delivers upon them day by day.' In its context, the passage finds Odysseus strategically emphasizing resignation to fate, before which we are passive. Evidently, Aristotle holds him to mean that the contents of mind vary, in a passive way, with the variations visited upon the body by its environment.

Aristotle ascribes such a view to the ancients, as he had done earlier in I 2, in part because, he maintains, (i) they regard reasoning to be no less corporeal than perceiving is, and (ii) they adhere to the like-like theory (cf. note to 404b11–b27). He implies without rigorous reconstruction that these two theses jointly commit both Empedocles and Homer to the identification of perception of thought. Plainly, several additional steps must be supplied if his ascriptive argument is to succeed.

**427a29–b14: Criticism of this Identification:** Perception is, in any case, not to be identified with either judging or understanding. In the first instance, implies Aristotle, those inclined to identify perceiving and understanding ought to have paid closer attention to the phenomenon of error. Those who reflected at all upon error—the state Aristotle gamely characterizes as more typical in animals than its opposite and as that in which the soul spends the lion's share of its time—were constrained to hold either that all perception is true (since understanding is truth-entailing) or that error results when like comes into contact with unlike. Neither is appealing. Aristotle comments on the latter, dismissing it as a facile suggestion. If *S* knows that white is not black, then the contrary states known to be distinct, namely black and white, are also the objects of the befuddled person who for some reason judges that they are the same. So, there is no hope in appealing to an unlike-unlike theory to explain error. For Aristotle's appropriately arch attitude to the suggestion that appearance is the same as understanding, see *Met.* 1010b1–1011a2 (where, however, the text is troubled). Although pertinent to the main thrust of this section, Aristotle's foray into error has the air of an aside. His principal argument for distinguishing perceiving (*aisthanesthai*) and understanding (*phronein*) is direct: they are not even extensionally equivalent, since all animals perceive, while only a very few have understanding (427b7–9). This short and decisive argument comes at the conclusion of a long meandering and ungrammatical sentence which had begun at the beginning of the chapter and only now reaches its climax. (For purposes of clarity, in the translation that sentence is broken down into nine distinct sentences, counting those ascribed to Homer and Empedocles.) Not content to rest his case there, Aristotle adds that perception is not to be identified with reasoning (*noein*), used here as a generic term covering understanding (*phronêsis*), knowledge (*epistêmê*), and true belief (*alêthês doxa*), together with their opposites (427b9–11). Perception of exclusive (*idia*) objects he maintains here, in keeping with his dominant contention, is always true (418a12, regarding which, see note; 428a11, 430b29; *De Sensu* 442b8; *Met.* 1010b2–26; this contrasts with 428b19, where a moderating qualification is entered). By contrast, reasoning is sometimes right and sometimes wrong.

The argument thus stated is insufficient. One might in principle maintain, having granted that reasoning often gets it wrong, that certain sorts of *de re* thoughts are, nonetheless, equally immune to error. The possibility is not an idle one, since Aristotle will later suggest that some acts of intellection, those concerning what something is, that is, concerning an essence (*to ti ên einai*)—are likewise always true. Indeed, there he goes so far as to align perception of exclusive objects with thoughts of essences in precisely this regard (430b27–9). If that is so, Aristotle's implicit appeal to the indiscernibility of identicals in this argument is insecure.

**427b14–26: Imagination is not the Same as Conceiving:** In one of his principal anti-reductive contentions of the chapter, Aristotle argues that imagination is not the same as conceiving (*hupolêpsis*). Aristotle's notion of conceiving is a bit slippery; among other problems, he does not use the term for it univocally.

Sometimes it is virtually the same as belief (*doxa*), especially when belief is feeble or thin, where it might be rendered as 'supposition' or 'view' (*Met.* 1010a10; *EE* 1235a20, 29), or as indifferently strong or weak, where simple 'belief' seems best (*EN* 1145b36). At the end of the current passage, it is rather a generic term, encompassing belief (*doxa*) as one of its species, along with knowledge (*epistêmê*) and understanding (*phronêsis*), together with their opposites (427b24–6). In the generic sense it is better rendered 'conceiving', as here, or in some cases perhaps as 'entertaining' (cf. *Top.* 125b30–126a2). In any event, if it is to range over the contrary of belief as well as belief, then it cannot be thought to require a pro-attitude or positive doxastic commitment of any sort.

That said, the actual argument used to differentiate imagination from conceiving seems to turn on some lack of voluntarism pertinent to belief, but not therefore to conceiving in the generic sense. We can produce an image for ourselves at will, whereas belief formation respects constraints imposed by truth and falsity. To take a case favourable to Aristotle, when asked to picture for ourselves a rotund man blocking our egress through a doorway, we might easily comply. When further instructed now to *believe* that there is such a man at present blocking the doorway, even though we can see that it is unobstructed, we will have difficulty following directions.

Aristotle's own illustration of the difference between believing and imagining invokes the mnemonic systems employed in his day, which require a subject to hold before the mind an articulated fixed image, perhaps a house with seven rooms of seven distinct colours, and to place into the rooms the items to be remembered, lines of Homer, for instance, rotating them sequentially. He mentions mnemonic techniques in *De Mem.* 451a12–15 and *De Insomn.* 458b17–23; cf. Plato, *Hipp. Maj.* 285e7. (For a full discussion of the mnemonic systems, see Sorabji, 1972). Again, in the present context, what matters is that, in such systems, people can produce and shuffle images around in ways untethered to their beliefs. Hence, Aristotle concludes, the faculties of imagination and belief cannot be identified. It would follow that imagination cannot be conception, but only in this narrow sense. For more on the relation between imagination and belief, see 428a18–24 and 428a24–b9.

**427b27–428a5: Possible Identifications:** If it is now agreed that imagination is not conception (*hupolêpsis*), the question arises as to whether it is one form or another of reasoning. When Aristotle turns to this possibility, he does so in a way which treats reasoning (*noein*) very broadly and generically, so that it covers not only reasoning narrowly construed but also perception (*aisthêsis*), belief (*doxa*), and knowledge (*epistêmê*) (428a4–5); unlike conception (*hupolêpsis*), reasoning (*noien*) is not characterized as embracing the opposites of these states. Importantly, in this preliminary set-up, Aristotle approaches offering a positive characterization of imagination, but only in general, functional terms, as 'that in virtue of which a particular image comes about for us' (428a1–2). This general characterization holds, he suggests, so long as we refrain from speaking 'metaphorically' (428a2). Aristotle does not say directly, however, what metaphorical language about imagination would be. Presumably our speaking in this way would implicate us in thinking of imagination not merely in terms of image manipulation, but in an extended way so as to cover all instances of mental imagery, including those implicated in perception. Greek draws a linguistic distinction tracking the broader and narrower conception of image use: *phainesthai*, to appear, and *phantazesthai*, to produce or call up an image for oneself. The 'metaphorical' sense is the unrestricted appearance which embraces but does not require production or agency. In speaking of the unrestricted notion as 'metaphorical', Aristotle is not suggesting an impropriety of use, but simply noting that there are extended and non-extended senses available; in its root sense, a metaphor is a transference of meaning from one term to another, in this case from a restricted to a more liberal sense, but nothing more (cf. *Top.* 112a32; *Rhet.* 1410b36; *Poet.* 1457b6). Elsewhere, Aristotle himself happily assumes the broader notion (*De Insomn.* 458b29). The effect, then, is simply to draw attention to a regimented way of speaking and a more relaxed way of speaking about imagination. (In English sometimes we speak of human beings as conscious, when contrasting them with non-conscious animals or machines, and sometimes we contrast our conscious states with other states of ours which are mental but unconscious. Neither the more encompassing use nor the more restrictive use of 'conscious' is improper.)

In any event, Aristotle now wants to introduce a series of candidates for possible reductive identification, all to be rejected as indefensible. Perhaps imagination is: (i) perception (*aisthêsis*), answered at 428a5–14; (ii) knowledge (*epistêmê*) or reason (*nous*), answered at 428a16–18; (iii) belief (*doxa*), answered at 428a18–24; or (iv) some combination of belief and perception, answered at 428a24–b9.

**428a5–16: Imagination is not Perception:** Aristotle retails a series of brief and underdeveloped arguments, each intended to show that perception has some feature lacked by imagination, or vice versa, with the result that they cannot be identified. Because they are brief, it is easy to imagine rejoinders to Aristotle's arguments. These rejoinders are themselves hardly decisive; on the contrary, most of Aristotle's arguments have some initial plausibility. The arguments in order are:

(1) Imagination is active during sleep, when perception is dormant. Hence, imagination and perception are distinct.

(2) All animals have perception, but some lack imagination, including, for instance, the lowly grub. Hence, since they are not even coextensive, imagination and perception are distinct.

(3) Perceptions are always true, whereas instances of imagination are mainly false. Hence, imagination and perception are distinct.

(4) We speak of things appearing in the realm of perception only in cases of indistinctness or unclarity, whereas all cases of imagination (*phantasia*) invite talk of appearing (*phainesthai*). Hence, imagination and perception are distinct.

(5) Visual images appear to those with eyes closed, whereas no one sees in this condition. Hence, seeing and imagining are distinct. Generalizing, then, imagination and perception are distinct.

The arguments admit of rejoinders, and in some cases invite them, especially when Aristotle seems to contravene views he has asserted elsewhere.

The first argument seeks to block the suggestion that perception is present in potentiality in someone who sleeps by countering that the imagination is *active* during dreams, whereas perception is dormant. When in a dream we have an image of a man in a yellow hat, even if we are, in some attenuated sense, then potentially seeing a man in a yellow hat, we cannot explain our image as an instance of perception.

The second argument has occasioned consternation and a spate of suggested emendations. One small problem is already attended to in the argument as formulated. The text says that 'perception is always present' (428a8), suggesting to some a contradiction even with what has just been asserted, viz. that perception is not present in sleep. The argument as formulated avoids this problem by treating 'always' (*aei*) non-temporally, as equivalent to 'in every case' or 'without exception' (cf. *EN* 1097b20; *Pol.* 1254a25, 1296a24, 1333a29), a translation deriving support from the contrast required in the present context, namely that perception is present without exception in all animals. More substantively, the manuscripts deny imagination indifferently to bees, ants, and grubs, something evidently at variance with Aristotle's tendency to be impressed by ants and bees. He regards bees as political animals, though presumably in a weaker of the various senses in which he uses that phrase (*Part. An.* 648a5–7, 650b24–7; cf. *Met.* 980b24). Grubs, by contrast, he does not hold in high regard (*Hist. An.* 489b12–13; *Gen. An.* 733a1–2). The translation accepts a suggestion owing in modern times to Torstrick, though with ancient support (in the paraphrase of Themistius 89, 35–90, 14) according to which Aristotle offers imagination to ants and bees but denies it to grubs.

On the other hand, if Aristotle vacillates about whether grubs have internal images, even while granting them to ants, we might, if we are willing to reflect on the matter, simply join him in doing so. It is not clear at what point we should forbear treating lower animal forms as capable of internal representation.

The third argument asserts unqualifiedly that perception is always true, though Aristotle is more guarded below at 428b18–19, where he claims, more in keeping with his normal position, that perception of exclusive objects (*idia*) admits least of all of falsehood (see notes to 418a11–17 and 418a24–5). A second mildly troubling feature of this argument pertains to Aristotle's conception of truth and falsity. Here he says that imagination is mainly false; earlier in the chapter (427b17–21), Aristotle had tied truth and falsity to the involuntariness of belief (*doxa*), suggesting implicitly that imagination was voluntary at least in part because it lacked such constraints. That in turn implies that truth and falsity simply do not pertain to imagination. One easy resolution understands Aristotle as asserting in the present passage that images are mainly not veridical, in the sense that they fail to represent anything, whereas earlier he had been suggesting that truth and falsity do not pertain to imagination as a faculty, in the sense that it is neither a constraint nor a goal of imagination that it aim for the truth. If so, then we are at liberty to say without contradiction that though images may in fact inadvertently represent something, their doing so is no part of the defining function of the faculty which trades in them, namely the imagination.

The fourth argument trades on some linguistic matters. While we say that objects in the distance appear small, we tend not to say that the page in the book we are reading *appears* to be printed; yet we always speak of appearing in the case of imagination. (This is an instance where 'appearance' would better capture the linguistic connection between *phantasia* and its root verb *phainesthai*, to appear; see headnote.) Our linguistic tendency suggests, defeasibly, of course, that we mainly think of imagination in ways other than we think of perception.

The final argument appeals directly to a putative fact about images: we can experience visual images when our eyes are closed. The back-reference in the text may be to the first argument, so that the visual images in questions are those occurring in dreams. If that is so, the argument mainly repeats the first argument, though at the level of the image rather than the faculty. Aristotle may also be thinking, however, of a remark at 425b24–5, where he speaks rather of after-images. If that is his point, the fifth argument adduces independent considerations, and does not draw upon the first.

**428a16–18: Imagination is not Knowledge or Understanding:** The points about truth and falsity re-emerge to differentiate imagination from knowledge (*epistêmê*) and understanding (*nous*). If imagination can be true, in the sense permitted in the third argument discussed in the note to 428a5–14, then it can also be false in that sense—indeed, it will usually be so, as that argument suggests. Aristotle's language here suggests that he is again allowing that both truth and falsity pertain to imagination.

For this reason, imagination cannot be knowledge or understanding, both of which are truth-entailing.

It should be noted that the translation of this section departs from its dominant practice of rendering *nous* as 'reason' or 'reasoning'. In *De Anima*, Aristotle uses the word *nous* primarily to name a faculty of the human soul, but occasionally, as here, he uses it in the sense it is given in, e.g., *Posterior Analytics* II 19, where it clearly characterizes not a faculty but a cognitive state in which a faculty or person may be. (See glossary entry for further references; see also the Introduction to III 4, for the proper understanding of the word in that chapter.) In this sense, the word *nous* functions a bit like the English word 'understanding', as in 'Humans, unlike dogs, are blessed with understanding' and 'Her quest for greater scientific understanding was frustrated by war.' In the current passage, Aristotle uses *nous* to refer to a truth-evaluable cognitive state—hence 'understanding' rather than the more common 'reason'.

**428a18–24: Imagination is not Belief:**    In contrast with his non-reductive arguments thus far, Aristotle's primary arguments against the reduction of belief (*doxa*) to imagination involve conviction, or perhaps feelings of conviction. Although it may be distinguished from other capacities and states in respect of truth and falsity (perception, knowledge, and understanding being always true), imagination may yet be belief: both are sometimes true and sometimes false. Still, belief, unlike imagination, involves conviction (*pistis*). The arguments appealing to this difference are variations on the same theme, each appealing to extensional non-equivalence:

An Argument from Belief and Conviction (428a19–22) is:

(1) Necessarily, if S has belief, then S has conviction.
(2) No beast has conviction.
(3) So, no beast has belief.
(4) Some beasts have imagination.
(5) Hence, belief and imagination are not even coextensive.
(6) Hence, imagination is not the same as belief.

An Argument from Persuasion and Reason (428a22–4):

(1) Necessarily, if S has belief, then S has conviction.
(2) Necessarily, if S has conviction, then S admits of persuasion.

(3) Necessarily, if S admits of persuasion, then S has reason (*logos*).
(4) Some beasts have imagination.
(5) No beast has reason (*logos*).
(6) Hence, again, belief and imagination are not even co-extensive.
(7) Hence, imagination is not the same as belief.

This second argument, from persuasion and reason, is of dubious authenticity, since the lines in which it occurs may well be an interpolation or expansion. In any event, both arguments develop the same root idea, that belief, but not imagination, is conviction-entailing.

Plainly these arguments succeed only if the conception of conviction (*pistis*) they employ is defensible. Conviction (*pistis*) may be stronger or weaker in Aristotle, ranging from acquiescence to robust confidence; minimally, though, it is a form of endorsement or pro-attitude (*Top.* 125b30–126a2). Crucially, imagination operates without any such implication. It is possible to have an image of *x's being F* without forming the belief *that x is F*. I might be neutral as to the question of whether *x is F* or, indeed, as Aristotle will later suggest (428b3–4), I may positively deny that *x is F* even while entertaining an image of its being so. This commends a decoupling of imagination and belief.

That said, the appeal to extensional non-equivalence is troubling, since Aristotle elsewhere evidently allows that non-human animals do have belief (see note to 434a10). The second, textually troubled argument perhaps provides a reason for Aristotle's current denial: if we suppose that belief in the end requires reason, then we will have, he supposes, good reason to deny belief to beasts.

In order to avoid a contradiction, it may be open to Aristotle to draw a distinction between kinds of beliefs, in the way that he later distinguishes kinds of imagination, as perceptual or rational (see note to 433b29). Unfortunately, although allowing him to ascribe and withhold belief to beasts, any such distinction would threaten the grounds for extensional non-equivalence here. Moreover, it is difficult to grasp a notion of belief indifferent to some kind of conviction, even if it is non-evidentiary in its basis. That said, Aristotle's subsequent distinction between rational and perceptual imagination (433b29), which carries with it the contention that non-human animals have only perceptual imagination (433b29–30), helps explain the way he divides rational and non-rational faculties: rationality may bleed down into other faculties, imbuing them with features they lack in its absence. Here, then, he may be assuming that animals lack rationally attuned beliefs, which would suffice to ground the arguments for non-extensionality.

**428a24–b9: Imagination is not the Interweaving of Belief and Perception:** We may agree that imagination is not perception (*aisthêsis*) on the grounds that the two come apart operationally (see note to 428a5–14), and that it is not belief (*doxa*), because belief requires conviction, whereas imagination does not (see note to 428a18–24). Even so, imagination may yet be a combination of the two, non-conviction-entailing insofar as it has a perceptual component, and operationally distinct from perception insofar as it is doxastic. The possibility is not an idle one, simply hanging in logical space for eventual refutation: it seems to have a Platonic pedigree (*Tim.* 52a7; *Soph.* 264a1–b3). If that is correct, then we can appreciate why Aristotle would feel the need in general to rebut reductive treatments of imagination. There are more parsimonious approaches to the faculty in the air which he regards as impoverished in their explanatory resources.

Properly, Aristotle begins by setting out three possibilities regarding imagination's relation to belief and perception, considered jointly. Imagination might be: (i) belief accompanied by (*meta*) perception; (ii) belief got through (*dia*) perception; or (iii) an interweaving (*sumplokê*) of belief and perception (428a24–6). The first two possibilities suggested are in fact already ruled out, since each involves an identification of imagination with belief. That leaves (iii), the suggestion that imagination is an interweaving (*sumplokê*) of belief and perception. The word is already rich in Academic overtones and has a quasi-technical meaning. Plato had said, for example, that 'reason (*logos*) comes to be for us through an interweaving of Forms with one another' (*Soph.* 259e5–6), where the sort of relation envisaged is plainly not any kind of aggregation or simple inter-stitching. In this sense, the position on the table is sophisticated, relative to those already canvassed in the chapter.

Aristotle's refutation is similarly sophisticated. (It has been subject to various interpretations. See Lycos (1964), Wedin (1988: 71–84), and Heil (2003) for reconstructions.) In general, Aristotle proceeds via a reductive dilemma. He regards the theory, crucially, as committed to treating the objects of belief and perception as one and the same (428a26–9), though his reason for doing so is initially a bit obscure, namely that it will not do to have an interweaving of a belief of something good and a perception of something white (428a29–b1). Presumably Aristotle is contrasting two sorts of cases: (i) my perceiving something white and my believing it to be white, where the overlap is non-co-incidental; and (ii) my perceiving something white and believing it to be good, where the overlap is co-incidental.

Once he has secured the non-co-incidental sameness of an object, Aristotle observes that, in fact, one and the same object may appear φ even while we do not believe it to be φ. The sun appears to us one foot across, even while we hold to the conviction that it is larger than the inhabited world. (So, e.g., with the Müller-Lyer lines: we stare at them, allowing that one set appears larger than the other, while believing, because we know the illusion, that they are equal in length.) Since belief and appearance come apart, and since we have agreed that what is believed is also what is perceived, we have the following argument:

(1) It is possible to imagine *x's being F* while believing *that x is not F*.

(2) If (1), and imagination is the interweaving of belief and perception, then either (a) one subordinates belief to imagination, or (b) one maintains both the belief and the image.

(3) If (2a), then one mysteriously gives up a belief, though no new evidence or grounds for persuasion have come to light.

(4) It is implausible and unmotivated to maintain that we should change our beliefs in the absence of new evidence or shifting grounds.

(5) If (2b), then, according to the theory in view, one and the same thing will be both true and false.

(6) (5) cannot be.

(7) Hence, either not (1) or imagination is not the interweaving of belief and perception.

Since we have no grounds to deny (1), and indeed perfectly plain reasons to affirm it, the theory according to which imagination is an interweaving of belief and perception is to be rejected. (1) seems a datum, especially if we bear in mind that imagination, as understood by Aristotle, does not require conviction (428a19–22). (2) sets the dilemma. Normally, in the case of conflict between belief and imagination, imagination bows to belief (we do not believe that the sun is one foot across). On the theory proposed it must either be the other way around, as (2a) suggests, or it will turn out that nothing gives way to anything, as (2b) contends. These seem the only alternatives if imagination takes as its object the object of belief and perception, which are non-co-incidentally the same (428b1–2; cf. *De Insom.* 458b29, 460b18). Neither alternative is palatable. Taking (2a) first: if I believe that the Müller-Lyer lines are the same length, then if my image of them is partly constituted by that belief, I will have to suppose that my belief came around to my image, so that my belief will have changed, unbidden by evidence, to conform to my image. Alternatively, according to (2b), my belief, which is true, will remain unchanged. Yet my belief, according to the theory, will constitute my image, which is not true. Hence, this same thing will be true and not true. Note that Aristotle does not assert, as he is easily and often understood to assert, that the theory commits its proponents to the view that one can believe and disbelieve the same thing or even that one can believe incompatible propositions. Rather, the complaint of alternative (2b) is that the belief itself will be both true and false, true because it was hypothesized to have been true and nothing has changed with respect to it when it came to be identified with an image, and false because it constitutes an instance of imagination which, as our datum (1) requires, is false and so not true.

Taking all that together, imagination can be neither belief alongside perception, nor belief got through perception, nor an interweaving of perception and belief.

**428b10–30: The Connection between Imagination and Perception:** Although imagination is neither perception (*aisthêsis*) (see note to 428a5–14), nor belief (*doxa*) (see note to 428a18–24), nor an interweaving of belief and perception (see note to 428a24–b9), there is, nonetheless, an important connection between imagination and perception. The discussion in this section changes tack from what has preceded, treating imagination now in primarily physiological terms. The first set of observations, too loose to constitute a proper argument, contend that imagination could not occur in beings lacking perception, and, more narrowly, that imagination could not occur without perception.

Aristotle proceeds to a more fine-grained discussion of the relation between imagination and perception by suggesting a threefold classification of perception in terms of truth and falsity. His distinction overlaps but is not completely coordinated with the classifications of objects introduced in II 6 (for which, see the Introduction to that chapter): exclusive (*idion*), common (*koinon*), and co-incidental (or co-inciding; *kata sumbebêkos*). Here he mentions the exclusive, a second class, and the common. Aristotle's presentation of the second class is unfortunately garbled in the text, but it differs from the exclusive inasmuch as it admits of falsity, whereas perception of the exclusive tends to be truth-preserving. The text as translated treats Aristotle as distinguishing not between exclusive and co-incidental objects, but as between broad and narrow conceptions of objects of perception (on which, see the General Introduction § III.B, and notes to 418a25, 424a29–b31, 426a23, 432a3–6). Taken this way, his point is that perceiving not narrowly and exclusively *white* but rather more broadly some *white thing* gives way to predicational complexes which admit of falsity (cf. *Cat.* 2a4–10; *De. Interp.* 16a9–18; *Met.* 1027b17–28), of the form *the thing is white*. About such complexes one may go wrong. This would contrast with perceiving an exclusive object, white, which Aristotle suggests is always true or, as he qualifies, 'is subject to falsity in the smallest degree' (428b19).

This qualification regarding exclusive objects represents a significant divergence from the uncompromising line taken in II 6 (cf. 427b12, 428a11, 430b29; *De Sensu* 442b8; *Met.* 1010b2–26). It is sometimes thought that the difference stems from a shift in specificity in Aristotle's characterization of exclusive objects. In II 6 it was the more generic colour (*chrôma*, 418a13), whereas here is the more specific white (*leukon*, 428b21). There is this difference, but it does not suggest any immediately defensible way of reconciling Aristotle's current rider with his earlier unqualified contention.

Moreover, Aristotle implicitly rescinds the qualification just a bit further on in the present chapter when he teases out the consequences of his distinction for imagination: those deriving from the first class, i.e. from perception of exclusive objects, are true when the perception is present, whereas the other two classes admit of falsity in degrees corresponding to the remoteness of the object.

**428b30–429a2: A Positive Characterization of Imagination:** Aristotle's reflections on imagination as a sort of perceptual afterbirth induce him to put forward, if only briefly, a positive characterization of the faculty, or quasi-faculty, which draws also more generally on the entire chapter, the thrust of which has been to parry a series of reductive hypotheses. He contends, by way of concluding, that 'imagination would be a motion effected by actual perception' (429a1–2; cf. *De Insom.* 459a17). It is unclear whether Aristotle supposes this last contention to approach being a definition of imagination, or, more weakly, a constraint on any adequate defining condition of imagination, or, more weakly still, a simple observation about the causal antecedents of every instance of imagination. (Someone might agree that every instance of perception is caused by distal stimulation without thereby being constrained to accept a causal theory of perception.)

**429a2–9: Closing Observations:** Aristotle closes with two observations, the first of which involves him in his occasional indulgence in bad etymology. Given the tight connection between perception and imagination, whereby perception gives rise to imagination, and given that sight is the paramount sense (cf. *Met.* 998a23; *De Sensu* 437a3), Aristotle suggests that the word 'imagination' (*phantasia*) developed from the word '*light*' (*phôs*). This is the sort of bad etymologizing for which Aristotle had elsewhere justly castigated others (see note to 405b11–30).

The last substantive observation looks forward to Aristotle's action theory, which he develops in III 9–10. He observes that imagination suffices for action in beasts, which lack reason (cf. note to 428a18–24), and in humans, when they have taken leave of theirs.

## CHAPTER 4

### Introduction to III 4

Aristotle's treatment of reason (*nous*) represents his third and final major deployment of hylomorphic analysis in *De Anima*, the first having been to soul and body in general and the second to perception (*aisthêsis*). The translation of *nous* as 'reason' reflects a decision regarding Aristotle's approach to the psychic faculty he characterizes here but also a somewhat unstable judgement about the shifting semantic fields of the relevant English alternatives, namely 'reason', 'understanding', 'intellect', and 'mind'. Each translation has some advantages and some disadvantages, and none is uniquely superior to the others. One important consideration concerns the fact that *nous* is pressed into service in a variety of ways in the Greek of Aristotle's time, sometimes indicating a faculty and sometimes indicating a state of a faculty, sometimes referring to a kind of cosmic principle or entity. To do something 'with *nous*' (*sun nô(i)*) is to do it wisely or prudently or reasonably; to 'have *nous*' (*echein noun*) is to be sensible or to pay attention to something or someone. More broadly, Anaxagoras (fr. 12) and Plato (*Soph*. 41a, *Tim*. 249a, *Phlb*. 30c) speak readily of the *nous* of the cosmos. This is a view with a resonance in Aristotle as well (*Met*. 1070b20; some would point additionally to the whole of *DA* III 5; see the Introduction to the next chapter). Aristotle several times draws reservedly favourable attention to Anaximander's characterization of *nous* in *De Anima* (404b1, 405a13, b19–20, including in the present chapter at 429a19). In Aristotle, *nous* does at least double duty: to reach a state of *nous* is to achieve a kind of understanding or insight (cf. 433a26, *A Po*. 88a15–17); to have a faculty of *nous* involves being able to engage in the kinds of activities characteristic of human animals, including thinking, reasoning, and intellection (404a28). Back in *De Anima* I, Aristotle wanted to raise and leave open the question of whether *nous* might be a certain sort of substance: 'But reason (*nous*) would seem to come about in us as a certain substance and not to be destroyed' (408b18–19).

Plausibly, 'reasoning' splits the difference between 'thinking' and 'intellection,' and also, on balance, 'reason' seems best to capture Aristotle's range of meanings when talking about both the faculty and the state; but not too much should be invested in any such determination. One disadvantage of this translation: it tends to lose the connection with some verbal forms, where 'thinking' is to be preferred, given the easier transitivity of 'to think' in comparison with 'to reason'. One can 'reason something through' but it is hard to say that 'one reasons what is undivided' in preference to 'one thinks what is undivided', which is the translation given for the verb 'to reason' or 'to think' (*noein*) in *DA* III 6 (*noein to adiaireton*; 430b7).

One other important point, also a potential disadvantage for this rendering, but equally a concern for any other translation as well: 'object of reason' is given for *noêton*, in preference to 'object of thought' or 'intelligible'. It should be emphasized that *noêton* is directly parallel to *aisthêton*, object of perception, and that both can be either factive or modal. That is, for *aisthêton* we sometimes want 'object of perception', i.e. something actually perceived, and sometimes 'perceptible', i.e. the kind of object that can be perceived. (Colours, not sounds, are objects of sight.) Similarly, *noêton* may be used factively or modally, but for the modal use 'reasonable object' simply will not do. So, it should be borne in mind that 'objects of reason' means either 'objects actually thought' (= factive) or 'objects which can be thought' or 'can be engaged by reason' (= modal). Thus one might say, e.g., 'An abstract mathematical function is an object of reason, not of perception'—that is, it is the kind of thing which can be thought but not perceived. The two can, of course, overlap: if Grüber is just now contemplating the cosine function, then the cosine function is the current object of his thought as well as an intelligible, the kind of thing which can be thought but not perceived. At the risk of straining the English unduly, the translation prefers 'objects of reason' for *noêta* simply to retain the wanted connection with 'reason' (*nous*), the faculty whose objects *noêta* are.

On the general principles of hylomorphic analysis pertinent to this faculty, see the General Introduction § II; on the special issues arising from its application to reason, see the General Introduction § IV.C.

Early in the chapter Aristotle draws attention to the fact that his analysis of reasoning (or thinking, *noêsis*) will proceed along the same lines as perception, namely that it is to be treated as a further instance of form reception (see notes to 429a13–18 and 429a29–b9). Still, he finds an immediate disanalogy between reasoning and perceiving, insofar as reason (*nous*) lacks an organ and indeed 'is in actuality none of the things which are before it reasons' (429a24), a surprising contention given the general hylomorphic model in terms of which Aristotle's analysis of reasoning is couched. In that framework, standard hylomorphic alterations require categorially paired agents and patients, where the patient manifests a suitable passive capacity, which capacity is rooted in some actual feature of the altered object. Thus, a white fence is made grey by receiving the form of grey already realized in a quantity of paint, but only then if there is a surface present to receive that form. We might by parity of reasoning expect there to be a recipient, material or otherwise, suited to acquire a form involved in reasoning. Some have thought Aristotle's reluctance to locate such a recipient a consequence of his woeful empirical ignorance: he simply had no inkling of the brain or central nervous system. In fact, however, as an analysis of this chapter shows, for better or worse, his reasoning in this regard is not a consequence of any simple empirical ignorance. On the contrary, he maintains that there are in-principle objections to reason's having an organ. These in-principle objections stem from reason's *plasticity*, that is from reason's being unconstrained with respect to its potential objects (see note to 429a18–29).

The chapter is fairly orderly, and may be divided into the following main sections: (i) introduction (429a10–13); (ii) an analogy between reasoning and perceiving (429a13–18); (iii) the plasticity of mind and the ramifications of its being so (429a18–29); (iv) a disanalogy between reasoning and perceiving (429a29–b9); (v) reflections on abstraction and the relation of reason to what has magnitude (429b10–21); (vi) two puzzles about reason (429b22–9); and (vii) solutions to these puzzles (429b29–430a9).

**429a10–13: Introductory Matter; an Analogy between Reason and Perception:** Aristotle opens the chapter by speaking of the part of the soul by which *the soul* (*hê psuchê*) knows and understands (429a10–11; cf. 411b5–7, 413a5, 429a23), thus putting some pressure on a stricture advanced in *DA* I 4 (408b1–15), where he seems to insist that it is the human being (*ho anthrôpos*) rather than the soul which is appropriately said to pity or learn or think. The remark made in the earlier passage has induced some ancient commentators, including Themistius (*in DA* 92, 32) to substitute 'human being' for 'soul' in the present passage. This is unnecessary, however, since Aristotle is not in the earlier passage denying that the soul is the subject of such psychological predicates, but rather claiming only that it is not subject to any intrinsic motions as may be implicated by the manifestation of such predicates (see note to 408a29–b18).

Aristotle introduces as topics for consideration in the present chapter the general question of how reasoning comes about and what the differentia of reason is. In recommending a consideration of reason's differentia, Aristotle is probably not using the term in its most technical taxonomical sense, where it specifies the feature whose presence sorts one species under a genus into another (*Top.* 122b12–24, 128a20–37, *Met.* 1020a33–b1), but is speaking in a more relaxed sense, as at 413b19, such that he is merely asking what the distinguishing feature or mark of reason might be.

This first sentence also contains a more vexing clause. Aristotle raises as a topic for investigation regarding reason 'whether it is separable or is not separable in magnitude but only in account' (429a11–12). The grammar of the sentence strongly suggests that this is not a free-standing question, on a par with the others it mentions as worth investigating. Rather, Aristotle is suggesting that reason is *at least* separable (or separate, *chôriston*) in account (*kata logon*; 429a12) and that it may also be separable (separate) in magnitude (*kata megethos*; 429a12) as well; at any rate, this seems to be the purport of the contrast as it is drawn. In the remainder of the chapter, however, he speaks simply of what is separate, without specifying the sort of separation he has in mind.

It is puzzling, however, that Aristotle should introduce as a topic of consideration whether reason is possibly separable in magnitude (*chôristos kata megethos*), since he does not seem to conceive of it as a magnitude in the first place (429a24–5; see note to 429a18–29). It may be that he is drawing the intended contrast somewhat loosely, so that he means not that reason is itself a magnitude, but that it is separate by not being related to the magnitude of the body as the faculty of perception is. He elsewhere in *De Anima* tends to speak not of separation in magnitude but rather of separation in place (*en topô(i)*) (though cf. 432a20, where we have the same contrast between separation in account (*logo(i)* and in magnitude (*megethei*)), and seems to use the expressions interchangeably, or at least to contrast them both with separation in account (*kata logon*) in similar ways (403a11, 413b15, 427a5, 432a20, 433b24–5). If that is right, then the intended contrast here may simply amount to his first suggesting that reason is separate in account from the other capacities of soul, and then wondering in passing whether it is also separate in place. That is, however, not strictly what he says here.

See the Introduction to I 1 for a review of types of separation in Aristotle; Miller (2012) reviews them and investigates in detail Aristotle's attitudes towards the separability of reason.

One final point about this first sentence concerns Aristotle's manner of framing his question about reasoning (*to noein*): 'it is necessary to consider what its differentia is and how reasoning ever comes about' (429a12–13). The phrase translated as 'how reasoning ever comes about' (*pôs pote ginetai to noein*; 429a13) is intended to be, so far as possible, neutral as between two ways of understanding Aristotle's question, one genetic and the other analytical. The genetic version: how does reasoning (*to noein*) ever develop in a human being? The analytical version: what in the world is reasoning (*to noein*)?

The questions have very different emphases. The genetic question is most naturally asked of reasoning considered as a cognitive activity, to the effect of wondering how human reasoning, which is, for instance, able to grasp necessary truths, develops out of sense perception (*aisthêsis*) and experience (*empeiria*). On this approach, his concern is continuous with the sorts of discussions he conducts about the development of reasoning in humans in *Metaphysics* A 1 and *Posterior Analytics* II 19. If it is taken as an analytical question, Aristotle is introducing as a topic for investigation the nature of the reasoning (*to noein*), together with the related question of the nature of the faculty of reason (*nous*). On this approach, he is asking: what sort of thing is reasoning (*to noein*), such that its faculty, reason (*nous*), is affected by the objects of reason (*noêta*), as general hylomorphism requires when applied in this domain, even though this faculty is unaffected (*apathês*) and unmixed with the body?

It would be appropriate for Aristotle to pose either sort of question, given where he has come thus far in *De Anima*. It is not inconceivable that he is asking both sorts of questions, but then he would be packing a surprising amount into a pithy phrase. As it turns out, with respect to the phrase itself, we have little guidance from parallel constructions in Aristotle. One reasonably close parallel, which may shed some modest light on his orientation here, is found in the *Prior Analytics* in a report that it has been shown 'when *and* how a deduction comes about' (*pote kai pôs ginetai sullogismos*; *A. Pr.* 52b39; cf. 25b27, 66b4)—though, again, that is not a strict linguistic parallel. See also, however, *Gen. An.* 733b23–34 and 734b5–6, where the genetic meaning seems more prominent.

In view of this paucity of guidance, one can best come to a fuller understanding of Aristotle's orienting interest by reflecting on the sorts of concerns he evinces with respect to reason (*nous*) and reasoning (*noein*) in this and subsequent chapters.

**429a13–18: An Analogy Between Reasoning and Perceiving:** Strictly, Aristotle does not directly assert that reasoning and perceiving are analogous. Instead, the analogy emerges in the antecedent of a conditional, though one evidently endorsed by Aristotle in what follows, and the commentary on this chapter assumes that this is so. A salutary cautionary note regarding this assumption can be found in Lowe (1983), who also offers a useful way of connecting this and the next chapter with III 7 and 8.

Aristotle immediately teases out four apparent implications of his analogy, and also along the way highlights one point of disanalogy:

(1) Reason is somehow affected by the object of reason, or something else of this sort (429a14–15).
(2) The disanalogy: Reason is, nonetheless, unaffected (*apathes*; 429a15).
(3) Reason is capable of receiving forms (429a15–16).
(4) Reason is potentially the sort of thing its object is, but is not its object (429a16).
(5) Reason will be in general disposed to its objects as the perceptual faculty is to the objects of perception (429a17–19).

Of these, (5) is unproblematic; (3) simply asserts that reason falls under the hylomorphic account of change, broadly construed (see the General Introduction § II); and to appreciate (4), it is only necessary to recall that just as there are two notions of 'object' in 'object of perception', one broad and one narrow (a rose versus the scent of a rose; see the General Introduction § IV.B), so there are two notions of 'object' in 'object of reason' (*noêton*). The locution 'object of reason' thus may be taken broadly as, e.g., the species considered as a collection of animals, or narrowly as the form of the species gorilla, that is, as the property in virtue of which all those animals qualify as gorillas. Put in these terms (4) is pointing out that when reason is enformed by the form of the species gorilla, it does not itself become a gorilla (cf. 432a3). In some instances of reasoning, however, the distinction between broad and narrow object may collapse (see note to 430b6).

So much is reasonably straightforward. By contrast, (1) and (2) present difficulties. It is noteworthy that Aristotle qualifies (1) as he does. Applied strictly, the analogy with perception would have him asserting directly that form reception in reasoning proceeds just as form reception in perceiving does (though exactly how that is to be understood has itself proven controversial; see the General Introduction § IV.B and the Introduction to II 12). The qualification 'or in something else of this sort' (*ê ti toiouton heteron*; 429a14–15) suggests that he resists this implication. Importantly, the qualification ranges not over the object of reason but rather over the process of being affected. That is, Aristotle is claiming not that in reasoning reason is affected by an object of reason *or* something else like an object of reason, but rather that it consists either in *being affected* by such an object or in *something like being affected* by such an object. His hesitation to accept the implication of his own analogy of thought with perception presumably derives from several sources, including: (i) the two notions of potentiality marked in 417b2–29, which ends with a forward reference, evidently to the current discussion (see note to 417b2–16; cf. notes to 412a21–7 and 417a14–20), according to which some cases of being affected involve the destruction of a contrary by a contrary, while others preserve and enhance what is affected; (ii) his contention that reason lacks a bodily organ (see note to 429a18–29); and (iii) his need to avoid an obvious contradiction between (1) and (2).

This last point is clearly the most immediate concern he should have in the current context. In (1) we find Aristotle claiming that reason is somehow affected, while in (2), which follows one line later, he asserts that it is unaffected (*apathes*) (429a15). Worse still, he represents (2) as an inference from (1), with the result that, if he were speaking unqualifiedly, he would be saying something of this sort: since reason, like perception, is *affected* by its objects, it must be *unaffected*—which would be rather like his saying that since a boxer, like a martial arts warrior, is sometimes bloodied when fighting, boxers must be unscathed in the ring. In fact, though, the qualification in (1) shows that he is making no such coarse inference, and is sensitive to the relation between something's being affected in the sense of suffering something (*paschein*) and its being itself unaffected by the thing which it suffers (*apathes*).

Aristotle is claiming, in effect, that, *when suitably understood,* reason's being affected—after a fashion—is consistent with its being unaffected. Here the related distinctions between two notions of being affected (*paschein*) and of alteration (*alloiôsis*) distinguished at 417b2–16 prove crucial. A child is altered by being fed and nurtured; but food does not affect her nature as a human being. On the contrary, her growing to maturity involves her realizing her fullest potential from a state which is already in place and not acquired in the process of her being affected, namely her nature as a human being. Similarly, reason is never altered in its nature when affected by its objects. There is an important wrinkle, however, which undermines this easy illustration to some extent, in that reason seems to have no nature beyond its being potential (429a21–2; see note to 429a18–29 for further discussion).

That allowed, the suggestion that reason is both unaffected and somehow brought about by the efficacy of its objects strains Aristotle's hylomorphic analysis of change almost beyond recognition (see the General Introduction § IV.C). Aristotle has, however, more to say on this matter in the present chapter at 429b23–4 (see notes to 429b21–9 and 429b29–430a9).

**429a18–27: The Plasticity of Reason:**  This complex section contains the crux of Aristotle's positive doctrine about the faculty of reason. It comprises a single continuous argument whose outlines are clear, but whose precise commitments and assumptions have occasioned severe controversy. The overarching argument is:

(1) Reason thinks all things (429a18).

(2) [If (1), then reason must be unmixed.]

(3) Hence, reason is unmixed (*amigê*; 429a18).

(4) [If it is unmixed, the nature of reason must be nothing other than something potential.]

(5) Hence, the nature of reason is nothing other than something potential (429a21–2).

(6) [If its nature is nothing other than something potential, then reason is in actuality none of the things existing before it thinks.]

(7) Hence, reason is in actuality none of the things existing before it thinks (429a22–4).

(8) [If reason is in actuality none of the things before it thinks, then it is not mixed with the body.]

(9) Hence, reason is not mixed with the body (429a24–5).

With the exception of (1), the odd-numbered premises represent the inferences drawn explicitly in the text; the even-numbered premises have been supplied to trace the enthymematic premises. (1) is itself simply asserted without argument, evidently as some manner of datum (429a18).

There immediately follows an additional argument for (9), which also serves to give some content to the claim that reason is not mixed with the body:

(10) If reason could come to be qualified in one way or another, e.g. if it could come to be hot or cold, there would be an organ for it, just as there is for the perceptual faculty (429a25–6).

(11) As things are, however: (a) there is no organ for it; or (b) it is nothing (429a27).

(12) (a) Since there is no organ for reason (accepting 11a), it cannot come to be qualified; or (b) since it is nothing in actuality (accepting 11b), reason cannot come to be qualified, and hence there is no organ for it.

(13) If either (3a) or (3b), reason is not mixed with the body (429a24–5).

(14) Hence, reason is not mixed with the body (429a24–5).

The disjunction in (11) and the concomitant disjunction in (12) reflect two distinct ways of understanding Aristotle's argument for his contention that reason lacks an organ.

If we accept (11a), which is the standard understanding of the argument, then the sense of being unmixed with the body will be precisely that reason lacks an organ. (11a) reflects an implicit addition, not in the text, but accepted by many translators, who understand Aristotle to be saying 'but as things are, there is no organ *for it* (*tô(i), sc.* for *nous*).

On this understanding, Aristotle's reasoning, in paraphrase, is: (a.i) if reason could be qualified by being hot or cold, then there would be an organ for it (= it would have its own organ); but (a.ii) it does not have any organ; so (a.iii) reason is unmixed with the body. This interpretation could be helped along by a reading having some manuscript warrant, according to which the word 'or' (*ê*) is placed before the claim that 'there would be an organ', thus representing this as an independent hypothesis about the requisites of reason's being mixed with the body. The translation does not accept this emendation.

If we accept (11b), which reflects a text without the inclusion of the 'or', Aristotle's point will be that since reason is nothing in actuality, it cannot come to be qualified, which is a condition of anything's having an organ. Periphrastically, then: (b.i) if reason were mixed with the body, it would be able to take on various qualities and would have an organ; but (b. ii) since it is nothing in actuality before reasoning, neither of these results obtains; so (b.iii) reason is not mixed with the body.

On either reading, the ultimate conclusion will be the same, that reason is unmixed with the body; so, it may seem indifferent as to whether we prefer (11a) or (11b). For the purposes of assessing his argument, however, it matters crucially how Aristotle arrives at his ultimate conclusion. (11a) represents him as simply asserting (in a.ii) that reason lacks any organ, perhaps as a result of the impoverished state of empirical science in his time. (11b), by contrast, represents him as relying on a point already established, to the effect that reason is nothing in actuality. Reasons for preferring (11b) are found in Shields (1995); contrasting accounts may be found in Caston (1998), Sisko (1999), and Heinaman (2007); the literature is fairly and clearly reviewed and assessed by Miller (2012). One should, in view of these complexities tread lightly regarding this passage. There has been a tendency, at least as old as ps.-Simplicius, to maintain, that 'since there is no organ for it, reason (*nous*) is completely separate from bodies' (*in de An.* 227, 30); such precipitate interpretations are consistent with the argument of this passage, but not required by it.

However one understands its final phase, the bulk of the argument proceeds in (1)–(9). Each of the premises has proven challenging. As presented, the argument ultimately rests upon a single, slender claim, namely that reason thinks all things (*panta noei*; 429a18). This is not the false claim that reason at any time, or even over all of time, thinks everything which can be thought; it is, rather, the intriguing claim that reason is unconstrained with respect to its objects. In this respect reason is, in Aristotle's estimation, unlike perception. A too intense light, though being an instance of the kind of thing which can be perceived, blinds; an intense thought, Aristotle contends, only sharpens the mind (cf. 424a28–34, 426a30–b3; notes to 422a20–31 and 429a29–b9). He infers, on this basis, that reason cannot have any positive features of its own.

One factor influencing Aristotle in drawing out this consequence of unrestricted plasticity is precisely the hylomorphic framework within which reasoning (or thinking, *noêsis*) is being articulated here: something cannot change into what it already is, either where the destruction of contraries is concerned, as in the base case, nor with respect to a level of actuality, as in the more attenuated case of alteration (see 417b2–16 and note to 429a18–29 for the distinction). Hence, if reason were a certain way, it could not be made to become that way; accordingly, it could not change in that respect; and consequently it could not think what it already was and so could not think all things. See Brentano (1867) for a philosophically penetrating development of this line of thought, though one which also swiftly leaves behind the contours of Aristotle's text as we have it. Shields (1995) attempts a detailed reconstruction of the argument of this passage.

Among the many remaining difficulties with the argument, some of the most severe are those attending to (7), the interim conclusion that reason is none of the things existing in actuality before it thinks (429a22–4). (See the General Introduction § IV.D for an exposition of this worry.) One might think that Aristotle's view is simply untenable here, on the grounds that, necessarily, if *x* is to be affected by an object of reason, then *x* must in the first instance exist in actuality in order to be affected. After all, if there is nothing actual to be affected in some alteration, then evidently no affection can take place: one cannot paint a fence white when there is no fence to be painted. There is some latitude for Aristotle here, however. He may be supposing only that reason exists in potentiality *as a faculty* of a human being before it thinks, at which time it becomes something actual. Thus, *S*'s capacity to swim across the English Channel, although grounded in actual facts about *S*'s physical constitution, is nothing in actuality before *S* learns to swim. One must in this vein distinguish between: (a) *S*'s actually having this or that capacity (Getrude has a capacity to swim, whereas her copy of *The Mill on the Floss* does not); and (b) *S*'s capacity being actualized or not (because he is a swimmer, Tom's capacity was actualized when he learned to swim and then again, in a different way, when he swam across the Channel, whereas Maggie's was never actualized at all because she never learned to swim). This much would respect what seems a minimal condition of adequacy, namely that necessarily if *x* is potentially φ, then there is some *y* such that *y* is actually ψ, and *y*'s being actually ψ grounds *x*'s being potentially φ. This would perhaps be a rather deflationary way of looking at Aristotle's striking claim, though it would still at least serve to distinguish reason from the faculty of perception, which is actual in sense (b) from the outset of life (see note to 417b16–27).

In any event, Aristotle's contention in this regard would seem to undermine, or rather to answer, his tentative query in 408b18–19 as to whether reason might not be a *substance* (*ousia*). For it seems impossible that something which is in its nature nothing other than potential could be a substance.

**429a27–9: Qualified Praise for Plato:** Aristotle punctuates his core argument regarding the nature of reason with qualified praise, evidently for Plato. He does not, however, mention Plato by name; nor are there any clear expressions of this view in the Platonic dialogues given in just the terms used here by Aristotle (though there are some remarks tending in the direction in mainly critical passages in the *Parmenides* at 132b5, 133c5, and 134a10).

He may also be alluding to Plato's doctrine of recollection, as at *Meno* 80e–86d. If this is intended, then the second of Aristotle's qualifications is so severe as to eviscerate Plato's intended meaning. For, on this approach, if we wish to think of the soul as 'a place of forms' (*topon eidôn*; 429a27–8), Aristotle recommends that: (i) we should not speak of the whole soul, but only the rational soul as this place of forms; and (ii) that forms are only potentially in the soul, and not actually.

Whoever the intended target may be, Aristotle does adhere to his own formulation of this doctrine at 410a10–13, 417b22–4, and 431b28.

**429a29–b9: A Disanalogy between Reason and Perception; the Separability of Reason:**  So far we have seen that Aristotle's analogy between reasoning and perceiving, if imperfect in several respects, at least provides a familiar framework for articulating the nature of reason. Aristotle now proceeds to draw attention to significant features of disanalogy between reasoning and perceiving and draws some striking consequences for reason. Earlier he had claimed that sensory organs (*aisthêtêria*) were that in which the capacity (*dunamis*) of perception (*aisthêsis*) is located (424a24). Now, on the basis, in part, of differences between reasoning and perceiving, Aristotle asserts that reason is separate (*chôristos*), evidently from the body (429b5).

It is essential in evaluating this passage to recall the striking claim of *DA* I 1, that a sufficient condition for the *soul* (*psuchê*) to be separate was its having affections peculiar to it (403a10). He seems here to make a directly analogous point regarding reason (*nous*) and also to derive the consequence left undrawn regarding the whole soul. The precise connection between these two consequences is partly a function of the mereology of soul presupposed by Aristotle (on which topic, see notes to 403a3–27, 410a13–22, 411a26–b14, and 413b11–414a3).

In the current passage, the source of disanalogy highlighted by Aristotle pertains to the way in which perception and reason fail to be affected by their corresponding objects. Undue intensity in its objects deadens or destroys the faculty of perception, whereas more elevated objects enhance the power of reason (cf. 424a28–34, 426a30–b3; note to 422a20–31). The argument of the passage appears abductive: we observe a marked difference between perception and reason; the best or only explanation is that reason is without the body; hence, reason is without the body, and so is separate.

That said, on a second possible interpretation, Aristotle is not arguing here for the separability of reason so much as accepting it as already established by the argument of 429a18–27, in which case he is merely appealing to the fact to explain and ground the disanalogy he observes between reasoning and perceiving.

**429b5–9: Self-Moving Reason:** In this passage, Aristotle relies on his distinction between grades of potentiality and actuality (discussed in notes to 412a21–7 and 417a14–20; cf. *Phys.* 255a33, *Met.* 1050a21–3), according to which an actualized potentiality which is not actively operative is a first but not a second actuality: if someone learns to read Old Church Slavonic, then they are actual readers of that language, even if they are at present reading the *New York Times*. When they put down the newspaper and turn to the appropriate liturgical texts, they are actual readers of Old Church Slavonic to a higher degree. This is also the kind of change which does not involve destruction, but rather preservation and development into a full actuality (as discussed in note to 429a18–29).

In the present connection, Aristotle says, on the reading adopted in the translation, that when one is in the relevant first actuality, one can move to the highest level, a second actuality, of one's own accord. This seems to have the consequence that reason is a sort of self-mover (cf. 417a27–8, b23–4). On the sometimes problematical results of this consequence, see Wedin (1994), Shields (1994), Burnyeat (2002), and Heinaman (2007).

It should be noted, however, that the text translated is controversial, and owes to an emendation at 429b9 proposed by Bywater in 1885, who argued that the text as transmitted 'itself' (*de hauton*) should be altered to 'through itself' (*di' hautou*). With the emendation, 'And then one is able to move to actuality through oneself,' Aristotle's point is that once intellectual forms have been acquired, one can reason at will, a reading deriving some, though hardly conclusive support from 417a27. Without the emendation, 'And then it is able to think itself,' the reasoning or thinking in question is reflexive, so that Aristotle's point will be that only when it has acquired some intellectual forms and so has moved from potentiality into actuality, is reason able to think itself. This reading gains some support, again hardly conclusive, from Aristotle's remark earlier in the chapter that reason is nothing in actuality before reasoning (see note to 429a18–27). It is possible that the unemended text should stand, but it is difficult to grasp why Aristotle should suddenly, without warning or following comment, wish to make a point about reflexive reasoning or self-awareness. The issue is comprehensively and intelligently discussed by Owens (1976), who makes the plausible but not overwhelming case for avoiding Bywater's proposal.

**429b10–21: Magnitudes, Abstraction, and Reason:**     This section concludes with a claim which recommends careful study of the entire passage, namely that reason's own separation somehow tracks the ways in which its objects are themselves separate from matter. Unfortunately, in view of its interlocking textual and interpretive difficulties, the passage has proven vexing to commentators. Malcolm (1983) reviews some of the issues regarding this passage and offers a reading which seeks to situate it in the programme of the chapter as a whole.

Aristotle distinguishes magnitude and water from what it is to be a magnitude and what it is to be water—or more literally 'being a magnitude' (appropriately also translated as 'being for a magnitude', *to einai megethei*; 429b10) and 'being water' ('being for water', *einai hudati*; 429b11), where the contrast intended is one between a thing and its being or essence (*einai*). In these cases, the things in question, water and magnitude, are not the same as their essences. To this class of entity, Aristotle opposes two other sorts which, he says, *are* the same as their being or essence. So, we have two interlocking distinctions: (i) things and their being or essence; and (ii) things which are identical with their being or essence and things which are not. These distinctions evidently draw upon *Metaphysics* Z 6, a chapter which should be read in connection with this passage, but which has, unfortunately, itself been subject to a variety of interpretations.

For the present, however, let us focus on the second distinction, and following Aristotle's illustration, call members of the first class *snub kinds* and members of the second class *formal kinds*. The snub (*to simon*) is Aristotle's preferred example of a thing whose definition requires that it be realized in matter of a specifiable sort: snub is concavity in a nose (cf. *Met.* 1025b32, 1030b28, 1064a23). The main function of the distinction between formal and snub kinds in the current passage is to draw attention to two ways of judging or discriminating snub kinds. It is entirely possible to make judgements about the being or essence (*einai*) of water or the being or essence (*einai*) of magnitude; but, according to Aristotle, one manages to do so only by means of a faculty other than the faculty required to make judgements about water or magnitude themselves. Or, at any rate, Aristotle allows, in a retreat from the surprising strength of his initial conclusion, that if one does in fact judge by means of the same faculty, this faculty must be in different conditions when judging in these different ways.

Presumably Aristotle intends to accept the first of these alternatives, suggesting that reason discriminates formal kinds and the essences of snub kinds, while perception discriminates snub kinds insofar as they have sensible qualities. If that is so, it is a bit puzzling as to why he allows that the diverse tasks might be handled by a single faculty in two distinct conditions. Probably Aristotle introduces the unfavoured alternative simply because the argument offered here is a bit slight, unless augmented by additional considerations. In any event, his entrenched policy of individuating faculties by their objects forces him towards the first alternative, that different faculties discriminate these different kinds (for this policy, see 402b9–16, 415a14–22, Introduction to II 4, and note to 418a11–17).

The concluding sentence of this section asserts that as things stand in the case of entities without matter, either formal kinds or essences abstracted from snub kinds, so too do they stand with respect to reason. Aristotle's precise intention in drawing this comparison is disputed. Some ancient commentators took the extreme view that in this passage Aristotle committed himself to a multiplicity of distinct human reasons, ranging from the enmattered reason (*enhulos nous*) to the immaterial reason (*anhulos nous*), corresponding to different kinds of abstract entities, belonging to snub kinds and formal kinds respectively (see, e.g., *Them.* 97, 5). This seems an extravagant overinterpretation, however. Aristotle's more likely meaning is that reason tracks degrees and kinds of abstractness or separation from matter by its own abstractive activities: it must abstract essences from snub kinds, which are separate only then and only in definition, but kinds existing separately *simpliciter* may be grasped directly and completely as they are, without any abstractive activity on the part of reason. For the distinction between kinds of separation (*chôriston*), see the Introduction to I 1 (cf. *Gen et. Cor.* 317b10, 329a25; *Met.* 1019a1–4, 1028a33–4, 1042a29; *EN* 1102a28–32); for the types of separation as they pertain to reason (*nous*), see Miller (2012).

**429b22–9: Two Puzzles:** Aristotle closes the chapter by framing two puzzles which threaten his account. The first puzzle is fairly clear, as is its solution; the second puzzle, along with the solution proffered to it, is comparatively obscure. That said, both puzzles seem appropriate, in view of the commitments of the chapter thus far.

*Puzzle One*: How can reasoning occur if reason is unaffected? The aporetic argument confronting Aristotle is:

(1) Reason is unaffected.
(2) Reasoning is a kind of being affected.
(3) If (2), then since it reason, reason is itself affected.
(4) Hence, reason is affected ((2) and (3)).
(5) Hence, reason is and is not affected in reasoning (by (1) and (4)).

This puzzle should concern Aristotle. He has articulated (1) at 429a15, and (2) at 429a14–15, having accepted them both ((1) somewhat surprisingly) as consequences of the analogy between reasoning and perceiving; see note to 429a13–18; cf. *Gen. et Corr.* 314b26–7, 324a34–b7. Together (1) and (2) suffice to generate a prima facie puzzle.

*Puzzle Two*: How can reason think itself? Here the aporetic argument is a bit more complex and also a bit more impressionistically put:

(1) If reason thinks itself, then either it is present in other things or it will have present in it something rendering it a suitable object of reason.
(2) If reason is present in all other things, then everything can reason.
(3) It is not the case that everything can reason.

308

(4) Hence, reason is not present in all things (by (2) and (3)).
(5) If reason has something present in it rendering it a suitable object of reason, then it will not be unmixed.
(6) Reason is unmixed.
(7) Hence, there is nothing present in reason capable of rendering a suitable object of reason (by (5) and (6)).
(8) Hence, reason cannot reason itself (by (1), (4), and (7)).

Here again an earlier commitment of the chapter engenders a problem, for Aristotle had accepted (6) at 429a18 and 429a2–4 as a consequence of the plasticity of reason (on which, see note to 429a18–27).

**429b29–430a9: Solutions to these Puzzles:**    In an effort to solve Puzzle One, Aristotle reaches back to his distinction between ways of being affected. See, in this chapter, note to 429a13–18; this should be read together with 417b2–29 and notes to 412a21–7, 417a14–20, and 417b2–16.

In the current context, Aristotle mainly seeks to explain the relevant kind of being affected by appeal to the potentiality exhibited by a writing tablet. Significantly, this analogy is not intended to represent reason as a kind of Lockean *tabula rasa*. Aristotle has, rather, a more limited illustration in view, pertaining to the kind of potentiality displayed by a writing tablet. There are some actual facts about a tablet which make it suitable to receive an inscription; but these facts are consistent with its being in potentiality relative to *all* letters, at least before it is written upon. So, it is in potentiality with respect to all of them, and is thus nothing, so to speak, inscribed in actuality before being written upon.

If this is Aristotle's intended meaning, two consequences follow. First, in repeating that reason is 'in actuality none of the things which are before it reasons' (429b31; cf. 429a24), Aristotle is supposing, as was suggested in the note to 429a18–27, not that reason mysteriously pops into existence when it begins reasoning, but rather only that its capacities, being infinitely plastic and grounded in actual features of a cognizer, are not actualized until reasoning in fact begins. Second, he is thus evidently intending to deny (3), which holds that if reasoning is itself a kind of being affected, then since reason thinks, it is affected. Reason remains in its essence fully potential, just as a writing tablet remains unaffected in its nature as potentially inscribed, until such time as letters are written upon it. Even then it retains the grounding potentiality of being able to have letters inscribed upon it. So, reasoning may itself be a kind of being affected without reason's being affected in its nature by the activity of reasoning. Aristotle's solution to Puzzle Two is a bit more vexing. He seems implicitly to advert to the distinction drawn earlier between what we called *snub kinds* and *formal kinds,* as discussed in the note to 429b10–21. The puzzle proceeds by forging a dilemma: either reason is capable of being thought through its own nature and so is actually something, and hence is not unmixed; or it is unmixed but it is capable of being thought by virtue of things other than itself. If the latter, however, and if what is thought and what thinks are the same in form, it will follow that other things are not only intelligible, but are in fact instances of intellect, or reason. Neither alternative seems happy, since if everything has reason, then everything thinks. On the other hand, if reason is actually in some determinate state or is some definite thing, then it is not unmixed, and so not infinitely plastic.

Aristotle evidently seeks to deny both horns of the dilemma. As for things thought, they do not therefore have reason simply in virtue of their being thought; for the sense in which reason is identified with them is only without their matter (430a2), just as reason thinks snub kinds only having first abstracted their essences. So, the sense in which it is right to say that water is one with reason is just to say that the essence of water enforms reason and is one with it formally. This leaves no temptation to ascribe mindedness to water. Unfortunately, however, this observation provides no ready reason for thinking that one or another of the premises in the second puzzle, as explicated, is false.

On the other side of the dilemma, matters are at least a bit more hopeful. Things without matter can be one with reason; if the pure or formal kinds at least include intellectual beings, as presumably they do (*Met.* 1074b29–1075a5), then reason can, so to speak, think reason by being actualized by them. Presumably the subsidiary worry voiced by Aristotle (430a5–6) confirms that he is proceeding along these lines: if a sufficient condition for reason to reason is the actual presence to it of an existing reason as an instance of a pure or formal kind, something, accordingly, standing in no need of abstraction, then why is reason not forever reasoning reason? If this captures the outlines of Aristotle's solution, three additional observations are pertinent. First, in some instances, Aristotle will refer to the form without the matter, even though he is not thinking of elevated immaterial beings, as in *De Anima* II 12, where he speaks of receiving forms without matter in connection with perception (see note to 424a17–24). Second, even if we adopt this approach, it will remain unclear precisely how Aristotle rejects either of the premises in his second aporetic dilemma. Finally, and more importantly, if this accurately tracks Aristotle's intended solution, then the puzzle itself may have to be reconfigured. It sounds initially as if it is a puzzle about the reflexive reasoning in which individual minds engage when they think of themselves. The solution sketched seems rather a solution to a more general puzzle about how reason as such can think reason as such, whether or not that reasoning is reflexive. If, that is, reason's reasoning, e.g. of the divine intellect, qualifies as reason thinking itself, then there is no immediate suggestion that the puzzle requires reflexivity to be generated (as, by contrast, a somewhat similar puzzle does about perception; cf. note to 417a2–14). Note, in this connection that Aristotle's language in setting the puzzle is somewhat circumspect: he wonders 'whether it [reason] is itself an object of reason' (*ei noêtos kai autos*; 429b26). Perhaps, then, the puzzle never was one directly concerned with reflexive thought. Conversely, if it really was intended to be a puzzle about reflexive thought, then it is unclear how this response qualifies as any kind of solution.

Further discussion of the puzzling features of these puzzles may be found in Kahn (1966) and De Koninck (1994), who connect them with thought about the divine intelligences discussed in *Metaphysics* Λ; Lewis (2003), who rightly stresses their connection to some Anaxagorean theses which Aristotle finds congenial; Caston (1999), who draws from them data about Aristotle's approach to consciousness; and Kosman (1975) and Gill (1991), who see them as presaging problems addressed only in the next chapter. Miller (2012: 319–20) provides a crisp overview of the problems and some approaches to them, and then also provides a plausible account of Aristotle's reasons for introducing them.

## CHAPTER 5

### Introduction to III 5

This terse, suggestive chapter has excited more exegetical controversy than any other in the Aristotelian corpus. Even though we
have seen Aristotle reserving reason (*nous*) for special treatment
throughout *De Anima*, and even though the previous chapter
characterizes reason as unmixed (*amigê*; 429a18) and unaffected
(*apathes*; 429a15), nothing has quite prepared the reader for the
striking claims of *De Anima* III 5. Aristotle now distinguishes an
active from a passive reason (or a productive from an affected
reason; *nous poiêtikos* from *nous pathêtikos*—though he does not,
in fact, ever use the term '*nous poiêtikos*' directly), and contends
that active reason is not only unaffected and unmixed and separable, but also 'in its essence actuality' (*tê(i) ousia(i) ôn energeia*;
430a17–18), and moreover 'deathless and everlasting' (*athanaton
kai aïdion*; 430a23). All of this raises the prospect that despite his
plain denial that the whole soul is separable in *De Anima* II 1,
reason, taken by itself, may yet be separable, with the consequent
result that perhaps he regards personal immortality as compatible
with hylomorphism after all. This possibility in turn brings into
sharper relief the qualification Aristotle immediately offers even
when issuing his 'plain denial' of the separability of the soul:
'Therefore, that the soul is not separable from the body, *or some
parts of it if it naturally has parts*, is not unclear' (413a2–5). Others
find little connection to the apparent qualification of *De Anima* II 1,
reading this chapter instead as isolated from the rest of *De Anima*,
and as a change of topic from human reason to divine reason.

We find, accordingly, two dominant exegetical tendencies in
response to this chapter. The first, a *Divine Interpretation* (DI),
holds that the reason (*nous*) as characterized by Aristotle in this
chapter is not a human faculty at all, but rather a detached and
everlasting divine mind. The second, a *Human Interpretation*
(HI), maintains, on the contrary, that the reason (*nous*) described
in this chapter is precisely human reason. HI, but not DI, thus
treats the reason under consideration in this chapter as the same
reason (*nous*) he has been characterizing in III 4 and will carry on
characterizing in the chapters which follow.

HI was typically espoused by exegetes in the medieval Latin
tradition seeking to develop a form of hylomorphism congenial to

Christian doctrine. An especially ingenious and powerful exponent of this general approach is to be found in Thomas Aquinas, who revisits the chapter again and again in his writings, both within and without his Aristotelian commentaries. Those pursuing a version of DI robustly reject this entire orientation. On this general approach, which found a powerful exponent already in Late Antiquity in the commentaries of Alexander of Aphrodisias, the active reason Aristotle finds cause to characterize in this chapter as deathless and everlasting is not a faculty of human beings at all, and so has nothing to do with the apparent qualification of *De Anima* II 1. According to this approach, the subject of this chapter is rather the divine intellect to which Aristotle elsewhere commits himself (*Met.* Λ 7 and 9).

Although at most one of these interpretations makes maximal sense of the chapter, neither can be ruled out on narrowly textual grounds. Further, in view of the strong proponents on either side, each deserves an equal hearing. Consequently, the commentary proceeds as follows. For each section of the chapter, it advances—so far as possible—a neutral exposition, followed by two running commentaries in tandem.

The Divine and Human Interpretations introduced in this section of the commentary are regrettably generic, and little effort is made to trace out the many sub-variations within each approach. Still, each individually represents one of the dominant lines of interpretation of this rich and provocative chapter; it is hoped that they jointly offer a glimpse of the lively dialectic which has characterized debates regarding *nous poiêtikos* (active reason) down through the centuries. At a minimum, the presentation of these contrasting approaches is intended to equip those readers wishing to enter the debate themselves to do so with at least a rudimentary map of the terrain in hand.

Unsurprisingly in view of the heated exegetical controversies over *nous poiêtikos*, the literature on this chapter is vast. Among the works cited in the bibliography, the most detailed, thorough, and philosophically uncompromising is Brentano (1867/1977: 163–229); others, including Hicks (1907), provide more philologically and historically sensitive running commentaries. Whether or not one adopts Brentano's interpretation, it is salutary to appreciate how well his discussion illustrates the complexity occasioned by this one short stretch of text: his commentary on a chapter of fifteen lines runs to sixty-six pages.

For a very clear and succinct taxonomy of the main approaches to this chapter, see Miller (2012), who uses a slightly different manner of classification from that employed here. He divides the schools of interpretation into *internal* and *external* interpretations, based upon whether the interpretations treat *nous poiêtikos* as internal or external to the human soul. Beyond offering a judicious overview, Miller provides a succinct and useful taxonomy of various sub-variations of his two main approaches (321, with 333, n.47). It should be noted that Miller's taxonomy shows one way in which the division employed here is not exhaustive: one could, for instance, believe that the active reason is not a human faculty all, without thereby identifying it with the divine mind. One might think, for example, as a very few commentators have thought, that the active reason Aristotle describes is a not a human capacity, but not the divine mind either. It could, for instance, be a common, non-divine mind, perhaps a kind of active principle of nature. The overview here sets aside such (minority, but not therefore false) views. It, nonetheless, provides references to the minority views, alongside the dominant approaches, where appropriate.

**General Orientations of the Divine and Human Interpretations:**
**DI**: As was already seen by the greatest of the ancient commentators on Aristotle, namely Alexander of Aphrodisias (*DA* 89. 9–10), active reason is pure actuality, and thus devoid of all matter and free from potentiality. This is the same intellect called by Aristotle the one which enters 'from without' (*thurathen*; *GA* 736b27). This intellectual being is not a human being, nor a part of a human being, and so not a faculty of the individual human soul. This being is the deity whose illuminating activity makes thought possible for otherwise benighted humans.

As we have already learned in *De Anima* II 1, Aristotle believes (i) that the human soul is not separable (413a4–6; see note to 413a3–7), and (ii) that the rational soul is not merely a detachable stratum on top of the perceptual soul which might be peeled off like the top layer of a cake (see note to 415b8–27). On the contrary, the rational soul is an essential unity—and indeed an entity whose primary function is to provide for the unity of the body. Together, these commitments combine to undermine any suggestion that, while the whole soul is inseparable, one part of it, active reason, is. Since, then, active reason *is* separate and the human soul is not, active reason cannot be—or be any part of—the human soul.

Further, when we turn to the governing characterizations of active reason in the present chapter, we find Aristotle comparing it most prominently to light (see note to 430a15–17). In speaking of it this way, he clearly treats it as something external to the human soul, as an enabling condition of a certain sort. So, it would be perverse to regard active reason as somehow internal to the soul, on a par with treating the light which makes colours visible as residing somehow within the eyes themselves. Rather, active reason, as conceived by Aristotle, is something wholly impersonal, existing externally to the individual human soul. It is the divine being characterized in *Metaphysics* Λ.

It may be that the consequences of the divine interpretation are welcome or it may be that they are unwelcome; but in either case, we would be wrong to foist upon Aristotle a Platonic, or still more anachronistically, a Christian conception of personal human immortality. Such an approach is, inter alia, out of keeping with the pervasively naturalistic and biological tenor of *De Anima*, which treats human beings as natural, rational, corporeal beings.

Some proponents of DI, in addition to Alexander of Aphrodisias, are: among the most prominent older writers, Avicenna, *De An.*, 221; Averroes, *Long Comm. in DA* III 18–20; and among more recent writers, Barnes (1971), Clark (1975), Rist (1966), Frede (1996), Caston (1999), and Burnyeat (2008).

**HI**: As the most ancient of all commentators on Aristotle, as well as the only interpreter of the doctrine who actually knew Aristotle, Theophrastus rightly saw that active and passive reason are simply two features of human reason: reason is active insofar as reasoning is hardly a purely passive affair, but reason itself is also, nonetheless, passive, in so far as it involves form reception and so is affected by the objects of reason given to it (*In DA* 110.18–28). This view at first also seems to find an early expression in Themistius, who at one point says: 'active reason is in the soul and it is like the most honourable part of the human soul' (*In DA* 103.4–5). As it turns out, however, Themistius denies that active reason is a personal individual faculty belonging to individual humans (*In DA* 105.28–9). So, Themistius points in the right direction without taking the needed additional steps himself. HI finds a full expression in Philoponus (*De intell.* 57.70–4) and in Aquinas (*In de an.* 742–3), who observed that any suggestion that active reason is external to the human soul, whether it is conceived as divine or not, seems to require that human beings depend upon the agency of an external actor in order to operate. This threatens to render humans essentially incapable of achieving their own good, since human flourishing consists in the activity of reason (*EN* x 6–8); but plainly any such suggestion is anathema to Aristotle's unambiguously stated belief that human flourishing consists in the realization of essential human capacities—that is, of capacities belonging to human beings themselves.

More importantly, when we turn to the text before us, we discover nothing in the course of *De Anima* which even remotely suggests an abrupt change of subject, as DI requires: throughout, we have been talking about the souls of natural beings, namely plants, animals, and humans, and neither before nor after the present chapter is there the slightest hint that the topic has temporarily shifted to another sort of being altogether. On the contrary, the reason under discussion in *De Anima* III 5 is the same reason under discussion in *De Anima* III 4 and III 6. These chapters are, however, plainly concerned with human reasoning. It is thus unsurprising that *De Anima* III 4 and III 5 both make free use of the sort of vocabulary reserved here for active reason, namely that its being unaffected and unmixed (*apathes* in III 4 at 429a15 and *apathês* in III 5 at 430a18; and *amigê* in III 4 at 429a18 and *amigês* in III 5 at 430a18).

Finally, as for the soul's parts, Aristotle had said plainly in the first chapter of the work that a sufficient condition of the whole soul's being separable is there being some affection peculiar to it and not shared with the body (see note to 403a3–27). He has now affirmed the antecedent of that conditional several times over, not least by asserting that the intellect lacks an organ (429a25–6; see note to 429a18–29) and is unmixed with the body (429a18, 24–5). Nor does his doing so contradict any claim about the inseparability of soul: Aristotle did not simply assert that the soul was inseparable from the body, but took pains to qualify his remark even as he introduced it: it is clear, he asserts, 'that the soul is not separable from the body, *or some parts of it if it naturally has parts'* (413a3–5). He then straight away hastened to insist that 'nothing hinders some parts from being separable' (413a6–7). See notes to 403a3–27 and 413a3–7.

It may be that the consequences of the personal interpretation are welcome, or it may be that they are unwelcome. That will in turn be partly a function of what the precise consequences are understood to be. For it must be stressed that so far HI is generic in its formulation and so is consistent with a wide range of more fine-grained interpretations. In fact, the (putative) consequences of HI vary greatly from proponent to proponent, since some hold to this general interpretation while insisting that the human active intellect is separable only in account or definition (*logô(i)*), and not ontologically, in its own right, or unqualifiedly (*haplôs*), while others understand Aristotle to be envisaging a form of personal immortality. Depending on the form of HI adopted and developed, then, Aristotle's doctrine will begin to look more or less markedly Platonic.

Some proponents of HI, in addition to Philoponus and Aquinas: among the most prominent older writers is ps.-Simplicius *in de An.* 240.1–248.18; among more recent writers those who hold that the human intellect is ontologically separate include Rodier (1900), Ross (1961), Robinson (1983), Sisko (2000), and Gerson (2004); and, finally, among more recent writers those who hold that the human active intellect is only definitionally separate are Hicks (1907), Wedin (1988), and Caston (1999).

**430a10–14: Active and Passive Factors in Nature and in the Soul:** In nature in general, there are active and passive elements. Indeed, it is at the core of Aristotle's hylomorphic analysis of change that in episodes of alteration something acts while something is affected: a lump of clay does not spontaneously organize itself into a statue, but is made into one by the agency of the sculptor; nor does the sculptor sculpt something from nothing, but only by acting upon a suitable subject. The clay, as matter, is thus passive and in potentiality, and the sculptor, as efficient cause, is thus active, exercising a power when actualizing the clay's passive potential to be a statue. So too in the case of the soul: the changes involved in perception and reasoning must conform to these general principles. Hence, we must find in the case of the soul, here in the case of the reasoning soul, active and passive factors. This seems a straight application of Aristotle's general hylomorphism. (Cf. *Phys.* I 7– II 8 and *Met.* Z 7–9, esp. 1045a30–2); see also the General Introduction § II on the general principles of hylomorphic explanation.)

**DI**: Aristotle says that the general division of active and passive powers found in all of nature are equally evident 'in the soul', which might be taken to mean that he is here characterizing a distinction internal to the individual soul. The phrase 'in the soul' (*en tê(i) psuchê(i)*, 430a13), however, need not mean 'in the individual soul'. Rather, Aristotle means only 'in case of the soul' or, more loosely, 'where the soul is concerned'. Of course, in this realm, as in others, the basic principles of hylomorphism apply: if reasoning and perceiving are attenuated species of alter-ation, then both active and passive components must be at play in episodes of these alterations (see the General Introduction § II for general principles of hylomorphic explanation). More than that would not be warranted by Aristotle's general appeal to hylo-morphism. On the contrary, it would seem a straightforward fallacy of division to move from (a) in every change in the natural sphere, active and passive elements are present to (b) in every part of the natural sphere, such as the individual soul, active and passive elements must be present. That would be rather like saying that since final causation is present in the whole of nature, it must likewise be present in cases of seeming co-incidence, so that when a creditor happens by chance upon his debtor in the marketplace the meeting must in fact be for the sake of something—an inference Aristotle clearly and rightly rejects (*Phys.* 196b33–197a19).

**HI**: Aristotle maintains that the active and passive elements which are present everywhere in nature are also present 'in the soul' (*en tê(i) psuchê(i);* 430a13). As Ross (1961: 45) observes, this 'can only mean the human soul'. We are, after all, in the midst of a discussion of the human soul, one according to which, as we have already seen, both active and passive features are required. In particular, Aristotle holds that for reasoning to occur some abstractive *activity* must take place (see note to 429b10–21), so that objects of reason (*noêta*) may be made avail-able for the individual episodes of thought of individual human beings. Any suggestion to the effect that abstraction is effected for humans by a unified external active intellect, or active reason, has an unacceptable and bizarre result, namely that everyone will forever think the same thoughts at precisely the same times. If the counter will be that this does not follow, since individual souls must still turn themselves towards externally abstracted forms as objects of reason (*noêta*), then that is to concede that both active and passive principles must be present in the individual soul, and nothing will be gained by trying to forestall that consequence. What Aristotle means is that reasoning involves activity and receptivity on the part of reason; and he is surely right about that.

**430a14–15: Producing and Coming to be All Things:** It is not immediately clear what is meant by reason's being active by somehow coming to produce or make all things (*tô(i) poiein panta*; 430a12). A useful clue comes from *Met.* 1033a31, where Aristotle speaks of making (*poiein*) some particular thing from a substrate (cf. *Met.* 1033b2, b22); a second, more local clue, comes from the comparison of reason's agency to the activity of a craft (*technê*; 430a12). Crafts do not produce something from nothing, but rather *fashion* something already in potentiality into something actual. If we combine these two thoughts, then Aristotle is not ascribing any unrestricted creative powers to active reason, but is rather suggesting that reason actively works on something potential to bring about something actual. To take this line of reasoning one step further, it will be natural to understand him as engaging in the kinds of abstractive activities in which reason is implicated (see again note to 429a18–27). If we are prepared to expand Aristotle's meaning in this direction, then the productivity of reason will reside in ordinary intellectual tasks such as concept formation, isolating commonalities between objects in thought, abstracting *in rebus* universals for analysis, and engaging in drawing inferences from one set of propositions to another. In all these ways, reason is appropriately described as active, as *doing* something or other. Note in this connection that Aristotle's general tendency is to think of universals as appropriate objects of reason (*APo.* 81b6, 87b28–37, 87b39–88a7; cf. note to 417a21–b2; *Met.* 1039b28–1040a7, 1087a15–20).

This somewhat deflationary understanding of Aristotle's meaning offers him little motivation to characterize active reason as deathless and everlasting, as he in fact proceeds to do (430a23). Still, it does fit his remarks in a broader and familiar pattern of Aristotelian explanation. If correct, it also suggests that some who proceed by speaking of '*nous poiêtikos*'—which exact term is in fact never used by Aristotle—as 'the creative intellect' or 'the maker mind' are overblown and potentially misleading. Safer and more appropriate would be characterizations in the neighbourhood of 'active intellect', or 'active mind', or, as the translation prefers, simply 'active reason'. Aristotle does speak of a passive reason, or reason which is passive (*ho de pathêtikos nous;* 43a24–5), where the implied contrast is a reason which is active, or active reason.

Note too in this connection that the definite article 'the' found in most English presentations of 'the active intellect' may tend to prejudice one's interpretation in favour of substantival views of active reason. Here some circumspection is warranted. In Aristotle's Greek, 'the active intellect' and 'the passive intellect' might be used to refer to two distinct intellects, or to one and the same intellect, where it might mean 'the intellect, insofar as it is active' or 'the intellect insofar as it is passive.' This would be roughly the difference observed in English between 'The cowardly man always defers to the courageous man' and 'When sober, she is unfailingly polite, but when intoxicated she can be really unpleasant, and, I can tell you, the sober woman is more agreeable than the drunken woman.' So in Greek we may distinguish 'Active reason—*sc.* the one which is active and never passive— is not affected by objects of reason' from 'Insofar as it is active, reason is not affected by objects of reason.' The substantival interpretation of the implied phrase *nous poiêtikos* ('the active intellect') may or may not be correct as an interpretation of the chapter; but as a matter of representation of the actual contents of the chapter, the other, less committal rendering ('active reason') leaves open the possibility that Aristotle means only to speak of reason (*nous*) insofar as it is active.

**DI**: If in its agency reason makes all things, then it is unrestricted in scope or power. No human intellect is so powerful. Clearly, then, active reason is a kind of superhuman agency, something appropriately described by Aristotle later in the chapter as 'deathless and everlasting' (430a23) and elsewhere as 'divine' (*Gen. An. GA* 736b27).

**HI**: Presumably, 'all' in 'all things' is implicitly restricted in its domain. Aristotle had said in the previous chapter that reason 'thinks all things' (429a18), where this meant only that it was unrestricted with respect to its objects, that nothing internal to it would hinder its reception of any intelligible form (see note to 429a18–27; and Shields (1995)). Here he means that reason, insofar as it is affected by intelligible objects existing in actuality, comes to be one in form with them (cf. 4 note to 431b24–432a1), but only after it has prepared itself and its potential objects appropriately.

**430a15–17: Like Light:** Aristotle appeals to light as a kind of positive state (*hexis*) in an effort to explain how it is that active reason is active in producing all things. We have seen earlier how light works in the case of colours. At 418b9–10, Aristotle characterized light as 'the actuality of . . . the transparent, insofar as it is transparent,' and observed further that 'darkness is the absence of this sort of positive state (*hexis*) from the transparent; the result is plainly that its presence is light' (418b18–20). This makes light a kind of enabling condition for the seeing of colour. Light does not make colour seen, though it does make it visible, as Aristotle himself highlights. If that is right, then the point of the comparison is to suggest that objects of reason (*noêta*) may be only potentially such until they are suitably actualized by reason's agency.

On this general approach then, active reason somehow makes the objects of reason available to passive reason, which is en- formed in the process of coming to think. For instance, if it is true that all kinetic energy ceases at 0° Kelvin, then this is a fact about the universe, captured by the Third Law of Thermodynamics, and this fact can be thought by a sufficiently trained and attuned mind. It is not, however, a simple thought which one might grasp more or less directly by looking out across a (seemingly) motion- less meadow. Rather, a fair bit of preparation must first be effected in order for it to be brought into focus; the law must, so to speak, be isolated and revealed to a discerning mind by a process of study. If reason's activity enables thought in this way, as light brings colours into a condition in which they can affect the perceptual faculty, then active reason proceeds by making the medium between mind and object transparent. It illuminates the conceptual space between an object of reason (*noêton*) and the reason (*nous*) which grasps it.

Of course, that much development is already speculative and also somewhat strained: a conceptual space is in fact not a space.

**DI**: As light is external to the perceptual faculty, and is caused, says Aristotle, by 'the presence of fire or something of this sort in the transparent' (418b16–17), so the agent intellect, which makes objects of reason fit for reasoning, is something external to human reason. It illuminates conceptual space as the sun illuminates physical space. It is not as if the eyes send out beams to illuminate colours through the darkness; rather, when light is made present by the agency of fire or the sun, then and only then are colours actually perceptible in the transparent. The terms of the analogy thus dictate that active reason is external to the human soul, no less than the sun is external to an animal's eyes.

**HI**: The analogy does not turn on the *source* but on the *presence* of light. Aristotle appeals to light to explain how active reason makes thought possible. The terms of the implicit analogy are precisely those he specifies, namely that just as light makes colours existing in potentiality into colours existing in actuality (430a16–17; cf. 418b18–20), so active reason makes objects of reason exist in actuality and thus thinkable. On this last point, careful readers will note that Aristotle has said only that light makes colours actual 'in a certain way' (*tropon*; 430a16). This is as it should be, since colours are fully actual as objects of perception only when perceived. As Aristotle claims, 'the actuality of the object of perception and of the senses are one and the same, though their being is different' (425b26–7; cf. 426a15–16 and note to 425b26–426a26). The relevance of his circumspection here is that something is a fully actual object of reason only when it is in fact thought, but it is made capable of being thought only by some act of abstraction, something accomplished in a specific time and place by the agency of an individual human thinker. Here again active reason is simply reason insofar as it is active.

**415a17–19: The Traits of Active Reason:** Aristotle lists the core traits of active reason. It is: (i) separate (*chôristos*; 430a17); unaffected (*apathês*; 430a18); (iii) unmixed (*amigês*; 430a18); and (iv) in its essence actuality (*tê(i) ousia(i) ôn energeia*; 430a18). Aristotle reels off this list rather abruptly, with no inference made from what precedes, though he does give a glimmer of a justification in what follows by asserting that 'what produces is always superior to what is affected' (429a18–19). There seems a fair distance still to travel, however. If we think that there is a dimension along which a sculptor is superior to clay she moulds, it will not follow that the sculptor is, e.g., unaffected or in her essence actuality.

That said, it would be wrong to read Aristotle as having failed to *establish* that active reason has these traits, because he has not really made any such attempt. Rather, he seems content simply to report his views on the matter. This is unfortunate inasmuch as we are left without the interpretative guidance of a grounding argument, and hence have little determinate evidence about how he understands these traits.

Such guidance as we do have stems primarily from what Aristotle has already said about reason in general in the previous chapter—and it is not uncontroversial that the data of that chapter is relevant to the form of reason characterized in this chapter. Assuming, though, that we can accept guidance from the linguistic data of that chapter, we might come to a clearer understanding of what is being asserted here.

In III 4, it seemed that reason was unaffected insofar as its essence was not altered by reasoning, inasmuch as it was held to be infinitely plastic (see note to 429a18–27); that it was unmixed with the body, in the sense of its lacking an organ (429a24–7; see note to 429a18–27) and being devoid of any intrinsic features, physical or otherwise (429a25–7; see note to 429a18–27); and that it was separate, where that might in principle be construed in a number of different ways (Introduction to I 1), but as 429a10–13 maintains, reason is separable at least in definition, where there is an open question as to whether it is separate also with respect to magnitude (see note to 429a10–15; cf. 413b15, 427a5, 432a20, and 433b24–5).

The brief grounds he gives for claiming that reason is essentially activity, namely that 'what produces is always superior to what is affected' (430a18), draws on a common theme for Aristotle, who adheres consistently to principles of priority for cause over effect, and more generally to the priority of the actual over the potential. Often these principles are mainly descriptive (e.g. that a cause is prior in time to its effects), but at times, as here, they are also evaluative. Cf. *Met.* 1049b27, 1051a4, 1072b2–24; *Gen. An.* 723a3–10; *A. Po.* 88a5; *Phys.* 265a22.

**DI**: Key among these traits, and new relative to the characterizations of the last chapter, is Aristotle's contention that reason is in its essence actuality (*tê(i) ousia(i) ôn energeia*; 430a18). This is precisely the sort of language he uses to characterize the divine intellect in the *Metaphysics* at 1071b17–22, 1072b26–7, and 1074b18. This is unsurprising, since he is talking about the divine mind in this chapter. What is more, in characterizing active reason as *essentially* actual, Aristotle commits himself to its being without potentiality altogether. It is difficult to appreciate how human reason could be so characterized.

**HI**: As we have seen, most of the traits of reason listed here have already been mentioned in general in the last chapter. What is new is the characterization of active reason as in its operation essentially active. We have already seen that reason is both affected, in a way, but also unaffected (see note to 429a13–18). This is no contradiction, so long as it is not affected and unaffected in the same respect, or with reference to the same part or features of itself. If we follow that same line of thought, the appropriate way to understand this passage is to read Aristotle as asserting that reason, *insofar as it is active*, is essentially in actuality. This is compatible with its being affected, insofar as it is passive. There is no mystery in this. If a rabid fan of Manchester City Football Club paints his chest blue before the big game, then he is wholly active insofar as he *is painting* his chest, but wholly passive insofar as his chest is a surface *being painted*. Reasoning, as we have already noted, essentially involves both active and passive elements (see note to 430a10–14: HI).

**430a19–21: Interpolation:**    These lines recur in their entirety in III 7 at 431a1–4 (see note to which). Here it seems likely that they are an interpolation by a scribe seeking to gloss the sense in which active reason is prior to passive reason, though the attempt adds little. We could decide that they definitely do not belong here, if we had good reason to suppose that they definitely do belong in the later chapter. Unfortunately, they fare only a bit better in the context in which they occur in the later chapter (see the Introduction to III 7).

**430a22: Not Sometimes Reasoning and Sometimes Not:**    This line is also sometimes thought to be an interpolation, perhaps trailing after the intrusive words immediately preceding it. (So, for instance, already in late antiquity Philoponus (*De intell.* 60.31) relays the information that some commentators known to him thought this line needed to be excised; and it is not present in ps.-Simplicius (*in de An.* 245.5).) That may be; it does seem disconnected with what has immediately preceded the interpolation. If it is retained, it is best regarded as parenthetical.

On the somewhat dubious assumption that they belong here, these lines would be picking up on a promissory note at 430a5–6 to investigate why reason is not always reasoning. The problem there, at least on one understanding (see note to 429b29–430a9), is that if a sufficient condition of reason's reasoning is the presence to it of a suitable object of reason (*noêton*), then, since there are always such objects available, it should always be reasoning.

If that is the correct parallel, then we cannot regard Aristotle as providing the wanted answer here, unless he is simply understood as conceding the point that reason always reasons. For here we have only a simple denial: reason in fact does not reason intermittently. Since it presumably reasons at some times, it must always be reasoning.

**DI**: As we have just seen, since reason sometimes reasons, and since it does not reason intermittently, it must always reason. Human reason does not always reason; it is not always active. Indeed, human reason 'is in actuality none of the things which are before it reasons' (429a24). So, the reason we are characterizing here must be the divine intellect, and not human reason at all.

**HI**: Because we are speaking of reason insofar as it is active, Aristotle will naturally avoid describing it as something operating intermittently. Fire does not sometimes burn and sometimes not burn. When there is fire, it burns in actuality, and not intermittently. Here active reason, like fire, being 'in actuality none of the things which are before it reasons' (429a24), is either actual or nothing at all. This is the sense in which 'it is not the case that sometimes it reasons and sometimes it does not' (430a21).

**430a22–25: Once Separated:** These lines in some ways encapsulate the high controversy surrounding this entire chapter. They contain, in neutral terms, the following claims:

    (i) once separated, this alone is just as it is;
    (ii) this alone is deathless and everlasting;

(iii) we do not remember; because
(iv) this is unaffected, whereas
(v) passive reason is perishable; and
(vi) without this nothing reasons.

The first and most obvious question concerns the referent of 'this' in (i), (ii), (iv), and (vi); in (i), (ii), and (iv)) it is most natural to assume that the referent is active reason, whereas in (vi), linguistically speaking it might equally be active or passive reason. We may assume that the natural referent is the right one in (i)–(v), while leaving open the question regarding (vi). If so, Aristotle here claims:

(i) once separated, active reason alone is just as it is;
(ii) active reason alone is deathless and everlasting;
(iii) we do not remember; because
(iv) active reason is unaffected, whereas
(v) passive reason is perishable; and
(vi) without this [either active or passive reason] nothing reasons.

On this account, Aristotle concludes the chapter by offering a final summary of the features of active reason.

With that in place, one may begin by asking about the relation between (i) and (ii), the claims that once active reason has been separated, it alone is just as it is. The tense and aspect of Aristotle's Greek lead one to assume that he means that active reason is at some time not separated, and then comes to be separated. This does not immediately entail that it is a personal capacity (the divine intellect never having been non-separated), since: (a) there are different types of separation (on which, see the Introduction to I 1); and (b) the natural way of taking Aristotle's Greek is certainly not the only acceptable way. As regards (a), if one supposes that the separation in question is separation *simpliciter*, then the claim suggests a resolution to the disjunct given at 429a11–12 to the effect that reason, at least insofar as it is active, is indeed separate more than in account or definition (*logô(i)*). Still, Aristotle may mean something much less striking, suggesting only, for example, that when active reason is isolated in thought, it is purely what it is.

326

As for (b), the tense and aspect of the word translated as 'having been separated' (*chôristheis*) need not be ingressive, as is sometimes assumed (where it would signal that reason is entering into a state or condition that it had not been in before), but rather simply indicating the complete state of its subject, regarded in its totality.

The claim translated as (ii) that active reason 'alone is just as it is' reflects a decision about what 'alone' (*monon*) modifies. An alternative translation, less likely but still possible, would be: 'only having been separated, this is as it is'. The difference in paraphrase would be: 'having been separated, active reason, taken by itself, is purely what it is,' vs 'only when it has been separated is active reason just as it is'. Perhaps the difference is only one of nuance, but the suggestion of the alternative translation would be that it is only by its being separated that active reason becomes untrammelled by matter and thus something which is purely its own nature, whereas the translation adopted suggests something less determinant, that it is the only thing surviving separation and emerging just as it is. Similar considerations affect (iii).

The claim (iv), that we do not remember, requires some explanation from Aristotle. Why and how is our not remembering relevant? As we shall see, both Divine and Human Interpretations are possible.

That passive reason is perishable (v) is now stated directly, by contrast with active reason (430a24–5), which has already been characterized as deathless and everlasting. The passage calls to mind 413b24–6, where Aristotle had maintained that things were unclear with respect to reason, as to whether it might be separated, 'in the way the everlasting is from the perishable'. Here, by contrast, he seems clear, at least as regards active and passive reason.

The chapter's closing claim (vi), that without this nothing thinks, might linguistically be taken as making a claim about active or passive reason. If active reason is intended, Aristotle is simply tidying up a bit, and reminding the reader of the opening of the chapter (on which, see note to 430a10–14). If it is rather passive reason that Aristotle has in view, then the closing is more consequential, and we would probably best understand him as connecting (v) and (vi) and as explaining the fact that we do not remember when active reason is separated, in fact or in thought, because passive reason is required for remembering. Aristotle might have grounds for reasoning this because he supposes that reasoning requires images (*phantasmata*) and that passive reason has a special role to play in their collection and storage. Clearly, though, such a thought is speculative. See, however, note to 432a3–9 on the role of images in thought.

**DI**: While an HI-style interpretation of these last remarks cannot be ruled out on narrow linguistic grounds, any such interpretation of them is, nonetheless, unnecessary and unwelcome, especially given what Aristotle has already said in the chapter. To begin, the claim about separation need not mean 'when active reason becomes in fact separate' from the other faculties of the soul or the body. Rather, Aristotle is suggesting only that when the divine intellect, which is active reason, is isolated in thought, it alone is appreciated as what it is, something deathless and everlasting. This is because the divine mind is fully actual, and anything with any kind of matter is somehow potential (*Met.* 1050b27). Indeed, as Aristotle asserts, all and only those entities which are everlasting qualify as utterly bereft of potentiality (*Met.* 1050b6–18). Further, the claim that we do not remember indicates only that we do not remember the agency of active reason in its preparation of objects of reason for our intellection because we are ourselves not involved in any such agency. On the contrary, it is precisely because it is the activity of a divine active reason which prepares objects for our contemplation that we are in a position to think at all.

Finally, given that nothing is both everlasting and perishable, it follows that active reason is numerically distinct from passive reason.

**HI**: While a DI-style interpretation of these last remarks cannot be ruled out on narrow linguistic grounds, any such interpretation of them is, nonetheless, unnecessary and unwelcome, especially given what Aristotle has already said in the chapter. For in fact, any such interpretation is contorted as a rendering of Aristotle's Greek. To begin, the claim that active reason is at some time separated is clearly stated, and this implies that there was a time when it was not separated. This is not, however, the divinity. First, the divinity never was anything but separate; and, further, any suggestion to the effect that the separation in question was merely conceptual is implausible in the extreme, since there is no reason at all to believe that the divine mind is deathless and everlasting only when it is isolated in abstraction. That is false: it is never anything but.

Aristotle's plain meaning is that active reason is purely what it is when it has been separated from the body and other faculties of the soul, which is just the possibility he had entertained at 429a11. It being unfathomable that he was thinking of the divine mind in the earlier passage, it is hard to credit the suggestion that he is doing so here. Moreover, the claim that *we* do not remember serves as confirmation of the personal interpretation: Aristotle is making a direct claim about *us* and our activities. He is speaking about our active reason. Here too there is an earlier passage which serves to secure both the referent and the content of his current claim, namely 408b24–9:

> Reasoning and loving or hating are not affections of reason, but rather of that which has reason, insofar as it has it. As a consequence, when this is destroyed, one neither remembers nor loves. For these did not belong to reason alone, but to the common thing, which has perished. But reason is presumably something more divine and unaffected.

Finally, we should not even suppose on the basis of these lines that active and passive reason are distinct in the manner of distinct substances, the first being everlasting and the second perishable. Rather, reason, as a whole, is everlasting, as it plainly must be if one of its capacities is everlasting. Reason is, after all, one being with active and passive abilities, each of which is required for human concept acquisition and cognition. Furthermore, Aristotle has just said that reason, when separated, is just as it is, and in its essence actuality. When reason is separated from the body and the other faculties of the soul, its passive capacities run dormant, and it becomes essentially activity.

His point, then, is not terribly complicated. Reason is like a doctor who is ill and yet able to treat herself with a course of medication. While ill, she has the passive ability to be cured no more or less than the active ability to cure. Once better, she has lost that passive ability. Plainly, it would be fallacious to infer that there were two doctors there all along, the ill doctor and the curing doctor. Rather, there was, and is, but one doctor, who was not but is now whole and healthy.

## CHAPTER 6

### Introduction to III 6

This chapter, like the two following, is a bit scrappy. It does not follow upon the preceding chapter in any obvious way; nor does it bridge in an orderly fashion to the next. Moreover, again like the following chapter, it offers very little by way of the internal argumentative or linguistic signposts characteristically found in Aristotle's writing. In this way, both chapters are unusual relative to Aristotle's typical manner of expressing himself. Though there seems to be no reason to doubt their authenticity, both chapters show signs of incompletion.

The current chapter does, however, have a main focus, namely the intellection of what is undivided *or* what is indivisible (*adiaireton*). Even so, commentators have struggled to specify the precise character of this main focus. What, precisely, are the divided or indivisible things under consideration? The disjunction in this question already reflects a problem of translation and interpretation. In narrow linguistic terms, Aristotle's word *adiaireton* may mean either *undivided* or *indivisible*. Thus, in principle, Aristotle might be talking about thought of objects which are de facto undivided, or rather, those which are in their nature indivisible; or he may be talking about both indifferently. The issue may seem settled by the fact that in the midst of his discussion he mentions objects which, though potentially divisible, are, at least as thought, actually undivided, e.g. a length (or line; *mêkos*, 430b8). So, Aristotle must mean at least to include divisible but undivided objects under the term *adiaireton*.

At the same time, Aristotle considers some objects which are indivisible, like points (*stigmê*; 430b20), and some others whose status might be debated, including essences (*to ti ên einai*; 430b28), as well as all objects bereft of matter (430b30). So, the question arises as to whether Aristotle has identified a clear class of objects for discussion. For this reason, the worry about the translation of *adiaireton* is not a simple linguistic matter, but reflects a deeper concern about the subject matter of the chapter.

Fortunately, however, the issue about translation, along with the underlying worry about the class of objects under consideration, can be handled with reasonable confidence. In all likelihood Aristotle is concerned not with objects regarded as undivided or indivisible in absolute terms, but rather with objects which are undivided or indivisible *relative to a domain*. That is, something may appropriately be considered indivisible in one respect, but divisible in another. For example, when linguists speak of phonemes or morphemes as being indivisible or without parts, they mean only relative to the context of appraisal: these are the simplest, indivisible units of linguistic theory. We may say indifferently, and without any threat of incoherence, that a phoneme is an indivisible unit of sound and a morpheme an indivisible unit of meaning, even though either is, relative to a variety of different, non-linguistic frameworks, perfectly analysable into parts and so not simple. A phoneme is a quantity of sound, and as such is infinitely divisible as a continuous duration of noise; still, it is the basic, indivisible unit of sound relative to the combinatorial demands of word construction.

Similarly, in the current chapter, Aristotle is mainly concerned with what is indivisible relative to the constitution of thought. His discussion, in fact, makes clear that he is working with a distinction along the lines of concepts and judgements. One might well say that judgements are necessarily truth-evaluable and divisible (or decomposable) into concepts, whereas concepts are simple in the sense of not yet being true or false. This is precisely the sort of language Aristotle uses with respect to thought concerning the undivided and the combined, or the simple and the synthesized (430a26–8).

Consequently, the translation sometimes renders '*adiaireton*' as 'undivided' and sometimes as 'indivisible'. This seems unavoidable, but does not reflect any conflation on Aristotle's part. A pupil's *undivided* attention might be *indivisible* with respect to its object of focus but yet readily *divided* into time segments, and so in this sense also *divisible*. Closer to Aristotle's treatment of lines, one may say that it is the nature of a continuum to be an *undivided* whole which is not therefore *indivisible*, but is, on the contrary, divisible without limit. Aristotle will use one word, *adiaireton*, for both 'inidivisible' and 'undivided' in these sentences. Berti (1978) reviews this matter helpfully; see also Pritzl (1984) for an assessment of the role of the intellection of indivisibles in Aristotle's broader theory of cognition.

Aristotle is in any event not interested in this chapter in thoughts about the *adiaireton* exclusively insofar as they are thoughts of what is undivided or indivisible. He draws an analogy between indivisible objects of reason and exclusive (*idia*) objects of perception (on which, see the Introduction to II 6 and note to 418a11–17). One consequence of this comparison, recognized and endorsed by Aristotle, is that one is immune from error, or almost immune from error, with respect to them. (On the question of truth and immunity to error with respect to exclusive objects of reason, see 427b12, 428a11, 430b29; *De Sensu* 442b8; *Met.* 1010b2–26; but cf. 428b18, where it is qualified). In the present chapter, Aristotle again uses the language of truth and falsity (43b26–7), as he had for exclusive objects of sense (427b12, 428a11–15, 428b18). In both cases he presumably has in view the notion of truth deployed at *Met.* 1051b17–1052a11, where it is explicated as the touching of an object. This sort of truth is evidently below the threshold of propositional truth, being more closely akin to the notion of truth where *being true* is a sort of success condition or a sign of authenticity, as when ornithologists distinguish a true sighting of an ivory-billed woodpecker from a false one. In this sense, the indivisible objects of reason discussed in this chapter function in reasoning as exclusive objects (*idia*) function in perception (*aisthêsis*): they are the basic concepts serving as constituents of thoughts, below which we are no longer in the realm of reason (*nous*).

**430a26-b6: Indivisible Thoughts, Truth and Falsity:**  This first section of the chapter is easily its most coherent. Thought of the indivisible is not yet true or false, but is never false. In saying that truth and falsity obtain only when there is already a combination of the objects of reason, Aristotle has in mind the sort of truth and falsity appropriate to propositions and assertoric sentences. By contrast, when he says that there is no falsity for the indivisible, Aristotle has in view a notion of falsity whose correlate is a sub-propositional notion of truth. Aristotle offers similar observations at *Met.* 1027b25–8, as at *De Interp.* 16a9–11 and 18a13–17. For these reasons, this section of text should also be in read in conjunction with the beginning of *De Interp.* 1 and the whole of *De Interp.* 5 and 8.

It is fairly clear that Aristotle's distinction between synthesized and unsynthesized objects of reason approximates, if inchoately, a familiar distinction between concepts and propositions.

If that is correct, then in speaking of the thought of what is undivided in this chapter, Aristotle is characterizing a kind of non-discursive thought, something which is sometimes held to be mysterious or indeed impossible (see, e.g., Lloyd 1970), but which may be nothing more complicated than our thinking of blue—not *that* blue is a colour, or *that* blue is not red, but simply *of* blue, or, to use a non-sensory concept, not thinking that hope is a virtue, but simply thinking *of* hope. That much would make sense of Aristotle's suggesting that thoughts of the indivisible are never false but not yet the sorts of things which admit of truth *and* falsity. They do not admit of truth and falsity, because they are sub-judgemental or sub-assertoric; and yet they are not false, in that the grasping of a colour other than blue, or of something else altogether, is not a false grasping of blue, but simply not a grasping of blue at all. Consequently, relative to this framework of appraisal, thoughts of uncombined concepts are indivisible, while thoughts of synthesized concepts, e.g., *that white is not black*, are divisible.

**430b6–b20: Potential and Actual Division:** The text of this section is troubled and has occasioned a good deal of comment. Some of the difficulty, but only some, has resulted from an unnecessary concern about Aristotle's understanding of the undivided or the indivisible (*adiaireton*). Much of that concern, though not all, may be addressed by appreciating that his main point about divisibility, as was suggested in the note to 430a26–b6, has primarily to do with propositional truth and falsity, and is, therefore, domain-relative (see the Introduction to this chapter). If that is correct, Aristotle is best now understood as addressing a potential objection to his earlier claim concerning the intellection of indivisibles. Someone might object that thought *of a line*, though not yet truth-evaluable, is, nonetheless, not simple. For every line is divisible; and one can, as it were, treat the thought as inheriting its complexity from the infinite divisibility of the line, with the result that the thought is divisible precisely because the line is (necessarily) divisible.

Aristotle's response, 'that the undivided is spoken of in two ways, either in potentiality or in actuality' (430b6), holds that a line is potentially divisible, but not therefore actually divided. Its being potentially divisible, because continuous, will therefore be irrelevant to the question of whether a thought of it is or is not divisible, in the semantic sense under consideration. Further, if one actually divides it, and thinks first of one half and then the other, the time of the thinking is itself divided as well. Cf. 426a23; *Phys.* 218b29, 299a20; *De Sensu* 446a30.

**430b20–6: Being Indivisible as Limit; Knowledge of Privation and Opposites:**   For reasons that are not immediately perspicuous, Aristotle changes to a consideration of another kind of indivisible object, a limit, like a point. Perhaps the shift reflects a change to a new kind of undivided object. So far, he has considered objects which are potentially divisible, but not actually divided, like lines, which are continuous. He first introduces points, which are not only actually undivided, but in fact indivisible, because of their lacking magnitude, but he then segues without obvious warrant to a consideration of privations and opposites more generally. The text is a bit patchy and may suffer from corruption or interpolation.

It seems likely that the last sentence of this section is an allusion to the divine mind, which at *Met.* 1075b20–4 is said to lack an opposite. Again, however, it bears only a tangential connection to the rest of the chapter.

**430b26–30: A Return to Topic:**   This concluding section returns to the main thread of the first part of the chapter, though Aristotle now advances his point in a manifestly linguistic idiom. Every assertion predicates one thing of another and is thus truth-evaluable; but not every instance of reason (*nous*) is synthetic and so not every instance is true or false in the propositional sense. Reason (*nous*) is presumably used here in the sense of a state of the faculty, rather than as the faculty itself (cf. note to 428a17–18, together with the glossary entry on *reason*).

Aristotle draws attention to one significant instance of sub-propositional thought, namely the grasping of an essence (*to ti ên einai*; 430b28), which he likens to a perceptual grasping of an exclusive (*idion*) object of perception (on the force of which comparison, see the Introduction to the present chapter). He extends his range of objects, in a closing remark, to those without matter in general. It is unclear whether he is thinking of those objects which exist without matter in abstraction, including the points and lines already discussed in the chapter, or has in mind the prime mover of *Met.* Λ 6–10, which exists permanently without matter, and thus stands in no need of abstraction. Perhaps he has both in view.

However that may be, if the general account of being divided or indivisible (*adiaireton*) given in the Introduction to this chapter is apt, Aristotle's emphasis should not be primarily on the character of objects taken in isolation, but rather on their ability to be grasped in a sub-judgemental act of intellection. It is probable that he has in mind two categories of such objects: (i) lines and other continua which may be grasped as simple but are in themselves potentially divisible (as discussed at 430b6–20); and (ii) points and things existing without matter which are simple and not potentially divisible (as discussed at 430b20–6). Here he groups essences with those in the second category (cf. *Topics* 142b27).

## CHAPTER 7

### Introduction to III 7

This chapter, like the next, is plainly a collection of fragments. Like both the preceding and the following chapters, it is conspicuously lacking in the kinds of connective and inferential particles characteristic of Aristotle's prose style. It was perhaps assembled by Aristotle for an eventual but never executed reworking or, more probably, by a later editor compiling otherwise unattached texts. In either case, it has no unifying topic or common theme.

That said, the chapter does contain some important doctrine and does seem, in its various fragments, authentically Aristotelian.

### 431a1–4: Relations of Priority and Posteriority in Knowledge:

Considered temporally, potential knowledge (*epistêmê*) is prior to actual knowledge in an actual knower, since one *can* know before one *does* know. Still, potential knowledge is not in general prior in time, since whatever comes to be actual, including knowledge, comes to be from something existing in actuality. Aristotle is thus relying on the general principle that only what exists in actuality can bring it about that something existing in potentiality comes to exist in actuality.

One may object that this general principle, whatever its merits, is insufficient in the present context. For it does not by itself require that what is potentially φ is made actually φ only by what is already itself actually φ. For this result, the priority of actuality must be wed to some version of a causal synonymy principle according to which only φ-things can make non-φ-things φ (e.g. only what is already hot can make what is not hot hot). Hence, one need not agree on the basis of the priority of actuality alone that what knows in potentiality comes to know in actuality only by the agency of actual knowledge. That said, Aristotle may be in a position to develop this general principle suitably to bridge the gap. On the priority of actuality to potentiality, see the whole of *Met.* Θ 8, but especially 1049b24–7; cf. *Met.* 1069b5–20, *Gen. An.* 734a29–30.

**431a4–6: Actualization, Change, and Being Altered:**   Aristotle continues on the theme of actuality and potentiality by pinpointing the actualizer in the case of perception (*aisthêsis*) as the object of perception (*aisthêton*). It is striking that in this connection Aristotle moves further along the course of distancing the process of perception from alteration and being affected. Earlier, he had hesitated a bit in suggesting that the alteration involved in perception was an attenuated kind of being affected (see notes to 416b32–417a2, 417a14–20, 417b2–16, and 418b3–5). Now he says, when speaking of the perceptual faculty (*aisthêtikon*), that it is neither affected nor altered. This seems to bring the perceptual faculty closer in character to reason (*nous*) than it had previously seemed to be. See note to 429a13–18.

**431a7–14: Perception, Pursuit, and Avoidance:**   Partly on the basis of its analogy with reasoning (on which, see note to 429a13–18), perception (*to aisthanesthai*, 431a8; and *aisthêsis*, assumed at 431a9) may be said to be, in a sense, similar to affirmation and denial, insofar as perception issues in pursuit or avoidance behaviour when in the face of pleasure or pain. Thus, a lamb may perceive something as pleasurable, and then by way of affirming this, move towards it, or may by contrast perceive something as painful, a threatening wolf, and by way of denying that, move away towards shelter. Aristotle is not saying that perception is a form of linguistic behaviour, or that perception has an internal linguistic syntax, but rather that its motions are characterizable in ways paralleling the linguistic output of creatures with reason (cf. *EN* 1139a21–3). On perception as involving a mean, see 424a4 and 424a28–b3, with notes to 423b27–424a10 and 424a28–b3.

Aristotle's next claims are, unless interpreted in a somewhat deflationary and implausible manner, rather baffling. He says: (i) 'avoidance and desire are the same, in respect of their actuality' (431a12) and (ii) 'the capacity for desire and the capacity for avoidance do not differ either from one another or from the perceptual faculty' (431a14–15). The second claim is made slightly less jarring by the addition that 'they do differ in being' (431a14), where the suggestion is that they overlap extensionally, even though these capacities are not identical. Thus, the capacity to organize auditory signals and the capacity to organize visual signals may equally be located in the tectum, but these organizational functions are nonetheless distinct. On differing in being, see note to 424a24–8; cf. *Met.* 1037b6; *Phys.* 202a18–20, b11–16.

That said, both (i) and (ii) remain rather puzzling. As for (i), plainly actual pursuit is not the same as actual avoidance. It is sometimes said, implausibly, that every pursuit of $x$ is at the same time an avoidance of $y$ and vice versa, on the grounds that whenever $S$ pursues some object, its opposite is avoided. What, though, is the opposite of *crème brûlée*? It does not seem plausible that a decision to order *crème brûlée* is a flight from *flan*, or more generally a flight from *crème brûlée*-lessness. Perhaps one might suppose more weakly still, then, that Aristotle is speaking not of desire as such, but, indirectly, of the faculty of desire, the actualization of which involves pursuit or flight. That is, however, not how he expresses himself; on the contrary, he seems to move on to offer this latter point as an additional observation. Still, unless some such expedient is adopted, it is difficult to construe Aristotle's point.

The second claim (ii) is still more difficult. One can treat the capacities of desire and flight as the same along the lines sketched under (i); but Aristotle fails to explain why he should regard these capacities as the same as the perceptual faculty. Here too one can fathom deflationary treatments, along the lines of Ross (1961: 305) to the effect that 'both faculties appear at the same point in the kingdom of living things—animals both perceive and desire, plants do neither; it seems possible that this is what A. has in mind—that perception and desire-or-repulsion are simply two elements in an animal's reaction to the things it perceives.' As Ross is aware, however, any such interpretation must then treat what Aristotle in fact says as an 'overstatement'—and, one might add, as an extravagant and misleading overstatement at that. In fact, nothing in *De Anima* prepares the reader for (ii). Perhaps it is a misguided interpolation.

**431a14–20: Images and the Rational Soul:**   Aristotle further develops his reflections on the perception of the pleasant or painful by extending his comments about pursuit and flight to the rational soul (*dianoêtikê psuchê*; 431a14). Where he had mentioned the pleasurable and the painful in the case of perception, he now adverts instead to a more conceptually laden way of speaking, in terms of affirming or denying that something is good or bad (*agathon ê kakon*; 431a15–16).

Surprisingly, Aristotle draws an underpowered inference from these observations, to the effect that 'the soul never thinks without an image' (431a16–17). The necessity of images in the rational soul is elsewhere asserted by Aristotle, including later in the next chapter, where it may, however, be qualified, and where it is added that images in the soul are like perceptions (see note to 431b2–17; cf. 403a8, 432a8–10; *De Mem.* 1, esp. 449b31–450a4, and 451a1–4). The instability in the current inference does not attach to the conclusion itself, which may or may not be defensible, but to the grounds for the derivation of this conclusion. As we have the text, Aristotle argues: (1) Images (*phantasmata*) function in the rational soul just as perceptions (*aisthêmata*) function in the perceptual soul; [(2) the affirmation of pleasurable perception yields pursuit, and the denial of painful perception yields flight;] hence, (3) affirmation of something as good in the rational soul yields pursuit, while denial of something as bad yields flight; consequently (4) the soul does not think without an image. If one is prepared to grant the analogy asserted in (1), and to accept (2) on the basis of 431a7–14, then (3) seems a reasonable inference, though even then, as Aristotle himself elsewhere discusses in detail, a continent person might avoid pursuit when tempted and a courageous person avoid flight when given a fright. The move from (3) to (4) also requires amplification. The problem arises both because some further assumption is needed to bridge the gap and because, even with ancillary premises, (4) seems overly general as stated. It is unclear why, even if images, as implicated in action, are required for practical reason, they should likewise be necessary for theoretical reason, which is not engaged in pursuit or flight. See 432b27–9: 'neither is the rational faculty or what is called reason what initiates motion, for the faculty of contemplation does not contemplate what is to be done, nor does it say anything at all about what is to be pursued or avoided.'

**431a20–b1: Discriminating Contraries and Cross Contraries:** This is another difficult passage, textually corrupt, and possibly a scholiast's interpolation. Any attempt to trace the reasoning of this passage beyond its initial set-up must be regarded as conjectural. That acknowledged, one can make an effort, proceeding on the dubious assumption that this section is both authentic and well-placed.

Aristotle remarks that it is necessary to return to the topic of how one discriminates sweet and hot things, where he is apparently referring back to 426b8–29 (see note to which; cf. also note to 425a14–b3), though he had spoken there not of sweet and hot things, but rather of sweet and white things. The difference is inconsequential, since he is concerned in each case with discriminating across sensory modalities.

Aristotle wonders how one manages to discriminate things not of the same modality. He elsewhere holds that in the case of opposites within one modality, like black and white, which are of the same kind though differing in species, perception (*aisthêsis*) itself discriminates (422b23–7; *De Sensu* 447b26, 448a3; *Gen. et Corr.* 323b9). How does this occur with objects of perception which are not opposites arranged along a single continuum, as when we have sensibles in distinct modalities? Perhaps as follows. Let sweet and bitter be unified, by being opposites along a single taste continuum. Now set alongside them another equally unified pair, say, hot and cold, again subordinate to a single, though distinct genus of quality. There remains something held fixed between the pairs, namely their proportion of opposition, which is the same in each case, since both define the termini of their continuous quality spaces. Now if hot and cold were to belong to a single thing, in different respects, of course, then one could hold the hot fixed, along with its proportion to the cold, subtract the cold from the equation, perform the same task with the sweet and bitter, subtracting the bitter, and then see that the sweet and the hot were distinct, since they were originally paired to distinct opposites along distinct continua. (This subtracting and re-contrasting operation seems to be what Aristotle has in mind by the phrase 'converting as appropriate', which is a periphrastic expansion of *'enallax'*, often rendered by a Latin logical term, such as *'convertendo'* or *'alternando'* (431a27; cf. *EN* 1131b5; *APo.* 74a18, 99a8).)

What, then, is the 'one thing' (431b21–2) which performs these operations? It cannot be either one of the individual sensory modalities, since these are keyed to limited ranges of oppositions given, ultimately, by their relative exclusive objects (see the Introduction to II 6, with note to 418a7–11). Presumably, then, the faculty in question is common perception (*koinê aisthêsis*), on which, see 425a14–b3; cf, *De Sensu* 437a9, 442b4–10, and *De Memoria* 450a9–12, 452b7–13.

Extracting even that much meaning from this difficult section presupposes various decisions about the constitution of the text, and about the referents of some free-floating demonstratives, as reflected in the translation. None of these decisions is universally accepted.

**431b2–17: Images, Pursuit and Flight:** Heightening the sense that the preceding section is an interpolation, or at best a digression, the text returns to the topic of 431a14–17, namely the role of images in the antecedents of action.

Although the text here too is ungainly, Aristotle seems to draw a contrast suggesting a modification of the unqualified assertion discussed earlier that one always thinks in images (431a16–17). If the doctrine of reasoning in images is unrestricted, then one may wonder why Aristotle connects imagistic thinking so closely to action (see the concern expressed in note to 431a14–17). The contrast suggested here ('some', *ta men* at 431b2, evidently answered by 'other things', *ta de* at 431b12) would have it that practical reason is imagistic, but that thinking of what exists in abstraction is not. The latter sort of thinking encompasses, e.g., thinking of the snub not as concavity in a nose, but of concavity as such, which one thinks of as one thinks of mathematical objects, whenever one thinks of them in their abstracted state and just as they are.

Given the instability of the text, it would be wrong to rely too heavily on its contrast between the role, or non-role, of images for different kinds of thinking. Still, if we accept the text as given, the general tenor of this section is as follows. Outside the sphere of perception, one may act on the basis of such images in the soul as portend the good or the bad. Just as is the case with perception of the pleasant and the painful, when conceptualizing an anticipated outcome of action, one moves towards or flees an object represented according to its apparent goodness or badness. (This seems the point of Aristotle's illustration of a moving beacon. According to Thucydides II 94, a stationary torch in a military context is friendly, while an approaching torch augurs hostility.) In other cases, where action is not implicated, as when one thinks of abstractions of various kinds, images need have no role. In any event, if there is to be an argument for concluding that images are required for contemplation, it will not be readily drawn from the sphere of practical reason. In the theoretical sphere, one thinks of objects as they are, with no practical end indicated by or issuing from the thought. Cf. 433a14–15; *EN* 1139a26–35.

**431b17–19: Concluding Remarks:** The chapter's summary reiterates its opening. The closing question has an analogue in *De Memoria* 450a7, though there, as here, it remains in effect an unanswered promissory note.

CHAPTER 8

### Introduction to III 8

Like the preceding chapter, this chapter contains little connected argumentation. Although it purports to be a summary of what has come so far, it serves this purpose in only the most general terms, and even then only partially. That said, it does contain a number of striking figures and consequential claims.

**431b20–4: The Soul is in a Way All Things:** The soul is potentially one in form with its objects insofar as it knows or perceives them. There is some emphasis in this section on the fact that the soul knows *all* things: if reason knows the objects of reason and perception the objects of perception, then if these two kinds of objects exhaust all there is, as Aristotle contends here, there is nothing the soul cannot be. The caution Aristotle expresses in 'in a way' (*pôs*; 431b23) prefigures the argument at 431b28–9, according to which the soul's faculties are not numerically identical with their objects taken broadly, but with the forms of those objects (see note to 431b24–432a1).

**431b24–432a1: The Way in which the Soul is All Things:** Although Aristotle's initial claim is reasonably clear, the Greek of this section is nonstandard and is not readily explained in terms of Aristotelian idiom. That said, the claim is plain enough: the faculties of knowledge (*epistêmê*) and perception (*aisthêsis*) are divided from one another in a manner corresponding to the division we find between the objects of knowledge and the objects of perception. This seems a corollary of his standard practice of individuating faculties by reference to their objects. (On this practice, see the Introduction to II 4, together with note to 415a14–22.) The rider that the faculties and their objects co-vary with respect to potentiality and actuality is not idle. Instead, it recalls Aristotle's contention that an object of perception is an object of perception only when perceived (see notes to 417a14–20, 417a21–b2, and esp. 425b26–426a26); thus, a faculty of the soul is actualized when and only when its correlative objects are.

If we think that the soul's capacities *are* their objects, suggests Aristotle, then only two possibilities appear open to us: (i) a given capacity is identical with an object taken broadly, that is, with a compound of matter and form; or (ii) that capacity is identical with its object taken narrowly, that is, with the form of its object. (For the broad versus narrow conceptions of objects, see the General Introduction § IV. B; cf. note to 424a17–24). Plainly, (i) will not do: when Alcibiades thinks of a stone, it is the form of the stone and not the stone itself which is found within his soul (cf. 410a10–13, 417b22–4). Thus, Aristotle holds that the soul becomes one in form, or isomorphic, with its objects. Note, moreover, that any such notion of isomorphism must already fall short of numerical identity. Otherwise, when Alcibiades and Socrates think of the same object, even taken narrowly, the reason (*nous*) of the one will, by the transitivity of identity, become numerically identical with the reason (*nous*) of the other. On the receptivity of form and isomorphism, see the General Introduction § IV.4.

**432a1–3: Two Striking Figures:** As a loose consequence of his commitment to form receptivity, Aristotle draws two striking images. Each has been subjected to various interpretations and expansions since antiquity.

The first compares the soul to a hand: each is a 'tool of tools' (*organan...organôn*; 432a2). It has been tempting to some to understand Aristotle as suggesting that the soul is a tool (*organon*) used by the body, which then itself uses tools, namely its several faculties, to accomplish its ends on behalf of the body. This, however, gets the order of directionality backwards: 'all ensouled natural bodies are organs of the soul' (415b18–19; cf. 407b25 with note to 415b8–27; *Part. An.* 641a14–32, 642a9–11, 645b14–18, 646b10–35). Aristotle argues consistently that form has priority over matter, and that the soul arranges the body in ways best suited to pursuing the living being's ends (on which, see Shields (2009)).

In this connection, it is noteworthy that Aristotle uses a similar sort of locution in *De Partibus Animalium* 687a18–19, where it is held that nature has outfitted human beings with hands as a 'tool for tools' (*organon pro organôn*; 687a21). In that passage, his express meaning is that the hand is not one tool but many, in virtue of its functional flexibility. The context is one in which Aristotle is arguing against Anaxagoras, whom he represents as having explained human intelligence as resulting from the possession of hands. On the contrary, claims Aristotle, nature, always seeking the best course, has equipped humans with hands because it suits their intelligence, the presence of which in turn suits them to use versatile appendages well. If part of that meaning carries over to the present passage, then Aristotle's point is that the soul is at once one tool and many, one tool *constituted out of* tools, or one functionally plastic organ constituted out of other such organs, including the perceptual faculty (*aisthêtikon*) and the faculty of reason (*noêtikon*). The soul would then be a tool of tools in the way that an umbrella association is 'an association of associations'. Care is required, however, in how the constitution

343

relation invoked here is to be explicated (on which, see note to 414b19–415a11 and the General Introduction § IV, n.9). The second figure is slightly more direct: Aristotle says that 'reason is a form of forms' (432a2). It is possible, as Bywater (1888) has contended, that this phrase should be expanded to 'reason is a form of intelligible forms', the word 'intelligible' (*noêtôn*) having dropped out of the text. That would come closer to completing the parallel with perception which follows immediately (432a2–3), since perception is said to be a 'form of the objects of perception'. While Bywater's emendation is unnecessary, his basic point is, nonetheless, apt. Reason and perception are forms of forms because the soul is a form of the body and yet receptive of forms, whether perceptible or intelligible.

**432a3–9: A Problematic Inference; Aristotle's Empiricism:** This passage is often cited as an exceptionally clear expression of Aristotle's empiricism. He claims, directly, that 'one who did not perceive anything would neither learn nor understand anything' (432a7–8). This claim is supposed to follow as one of two conclusions from the following argument:

(1) There is nothing beyond perceptible magnitudes (432a3–4).
(2) If (1), then the objects of reason (*noêta*) are in perceptible forms (either as existing in abstraction or as states and affections (*hexeis kai pathê*) of objects of perception (*aisthêta*)) (432a5–6).
(3) Hence, the objects of reason (*noêta*) are in perceptible forms (432a4–5).
(4) If (3), then: (a) one who never perceived would neither learn nor understand; and (b) whenever one contemplates, one at the same time contemplates a sort of image.
(5) Hence, one who never perceived would neither learn nor understand (432a6–7); and
(6) Hence, whenever one contemplates, one at the same time contemplates a sort of image (432a7–8).

The argument is plainly valid. The only questions, then, pertain to the non-inferred premises, namely (1), (2), and then also (4).

Trouble begins with (1), a premise which had already caught the attention of Aristotle's commentators in antiquity (so Alexander, as reported by ps.-Simplicius, 284, 23 and ps.-Simplicius himself 284, 13–22). They seem right to be concerned. The problem is that this claim appears plainly inconsistent with Aristotle's commitment to separated substances, which are without matter. Moreover, Aristotle thinks that the prime mover is not in space (*De Caelo*, 279a18), and the other divine intelligences, again like the prime mover (*Met.* 1075a1–2, 1075a6–7), are unchangeable and so without matter (*Met.* 1072b2–4) and also without magnitude (*Met.* 1073a33; cf. 1038a6, 1045a34). So, unless he has changed his mind about core areas of his metaphysics and cosmology, Aristotle has contradicted himself. Or, perhaps, as some would have it, he does not really maintain (1), since in the text it is cagily qualified ('as it seems' (*hôs dokei*); 432a4). This last expedient seems unlikely, since, as the text proceeds, Aristotle's inferences depend upon a straightforward assertion of (1). Again, however, those disinclined to find Aristotle expressing any such sentiment suppose that he must be arguing on behalf of those who do accept (1), rather than *in propria persona*. The text gives no indication that this is so.

Bracketing that, or supposing that (1) is Aristotle's considered view, we may proceed to (2) and (4). (2) has at least this much plausibility: if forms do not exist in a separated state, then they must somehow be features of the material objects whose forms they are. It will not follow directly that they will be so by being contained *in* perceptible forms, but the thought may be that if they are to be cognitively available at all, objects of reason must be procured via perception. Nor does it follow that objects of reason, because acquired via perception, are therefore in any sense quasi-perceptual; this, on the contrary, is a view Aristotle forcefully rejects.

That noted, once having proceeded to (4), Aristotle derives two further consequences from the genetic reliance of thought on perception, first that perception is required for learning or understanding generally, and second that contemplation involves images. Neither consequence is unobjectionable, considered either itself or as a consequence of the role of perception in acquisition.

Our attitude to the plausibility of (4) will be partly determined by the strength of empiricism we understand (5) to represent. As stated, the argument seems preoccupied with the origin of objects of reason, and not with any question of justification with respect to them. (6) bears a still more tenuous relation to any thesis regarding our access relations to objects of reason. One should note in this connection, however, that the text of 432a8–9 as we have it is multiply ambiguous, as between: (a) one necessarily at the same time contemplates some image (*phatasma ti*); (b) one necessarily at the same time contemplates a sort of image (*phatasma ti*), where *ti* is understood in the so-called *alienans* sense, that is, as meaning 'an image . . . sort of' as opposed to a 'sort or type of image' (see note to 416b32–417a2); and (c) one necessarily at the same time contemplates by means of images (*phantasmati*). The translation accepts (b), partly in virtue of Aristotle's tendency to link the need for images in thought to practical reason alone, and not therefore in theoretical reasoning. Images are, he thinks, implicated in action, because we must represent what is to be pursued or avoided as either good or bad (see 432b27–9; cf. notes to 431a14–17 and 431b2–17); it will not follow that they are implicated when thinking, for instance, that Gandhi's coinage 'satyagraha' has no ready translation in English.

In any event, if we accept (b), then the claim is a very weak one, and more likely to find support in terms of the current argument; if we accept (a), then the claim is much stronger, and less likely to be underwritten by the current argument; and if we accept (c), then the claim might again be very weak, to the effect that images are instrumental for our thinking. The adverb rendered as 'at the same time' (*hama*; 432a8) makes (c) unlikely, especially if it is given the very weak reading just mooted.

Taking all this together, even though one consistent way of reading these lines makes Aristotle out to be a robust empiricist about concept acquisition, his readers should be cautious before finding in them any detailed or unambiguous statement tending in this direction. First, the lines are open to other, less committal interpretations, and, second, they seem in some ways at variance with deeply held commitments consistently expressed elsewhere in the corpus.

**432a10–15: The Relation between Images and Thoughts:** Aristotle concludes the chapter with a caution and a query. The caution is that we should not permit the reflections on the role of images in thought, however this is to be understood, to incline us to suppose that images are assertoric. Images (*phantasmata*) do not make claims, since expressions with assertoric force result only from some manner of combination, from an interweaving of thoughts (*noêmata*).

This salutary caution then prompts a reasonable query from Aristotle: how will 'first thoughts' (*prôta noêmata*; 432a12) differ from images (*phantasmata*)? In posing this sort of question, Aristotle is evidently, again reasonably, thinking of these 'first thoughts' as unwoven, as the sub-propositional concepts which come to be predicated of one another to yield truth-evaluable propositions. Perhaps, then, though this is highly conjectural, these thoughts (*noêmata*) are first (*prôta*) in the sense that they are closest to sense perception. Although he has not used the term 'first thoughts' earlier, such thoughts would be, or be akin to, the indivisible thoughts characterized in 430a26–b6 (see note to which, together with the Introduction to III 6). There would be a reasonable question as to how such thoughts should be distinguished from images: whereas complex thoughts are assertoric, images are not—but then neither are the first nor indivisible thoughts assertoric.

Unfortunately, the text as we have it at the end of the chapter is in a desperate state, and its reconstruction must be regarded as conjectural. As I have constituted it, Aristotle does not supply the differentiating feature, but simply asserts that thoughts are not images, leaving the more fine-grained query about first thoughts unaddressed.

## CHAPTER 9

### Introduction to III 9

This chapter rejoins the dominant thread of the discussion up to *De Anima* III 6, thus further strengthening the impression that chapters III 7–8 are probably interpolations, even if they are authentically Aristotelian. Their being so need not diminish such value as they have, of course, though insofar as *De Anima* III has any coherent overarching plan, these chapters seem not to form any integral part of it. By contrast, the current chapter re-engages, in a reasonably orderly fashion, Aristotle's discussion of the soul in terms of its defining capacities: he has thus far treated the nutritive soul (*DA* II 4), the perceptual soul (*DA* II 5–III 2), and the rational soul (*DA* III 4–6, with additional observations scattered through *DA* III 7–8). Now,

Aristotle turns to a further, highly significant fact about animals, as opposed to plants (432a15–16): animals move about. He naturally assumes that something must explain this ability. Should we say that the psychic faculties mentioned thus far, either individually or corporately, suffice to initiate motion? Or must we recognize a distinct faculty alongside those already recognized?

These sorts of questions quite reasonably prompt Aristotle to reflect upon the general principles of soul division and capacity individuation. If we assign one faculty to each and every ability we manifest, no matter how narrowly individuated, then the soul will have endless numbers of parts. Presumably, we do not want to say that since humans can whistle a happy tune, the human soul has a distinct whistling-a-happy-tune faculty. Rather, we should rely upon some coarser-grained principle of faculty individuation. (See, however, Gregoric (2007: 24, 38–9) for an argument to the contrary.)

So far, Aristotle has himself relied upon a reasonably stable policy of faculty individuation given in terms of the discreteness of psychic objects (see the Introductions to II 4 and III 3; 402b9–16 and 415a14–22, with their relevant notes; see also notes to 418a7–11 and 418a11–17). One question, then, concerns whether it is possible to extend that treatment by identifying discrete objects implicated in the initiation of motion. Presumably these will be the objects of desire (*orekta*; 433a28, b11).

**432a15–22: Introduction of the Topic:**    Aristotle justifies the present inquiry by noting that the souls of animals have been defined in terms of two faculties: the judgemental or critical faculty, which has been explained in terms of reason (*nous*) and perception (*aisthêsis*), and the capacity for locomotion, which awaits an account. Aristotle does not mention the nutritive faculty, which is common to all living compounds, no doubt because he is thinking exclusively of animals (432a15–16). His precise back reference is unclear, but it is presumably to 427a17–19.

What is responsible for initiating motion? Aristotle mentions two possibilities: (i) the whole soul; or (ii) some part of the soul, distinct in magnitude or definition. If (ii), then one must determine whether the single capacity is: (ii.a) identical with one of the faculties already delineated, or (ii.b) something distinct and dedicated to this purpose (something exclusive, or peculiar; *idion*).

Alternatively, perhaps when Aristotle addresses the options under (ii.a) at 432b19–433a6, he does not consider the possibility that the faculty in question might cut across parts of the two faculties already delineated, so that it will be identical with neither taken individually nor yet identical with the entire soul. He seemed alert to this sort of possibility in his treatment of imagination (*phantasia*), the discussion of which bears methodological similarities to the current inquiry (cf. note to 428a24–b9). Aristotle does, however, consider something akin to this possibility in the next chapter, at 433a17–27.

**432a22–432b3: A Concern about Soul Division:** These questions about the faculty responsible for initiating movement understandably prompt a prior question about faculty individuation. Animals have the ability to move themselves about. Must they, then, have a dedicated capacity or faculty (*dunamis*) for this purpose? Aristotle observes that we should exercise caution here. Presumably we do not want to introduce a psychic capacity or division of the soul corresponding to every action type in which we can engage.

The caution is intended quite generally. Aristotle has in view the fact that the soul can be differently divided. Thus, he is reflecting not only Plato's tripartite psychology of reason, spirit, and appetite (*Rep.* iv), but also on a different, bipartite division, one also ascribed to Plato in the *Magna Moralia* (1182a23–5), into the rational and irrational. (The two divisions are not necessarily in competition with one another.) Aristotle alludes to the same bipartite division as 'exoteric' in the *Nicomachean Ethics* (1102a26–8). Such exoteric writings are intended for a popular audience, and are of Aristotle's own composition (*Pol.* 1278b30; *EE* 1217b22, 1218b34). Aristotle's concern in the current connection also echoes his worries about imagination (see the Introduction to III 3), where he was concerned with whether we have grounds to regard imagination as its own faculty. Now, though, he is investigating a putative faculty capable of initiating motion. He acknowledges this concern here as it pertains to his own approach (431a31), but does not develop it.

**432b3–7: A Special Concern about the Faculty of Desire:** One reasonable principle of part individuation seems to yield as a separate capacity the faculty of desire (*orektikon*; 432b3). The faculty of desire qualifies as distinct in terms of its potentialities and in terms of its account. It presumably tracks objects of desire, and what it is to desire something is not the same as what it is to reason about it, nor again is it merely to adopt a spirited demeanour with respect to it, nor even merely to have appetite for it, if, at any rate, we are thinking, as Plato seems to be thinking in *Republic* iv, of appetite (*epithumia*) as markedly less cognitive than desire (*orexis*). Here, though, we must proceed with caution, since we should probably be wary of presuming that 'appetite' and 'desire' have terribly clear boundaries in their English usage. Sometimes appetite seems a species of desire, at other times it seems opposable to desire. One might have an appetite for pizza and so desire one; but one might desire to discover the perpetrator of a heinous crime, without having any appetite for the job in any of its aspects. With that caution in mind, though, we might, nonetheless, want to refrain from making appetite coextensive with desire, even if we wanted to insist that appetite is one species of desire. These same concerns carry over to the Greek of Plato and Aristotle. (Cf. note to 414a29–b16 for a discussion of Aristotle's terminology in this regard.)

Aristotle contends that it would be absurd to break up the faculty of desire (*orektikon*). Adopting the bipartite division of soul, we find wish (*boulêsis*) in the rational division, and appetite (*epithumia*) and spirit (*thumos*) in the irrational; adopting the tripartite set-up, we find desire (*orexis*) in each.

Thinking evidently of Plato, Aristotle suggests that we have no grounds to fracture desire in this way, though it is not clear that Plato is liable to any such criticism; he may simply be thinking of desire as it ranges over distinct sorts of objects, without thereby thinking of it as itself intrinsically divided. (For a discussion of the principles and consequences of Platonic soul division, see Shields (2010).) It is conceivable, though, that Aristotle's discussion is not anti-Platonic so much as unsettled and so still searching with respect to its own ultimate commitments.

Here it should be noted that the verb translated as 'break this up' (*diaspan*) at 432b5, might conceivably mean 'break off from' (cf. *Rhet.* 1386a10). If it were taken that way, one might understand Aristotle as actually *agreeing* with Plato, by endorsing his suggestion that the faculty of desire cannot be hived off from the other faculties. There is so little argumentative development in the present digression that it is difficult to say with any certainty. In any event, it is clear that using different principles of differentiation yields distinct forms of soul division. Aristotle must guard that his own principles do not engender more faculties than he himself is prepared to countenance. As he observes, unless our principles of individuation are controlled, we will risk generating an infinite number of faculties (432a24).

**432b7–19: What Initiates Motion is not the Faculty of Nutrition:** Lending further credence to the thought that his brief excursion into soul division is primarily a methodological digression, Aristotle overtly refocuses the discussion to the issue at hand: what initiates motion in an animal?

He immediately points out that it is not the same as the nutritive and reproductive faculties. Here it is important to bear in mind that Aristotle holds reproductive and nutritive souls to be the same, and also to be the first, or most common soul (416a19–20; cf. notes to 415a22–b7, 416a19–b9, and 416b11–28). This leads naturally to Aristotle's first argument for the non-identification of the faculties of locomotion and nutrition/generation: the faculties in question are not even coextensive and so cannot be identified.

His second argument is mildly puzzling. Aristotle denies that the faculty of locomotion can be identified with the faculty of nutrition on the grounds that locomotion of this sort is always for the sake of something (*heneka tou*; 432b15). Surely, though, he also thinks that nutrition is for the sake of something. The probable resolution is that he is thinking here primarily of forward motion (432b14), especially voluntary motion (432b16–17), suggesting motion in pursuit, which requires imagination (*phantasia*) and desire (*orexis*). If that restriction is in place, then he is pointing out that certain kinds of locomotion require a capacity for representation, with the result that desire must be something beyond the nutritive capacity.

It should be noted that if this accurately represents Aristotle's second argument, then he is thinking of locomotion primarily as it occurs in animals and setting aside the sort of motion, or change, that we observe in plants as they put down roots and the like. He would be justified in doing so, if his argument is just that locomotion often involves representation, whereas nutrition never does; this would yield the non-coextensivity he seeks in the argument.

**432b19–25: What Initiates Motion is not the Faculty of Perception:** Aristotle at first appeals to the argument form already deployed in the case of nutrition (see note to 432b7–19), but he then augments the argument by a robust appeal to teleology. The argument itself is again simple: the faculties in question are not even coextensive and so cannot be identified. The source of the non-coextensivity prompts a broader appeal to some overarching teleological commitments. As for the non-coextensivity to which Aristotle appeals, there are some animals lacking all forms of locomotion, though, as animals, they must of course have perception. He had called attention to such animals earlier (410b19–20), there also drawing upon his marine biology in thinking of sea nettles, sponges, oysters, and certain Testacea (*Hist. An.* 487b6–9, 588b12; *Part. An.* 681b34, 683c8); he, in fact, denies that there are stationary land animals (*Hist. An.* 487b6–8, 621b2–5).

The broader appeal to teleology repeats a familiar refrain from Aristotle: nature does nothing in vain (415b15, 434a31; *Part. An.* 641b12–19; *Gen. An.* 788b20, *Pol.* 1256b20). In the present context he means to argue that since there exist fully mature, perfectly formed animals of a non-motive kind which, nonetheless, have perception (for all animals have perception (413b8–9, 415a5, 434a29, b13–19)), it is not possible, on the assumption that the capacity to initiate motion is the same as the perceptual faculty, for such animals to lack the organs requisite for locomotion. An inspection of stationary marine animals reveals no such organs. It follows, then, on the assumption of the teleological principle invoked, that the capacities cannot be identified.

**432b25–433a6: What Initiates Motion is not the Same as Reason:** Aristotle's argument against identifying the faculty of locomotion with reason is both subtler and more consequential than the earlier arguments of this chapter. Instead of appealing to simple non-coextensivity, which is no longer available to him, Aristotle uses a variety of arguments intended to show that the presence of intellectual activity is compatible with the absence of motion; hence, bare reason alone does not suffice. This style of argument is less secure than his earlier arguments, and seems to create some difficulties for him (see note to 433a6–8). In general, one might argue that the exercise of capacity φ is compatible with our not φ-ing, if we are thinking of φ-ing as requiring conditions for its success which are beyond the mere expression of φ. Thus, (i) the capacity to φ might be heterogeneous in its activities, as the capacity to burn might light or heat a room; or (ii) the capacity to φ may be overridden by a distinct, interposing capacity Ψ; or again (iii) the world may not cooperate, thus making our expression of φ ineffectual. Thus, fire might be able to burn wood, though be thwarted owing to this particular log's being saturated with water. (See also note to 433a6–8.)

That said, Aristotle draws attention to the comparatively narrow fact that in contemplating, one does not normally, in a theoretical context, contemplate what is to be done; nor does contemplation issue in directives to flee or pursue. He is not, or is not obviously, adopting the Humean posture that reason is *incapable* of initiating motion; for he says just below, at 433a1–3, that reason can enjoin action. Evidently, Aristotle is focusing here only on theoretical reason. So far, at least, he is mainly making the point that not every instance of the exercise of reason is sufficient for motion, not that no such exercise could be. To take a case favorable to Aristotle's suggestion, if S is thinking hard about transfinite numbers, then that activity will not direct S to begin preparing a meal, even if S is hungry.

The suggestion that all motion involves pursuit or flight might seem plainly false: a girl who idly runs her fingers through her hair while reading is moving but not thereby pursuing or fleeing anything; this, though, assumes that she is not acting intentionally, and, again, Aristotle is mainly concerned with intentional or voluntary behaviour (see note to 432b7–19), where the connection to pursuit or avoidance lies close, especially within Aristotle's teleological framework. Consequently, his position, suitably understood, does not seem obviously problematic. He is simply contending that intentional behaviour is end-directed.

On the involuntary motions associated with seeing the fearful or the pleasant, see 403a21 and 408b8.

The last stretch of this argument, beginning at 433a1, is the most significant, since in this stretch of text Aristotle turns to the rational faculty most likely to be identifiable with the faculty of locomotion. Surprisingly, Aristotle does not avail himself of a non-coextensivity argument, given that some animals move, but lack reason altogether. Instead, he considers a case where reason does command action. Even when that occurs, desire may direct one elsewhere, as happens in the case of the akratic, or weak-willed agent. (For Aristotle's treatment of *akrasia*, see *Nicomachean Ethics* VII 1–3. One should not, however, suppose that the treatment there is complete, such that the present passage must be shown to conform to it. On the contrary, as Moss (2009) persuasively argues, one can best understand Aristotle's general approach to *akrasia* only by appreciating the purport of the current passage for his broader treatment of that topic in the *Nicomachean Ethics* and elsewhere.) The weak-willed person reasons that action *a* is, all things considered, preferable to any alternative course of action *b*, and her reason accordingly directs the doing of *a*, but desire wells up and redirects the agent's attention to *b*, with the result that *b* is pursued in place of *a*. If *b* is indolence, then reason may fail to eventuate in action altogether. Here, evidently, Aristotle is thinking of practical rather than theoretical reason (cf. 433a14–16). His argument is, then, that the exercise of practical reason is compatible with inactivity, with the result that the faculty of locomotion cannot be the same as the faculty of reason, even in its practical mode.

All that taken together, then, the general structure of his argument is: (1) the operation of theoretical reason is compatible with inactivity; (2) the operation of practical reason is compatible with inactivity; (3) the operation of the faculty of locomotion is not compatible with inactivity; hence (4) the faculty of locomotion can be identified with neither theoretical nor practical reason. On a potential problem with this style of argument, see note to 433a6–8.

**433a6–8: A Perplexing Coda on Desire:** Given the differentiations and associations made thus far in this chapter, it seems natural at this juncture to conclude that the faculty of locomotion is none other than the faculty of desire (*orexis*). Thus, for example, it seemed to be assumed in the case of the akratic that desire could eventuate in action. Now even that thesis is challenged, by appeal to the enkratic, or self-controlled man. (Aristotle supposes that, in descending order of virtue: the completely virtuous person acts without a trace of internal struggle; the *enkratic* struggles but overcomes to pursue what is best; the *akratic* struggles only to succumb; and the vicious person simply pursues without a whiff of struggle or remorse whatever course her craven desire directs. See *EN* vii 1.) The case of the enkratic is introduced as the converse of the akratic (433a1): the akratic shows that the faculty of locomotion cannot be identified with reason, since desire can derail reason, while the enkratic shows that the faculty of locomotion cannot be identified with desire (*orexis*), since desire's bid can also prove impotent.

The argument is difficult on two counts. First, the general strategy of arguing that faculty φ cannot be identified with faculty Ψ on the grounds that an expression of φ may not result in successful Ψ-ing seems to prove too much if it proves anything at all. An internal combustion engine's ability to power the motion of a car might be expressed without the car's moving, because of any of a variety of internal or external impediments. Second, as an ad hominem point, Aristotle in the next chapter comes to the conclusion after all that 'there is one thing initiating motion: the faculty of desire' (*orektikon*; see note to 433a14–26). Some possibilities are: (i) Aristotle is here implicitly distinguishing between desire (*orexis*) and the faculty of desire (*orektikon*); (ii) he is here thinking of desire in isolation from other contributing faculties, though in the next chapter he is thinking of it as enmeshed in a functioning intentional psychology, including practical reason; or (iii) the current argument is preliminary and aporetic, and so does not represent Aristotle's own final assessment. Of these either (ii) or (iii) seems most likely. As stated, these need not be regarded as mutually exclusive explanations.

## CHAPTER 10

### Introduction to III 10

This chapter continues the discussion of the last. Aristotle now moves towards some more definite findings regarding the faculty of locomotion. In tone, the present chapter is less aporetic than the previous. Consequently, where there are occasional tensions between the two, they should probably be resolved in favour of the findings of III 10 over III 9.

At least initially, the chapters appear significantly at variance with one another regarding the faculty of desire and its role in initiating motion in animals. The bulk of III 9 was given over to distinguishing the faculty responsible for initiating motion from the acknowledged psychic faculties: it is not nutrition (432b7–19); it is not perception (432b19–25); and it is not reason (432b25–433a6). It then closed with the suggestion, advanced by relying on arguments analogous to those deployed for the case of reason, that the faculty responsible for motion could not be desire (*orexis*) (433a6–8). In the current chapter, however, Aristotle evidently concludes that 'there is one thing initiating motion: the faculty of desire' (*orektikon*; 433a21) ('evidently', because a second manuscript tradition prefers 'object of desire' (*orekton*) at 433a21; see note to 433a14–26). Further on in the chapter he reiterates, 'It is apparent, then, that what is called desire (*orexis*) is the sort of capacity in the soul which initiates motion' (433a31–b1).

This initial tension does not vitiate the contribution, however inchoate, Aristotle has to make to the philosophy of action. While it is true that these chapters find him struggling with the mixture of contributions to intentional action made by the various capacities of the soul, Aristotle does show himself sensitive to the very real difficulties which even today surround the question of the antecedents of intentional action: he observes that desire, practical reason, and imagination all have some role to play, though he does not arrive at a clear and unambiguous account of their relative contributions. It is, nonetheless, laudatory that he avoids the remorseless and prescriptive taxonomizing characteristic of some later, primarily Humean approaches to the aetiology of action. For some ways in which Aristotle's approach to action can and cannot be appropriately regarded as Humean, see Irwin (1975), and for an in-depth study of Aristotle's approach to action, see Charles (1984).

A carefully focused, textually alert discussion of this chapter can be found in Richardson (1995), whose contribution is noteworthy for distinguishing two orientating interpretations, namely what he terms a desire-based approach and a good-based approach, where the crucial difference pertains to the question of what Aristotle takes the ultimate source (*archê*) of motion to be: an internal faculty (the *orektikon*) or an object desire (the *orekton*) taken either as the good or the apparent good. (Richardson argues in favour of the object of desire, the *orekton*; see note 433a14–26 below for an argument in favour of the faculty, the *orektikon*, which is the text the translation presupposes.)

It should be noted in this connection that although Aristotle speaks of what initiates *motion* (*kinein*), he is primarily concerned in this chapter with intentional action, broadly construed, and not just with bodily motions taken indifferently. He is concerned with the kinds of motions characteristic of living beings capable of representing their environments, and focuses primarily and most narrowly on human beings, but then also thereafter on other, non-human animals. Ackrill (1978) explores some of the background features concerning Aristotle's approach to intentional action.

The current chapter divides reasonably clearly into three sections, even though the connection of the second to the first and third is rather thin: (i) preliminary suggestions regarding desire and reason, with the finding that desire is the primary source of motion (433a9–b1); (ii) an excursus into the parts and faculties of the soul (433b1–13); and (iii) summary and specification (433b13–30).

**433a9–13: Desire and Reason as Initiating Motion:**   Aristotle opens the chapter by recording the *phainomena*, that is, how things appear: desire (*orexis*) and reason (*nous*) appear to have some role to play in initiating action. This undercuts the tenor of the previous chapter, though there is no direct contradiction, at least on the assumption that Aristotle was there thinking of the faculties of the soul as taken in isolation from one another (cf. note to 433a6–8), or, more generally, that the earlier chapter was intended as principally aporetic.

What is a bit more surprising is that Aristotle seems to justify the suggestion that reason initiates motion by implying that imagination (*phantasia*) may be regarded as a kind of reasoning (*noêsis*), or at least as suitably akin to reasoning. To be sure, Aristotle has already indicated that imagination has a role to play in initiating action, in both the non-rational beast and in the temporarily irrational human (see note to 429a2–9). What he has not suggested so far is that imagination (*phantasia*) might be a kind of thinking or reasoning. Indeed the possibility of the converse, that reason might be a kind of imagination (*phantasia tis*), was floated at 403a8–9. Contrary, then, to the current suggestion,

Aristotle has earlier argued that imagination is neither knowledge (*epistêmê*) nor understanding (nor reason, *nous*—see note to 433a26–30 below), on the grounds that these states or faculties are truth-entailing, whereas imagination can be false (see note to 428a17–18). In this chapter Aristotle reaffirms the superiority of understanding (or reason, *nous*) in related but distinct terms, by contending that it is always right (*orthos*; 433a26). Presumably Aristotle feels a legitimate pressure to treat imagination (*phantasia*) as capable of initiating action, especially, but perhaps not exclusively, in non-rational animals; what is less clear is why this should incline him to entertain the hypothesis that imagination (*phantasia*) is a kind of reasoning (*noêsis*). One possible, deflationary resolution would be to translate the passage in a more attenuated and paraphrastic way, as 'if one were to treat imagination as reasoning—of a sort'. (See note to 416b32–417a2 for an explanation of Aristotle's idiom here.) In any event, it should be noted that Aristotle's language here is both conditional and tentative. Frede (2008) explores some ways in which imagination (*phantasia*) might be thought akin to reasoning (*noêsis*).

**433a14–26: Practical Reason and the Primacy of Desire:**  The sort of reason (*nous*) implicated in action is, appropriately enough, *practical reason*, the kind engaged in calculating rather than contemplating. Aristotle makes similar points elsewhere (431a14–17, 433a26–9; cf. *EN* 1139a26–35, 1143b2). Here Aristotle differentiates the two kinds of reason by appeal to their respective ends: practical reason engages an end as something to be done or accomplished and involves itself in calculating how to achieve that objective. In this respect, contends Aristotle, practical reason is like desire and the sort of imagination involved in initiating motion.

Aristotle treats practical reason as centrally implicated in action: the object of desire (*orekton*) initiates motion, and *because of this* thought (*dianoia*; 433a19—here equivalent to practical reason) initiates action. Where thought is lacking, in the case of non-human animals, imagination responds in an analogous way to the object of desire, so that imagination is akin to reason in failing to suffice for action in the absence of desire. The moral to draw, implies Aristotle, is that the faculty of desire (*orektikon*) is the *sole* initiator of motion. A more cautious conclusion would treat this faculty as the *primary* initiator of motion.

An alternative conclusion, favoured by Richardson (1995) and given some legitimacy by an alternative textual tradition, one already known in antiquity (ps.-Simplicius *in de An.* 297a30), would conclude rather that the object of desire (*orekton*), is the sole initiator of movement. The textual variance is plainly significant, but can also be overstated (as ps.-Simplicius judiciously remarks, *in DA* 298, 30–299, 7).

The basic difference between the readings is as follows. One reading locates the ultimate mover in the object desired (*orekton*), because it is conceived as good or as an apparent good; the other looks to the faculty (*orektikon*) as the ultimate locus in which motion is initiated. The second may be thought to emphasize the internal workings of the agent; the first will emphasize, in a manner more closely parallel to perception (*aisthêsis*) and reasoning (*noêsis*), the individuation-subordination of the faculty to the object of its concern. The translation accepts the text as Ross constitutes it, which follows neither manuscript tradition slavishly; it treats the faculty (the *orkektikon*) rather than the object (the *orekton*) as the source of motion, and treats the faculty as dependent on its object for its individuation conditions. This seems basically correct, since Aristotle's dominant goal in this passage is to argue for a unified capacity of desire (the *orektikon*), as is shown by the contrast which follows: 'For if there were two things which initiated motion—reason and desire—they would do so according to some common form.' 433a21–3). Since the contrast class involves faculties, Aristotle's conclusion likewise pertains to the faculty and not its object. In either case, however, the faculty of desire (*orektikon*) will play an indispensable role, one not to be parcelled out to either reason (*nous*) or imagination (*phantasia*).

That allowed, on the reading adopted in the translation, Aristotle will be arguing not only for the centrality of primacy of the faculty of desire (*orektikon*) in initiating motion, but more strongly for its exclusivity. Aristotle's argument for exclusivity over primacy is a bit diffuse, evidently running together two lines of thought: (i) if there were two faculties responsible for initiating motion, they would do so according to a common form, and since there is no common form, it can only be one faculty, the faculty of desire—something in any case always operative when motion is initiated—which is responsible for initiating motion; and (ii) reason is impotent without desire, since reason does nothing without wish (*boulêsis*) and wish is a kind of desire, whereas desire, in the form of appetite (*epithumia*), can initiate motion in a manner positively contrary to rational calculation.

The first argument relies on the rejection of an unexplored possibility, that something common to reason and desire might be the sole or primary cause of motion. Aristotle seems merely to advert to the brief characterization of the aetiology of action already provided: the object of desire moves practical reason, and because of this, practical reason initiates motion. Looked at this way, his argument is simple: if there is no object of desire, there is no motion; but where there is an object of desire, there is a faculty of desire. So, desire, unlike practical reason and imagination, is a *sine qua non* of motion in the case of animals and has thus at least this much claim to primacy. Put thus, however, the argument makes no use of Aristotle's contention that desire and reason share no common form. It also leads at best to a kind of primacy for the faculty of desire, thus falling short of establishing it as the faculty exclusively responsible for the initiation of motion.

The second argument is also independently troubling insofar as it seems at variance with the final argument of the previous chapter (see note to 433a6–8 and the Introduction to this chapter).

**433a26–30: Reason is Right; Imagination and Desire are Right and not Right:** It is initially jarring to learn that 'reason is always right'. Presumably, however, reason is always right only in the sense that when operating unimpaired it correctly identifies that object of desire which is in fact good, rather than the one merely seeming to be good. A second possibility, one built on the reading of 433a20 presupposed in the text (see note to 433a14–26), recommends a neat parallelism. On this approach, reason (*nous*) is not the faculty here, but is rather to be equated with a peerless state of that faculty, as it is in *Posterior Analytics* II 19. If so, then the sense in which 'reason' (*nous*) is always right is more elevated: when we attain a state of reason (or *understanding*, or *intuition*, or *intuitive grasping* as one might render *nous* in this connection), then reason, the faculty, is always right. The parallelism would then be: when we have attained this highest state of reason, we have grasped the good as it is, and not merely as it appears, whereas imagination and desire, shared with non-human animals, are restricted to the apparent good—which may be in fact good, but would not be cognized as such. 'Reason, then, is in every instance correct, while desire and imagination are both correct and not correct. Consequently, the object of desire always initiates motion; but this is either the good or the apparent good' (433a26–9). On this approach, reason attains the good, whereas desire and imagination present to us only the apparent good, and so cannot stably deliver us to our real good in intentional action.

However that may be, the relevance of mentioning both the apparent and the real good here is to highlight reason's indispensable role in the antecedents of human action. Given that we seek what is in fact good for ourselves, and not what merely seems to be good, and given that reason is required to make this determination, we must rely upon reason to secure our best end. In rational creatures, then, it would be wrong to say that the faculty of desire operates so as to exclude reason. Cf. *EN* 1113a15–b6, 1139a23–b5; *EE* 1235b25. For a nuanced treatment of the relation of the good to the apparent good, see Moss (2012).

**433b1–13: The Parts of the Soul:** Aristotle cautions that those who establish parts of the soul in accordance with discrete sets of objects run the risk of psychic fission. This is noteworthy insofar as Aristotle himself applies this very method earlier in *De Anima* (see the Introduction to II 4, and notes to 402b9–16, 415a14–22, 418a11–17, and 429b10–21), even if, as seems likely, his mention of appetite and spirit in the current passage is a glancing reference to Plato, *Republic* iv. It is also noteworthy that Aristotle now lists a deliberative faculty (*bouleutikon*; 433b33), whereas earlier he had mentioned a faculty of locomotion (*kinêtikon kata topon*; 414a32), omitted here.

As the discussion develops, it becomes clear that Aristotle is primarily concerned not with generating parts corresponding to the parties of every internal conflict, but rather with the more coarse-grained question of whether there is a faculty related to every discrete sort of object. He observes that objects of desire (*orekta*), no matter how variegated, nevertheless form a single class, precisely as objects of desire. This also explains his somewhat cumbersome suggestion that what initiates motion is the 'faculty of desire insofar as it is a faculty of desire' (433b11). Aristotle means that even though the objects of desire are many, and even though conflicting desires arise relative to distinct objects, the common source of all such motion is the faculty of desire simply doing its job as a faculty: conflicting desires are, after all, *desires*; so, no further faculty is required to explain conflicts among desires. These are all and only desires, because they issue from the operations of a single faculty, namely desire (*orexis*). There is thus no need to posit a multiplicity of soul parts to explain this common sort of internal conflict.

**433b13–18: The Three Factors of Motion:** We now have a precise specification of the factors involved in the aetiology of action. There are, contends Aristotle, three: (i) what initiates motion, identified as the good to be accomplished; (ii) that by which one initiates motion, the activity of the faculty of desire; and (iii) what is moved, the animal. This coheres closely with his account of motion in *Physics* 256b14–24 (cf. *Met.* 1072a24–30). It is sometimes thought that Aristotle departs from his earlier treatments by further subdividing (i) into (a) that which initiates motion while itself not moving, and (b) that which initiates motion while itself being in motion. The division in the current passage, however, is not subordinate to (i). Instead, Aristotle is allowing that while both the good sought and the faculty of desire initiate motion, only the faculty does so while being itself in motion. Thus, the object of desire initiates motion without itself being in motion.

**433b19–30: Summary of Principal Findings:** Aristotle moves towards a general summary, but in so doing, he does not refrain from adding a surprising innovation, namely a distinction between types of imagination (*phantasia*) not mentioned earlier in the work.

Aristotle precedes his summary by alluding to a fuller treatment of the bodily instrument employed by the faculty of desire. The most likely surviving discussion would be *De Motu Animalium* 698a14–b7, 702a21–b11.

When contending that the starting point (*archê*) in intentional action is the same as its end point (*teleutê*), Aristotle means that for a particular action, the goal first moves the faculty of desire as its final cause and then also serves as the terminus of the action, that in which it is completed. His illustration serves not to explicate how the first moving cause is also the terminus, however, but rather how one and the same state of affairs can yet differ in being, insofar as it is both the starting point and the end point. A hinge, as Aristotle is thinking of it, is a ball-and-socket joint, such as the hip. (The term translated as 'hinge' (*gigglumos*) is used in Greek both for a metal door hinge and for a ball-and-socket joint.) The idea is that the curvature of the swivel in such cases is both convex, from the standpoint of the ball, and concave, from the standpoint of the socket. In this sort of joint, the socket remains motionless while the ball pivots within. (Cf. *De Motu An.* 698a14–b4, 701a36–b32, 701b33–702b11 for a fuller treatment of the mechanisms involved.) In a similar manner, the same state of affairs may be considered first, from the standpoint of initiating an action, its source or starting point (*archê*) but then also, from the standpoint the ultimate result attained, its end point (*teleutê*). Thus, e.g., *being healthy* is both the impetus and outcome of my exercising.

Aristotle concludes by noting that there is no desire without imagination (*phantasia*), but then distinguishes, somewhat surprisingly, two forms of imagination, one perceptual and the other rational. He had not earlier availed himself of any such distinction, not even in the full treatment of imagination offered in III 3. Perhaps there has been some hint of the distinction, if only obliquely, at 403a8, 427b27, 431a14, and 432a12, but the distinction is reaffirmed plainly later, at 434a5–7. In the context of the present chapter, the distinction may serve as a corrective to the odd contention entertained at the outset to the effect that the exercise of imagination might be regarded as a kind of reasoning (see note to 433a8–13). As introduced, the distinction offers to non-human animals only perceptual imagination, with the result that the exercise of imagination would be functionally isomorphic across all animals insofar as the initiation of motion is concerned, even though the exercise of imagination in humans will typically be conceptually laden, with content inaccessible to the non-human animals. Thus, while all animals represent an apparently good end for themselves and so pursue it, only humans characterize the end for themselves *as good* and so as something *worthy of being pursued*; and only humans, owing to

the attainments of reason (*nous*), can distinguish the good from
the merely apparent good.

## CHAPTER 11

### Introduction to III 11

This brief chapter first continues the discussion of the aetiology of
animal motion begun in the last, but then segues into a brief but
suggestive discussion of the practical syllogism. It begins by focusing
on the kind of motion that occurs in very simple animals, those
endowed with only the sense of touch. This gives rise to a brief
consideration of the kinds of imagination we should recognize,
which in turn invites a brief discussion of the role of desire in animals
with different psychological economies. In this latter discussion,
Aristotle visits the topic of weakness of will (*akrasia*) in passing.

**433b31–434a5: Movement in Incompletely Developed Animals:**
Aristotle understandably finds something inherently puzzling
about the movements of incompletely developed animals (*atelē*),
by which he normally means neither mutants nor the maimed
(*pērōmata*), but rather either animals lacking the full range of
sensory faculties or, more often, those with sensory faculties not
completely developed (cf. 425a10). In the current passage, he
focuses on those animals which are incomplete in the sense of
lacking the full range of faculties enjoyed by other animals. He
has allowed that not all animals have all senses, but insists that
nothing is an animal without at least touch (cf. 413b3–5, 414b3,
434b24, 435b5–7; *De Sensu* 436b13, *Hist. An.* 489a17). While not
every animal with touch is able to move, since some animals are
sessile (434b7–8), the vast majority of animals do have locomotion, including most which live by touch alone. Aristotle wonders:
if a slug can move and evidently feels pleasure and pain in so
doing (as when it retracts), this then might seem to imply that it
has imagination (*phantasia*) and appetite (*epithumia*). Earlier he
had contended that simple animals must have desire on the
grounds that sensation requires awareness of pleasure and pain,
which in turn requires desire (*orexis*) (413b19–23).

Aristotle had also earlier allowed that some animals lack
imagination (*phantasia*) (415a10, 428a8). Here he suggests that

imagination might be present in lower animals after all, but in an indeterminate manner (*aoristôs*; 434a4), somehow commensurate with the indeterminate character of their movements. His meaning in calling movement and imagination indeterminate (*aoristôs*) is a little opaque, though it may be illuminated by his suggestion that thought (*dianoia*) can proceed indeterminately when multivocal terms have not been rendered precise (*DC* 276a21; cf. *Cat.* 8b10). The idea is that thought can proceed, even if it is a bit hazy owing to the presence of multivocity. Thus, for example, being a *citizen* might be spoken of in many ways, so that a citizen under a kingship is not the same thing as a citizen under a parliamentary democracy; still, one can make some progress in thinking about the ways in which citizens should regard their governments in general, before turning to such comparatively fine-grained considerations. If that illustration is apt, then one might say that while only humans have deliberative *imagination*, humans, in common with higher and lower animals, can also have indeterminate images; lower animals, however, are restricted to images of indeterminate (*aoristôs*) character. A slug's imagination may be similar: its images are hazy and indeterminate, like the idea of a citizen in general, but may yet function in an analogous way in its psychological economy. If so, then a slug's imagination, although suited to its purposes, will lack the precision of image found in higher non-human animals, and then lack to an even greater degree the precision of image found in human beings, as required for deliberate action. So, Aristotle's answer to the question posed by present-day cognitive scientists as to whether paramecia have mental representations is, in typical fashion: yes and no. Yes: slugs have images, as one may surmise from the role images play in locomotion. No: if the question is meant to ask whether they have fully determinate images of the sort rational beings have, then slugs do not. For in contrast with the images humans have, those of slugs are indeterminate (*aoristôs*), and so do not reach the level of precision found in human beings.

**434a5–10: Types of Imagination:** Aristotle has already recognized two forms of imagination, one perceptual and one rational (see note to 433b19–30), and now specifies what seems a version of the rational form, namely deliberative imagination (*bouleutikê phantasia*), which he restricts to animals with the faculty of reason. When speaking of this form of imagination, Aristotle highlights its role in assessing alternative ways to promote some end. He contends that deliberating about what is better or worse involves comparing distinct scenarios one with the other and so presupposes a common scale of valuation; this comparative activity activates the rational imagination insofar as it is required for measuring appearances jockeying for supremacy against this single standard (cf. *De Mem.* 453a13, *EN* 1112b11, *Met.* 1152b11). Here it bears recalling the linguistic connection in Aristotle's Greek between the verb to appear (*phainesthai*) and imagination (*phantasia*, also sometimes translated as *appearance*; see the Introduction to III 3). The appearances or images involved in this process need not be conceived pictorially; on the contrary, such appearances may be conceptually rich in ways making pictographic representation difficult to fathom.

**434a10–15: Desire and Deliberation:**     Since some animals move in the absence of reason, and animal movement requires desire (*orexis*), even while deliberation occurs in the sphere of reason alone, desire must not be of its own nature deliberative. It is striking that Aristotle speaks of desire as lacking a 'deliberative faculty' (*bouleutikon*), which might also be rendered by 'deliberative capacity' or 'deliberative ability'. In any rendering, however, Aristotle's point is that desire lacks the ability to deliberate of its own accord, presumably because it lacks the requisite facility for weighing competing appearances against a single scale in the manner of the rational faculty (*logistikon*).

The text of the next section is a bit corrupt. The translation reflects one probable reconstruction: 'Sometimes this desire overpowers that desire and initiates motion, and sometimes that one overpowers this one and initiates motion, like one ball overpowering another' (434a12–13). Taken this way, the illustration Aristotle uses to make his point about competing desires is straightforward: one desire may overpower another as one ball might overpower another when they collide. If this captures the force of his analogy, Aristotle will be conceiving of each individual desire as having its own independent strength and force. Once initiated, a desire rolls forward as a ball upon a croquet lawn, such that a dominant desire simply knocks its feebler competitors aside. Thus, a desire for cake may brush aside a desire for health as it impels an agent towards its own narrowly circumscribed satisfaction.

The translation must, however, be regarded as tentative, not least because it relies upon the introduction of a word not in our manuscripts. The phrase rendered 'like one ball overpowering another' reflects the acceptance of a conjecture of Essen, who writes *hôsper sphaira sphairan* at 434a13, that is, as one ball (*sphaira*) overpowering another ball (*sphairan*), when in fact our manuscripts and commentaries all have simply either 'like a ball' (either *sphaira* or *sphairan*, but not both). Moreover, since the word translated as 'ball' (*sphaira*) more regularly means 'sphere' in Aristotle, some ancient commentators, including Themistius (121, 34) and some unnamed exegetes known to ps.-Simplicius (310, 30), were inclined to offer much more elaborate interpretations of this passage, involving the rotations of the heavenly spheres discussed at length in Aristotle's *De Caelo* and elsewhere. Minimally, such accounts are unnecessary, since 'ball' is also a perfectly common meaning of *sphaira*, and one surely known to Aristotle. Moreover, the picture of one heavenly sphere overpowering another seems both strained and inappropriate to the context. It is, therefore, preferable to agree with ps.-Simplicius, who rejects the view of the exegetes he mentions (310, 30), by accepting the more mundane meaning of this term. That said, the more elaborate alternative cannot be rejected as impossible.

In any case, when Aristotle notes that the faculty of knowledge remains unmoved, he is not denying the possibility of *akrasia*, but is rather contrasting knowledge, which is always internally consistent and invariant in its outcomes, with beliefs and desires, which may be pitted one against the other. His suggestion, then, is that in cases of *akrasia*, when desires proceed insufficiently regulated because unstructured by reason, even a desire selected by an agent may be overwhelmed and knocked off course by a stronger desire left unchecked. When regulated by reason, however, desires are more tractable and well-ordered, because trenchantly channelled towards some identified good. This, presumably, is part of what Aristotle thinks Socrates, despite his overstating his case, got right about the extreme peculiarity of akratic conduct (*EN* vii 2–3).

**434a16–21: The Prominence of Particular Belief in the Aetiology of Action:** Aristotle's observation about the role of desire in rational and non-rational action precipitates a brief discussion of the practical syllogism, which he develops in more detail elsewhere, especially *Nicomachean Ethics* vii 3 and *De Motu Animalium* 7. To some extent, this discussion serves to reframe what has come before and so also serves as a corrective to a suggestion which might be thought implicit in the earlier sections of the chapter, namely that desire alone drives action. On the contrary, contends Aristotle, in rational animals belief (*doxa*) has an important role to play (cf. 428a18–24), both beliefs about particulars present to perception and general beliefs taking the form of universal premises which govern action (cf. *EN* 1147a25).

The general framework is clear. A universal premise is judged by an agent to obtain: All φ-things are to be done by ψ-type people (e.g. a moderate amount of wine is to be drunk by a healthy person). In fact, in framing this premise Aristotle speaks of 'conception' (*hupolêpsis*) rather than judgement or belief (*doxa*), though he is plainly using the term 'conception' such that it carries at least some conviction on the part of the agent. So, in speaking of conception, he means roughly that the agent begins by conceiving of φ-things as the sorts of things to be done by ψ-type people (cf. *APo.* 89a2. 89a38, *Met.* 981a5, 1005b25, 1073a17; *EN* 139b17 for similar uses).

Aristotle's characterization here agrees with *Nicomachean Ethics* vii 3 in that he implicitly envisages two distinct universal classes in the major premise of a practical syllogism, the first pertaining to the action type and the other pertaining to the type of agent (*EN* 1147a1-6; cf. *De Motu Anim.* 701a13). No such universal conviction suffices by itself for action, however. It is necessary to add a particular premise to the effect that *this* is the moderate amount of wine, and *I* am a healthy sort. Note that the second particular judgement (and here Aristotle does speak of judgement or belief; *doxa* at 434a20) has an indexical component, whereby the agent reflexively links the characterization in the universal premise to himself in the expression of the minor premise.

Aristotle first suggests that it is the particular judgement in the minor premise that begets motion, but then backs off slightly, contending finally that the universal judgement is also present, though it is 'more at rest' from the standpoint of inciting any given particular motion. The universal premise causes motion only as a sort of background directive. Thus, while one accepts the universal judgement *that fire alarms are to be pulled in cases of fire,* it is the perception of *this fire* which incites this action, this pulling of this alarm, by me, now. Still, the universal premise is present, playing its structuring role, though it is not such as to instigate a particular action as its proximate efficient cause. This leaves Aristotle with the options of saying either that the minor premise is the proximate cause, or, more plausibly, that the minor premise is the proximate cause only with the background enabling condition provided by the major premise. For a good discussion of some of the intricacies and difficulties of Aristotle's conception of the practical syllogism, see Price (2008).


CHAPTER 12

**Introduction to III 12**
Aristotle has several times in the treatise alluded to the hierarchical relations between the faculties of the soul, twice indicating that a fuller explanation of the reasons why they are distributed as they are would be undertaken (413b4–10, 413b33–414a3). This chapter offers that promised explanation; it is given in thoroughly teleological terms. Aristotle argues that life requires nutrition, which in turn in animals requires the sense of touch—where the modality given by 'requires' is neither logical nor metaphysical, but teleological. That is, there is no contradiction or other deep impossibility in the suggestion that there might be an animal lacking the sense of touch. It is rather the case, suggests Aristotle, that it would offend against the purposefulness of nature to require animals to eat without also endowing them with the wherewithal for acquiring food. This, then, provides the general basis for his contention that 'the primary form of perception which belongs to all animals is touch' (413b4–5).

For this reason, then, Aristotle first investigates the sense of touch (which will include taste as a sort of subordinate case) as necessary for life, because it is necessary for nutrition (434a22–b8); he then turns to the other senses as necessary for the sort of life found in the vast majority of animals, those having the higher forms of perception in addition to touch (434b24–435a10).

In keeping with the primarily naturalistic character of the entire work, Aristotle implicitly restricts the domain of inquiry in this chapter to mortal beings. Earlier he had made this restriction explicit (413a32; see note to 413a30–b10).

**434a22–6: The Minimal Requisites of Natural Life:** Anything alive is subject to growth and decline; nutrition is necessary for these activities; hence, every living thing, for the entire time it is alive, must have a nutritive soul. By contrast, not everything alive needs a perceptual soul. Indeed, some kinds of simple bodies cannot have such a soul, because they are materially unsuited to realize the activities of perception.

Two points are especially noteworthy regarding this opening passage. First, the modality employed here and throughout the chapter is a form of hypothetical necessity: *if* something is to be alive, then it must manifest various activities, and *if* it is to manifest these activities, *then* it is necessary that it have such and such a soul. He is not arguing that as a matter of metaphysical or logical necessity nothing could perceive without taking on nutrition, and still less that thought is impossible in this strong sense without perception. Elsewhere he commits himself to the denial of this stronger modality (*Met.* 991a10, 1050b16–29, 1069a30–33, 1071b3–5). On Aristotle's conception of hypothetical necessity, see *Physics* II 9, where he draws out some of the connections he sees between hypothetical necessity and material causation. For an exposition of this connection, see Cooper (1985) and especially Charles (1988).

This form of hypothetical modality is articulated within the overarching framework of Aristotle's general teleology: if some end is to be achieved, then such and such must obtain. Thus, if this saw is to cut wood, then it must be made of suitably rigid matter. Similarly, if this eye is to see, then it must be made of a material capable of being suitably affected by colour. It is useful to compare this passage, and indeed the whole of this chapter, with *De Partibus Animalium* I 1, where the priority of the final cause in natural explanation is made clear (so, e.g., 639 11–16), as is the mode of hypothetical necessity pertinent to teleological explanation (640a1–9, 642a1–13).

Second, in consequence, Aristotle does not suppose that the soul by itself is sufficient to render just any body capable of life.

Indeed, in this passage one can feel the force of Aristotle's better-known contention in *DA* II 1 that 'the soul will be an actuality of a *certain sort* of body' (*toioutou . . . sômatos*; 412a21–2). Only a body suitably endowed to realize the activities characteristic of life can be ensouled. Similarly, only bodies equipped to perceive can receive a perceptual soul, and, more generally, only bodies capable of taking on nutrition can receive a nutritive soul. Here too it is important to recall what Aristotle meant in calling the body suited to realize a soul 'organic'. Such a body is one suited to being the tool of the soul. (See note to 412a28–b4 for fuller discussion.) It is similarly salutary to recall that Aristotle had made this a theme of his criticisms of his predecessors, some of whom, he complains, proceed 'as if it were possible . . . for just any soul to be outfitted in just any body' (408a21–3; see note to 407b14–26 for fuller discussion).

Aristotle goes on to deny that simple bodies are suited to perceive, as is any body incapable of receiving a perceptual form without the matter (see note to 424a17–24). Aristotle develops this point below at 434b9–22.

**434a27–b8: Perception, Motion, and Sessile Animals:** This passage more than any other in *De Anima* makes explicit the teleological framework underpinning the entire work (though cf. also 432b19–26, where much the same point is made more briefly, using some of the same language). Aristotle argues that every animal must have perception if it is to move about in order to acquire nutrition. Otherwise, such animals would plainly perish, thus violating the principle that nature does nothing in vain: they lack the wherewithal required to engage in an activity necessary for their existence. Thus: (i) if an animal is to acquire nutrition, it must move itself about; (ii) if it is to move itself about, it must have perception; for (iii) otherwise, the animal would surely perish, because required but not resourced to move; which violates (iv) the overarching teleological thesis that nature does nothing in vain; so (v) every animal must have perception. It being thus structured, Aristotle effectively has two arguments, one on behalf of (v), his final conclusion, and an embedded one, on behalf of (ii), the claim that motion requires perception. It is the embedded argument that appeals most fully to Aristotle's broader teleology (cf. 415b15, 434a31; *Part. An.* 641b12–19; *Gen. An.* 775a20, 788b20; *Met.* 1021b24; *Pol.* 1256b20).

Assuming that this is Aristotle's general line of argument, his discussion of sessile creatures becomes apposite because their existence threatens (i), that if an animal is to acquire nutrition, it must move itself about. In fact, there are patent counterexamples to that claim of whose existence he is well aware: sessile animals take on nutrition without engaging in locomotion. He has in mind such sea creatures as sea nettles, sponges, oysters, and Testacea, all of which he describes in his biological works (*Hist. An.* 487b6–9, 588b12; *Part. An.* 681b34, 683c8).

His treatment of sessile animals is difficult to reconstruct, in part because the text of this passage is crucially corrupt. His final conclusion is clear enough, however, and simply reaffirms what he has already argued: 'no non-sessile body has a soul without also having perception' (434b7–8). If that is indeed his main concern, then his brief remark that 'nourishment comes to sessile animals from the areas where they naturally occur' (434b2) will dispatch the potential counterexample by granting it, only to embed it in a broader principle, that nature would not fail to provide the wherewithal for such an animal to reach its end (*telos*; 434b1). This would effectively neutralize the counterexample by limiting its force: (i) might easily be rewritten as (i$^i$): if a non-sessile animal is to acquire nutrition, it must move about. Since sessile animals do not violate the general principle that nature does nothing in vain, and the vast majority of animals are non-sessile, including all land animals (*Hist. An.* 487b6–8), the teleological structure of the argument could then proceed unhampered with the rewritten premise. Still, again on the assumption that this is his view of the matter, Aristotle's response seems to devolve into a form of special pleading: if (i$^i$) is his considered view, then it requires independent justification which Aristotle does not provide here. After all, if sessile animals can find food ready to hand without moving after it, then this could in principle—without some further barrier—equally be true of at least some non-sessile animals as well.

Between Aristotle's main argument and the statement of his final conclusion, our text has a brief discussion concerning the possibility of non-sessile animals endowed with a reason capable of discriminating (*nous kritikos*) but lacking in perception

(434b2–7). It is difficult to relate this discussion, which reads very much like an interpolation, to the main thread of the argument in this passage. Aristotle has not so far been talking about the relation between the higher critical faculties and perception, but rather about the relation between the perceptual and nutritive souls.

However that may be, Aristotle's discussion of non-sessile animals in this passage bears the marks of his detailed marine biological research, and reflects his judgement that 'nature moves so seamlessly from lifeless things to animals, passing through living beings which are not animals, that there seems to be scarcely a difference from one to the other, due to their proximity with one another' (*Part. An.* 681a12–15). Various stationary sea creatures, though animals in Aristotle's view, prove to be sufficiently plantlike that they require special comment from the standpoint of animal perception and motion.

**434b9–22: Touch and Taste:**   Aristotle argues that in order to have perception, a body must either be simple or something mixed; but it cannot be simple, since nothing simple is capable of touch and everything with perception has touch as the primary organ of sense (cf. 413b4–5). He provides another teleological argument for the claim that every animal must have touch, this one involving the absence of a medium for this sense (on problems pertaining to the medium of touch, see note to 423a22–b26).

The text is once again suspect, but, as translated, the argument appeals to a sort of non-futility principle similar to the teleological principle already introduced: since every animal unavoidably has a body capable of touching things, some potentially harmful and others potentially beneficial, if it is to survive, the animal must be able to perceive the tangible by the sense of touch. Otherwise, it could not discriminate the potentially harmful from the potentially beneficial amongst tactile objects before it, and so could not respond by flight or pursuit as appropriate. It follows that without this discriminatory ability the animal would perish. This, then, would prove inconsistent with nature's general purpose, which is to bring an animal to maturity so that it may reproduce. So, as a matter of hypothetical necessity, if an animal is to survive, it must be endowed with the sense of touch.

Animals do need touch, then, to survive. Aristotle adds that taste qualifies as a sort of touch, because what is capable of nourishing is also something tangible (cf. *De Sensu* 436b17; see note to 422a8–19). To complete the inference, he seems to assume the dubious ancillary thesis that touch is the *only* faculty capable of detecting what is tactile. Yet just as something both tactile and coloured is visible by sight without sight's being a kind of touch, so something capable of nourishing might be tactile without its being the case that taste is also a kind of touch. Aristotle may be thinking more narrowly of flavour (*chumos*) as itself something tangible, though this is not what he in fact says in this passage. This is, however, evidently the view expressed at *De Anima* 422a8–11, and then again more fully at *De Sensu* 441b19, where flavour is said to be a quality of something liquid capable of activating taste (*geustos*).

Aristotle does allow, in the next chapter, that all the sense organs (*aisthêtêria*) in a certain way perceive by touch (*DA* 435a17–19), though they involve a medium. None of these qualifies as a kind of touch, however, as Aristotle here says taste does.

However that may be, 'sound and colour and scent do not nourish' (430b19–20) an animal and are, accordingly, not even hypothetically necessary for animals as a class. Again, though, one might reasonably probe the implicit distinction made here between the other modalities and touch. After all, it does not nourish either, unless in connection with taste, and then only indirectly. Presumably the other senses can equally have an indirect relation to nourishment.

**434b22–7: Hypothetical Necessity for Senses other than Touch and Taste:**     For these reasons, then, only taste and touch are necessary to all animals. The remaining three senses, though not necessary to animals as a class, are necessary, that is, hypothetically necessary, for all animals that engage in locomotion. Moreover, they do contribute to the well-being even of those animals for which they are not even hypothetically necessary.

The argument for the hypothetical necessity of senses other than touch for animals capable of moving follows a now familiar pattern: if they are to engage in locomotion, then animals must be equipped with faculties capable of detecting objects through a medium, such as colour through air or water (cf. *DA* 418b6).

Otherwise, they would not be able to survive, and their failure in this respect would violate the non-futility principle to which Aristotle has several times appealed in this chapter. They would, in short, be endowed with an ability whose expression would be detrimental to them, a circumstance at variance with the normative teleology of nature assumed in this chapter. Cf. *De Sensu* 436b18–437a2, where Aristotle makes a similar argument, and expands upon it slightly by offering a further justification in terms of the additional epistemic functions of sight and hearing. These senses also discern features of the world, the apprehension of which yields understanding (*phronêsis*), both practical and theoretical, in animals endowed with reason.

**434b27–435a5: Reflections on the Medium:**   Aristotle's observation that senses beyond touch and taste are hypothetically necessary for animals capable of locomotion prompts him to reflect on some features of the medium involved in distal perception. Although intrinsically interesting, the passage does not contribute in any direct way to the general direction of the chapter, which has been to offer a teleological justification for the distribution of psychic faculties across the range of natural living beings.

Aristotle likens distal perception to locomotion, suggesting that the medium of perception is altered in a manner analogous to change in place: something initiates the motion without undergoing motion, transmits that motion to an intermediary which is both moved and moves something further along in the chain, until such time as the end of the chain is reached, where what is moved no longer moves anything further. So, to complete the analogy, the object of perception (the *aisthêton*) initiates a change in the medium, which in turn moves a further feature of the medium, until it reaches the sensory faculty (the *aisthêtikon*), which is affected but does not move anything further. Aristotle cautions that the analogy is importantly inexact, because in the sort of alteration involved in the perceptual chain, what is altered remains in the same location. Further, the final alteration involves no displacement at all. (On the sort of alteration involved in perception, see note to 416b32–417a2.)

Aristotle observes that the various media suitable for serving as intermediaries in instances of distal perception have their own intrinsic material features, with the result that some are more and

375

some less suited to static-free transmission of sensible forms over greater or lesser distances.

**435a5–10: Sight and Reflection:**    Aristotle closes the chapter by teasing out a consequence of his brief discussion of the process of the transmission of sensible qualities through a medium. He notes that the direction of transmission obviates any need for the thesis that sight reaches out to its object in perception. This theory, which may seem alien, had adherents in both Empedocles (DK B 84) and Plato (*Tim.* 45b–46c; cf. *Meno* 76c). Whatever its peculiarities (on which, see Long (1966)), Empedocles' theory shares with Aristotle's own approach the thought that distal perception requires some mechanism to explain action at a distance. In the next chapter he allows that all the sensory organs, including those activated through a medium, perceive by touch (*DA* 435b17–19).

Aristotle also discusses the theory that the eyes reach out to the objects of perception, in both its Platonic and Empedoclean formulations, at *De Sensu* 437b11–438a4. Briefly, Empedocles likened the eyes to a lantern whose fiery beams landed upon objects of perception and then reflected back (hence the mention of 'reflection' (*anaklasis*) at 435a5–6). In Aristotle's current rejection of the theory, its shortcomings are to be appreciated by the analogy with locomotion: the final object moved does not reach out to the first initiator of its own motion. In *De Sensu* 2, Aristotle also faults Empedocles and Plato for the empirical inadequacy of their theory.

CHAPTER 13

### Introduction to III 13

This final chapter of *De Anima* is something of a patchwork, reprising some of the main claims of the preceding chapter but also connecting them to some theses established earlier in the work. It does not introduce any new topic for sustained development. Even so, it draws out a number of implications and illuminates some of the earlier theses by showing how Aristotle is prepared to deploy them.

**435a11–b3: The Elemental Basis of Perceptual Bodies:** Aristotle repeats that no simple body could realize a perceptual soul (cf. *DA* 434a28, 434b9), but now makes clear that the notion of simplicity in question is not spatial but elemental: nothing composed of any one element could perceive. This holds even for touch, which serves as a sort of mean between the various objects of touch. (Aristotle had allowed a variety of oppositions in the objects of touch; see note to 422b23–423a21 for the difficulties associated with this suggestion.) Aristotle's reasoning is compressed, but he is relying on his conception of the elements advanced in *De Generatione et Corruptione* II 3, according to which each of the four elements has an essential pair of features: earth is cold and dry; air is hot and moist; water is cold and moist; and fire is hot and dry. Since touch can perceive all of these contrasts, and earth is limited to the cold and dry, the sensory organ of touch cannot be earthen alone. Thus, for the same reason, the earthen bits of the body, like hair and bone, are incapable of touch, and so incapable of all perception, since touch is presupposed by the remaining sensory modalities.

It is noteworthy that in this passage Aristotle seems to speak as if flesh were the organ of touch ('only touch seems to perceive through itself,' where 'through itself' is contrasted with 'through something else', namely through a medium; 435a17–19). Earlier he had introduced flesh as medium of touch (423b26; cf. also *Part. An.* 656a27–30; *De Iuv.* 469a4–27), locating the sensory organ within. The inconsistency suggests that at least this part of the present chapter may be drawn from a different, presumably earlier phase of Aristotle's thinking about this matter.

However that may be, owing to the same material constraint, and in contrast to a contention of Plato's (*Timaeus* 77b), Aristotle has at his disposal an explanation for his view that plants cannot perceive. What holds for flesh and bone holds equally for plants, which are no less earthen (cf. 410b23, 414a33, 415a2).

It is noteworthy that in advancing this view about bones, hair, and plants, Aristotle seems to be relying on a markedly literal notion of form receptivity (see the General Introduction § IV.B).

**435b4–19: Excessive Objects of Perception: the Special Case of Touch:** Aristotle had earlier appealed to the fact that the senses are destroyed by encountering overly intense objects of perception as a basis for distinguishing perception from reason, which by contrast is strengthened and improved by meeting with intense objects of reason (cf. 424a28–34, 426a30–6b3; for further discussion see notes to 422a20–1 and 429a29–b9). He now joins this observation to his contention that no animal exists without touch (on which, see note to 434b9–22) to conclude that an overly intense object of touch destroys not only the sensory organ, but the whole of the animal. Thus, he argues:

(1) A necessary condition of being an animal is having a perceptual soul.

(2) A necessary condition of having a perceptual soul is having the faculty of touch.

(3) Hence, nothing is an animal without the faculty of touch.

(4) An overly intense object of touch destroys the faculty of touch.

(5) Hence, an overly intense object of touch destroys the animal. Further, since animals may exist without the higher faculties of perception, overly intense objects in those modalities destroy their sensory organs only, permitting the animal to carry on living, if in a mutilated form.

**435b19–24: Higher Senses are for the Sake of Living Well:**    In contrast to touch, which alone is necessary for animal existence, the remaining senses exist for the sake of living well. Aristotle alludes to his earlier discussion of this point in the last chapter, at 434b24–5 (on which, see note to 434b22–7). The current passage adds only a little to the earlier discussion, by way of specifying the ways in which the higher senses contribute to a higher-quality life.

Aristotle's last remark in this passage, about hearing, is a little obscure as stated, but it is easily amplified by his fuller discussion in *De Sensu*. Because voice and significance co-incide with sound, which is the exclusive or proper object (*idion aisthêton*) of hearing, 'hearing contributes the greater part to the growth of intelligence (*phronêsis*)' in animals endowed with reason (*De Sensu* 437a10–11). Indeed, hazards Aristotle, this is why those blind from birth are more intelligent than those born without hearing or speech (*De Sensu* 437a15–17).

The end of this chapter also marks the end of Aristotle's teleological investigation of the faculties of soul. This ending comes rather abruptly, with Aristotle having considered only the perceptual faculties; we might have expected him to proceed in the same vein to a discussion of imagination and reason (cf. *DA* 414b33, 415a10).

The work, like the chapter, ends with no general summary. In this, Aristotle's *De Anima*, as it exists in our current manuscript configuration, contrasts sharply with many others among Aristotle's works, which self-consciously call attention to their own completion (e.g. *De Sensu* 449b1–4; *De Memoria* 453b8–11; *Part. An.* 697b26–30; *EN* 1179a33–b4). In all likelihood *De Anima* is an incomplete treatise.

# DISCURSIVE GLOSSARY OF ARISTOTELIAN TERMINOLOGY

This glossary focuses on (i) Aristotle's dedicated psychological vocabulary; (ii) technical terms initially developed in Aristotle's metaphysics or natural philosophy which are then deployed or appropriated and further developed in *De Anima*; and (iii) words most likely to cause confusion owing to the fact that the semantic fields of English and Ancient Greek rarely map directly onto one another. I stress that the truncated remarks given here may mislead if left unaugmented by considering the contexts in which the terms defined are used. For this reason, the glossary makes frequent reference to the text and notes, where fuller treatments are given, as relevant to specific contexts of use.[1]

Cross-references to other glossary entries are given in **bold**.

**Accident**, see **Co-incident**

**Account, Reason, Structure, Argument, Discourse, Statement, Ratio** (*logos*) A difficult term to render into English, *logos* divides roughly into two families of meanings, one broadly semantic and the other broadly metaphysical. On the semantic side, a *logos* might be a sentence or a statement, or a set of statements, which when appropriately connected qualify as an argument. In the other direction, *logos* is reason, held by Aristotle to be reserved to human beings among the animals. Also on the metaphysical side, a *logos* is the ratio or proportion in a mathematical formula; but it is also, more broadly, what is captured in a definition of something, where the term is virtually interchangeable with **form**. The two families of meanings are connected: a statement is produced by the rational **faculty** of a being with linguistic abilities and bears the marks of its production. Similarly, a definition, if considered as a linguistic expression, is a kind of *logos*, as what captures the **essence**—the **form** or *logos*—of something. In this sense, *logos* behaves something like the word 'defining' as it is used in such phrases as *defining account* and *defining feature*: the defining feature (metaphysical) is to be cited in a defining

[1] This glossary derives in part from the fuller list of Aristotelian terminology given in Shields (2014). It differs in that: (i) I emphasize here features pertaining to Aristotle's psychology; (ii) I discuss difficult terms more fully, with an eye on any special difficulties introduced in *De Anima*; and (iii) I occasionally add suggestions for fuller discussions elsewhere, for those wishing to pursue the questions raised but not answered here. I thank Routledge Publishers for permission to draw upon the more general glossary.

account (semantic). Similarly, an essence-specifying *logos* captures and displays the *logos* or **form** of some entity. See notes to 403a3–27, 418a7–11, and 424a17–24.

**Actuality, Activity** (*energeia, entelecheia*): These two terms appear to be Aristotelian neologisms; they are often interchangeable, though in some cases they differ slightly in meaning. They are best known by their contrasts: (i) *energeia* is regularly contrasted with its correlative **potentiality** (*dunamis*), where it means the actualization of some capacity, e.g. the capacity to see is actualized when one is actually seeing something; (ii) less often, most notably in ethical contexts, *energeia* is contrasted with **change** or **process** (*kinêsis*), in which case it means *activity* or *actuality* in the sense of being a *complete* activity, i.e. one whose performance does not require the attainment of any result beyond itself. In this sense, e.g., seeing qualifies as an actuality (*energeia*), whereas baking is a process (*kinêsis*). One of Aristotle's first questions about the soul in *De Anima* concerns whether it is an actuality (402a26; see note to 402a23–b8). He answers in *De Anima* II 1 that it is (see note to 412a6–11), but the matter is somewhat complicated by the fact that he also distinguishes in *De Anima* between a first and a second actuality (412a22–7, 417a21–b9), where the distinction corresponds to an entity's having a facility for $\phi$-ing, but not now $\phi$-ing (e.g. someone who has learnt how to swim but is now sitting or walking), and someone now exercising the capacity for $\phi$-ing (e.g. someone who is now swimming). The distinction is consequential not only for Aristotle's account of soul in general, but also for his theories of **perception** (*aisthêsis*) and **reasoning** (*noêsis*); see note to 417a14–20. For a fuller discussion of Aristotle's concept of actuality, see Shields (2009). For a rich but uncompelling argument that *energeia* is always best rendered—especially in *De Anima*—as 'activity', see Kosman (2013).

***Aition, Aitia***, see **Cause.**

**Animal** (*zô(i)on*): Among animate beings, animals differ from plants by having **perception** (*aisthêsis*) and **desire** (*orexis*), and among animals humans differ from non-human animals by having **reason** (*nous*). See 414a31–b6, 431a11, and 434a5. On Aristotle's hylomorphic analysis, animals are compounds of **soul** (= **form**) and **body** (= **matter**), on which, see the General Introduction § III.

**Appearance**, see **Imagination** (*phantasia*)

**Appearances** (*phainomena*): From the verb *phainesthai*, to appear, *phainomena* are simply *things which appear*, or, put as a simple substantive, *appearances*. As with the English word 'appearance', a *phainomenon* might be perceptual, whether veridical or non-veridical, or intellectual, again whether veridical or non-veridical. Perceptual (and veridical): 'Just at sunrise, the mountains give off a purplish appearance.' Intellectual (and non-veridical): 'Any appearance that the economy is rebounding after the recession is demonstrably illusory.' Fortunately, Greek marks a (non-rigid) syntactic distinction between *what appears to be so but is not really so* and *what, being a certain way, also appears that way.* These correspond roughly to the difference in English between 'The Müller-Lyer lines appear to be different lengths, though they are in fact the same' and 'Novalis impressed many from the moment he first appeared as a student in Jena.' Appearances play an important methodological role for Aristotle, since he self-consciously collects them as he begins an inquiry; he does so, however, without thereby either endorsing or questioning the ultimate veridicality of those appearances. He follows this procedure in *De Anima* I, while also collecting the **reputable beliefs** (*endoxa*), not least because the views of his predecessors, who have already thought hard about the soul and its characteristics, partly constitute the appearances he regards as worthy of consideration. While never slavishly beholden to the appearances, and perfectly willing to overturn them when they are unsustainable, Aristotle inclines towards the view that *ceteris paribus* appearances should be preserved. Thus, for example, it appears that we engage in deliberation about how we are to act, and it further appears that such deliberations regularly affect the course of future events (406b24–5); so, we should adhere to this appearance unless we are compelled to give it up. In *De Anima*, Aristotle recounts and endorses a broad range of appearances regarding the soul, including the foundational *phainomenon* that some things are living, or animate, and others not (412a13). See note to 402a23–b8.

**Archê**, see **Principle**

**Be, exist** (*einai*): Aristotle uses this verb in two ways: (i) predicatively ('Professor Flabbyface is boorish.'); (ii) existentially ('There is no Santa Claus.'). Aristotle sometimes faults his predecessors for failing to distinguish these uses and criticizes their views accordingly. Two special uses of the verb are paramount in *De Anima*: (i) Aristotle will often suggest that *x* and *y* are one and the same, though they differ in being (*to einai*), where this means that two things may **co-incide**, though their **accounts** are distinct, that is, that two things may be coextensive, though intensionally distinct. Thus, all and only rational beings are capable of grammar, though what it is to be rational is not the same as what it is to be capable of grammar; and (ii) the nutritive and generative souls **co-incide**, though the processes of generation and nutrition are distinct. See 416b25 and note to 416b11–28. See also **Substance**.

**Belief (*doxa*)**: a pro-attitude which may be true or false, a feature which distinguishes belief from **knowledge** (*epistêmê*). In Greek *doxa* is cognate with the verb *dokein*, to seem. One might accordingly expect it to belong to all **animals**, whether rational or not; but because it requires rational faculties, according to Aristotle, and **conception** (*hupolêpsis*) in particular, only human **animals** have belief. See 428a18–24, 434a10–11.

**Body (*sôma*)**: *Sôma* has a series of distinct but related meanings in Aristotle, just as 'body' does in English. Sometimes it is used of geometrical solids, and other times of quantities of matter (as at 416a28), and still other times it refers to an **animal**'s body, which Aristotle contends is the matter of the compound **animal**, of which the **soul** is the **form**. More precisely, the body which is the matter of the compound is the **organic** body, namely that body suited to be a tool for the life-activities of the **animal**, including nutrition, perception, and, in the case of humans, reasoning. Aristotle criticizes some of his predecessors for failing to reflect upon the fact that only suitably structured bodies are suited to be the matter of souls. See notes to 407b14–26 and 412a28–b4.

**Capacity**, see **Potentiality**

**Category**: In Aristotle, a basic kind or ultimate classification of beings. Aristotle poses a categorial question as one of the very first matters to determine regarding the soul (402a23–b1). This question he answers when beginning his own positive account in *DA* II 1 (412a19–21, 412b10–11) by contending that the soul is a **substance** (*ousia*) as **form** (*eidos*). See notes to 402a23–b8 and 412a6–11. For a basic introduction to Aristotle's theory of categories, which is very much presupposed in *De Anima*, see Shields (2014: Ch. Four).

**Cause, Explanation (*aitia, aition*)**: A basic explanatory factor, cited in response to questions concerning what is the case and why. There are four kinds of cause: material, formal, efficient, and final. For most domains of inquiry, citing all four causes is necessary and sufficient for explanatory adequacy. Aristotle regularly connects causation with **knowledge**, since he thinks that we have knowledge of something only when we know its causes. It is accordingly unsurprising that he should characterize the soul in four-causal terms, as the **form** of the body, but equally as a **final** and **efficient** cause. See note to 415b8–27. For a general introduction to Aristotle's four-causal theory of explanatory adequacy, see Shields (2014: Ch. Two).

**Change, Motion, Process (*kinêsis*)**: A change is the actualization of what is potentially φ insofar as it is potentially φ. No one English term has exactly the semantic field as *kinêsis*. We tend to reserve the term *motion* for one kind of change, namely change in location, so that

384

*motion* will often be too restrictive for *kinêsis*. In addition to change in location, Aristotle also recognizes growth, diminution, and simple alteration as kinds of *kinêsis*. Still, sometimes Aristotle uses *kinêsis* interchangeably with another term, usually restricted to alteration, namely *metabolê*. Then again he sometimes contrasts it with **energeia** (actuality or activity), where it is best rendered as *process*. In *De Anima*, Aristotle argues that the soul cannot move in its own right (*kath' hauto*) but can be moved only **co-incidentally** (*kata sumbebê-kos*), evidently because he does not regard the soul as a magnitude. See headnote to *DA* I 3, and notes to 405b31–406a12, 406a12–16, and especially 406a16–b25.

**Co-incident, Accident** (*sumbebêkos*): This word has stricter and more relaxed usages in Aristotle. Strict: (i) When two things co-incide, they overlap—though their overlapping will not constitute a 'coincidence' in our sense of the term. Co-incidents are significant in Aristotle's philosophy in a number of ways, in his theory of **causes** and in his efforts to disarm sophistic paradoxes of various sorts. If the prime minister of Poland and the best composer in Poland co-incide—if they are the same person—then it will be true, but misleading because of its being a mere co-incident cause, to say that 'The ineptness of Poland's best composer caused its economy to crumble.' (ii) Matters are slightly more complex in the arena of **demonstration**, where two distinct notions come into play, but are not always clearly distinguished. In the first, more technical use, x's being *F* co-incides with x's being *G* when *F* is x's essence and *G* is a non-essential but necessary feature of x consequent upon x's being *F* (e.g. if a square is essentially a four-sided closed plane figure, then its having internal angles equaling 360 degrees is a co-incident). Relaxed: In a second, more relaxed sense, a co-incident is simply any intrinsic feature of a thing other than its essence; here it is appropriate to render it as *accident*. For more on this term, see note to 402a7–10. The notion of co-incidence plays a significant role in *De Anima*, especially in connection (a) with Aristotle's conception of the soul's **motion** (see note to 406a16–b25); and (b) with Aristotle's theory of **perception** and the **objects of perception** (e.g. at 418a8–9; see note to 418a20–4).

**Conception, Conceiving, Supposition** (*hupolêpsis*): A somewhat slippery term, in some cases it is neutral as regards conviction, so that it might be rendered as 'entertaining' or perhaps 'supposition', as in 'Her endless entertaining of alternative possibilities left her finally frozen and unable to act' or 'On the supposition that what you say is true, we would be engulfed in flames by now.' Elsewhere, it is a generic term comprising both **knowledge** (*epistêmê*) and **belief** (*doxa*), where it evidently involves some pro-attitude beyond bare entertainment; in this sense, at least, it is restricted by Aristotle to humans among the animals (427b28; cf. *Met.* 1008b26, *EN* 1147b4). This is the use at play in *DA* III 11, where conception involves at least some modest conviction. In these cases, it has at least the level of conviction found in 'Given her conception of fair play, it's no surprise that she stooped to such shenanigans.' See notes to 427b27–428a5 and 434a16–21.

**Core-dependent homonymy**: A type of **homonymy** according to which some range of related definitions depend asymmetrically on a core notion. Aristotle's typical example is *healthy*, across the range of: (i) Socrates is healthy; (ii) Socrates' complexion is healthy; (iii) Socrates' exercise regimen is healthy. The illustration is supposed to make clear first that *healthy* in these applications is not **univocal**, but that the instances are, nonetheless, related, and related in a distinctive way, since accounts of *healthy* in (ii) and (iii) require reference to the account of (i), but not vice versa. If that is accepted, then claims to core-dependent homonymy may be extended to other, more interesting cases. Of course, appeals to core-dependent homonymy are likely to become controversial when extended to such notions as *justice, goodness*, and *being*. In *De Anima*, Aristotle appeals to the core-dependent homonymy of being at 410a13-15. See also **homonymy** and **univocity**.

**Demonstration (*apodeixis*)**: The currency of completed scientific inquiry, a demonstration is a kind of **deduction** featuring premises which are **necessary**, better known than their conclusions, and universal in scope. Aristotle considers the role of demonstration in *DA* I 1. See headnote to *DA* I 1, together with notes to 402a1–4 and 402a10–22.

**Deduction (*sullogismon*)**: 'A deduction is *logos* in which, certain things having been supposed, something different from those supposed results of **necessity** because of their being so' (*APr.* 24b18–20).

**Desire (*orexis*)**: There are three sorts of desire recognized in *De Anima*: rational desire (*boulêsis*), which is restricted to humans and takes as its object what is good; appetite (*epithumia*), which all animals share, and which takes as its object **pleasure** (*hêdonê*); and also spirit (*thumos*), which is concerned with social standing, including the avoidance of shame (414a29–b16, 432b4–7). See note to 414a29–b16. For the status of the capacity of desire (the *orektikon*) as a faculty of soul, see the General Introduction § IV and notes to 414b19–415a11 and 433a6–8.

**Dialectic (*dialektikê*)**: A form of inquiry and argumentation which begins with **reputable opinions** rather than universal and necessary premises (and hence not an instance of **demonstration** and so not used in **science** (*epistêmê*)). Dialectic may be destructive, by showing up faults in an interlocutor's reasoning, or, more problematically, constructive, when it permits a form of argumentative progress which falls short of the rigours of **science**. Aristotle raises a question about the role of dialectic in *De Anima*, though his answer is disputed. See note to 403a27–b16.

**Differentia (*diaphora*)**: Typically rendered in English by its Latin equivalent to mark that it is a technical term, the *differentia* (= difference) is what distinguishes one **species** under a **genus** from another. See notes to 402a10–22, 403b24–31, and 429a10–13.

**Discriminate, Judge (*krinein*)**: Because the senses can *krinein* (418a14, 422b23–7, 425b21, 427a30; cf. *De Sensu* 447b26, 448a3; *Gen. et Corr.* 323b9) but are not true or false in a propositional sense, *krinein* is usually best rendered as 'discriminate'. In some cases, however, when it issues in truth evaluable items, 'judgement' is preferable (so, e.g., *Met.* 1009b2). In some cases, Aristotle's intended meaning is difficult to determine. See, e.g., notes to 426b9–29 and 431a20–b1.

***Dunamis***, see **Potentiality**

**Efficient Cause**, see **Cause**

**End, Final Cause (*telos*)**, see **Cause**. Note that when *end* is used for the final cause, it is in neither its spatial nor its temporal sense (and so not, that is, the end of the valley or the end of the day). Having come into English via the Latin *finis*, *end* in this application is used purely as an equivalent for the final cause, *telos* in Greek. Closer to its meaning in Aristotle is its use in such expressions as 'It didn't serve his ends to be so truculent.'

***Endoxa***, see **Reputable Opinions**

***Energeia***, see **Actuality**

***Entelecheia***, see **Actuality**

***Epistêmê***, see **Science**

**Essence (*to einai, ousia, to ti ên einai, hoper*)**: As this list of Greek terms indicates, Aristotle has no single, set term for essence. Still, he is regularly keen to highlight the defining features of kinds, which he treats as essential. His approach to essentialism is non-modal: the essential features of a kind are not merely those features without which something would not be an instance of that kind, but must also be explanatorily prior to other necessary features of that kind. Thus, if rationality is the essence of human beings, necessarily human beings will be capable of grammar, capable of laughter, and so on; these latter features are jointly explained by rationality, but do not explain it. Each of the latter is an instance of a ***proprium***. Aristotle holds that the soul is essence (*to ti ên einai*) of an organic, living body (412b11), thus implicating himself in the thought that the body, which is the matter of the soul, ceases to exist when it has lost its soul. See the General Introduction § III.B for a presentation and brief discussion of the problem occasioned by this commitment. Aristotle equally sets as a task for *De Anima* a determination of the essence (*ousia*) of the soul (402a7). See note to 402a7–10.

**Exclusive**, see **Proprium**

**Explanation**, see **Cause**

**Faculty**, see **Potentiality**

**Final Cause**, see **Cause**

**Form** (*eidos, morphê*) In its most general application, a form is simply a positive attribute—what is gained or lost in an instance of **change**, whether accidental or substantial. In its most superficial sense, form is akin to *shape* (as in the form of a statue); but it typically has a deeper, more metaphysically loaded meaning, such as *character* or *kind*. When a form is substantial, then it is cited in an essence-specifying definition of a kind (as in the form (*eidos*) of humanity). When it is used in the sense of *character* or *kind*, *eidos* can also mean *species* (as in the species (*eidos*) horse). For an introduction to Aristotle's general understanding of form, see Shields (2104: Chs. Two and Three). Aristotle contends that the soul is the form of the body (412a20), thereby applying to soul-body relations his general hylomorphism, on which, see the General Introduction §§ II and III.

**Formal cause**, see **Cause**

**Function** (*ergon*) Typically a function is what something is *for*: the function of a computer is to compute, that of a kitchen blender to blend ingredients, and so on. Aristotle applies the notion broadly, beyond artefacts to include the characteristic activity of natural organisms, even though they have not been designed for any purpose. Aristotle also uses *ergon* to denote the **activity** involved in exercising a function. See also **cause**.

**Generation, Coming to be** (*genesis, gignesthai*): The word *genesis* (generation) is formed from the verb *gignesthai*, to come to be. Aristotle distinguishes two types of generation or coming to be: (i) unqualified generation, when a new **substance** comes into existence; and (ii) qualified generation, when something already existing comes to be something or other. (English tends to reserve the word *genesis* for Aristotle's first meaning.) Aristotle treats the soul as a **principle** of generation and holds that the nutritive soul is the same as the generative soul, though they differ in being (*to einai*) (see note to 415a22–b7).

**Genus** (*genos*): A genus is a kind, normally superordinate to some range of **species**, which are differentiated from one another by means of some *differentia*. Thus, human, dogs, and snakes are all species under the genus animal. Aristotle also speaks of the highest **categories** of being as genera, and poses as a central question concerning the soul what its genus of being might be (402a23–b1).

*Hêdonê*, see **Pleasure**

**Homonymous** (*homônumon*): Two things are homonymous when they share the same name but have different **accounts**. In extreme and easy cases, this will be obvious and uninteresting (e.g. riverbanks and savings banks). In other, more philosophically interesting cases, homonymy may be more difficult to detect (e.g. good singers and good opportunities). In these cases, its presence may also be disputed. In constructive contexts, Aristotle repeatedly adverts to the notion of **core-dependent homonymy**. Further, Aristotle tends to use the terms *homonymous* and *meant in many ways* or *spoken of in many ways* (*pollachôs legomenon*) coextensively and sometimes even interchangeably. In *De Anima*, he contends that **cause** (*aition*) and **principle** (*archê*) are meant in many ways, and argues that the soul is a cause and principle as a formal, final, and efficient cause (415b8–11). See note to 415b8–27.

**Hylomorphism**: The thesis that ordinary objects are compounds of **form** and **matter**. For a discussion of Aristotle's introduction of hylomorphism, which is for him a fundamental philosophical term, see the General Introduction § II.

**Imagination, Appearance** (*phantasia*): A capacity or faculty of the soul by means of which animals store and manipulate images or appearances. Because of its connection to the verbal form to appear (*phainesthai*), it is tempting to render *phantasia* as 'appearance'. This is strained in English, however, since we tend not to think of appearances as psychic faculties, as opposed to things appearing to psychic faculties. That said, 'imagination' will give the wrong impression if we are thinking of its common use, according to which it is an ability to think creatively or fancifully ('He's utterly lacking in imagination.') In fact, for Aristotle, no human lacks imagination, and all, or nearly all animals, have it as well (see note to 428a5–16). Aristotle distinguishes, however, between two forms of imagination (433b29–30), one rational and one perceptual, corresponding to the form the capacity takes in rational and non-rational animals, on which distinction, see note to 433b19–30. See also headnote to *DA* III 3.

**Intelligence, Prudential Wisdom, Understanding** (*phronêsis*): Sometimes reasonably rendered simply as *intelligence*, *phronêsis* has broad and narrow senses. In its broad application, it covers intelligence generally, so that it is the sort of thing a human has but a rosebush lacks. In its narrow application, it covers the kind of intelligence displayed in practical reasoning, where it is sometimes rendered as *prudential wisdom* or simply *wisdom* (as in, 'He displayed great wisdom in knowing when to quit.'). In its more narrow application, *phronêsis* is also contrasted with theoretical wisdom, *sophia*. Aristotle uses the term in its wider sense at 417b8.

**Intelligibles**, see **Objects of reason**
***Kinêsis***, see **Change**
**Knowledge (*epistêmê*)**, see **Science**
***Logos***, see **Account**
**Material cause**: see **Cause**
**Matter (*hulê*)**: The primary subject of change, introduced in conjunction with its regular correlative, **form**. In its simplest use, matter is simply the stuff of which something is made, something which underlies a change, e.g. a quantity of bronze is the matter of a statute. Matter becomes intricately wed to the notion of **potentiality** (a connection made at 412a9), as form does to **actuality** (412a10). The initial association of matter and potentiality is easy to fathom, since we may see that a quantity of bronze is potentially many different sorts of artefact, and is actually some artefact only when it is enformed in a certain way. Aristotle contends that the body is the matter of the animal, which is in turn treated as a compound of **form** and matter (412a6–9).
**Meant in many ways (*pollachôs legomenon*)**, see **Homonymous**
**Motion**, see **Change**
**Nature (*phusis*)**: Aristotle uses the term *nature* restrictively, when insisting that something has a nature only if it has an internal source of change, and then more expansively, in speaking of the whole of the natural universe. Typically, in the narrower sense, something's nature is its **essence**, e.g. the nature of a human being is to be rational. Using this narrower sense, Aristotle says that he wants to discover the nature of the soul (402a7). See note to 402a7–10.
**Objects of perception, Sensible objects (*aisthêta*)**: Often translated simply as 'sensibles', *aisthêta* are the objects of perception, literally things perceived or perceptible (see note to 416b9–11). Aristotle distinguishes three kinds of objects of perception: (i) **peculiar** or exclusive; (ii) **common**; and (iii) **co-incidental**. See note to 418a7–11, and also the General Introduction § IV.B, for a discussion of the broader and narrower sense of the term as it occurs in *De Anima* (418a25, 424a29–b31, 426a23, 431b21–3, 432a3–6). Aristotle's dominant practice is to understand **perception** as ranging over particular objects, whereas reason ranges over universals (*APo.* 81b6, 87b28–37, 87b39–88a7, *Met.* 1039b28–1040a7, 1087a15–20).
**Objects of reason, Objects of thought, Intelligibles (*noêta*)**: Aristotle regularly treats **reason (*nous*)** as ranging over universals, in contrast to perception (*aisthêsis*), the objects of which (*aisthêta*) are particulars

(*APo.* 81b6, 87b28–37, 87b39–88a7, *Met.* 1039b28–1040a7, 1087a15–20). Just as is the case with its correlate in the area of perception, *aisthêta, noêta*, can be used either modally (= things thinkable, often rendered as 'intelligibles') or factively (= things thought). 'Objects of reason' should be understood to have the same bivalence. 'Universals are never perceived but are only objects of reason' vs 'As a matter of fact, some principles of physics remain to be discovered and so thus far have never been objects of reason for anyone.' See headnote to *DA* III 4.

**Organic** (*organikon*): An adjective formed from the word *organ on*, or tool, which means, roughly, *capable of serving as a tool* or *suited to be a tool*. It is often rendered into English when applied to the body with phrases such as 'replete with organs' or 'equipped with organs', but this is incorrect: although a body suited to be a tool of the soul will be equipped with suitable organs, it is the body as a whole which is said to be *organikon*, which reflects two distinctive features of Aristotle's approach to **body** and **soul,** first that the soul is prior to the body, and second that the soul is the **final cause** for which the body is fitted. That is, the body, like other tools, is for the sake of something, and so has a final cause. See notes to 407b14–26 and 412a28–b4. Given that *organikon* is a theoretically embedded term, it is probably best to leave it basically untranslated as 'organic', though doing so unfortunately gives misleading connotations in English. See also **body**.

**Peculiar,** see **Proprium**.

**Perception** (*aisthêsis*): A subject perceives an object of perception when his sensory faculty is enformed by the sensible form of that object. See the General Introduction § IV.B for the general framework of Aristotle's approach to perception. The word *aisthêsis* is used in various ways, just as the word 'perception' is in English. In some cases it denotes the activity of perception, where 'perceiving' would be an acceptable translation ('Perception is not always conscious.'). It also refers to the faculty of perception, equally called the *aisthêtikon* ('Animals have perception; plants do not.'). Occasionally it is best rendered by 'sensation', as at 423a3, though in the interest of uniformity I have shied away from that rendering so far as possible— though we should not suppose that there is more uniformity or regimentation in English than there in fact is. It is also worth bearing in mind that the related verb *aisthanesthai* has both intellectual and perceptual uses, just as does 'to perceive' in English ('She was the first to perceive that the economy was about to collapse' vs 'He immediately perceived a rancid odour.'). See note to 425b12–25 on the relevance of this difference.

**Perceptual objects,** see **Objects of perception**

*Phainomena*, see **Appearances**

*Phronêsis*, see **Intelligence**

**Pleasure** (*hêdonê*): The object of appetite, pursued by rational and non-rational animals alike. Anything which can perceive, according to Aristotle, has an ability to experience pleasure, and so in turn has a capacity of **desire** (*orexis*). See note to 413b11–414a3.

**Possible, Possibility**: Aristotle works with two notions of possibility. The first is: *x* is not impossible—or, what comes to the same, it is not necessary that not *x*. The second is: *x* is neither necessary nor impossible. The first is one-sided possibility and the second two-sided. The difference may be illustrated with the phrase *it is possible that x is hot*. Since it is necessary that fire is hot, if we say that it is possible that fire is hot, we have one-sided possibility in view, since fire cannot be not hot. By contrast, since water may be either hot or not, when we say that it is possible that water is hot, we have two-sided possibility in view.

**Potentiality, Capacity, Faculty, Power** (*dunamis*): Closely associated with its regular correlate **actuality** (*energeia*), potentiality is a core concept for Aristotle. Something has a potentiality for $\phi$ when it has an internal **principle** for being $\phi$ or doing $\phi$ things. Thus, some wood is potentially a house, whereas water vapour is not, and an eye has the capacity to see, whereas the sole of a leather shoe does not. These illustrations show how Aristotle regards potentiality as more restrictive than bare **possibility**. In this connection, it is often natural to render *dunamis* as *capacity* or *faculty* or *power*. Although sometimes regarded as in competition, these proposed translations are often better regarded as determinables and determinates of one another, so that a human being who has developed his potentiality to swim also has this capacity; but we might wish to refrain from ascribing a swimming faculty to him, on a par, e.g., with the faculty of perception (*aisthêsis*). One substantive question concerns, then, when we should wish to ascribe a fullyfledged faculty to a subject with a given capacity. On Aristotle's approach to capacity and faculty individuation, see the Introduction to II 4, and notes to 418a11–17 and 429b10–2. Aristotle regards **matter** as potential and treats the two concepts as intimately connected.

**Principle, Source, Origin, Beginning, Rule** (*archê*): As this long list indicates, *archê* is an important and malleable word for Aristotle. In many contexts, Aristotle's treats the *archê* of something as its fundamental feature, as that in terms of which its other features are derived; non-fundamental features are to be explained by reference to the features from which they derive, even if they **co-incide**. Given this understanding of an *archê*, it is natural and appropriate for Aristotle to cast his inquiry into the soul in part as an investigation into its principles (*archai*) and also to treat his predecessors as having nominated an *archê* when they suggest, e.g., that the soul is made of this or that element (see note to 404b30–405b10). He likewise treats his own four **causes** as principles, suggesting that only in the terms given by them may we arrive at complete explanations. The verb *archein* also means *to rule*, so that the ruling power is called an *archê*. The connection across all these uses is that an *archê* is something *primary*. Aristotle maintains that in the case of animals the soul (*psuchê*) is an *archê*, in the sense of being the source and cause of their being living beings. See note to 402a4–7.

**Process**, see **Change**

*Proprium* (*idion*): Although it has non-technical uses, where it means *distinctive* or *private*, *idion* is also a technical term for Aristotle, referring to non-essential but necessary properties of something. Thus, for example, it is *idion* of human beings to be capable of grammar. In this sense, it is customary to mark its technical feature by reserving for it the Latin equivalent *proprium*. Somewhere between its technical and non-technical uses, Aristotle uses *idion* to refer to the exclusive or proper **objects of perception** in his theory of perception, in terms of which sensory faculties are individuated. An *idion* object of perception (*aisthêton*) is what is peculiar or exclusive to a sensory modality (colour to sight, scent to smell, and so on). See notes to 418a11–17 and 418a17–20. More generally, Aristotle thinks that an inquiry into the soul needs to determine which features are *idion* to it (403a4–5), where this is contrasted with what is common (*koinon*) to body and soul.

**Prudential wisdom**, see **Intelligence**

*Psuchê*, See **Soul**

**Reason, Intellect, Mind** (*nous*): (i) Aristotle identifies *nous* as the capacity of the soul by which it knows and understands (429a10–11), and compares it with perception, whose basic hylomorphic framework it shares (see note to 429a13–18), but from which it departs in not requiring an organ (429a27). See the General Introduction § IV.C, headnote to *DA* III 4, and notes to 408b18–29 and 429a18–27. (ii) *Nous* is equally a state or activity of mind, ranging from (a) any form of intellectual vs perceptual activity to (b) understanding, where truth is implied (as at 433a26), to (c) the grasping of indemonstrable first principles (as at *APo.* 88a15–17). Readers of *DA* III 4 should be alert to this range of meanings; arguably in that chapter Aristotle emphasizes the more restricted sense captured in (ii.b), though this a matter of dispute.

**Reasoning, Thinking, Understanding, Thought** (*noêsis*): the activity of *nous*, reasoning, or understanding, or simply thinking. Like *nous*, when considered as a state of activity (see **Reason**), *noêsis* is sometimes generic, where it is best rendered as 'thought' or 'thinking'; in other cases, it seems more restricted, so that 'understanding' would be preferable. The translation seeks uniformity in preferring 'reasoning', which also captures the linguistic connection in Greek to the verbal (*noein*) and noun (*nous*) forms.

**Reputable Opinions, Credible Opinions, Entrenched Beliefs, Common Beliefs** (*endoxa*): '*Endoxa* are those opinions accepted by everyone, or by the majority, or by the wise—and among the wise, by all or most of them, or by those who are the most notable and having the highest reputation' (*Topics* I 1, 100b21–3). Aristotle collects *endoxa* at the start of a **dialectical** inquiry, running through them both to bring a problem into focus and to consider what progress may have already been made with respect to the issue under consideration. The word *endoxon* is related to the verb *dokein*, to seem. When Aristotle records the *endoxa*, he is recounting how things have seemed, without taking a stance on whether what seems to be the case is or is not the case. Much of *De Anima* I is *endoxic*; consequently, it is often difficult to determine how much settled doctrine can be read into his remarks there. See also **appearance**.

**Science** (*epistêmê*): The word *science* comes into English from *scientia*, the Latin equivalent of *epistêmê*. In Aristotle *epistêmê* has two central uses: (i) an organized body of knowledge, presenting the completed results of inquiry, expressed using **demonstration**; (ii) the state of knowledge which someone knowing such a science has achieved. Note that the first use is broader in Aristotle than *science* is in contemporary English, where *science* is often equivalent to *natural science*; in Aristotle, science comprises any properly articulated body of knowledge—more in keeping with the English use which recognizes also the mathematical, social, and moral sciences.

**Sensation**, see **Perception**

**Sensible objects**, see **Objects of perception**

**Sensory organ, Perceptual organ** (*aisthêtêrion*): the organ of perception, the eye, for sight, the ears for hearing, and so on. Aristotle distinguishes the sensory organ from the faculty (*dunamis*), because the faculty, unlike the sensory organ, lacks magnitude. See notes to 424a17–24 and 424a24–8.

**Soul** (*psuchê*): the soul is the **form** and **actuality** of an organized body, which is the **matter** of the soul. Aristotle regards it as uncontroversial that animals have souls, because to have a soul is in his terms simply to be animate, or living (*psuchê* = *anima* in Latin). For the same reason, he regards plants as ensouled. The soul is thus a source or **principle** (*archê*) of all life. If we make the easy judgement that all living things have a soul, then the interesting philosophical question, as Aristotle sees it, pertains to the **nature** of this soul that all living things have. A further question, explored in *De Anima* II 3, concerns the relationship between the broadest form of soul, shared by all animate beings, and the increasingly less common perceptual and rational souls, which Aristotle regards as forming a kind of hierarchy. On the hierarchy and unity of souls, see 434a22–b18; cf. *Part. An.* 687a24–690a10; *Met.* 1075a16–25. See also note to 414b19–415a13.

**Substance, Essence** (*ousia*): (i) Aristotle's preferred way of referring to substances, or basic beings, is *ousia*, an abstract noun formed from the feminine participle *ousa* of the verb *einai*, to be. Thus, one might as readily speak in this connection of *beings* or *basic beings* rather than *substances*. For this reason, although *ousia* is traditionally translated as *substance*, this is a very misleading rendering if it is taken to indicate, as it sometimes does in English usage, some *stuff* or *quantity*, because neither of these qualifies as a substance in Aristotle's technical sense. Rather, a substance is a basic being, something capable of existing in its own right. (ii) Aristotle also uses the word *ousia* to refer to the essence of a kind of thing. Strikingly, in *De Anima*, he takes it as his task to discover and display the *ousia* of the soul, which is itself, as form, also the *ousia* of the *animal* (*zô(i)on*) (see note to 402a7–10). For a basic introduction to Aristotle's approach to *ousia*, see Shields (2014: Chs. Four and Six).

**Teleology,** see **End**
**Thinking,** see **Reasoning**
**Understanding,** see **Intelligence**
**Univocity**: A single, non-disjunctive essence-specifying definition. Aristotle assails Plato for his tendency to assume univocity. In these contexts, Aristotle often prefers **core-dependent homonymy**. One substantive question regarding *De Anima* concerns whether Aristotle understands himself to offer a univocal account of soul, on which, see note to 412b4–9.

# BIBLIOGRAPHY

The literature on *De Anima* is vast; no serviceable bibliography can aspire to be comprehensive. Accordingly, this bibliography proceeds with the readership of the Clarendon Aristotle Series foremost in view. It restricts itself primarily to landmark or indispensable works, especially significant secondary literature in English, and works cited in the present volume. Pavel Gregoric has prepared an extremely useful annotated biliography, 'Aristotle's Philosophy of Mind,' online at http://www.oxfordbibliographies. com. Like other online bibliographies, his is dynamic, and will be updated as new works appear.

## I. Texts, Translations, and Commentaries

ACKRIL, J. L. (1963), *Aristotle's Categories and De Interpretatione*, trans. with commentary (Oxford: Oxford University Press).

APOSTLE, HIPPOCRATES (1981), *Aristotle's On the Soul* (Grinell, IA: Peripatetic Press).

AQUINAS, THOMAS (1999), *A Commentary in Aristotle's De anima*, trans. Robert Pasnau (New Haven, CT: Yale University Press).

BARNES, JONATHAN (1994), *Aristotle's Posterior Analytics*, trans. with commentary (Oxford: Oxford University Press).

BEARE, J. I. and ROSS, G. R. T. (1908), *The Parva Naturalia* (Oxford: Clarendon Press).

BOS, A. P. (2003), *The Soul and Its Instrumental Body: A Reinterpretation of Arisotle's Philosophy of Living Nature* (Leiden: Brill).

FÖLLINGER, SABINE (2010), 'Was ist "Leben"? Aristoteles' Anschauungen zur Entstehung und Funktionsweise von Leben', 'Philosophie der Antike 27' (Stuttgart: Franz Steiner Verlag).

FÖRSTER, AURELIUS (1912), *Aristotelis De Anima Libri III* (Budapest: Academiae Litterarum Hungaricae).

HAMLYN, D. W. (1993) [1968], *Aristotle De anima, Books II and III (with passages from Book I)*, trans. with introduction and notes by D. W. Hamlyn, with a report on recent work and a revised bibliography by Christopher Shields (Oxford: Clarendon Press).

HICKS, ROBERT DREW (1907), *Aristotle, De anima*, trans. with introduction and notes (Cambridge: Cambridge University Press).

JANNONE, A. and BARBOTIN, E. (1966), *Aristote: De l'âme* (Paris: Bude).

LAWSON-TANCRED, H. (1986), *Aristotle: De Anima* (Harmondsworth: Penguin).

LEFÈVRE, CHARLES (1972), *Sur l'évolution d'Aristote en psychologie*, Éditions de l'Institut Supérieur de Philosophie de l'Université Catholique de Louvain (Louvain-la-Neuve: Université Catholique de Louvain).

POLANSKY, RONALD (2007), *Aristotle's De Anima* (Cambridge: Cambridge University Press).

RODIER, G. (1900), *Aristote: Traité de l'âme* (Paris: Leux).

ROSS, G. R. T. (1906), *Aristotle, De sensu and De memoria*, text and trans. with introduction and commentary (Cambridge: Cambridge University Press).

ROSS, W. D. (1955), *Aristotle: Parva Naturalia* (Oxford: Clarendon Press).

ROSS, W. D., ed. (1956), *Aristotelis: De Anima*, ed., Oxford Classical Texts (Oxford: Clarendon Press).

ROSS, W. D., ed. (1961), *Aristotle, De anima*, introduction and commentary (Oxford: Clarendon Press).

SIWEK, PAULUS (1965), *Tractatus De Anima, Graece et Latine* (Rome: Desclée et Cie).

THEILER, W. (1979), *Aristoteles: Über die Seele* (Berlin: Akademie Verlag).

TORSTRICK, ADOLPHUS (1862), *De Anima libri III* (Hildesheim: G. Olms).

## II. Anthologies and Monographs

BARNES, L., SCHOFIELD, M., and SORABJI, R., eds. (1979), *Articles on Aristotle*. 4 vols. *Vol. 4: Psychology and Aesthetics* (London: Duckworth).

BEARE, J. I. (1906), *Greek Theories of Elementary Cognition: From Alcmaeon to Aristotle* (Oxford: Clarendon Press).

BLUMENTHAL, HENRY (1996), *Aristotle and Neoplatonism in Late Antiquity: Interpretations of De Anima* (Ithaca, NY: Cornell University Press).

BRENTANO, FRANZ (1867), *Die Psychologie des Aristoteles, insbesondere seine Lehre vom Nous Poietikos* (Mainz: Verlag von Franz Kirchheim).

BRETANO, FRANZ (1977), *The Psychology of Aristotle*, ed. and trans. Rolf George (Berkeley, CA: University of California Press).

BURNYEAT, MYLES (2008), *Aristotle's Divine Intellect* (Milwaukee, WI: Marquette University Press).

CHARLES, DAVID, (1984), *Aristotle's Philosophy of Action* (Ithaca, NY: Cornell University Press).

CHARLES, DAVID (2000), *Aristotle on Meaning and Essence* (Oxford: Clarendon Press).

CLARK, STEPHEN (1975), *Aristotle's Man: Speculations upon Aristotelian Anthropology* (Oxford: Oxford University Press).

DEURETZBACHER, JAKUB (2014), 'Cardiocentrism in Aristotle and Alexander', Doctoral Dissertation, Humboldt-Universität zu Berlin.

DURRANT, M. (1993), *Aristotle's De Anima in Focus* (London: Routledge).

ELLIS, JOHN, ed. (1992), 'Ancient Minds', *The Southern Journal of Philosophy* 31, suppl.

EVERSON, STEPHEN (1997), *Aristotle on Perception* (Oxford: Clarendon Press).

GALLOP, DAVID (1990), *Aristotle on Sleep and Dreams*, text, trans., introduction, notes, and glossary (Peterborough, Ont.: Broadview Press Ltd.).

GILL, MARY LOUISE and LENNOX, JAMES G., eds. (1994), *Self-Motivation: From Aristotle to Newton* (Princeton, NJ: Princeton University Press).

GRANGER, HERBERT (1996), *Aristotle's Idea of the Soul* (Boston, MA: Kluwer Academic Press).

GREGORIC, PAVEL (2007), *Aristotle on the Common Sense* (Oxford: Oxford University Press).

HARTMAN, EDWIN (1977), *Substance, Body and Soul: Aristotelian Investigations* (Princeton, NJ: Princeton University Press).

JOHANSEN, THOMAS (1998), *Aristotle on the Sense-Organs* (Cambridge: Cambridge University Press).

LEAR, JONATHON (1988), *Aristotle: The Desire to Understand* (Cambridge: Cambridge University Press).

LLOYD, G. E. R. and OWEN, G. E. L., eds. (1978), *Aristotle on Mind and the Senses* (Cambridge: Cambridge University Press).

MARMODORO, ANNA (2014), *Aristotle on Perceiving Objects* (Oxford: Oxford University Press).

MODRAK, DEBORAH (1987), *Aristotle: The Power of Perception* (Chicago: University of Chicago Press).

MODRAK, DEBORAH (2001), *Aristotle's Theory of Language and Meaning* (New York: Cambridge University Press).

MOSS, JESSICA (2012), *Aristole on the Apparent Good: Perception, Phantasia, Thought, and Desire* (Oxford: Oxford University Press).

MOURACADE, JOHN, ed. (2008), *Aristotle on Life* (Kelowna, BC: Academic Printing and Publishing).

NUSSBAUM, MARTHA C. (1978), *Aristotle's De Motu Animalium*, text, trans., commentary, and interpretive essays (Princeton, NJ: Princeton University Press).

NUSSBAUM, MARTHA C. and RORTY, AMÉLIE OKSENBERG, eds. (1995) [1992], *Essays on Aristotle's De Anima*, first paperback edn, with an additional essay by M. F. Burnyeat (Oxford: Clarendon Press).

NUYENS, F. (1948), *L'Évolution de la psychologie d'Aristote* (Louvain: La Haye).

PERLER, DOMINIK (2015), *The Faculties: a History* (Oxford: Oxford Univeristy Press).

POPPELREUTER, H. (1891), *Zur Psychologie des Aristoteles, Theophrast, Strato* (Leipzig: Teubner).

SHIELDS, CHRISTOPHER (1999), *Order in Multiplicity: Homonymy in the Philosophy of Aristotle* (Oxford: Oxford University Press).

SHIELDS, CHRISTOPHER (2014), *Aristotle* (London: Routledge).

SORABJI, RICHARD (1972), *Aristotle on Memory* (Providence, RI: Brown University Press).

STRATTON, GEORGE MALCOLM (1917), *Theophrastus and the Greek Physiological Psychology before Aristotle* (London: George Allen & Unwin).

THEILER, WILLY (1983), *Über die Seele*. Aristoteles Werke in deutscher Übersetzung, v. 13, 2nd edn (Darmstadt: Wissenschaftliche Buchgesellschaft).

WEDIN, MICHAEL V. (1988), *Mind and Imagination in Aristotle* (New Haven, CT: Yale University Press).

ZELLER, EDUARD. (1879), *Die Philosohie der Griechen* Vol. 2.2 (Fues Verlag: Leipzig).

## III. Articles and Book Chapters

ACKRILL, J. L. (1978), 'Aristotle on Action', *Mind* 87: 595–601.

ACKRILL, J. L. (1979) [1972–3], 'Aristotle's Definitions of psuchê', *Proceedings of the Aristotelian Society* 73 (1972–3): 1991–33, repr. in Barnes, Schofield, and Sorabji (1979), 65–75.

ANNAS, JULIA. (1995) [1986], 'Aristotle on Memory and the Self', *Oxford Studies in Ancient Philosophy* 4: 99–117, repr. in Nussbaum and Rorty (1995) [1992], 297–311.

BARKER, A. (1981), 'Aristotle on Perception and Ratio', *Phronesis* 26: 248–66.

BARNES, JONATHAN (1979) [1971–2], 'Aristotle's Concept of Mind', *Proceedings of the Aristotelian Society* 72 (1971–2): 101–14, repr. in Barnes, Schofield, and Sorabji (1979), 32–41.

BERTI, ENRICO (1978), 'The Intellection of "Indivisibles" according to Aristotle *De Anima* III.6', in G. E. R. Lloyd and G. E. L. Owen eds., *Aristotle on the Mind and Senses* (Cambridge: Cambridge University Press), 141–79.

BIRONDO, NOELL (2001), 'Aristotle on Illusory Perception', *Ancient Philosophy* 21: 57–71.

BLOCK, IRVING (1960), 'Aristotle and the Physical Object', *Philosophy and Phenomenological Research* 21: 93–101.

BLOCK, IRVING (1961), 'Truth and Error in Aristotle's Theory of Sense Perception', *Philosophical Quarterly* 11: 1–9.

BLOCK, IRVING (1965), 'On the Commonness of the Common Sensibles', *Australasian Journal of Philosophy* 43: 189–95.

BLOCK, IRVING (1988), 'Aristotle on Common Sense: A Reply to Kahn and Others', *Ancient Philosophy* 8: 235–49.

BOLTON, ROBERT (1978), 'Aristotle's Definitions of the Soul: *De anima* II, 1–3', *Phronesis* 23: 258–78.

BOLTON, ROBERT (2005), 'Perception Naturalized in Aristotle's De Anima', in J. Salles, ed., *Metaphysics, Soul, and Ethics in Ancient Thought* (Oxford: Clarendon Press), 209–24.

BOS, ABRAHAM (2001), 'Aristotle's *De Anima* II.1: The Traditional Interpretation Rejected', in D. Sfendoni-Mentzou, J. Hattiangadi, and D. M. Johnson, eds., *Aristotle and Contemporary Science* vol 2 (Bern: Peter Lang), 187–201.

BOSTOCK, DAVID (2012), 'Aristotle's Philosophy of Mathematics', in C. Shields, ed., *The Oxford Handbook of Aristotle* (Oxford: Oxford University Press), 465–92.

BRADSHAW, D. (1997), 'Aristotle on Perception: The Dual-Logos Theory'. *Apeiron* 30: 143–61.

BRENTANO, FRANZ (1995), '*Nous Poêtikos*: Survey of Earlier Interpretations', in Nussbaum and Rorty (1995) [1992], 313–41.

BROACKES, JUSTIN (1999), 'Aristotle, Objectivity and Perception', *Oxford Studies in Ancient Philosophy* 17: 57–113.

BROADIE, SARAH (1993), 'Aristotle's Perceptual Realism', *Southern Journal of Philosophy*, suppl. 31, 137–59.

BROADIE, SARAH (1996), '*Nous* and Nature in Aristotle's De anima III'. *Proceedings of the Boston Area Colloquium in Ancient Philosophy* 12: 163–76.

BURNYEAT, MYLES (1995a), 'Is Aristotle's Philosophy of Mind Still Credible?', in Nussbaum and Rorty (1995) [1992], 15–26.

BURNYEAT, MYLES (1995b), 'How Much Happens When Aristotle Sees Red and Hears Middle C? Remarks on *De Anima* 2.7–8', in Nussbaum and Rorty (1995), 421–34.

BURNYEAT, MYLES (2001), 'Aquinas on 'Spiritual Change' in Perception', in D. Perler, ed., *Ancient and Medieval Theories of Intentionality* (Leiden: Brill), 129–153.

BURNYEAT, MYLES (2002), 'De Anima II 5', *Phronesis* 47: 28–90.

BYNUM, T. W. (1987), 'A New Look at Aristotle's Theory of Perception', *The History of Philosophy Quarterly* 4: 163–78.

CASHDOLLAR, S. (1973), 'Aristotle's Account of Incidental Perception', *Phronesis* 18: 156–75.

CASTON, VICTOR (1992), 'Aristotle and Supervenience', in Ellis (1992), 107–35.

CASTON, VICTOR (1996), 'Why Aristotle Needs Imagination', *Phronesis* 41: 20–55.

CASTON, VICTOR (1997), 'Epiphenomenalisms, Ancient and Modern', *The Philosophical Review* 106: 309–63.

CASTON, VICTOR (1998), 'Aristotle and the Problem of Intentionality', *Philosophy and Phenomenological Research* 58: 249–98.

CASTON, VICTOR (1999), 'Aristotle's Two Intellects: A Modest Proposal', *Phronesis* 44: 199–227.

CASTON, VICTOR (2000), 'Aristotle's Argument for Why the Understanding is not Compounded with the Body', *Proceedings of the Boston Area Colloquium in Ancient Philosophy* 16: 135–75.

CASTON, VICTOR (2002), 'Aristotle on Consciousness', *Mind* 111: 751–815.

CASTON, VICTOR (2005), 'The Spirit and the Letter: Aristotle on Perception', in Ricardo Salles, ed., *Metaphysics, Soul, and Ethics* (Oxford: Oxford University Press), 245–320.

CHARLES, DAVID (1988), 'Aristotle on Hypotheical Necessity and Irreducibility', *Pacific Philophical Quarterly* 69: 1–53.

CHARLES, DAVID (2009), 'Aristotle on Desire in Action', in D. Frede and B. Reis, eds., *Body and Soul in Ancient Philosophy* (Berlin: De Gruyter), 291–308.

CHARLTON, WILLIAM (1985), 'Aristotle and the *Harmonia* Theory', in Allan Gotthelf, ed., *Aristotle on Nature and Living Things* (Pittsburgh, PA: Mathesis Publications), 131–50.

CHARLTON, WILLIAM (1987), 'Aristotle on the Place of the Mind in Nature', in A. Gotthelf and J. G. Lennox, eds., *Philosophical Issues in Aristotle's Biology* (Cambridge: Cambridge University Press), 408–23.

CHARLTON, WILLIAM (1993), 'Aristotle's Definition of Soul', in M. Durrant, ed., *Aristotle's De Anima in Focus* (London and New York: 1993), 197–216.

CODE, ALAN (1987), 'Soul as Efficient Cause in Aristotle's Embryology', *Philosophical Topics* 15: 51–9.

CODE, ALAN (1991), 'Aristotle, Searle, and the Mind-Body Problem', in Ernest Lepore and Robert van Gulick, eds., *John Searle and his Critics* (Oxford: Basil Blackwell), 105–13.

CODE, ALAN and MORAVCSIK, JULIUS (1992) [1995], 'Explaining Various Forms of Living', in Nussbaum and Rorty (1995) [1992], 129–45.

COHEN, S. MARC. (1992) [1995], 'Hylomorphism and Functionalism', in Nussbaum and Rorty (1995) [1992], 57–73.

COOPER, JOHN (1985), 'Hypothetical Necessity', in A. Gotthelf, ed., *Aristotle on Nature and Living Things* (Pittsburgh, PA: Mathesis Publications), 150–167; repr in J. M. Cooper (2004), *Knowledge, Nature and the Good: Essays on Ancient Philosophy* (Princeton, NJ: Princeton University Press), 130–147.

CORCILIUS, K. and GREGORIC, P. (2010), 'Separability vs. Difference: Parts and Capacities of the Soul in Aristotle', *Oxford Studies in Ancient Philosophy* 39: 81–120.

CORKUM, P. (2010), 'Attention, Perception and Thought in Aristotle', *Dialogue* 42: 199–222.

DE KONINCK, CHARLES (1994), 'Aristotle on God as Thought Thinking Itself', *Review of Metaphysics* 47, 471–515

DE LEY, H. (1970), 'A Note on Aristotle, *De Anima*, A. 3, 406b1–3', *Classical Quarterly*, n.s. 20: 92–4.

EASTERLING, H. J. (1966), 'A Note on *De anima* 414a4–14', *Phronesis* 11: 159–62.

EBERT, T. (1983), 'Aristotle on What is Done in Perceiving', *Zeitschrift für philosophische Forschung* 37: 181–98.

ENGMANN, JOYCE (1976), 'Imagination and Truth in Aristotle', *Journal of the History of Philosophy* 14: 259–65.

EVERSON, STEPHEN (1995), 'Proper Sensibles and καθ' αὐτά Causes', *Phronesis* 40: 265–92.

FINE, GAIL (1984), 'Separation', *Oxford Studies in Ancient Philosophy* 2: 31–87.

FINE, GAIL (1993), 'The Object of Thought Argument: Forms and Thoughts', in Gail Fine, *On Ideas: Aristotle's Criticism of Plato's Theory of Forms* (Oxford: Clarendon Press), 120–41.

FINE, KIT (1995), 'The Problem of Mixture', *Pacific Philosophical Quarterly* 76: 266–369.

FREDE, DOROTHEA (1992), 'The Cognitive Role of *Phantasia* in Aristotle', in Nussbaum and Rorty (1995) [1992], 279–95.

FREDE, MICHAEL (1990), 'The Definition of Sensible Substances in *Metaphysics Z*', in D. Devereux and P. Pellegrin eds., *Biologie, logique et metaphysique chez Aristote* (Paris: Éditions du CNRS), 113–29.

FREDE, MICHAEL (1992) [1995], 'On Aristotle's Conception of Soul', in Nussbaum and Rorty (1995) [1992], 93–107.

FREDE, MICHAEL (1996), 'La Théorie aristotélicienne de l'intellect agent', in C. Viano ed., *Corps et âme: Sur De Anima d'Aristote* (Paris: Vrin), 376–90.

FREDE, MICHAEL (2008), 'Aristotle on Thinking', *Rhizai* 5: 287–301.

403

FREELAND, CYNTHIA. (1992) [1995], 'Aristotle on the Sense of Touch', in Nussbaum and Rorty (1995) [1992], 226–48.

FREELAND, CYNTHIA (1994), 'Aristotle on Perception, Appetition, and Self-Motion', in Gill and Lennox (1994), 35–63.

FREY, CHRISTOPHER (2007), 'Organic Unity and the Matter of Man', *Oxford Studies in Ancient Philosophy* 32: 167–204.

GALLOP, DAVID (1988), 'Aristotle on Sleep, Dreams, and Final Causes', *Proceedings of the Boston Area Colloquium in Ancient Philosophy* 4, 257–90.

GANSON, TODD STUART (1997), 'What's Wrong with the Aristotelian Theory of Sensible Qualities?', *Phronesis* 42: 263–82.

GANSON, TODD STUART (2000), 'Review of Johansen (1998)', *Philsophical Review* 109, 89–92.

GERSON, LLOYD (2004), 'The Unity of Intellect in Aristotle's *De Anima*', *Phronesis* 49: 348–73.

GILL, MARY LOUISE (1991), 'Aristotle on Self-Motion', in Lindsay Judson, ed., *Aristotle's Physics: A Collection of Essays,* (Oxford: Clarendon Press), 243–65.; repr. in Gill and Lennox (1994), 15–34.

GOTTSCHALK, H. B. (1971), 'Soul as Harmonia', *Phronesis* 16: 179–98.

GRANGER, HERBERT (1990), 'Aristotle and the Functionalist Debate', *Apeiron* 23: 27–49.

GRANGER, HERBERT (1993), 'Aristotle and the Concept of Supervenience', *The Southern Journal of Philosophy* 31: 161–77.

GRANGER, HERBERT (1994), 'Supervenient Dualism', *Ratio* 7: 1–13.

HAMLYN, D. W. (1959), 'Aristotle's Account of *aesthêsis* in the *De anima'. Classical Quarterly* 9: 6–16.

HAMLYN, D. W. (1968), 'Koine Aisthesis', *The Monist* 52: 195–209.

HARDIE, W. F. R. (1976), 'Concepts of Consciousness in Aristotle', *Mind*, n.s. 85: 388–411.

HEIL, JOHN (2003), 'Aristotle's Objection to Plato's Appearance', *Ancient Philosophy* 23: 319–35.

HEINAMAN, ROBERT (1981), 'Knowledge of Substance in Aristotle', *The Journal of Hellenic Studies* 101: 63–77.

HEINAMAN, ROBERT (1990), 'Aristotle and the Mind-Body Problem', *Phronesis* 35: 83–102.

HEINAMAN, ROBERT (2007), 'Actuality and Potentiality in *De Anima* II.5', *Phronesis* 52: 132–87.

HICKEN, W. F. (1954), '*Phaedo* 93a11–94b3', *Classical Quarterly* xlviii: 16–22.

HÜBNER, JOHANNES (1999), 'Die aristotelische Konzeption der Seele als Aktivität in *de Anima* II 1', *Archiv für Geschichte der Philosophie* 81: 1–32.

HUSSEY, EDWARD (2012), 'Aristotle on Earlier Natural Science', in C. Shields, ed., *The Oxford Handbook of Aristotle* (Oxford: Oxford University Press), 17–45

HUTCHINSON, D. S. (1987), 'Restoring the Order of Aristotle's *De Anima*', *Classical Quarterly*, n.s. 37: 373–81.

IRWIN, TERENCE (1975), 'Aristotle on Reason, Desire, and Virtue', *Journal of Philosophy* 72: 567–78.

IRWIN, TERENCE (1980), 'The Metaphysical and Psychological Basis of Aristotle's Ethics', in A. Rorty, ed., *Essays on Aristotle's Ethics* (Berkeley, CA: University of California Press), 35–53.

IRWIN, TERENCE (1991), 'Aristotle's Philosophy of Mind', in Stephen Everson, ed., *Companions to Ancient Thought 4: Psychology* (Cambridge: Cambridge University Press), 56–83.

JOHANSEN, THOMAS (1996), 'Aristotle on the Sense of Smell', *Phronesis* 41: 1–19.

JOHANSEN, THOMAS (2005), 'In Defense of Inner Sense: Aristotle on Perceiving that One Sees', *Proceedings of the Boston Area Colloquium in Ancient Philosophy* 21: 235–76.

KAHN, CHARLES, H. (1966) [1979], 'Sensation and Consciousness in Aristotle's Psychology', *Archiv für Geschichte der Philosophie* 48: 43–81, repr. in Barnes, Schofield, and Sorabji (1979), 1–31.

KAHN, CHARLES, H. (1995) [1992], 'Aristotle on Thinking', in Nussbaum and Rorty (1995) [1992], 359–80.

KAMTEKAR, RACHANA (2009), 'Knowledge by Likeness in Empedocles', *Phronesis* 54(3): 215–38.

KATAYAMA, ERROL (2008), 'Substantial Unity and Living Things in Aristotle', *Apeiron* 41: 99–128.

KOSLICKI, KATHRIN (2006), 'Aristotle's Mereology and the Status of Form', *Journal of Philosophy* CIII, 715–36.

KOSMAN, ARYEH (1969), 'Aristotle's Definition of Motion', *Phronesis*, 14: 40–62.

KOSMAN, ARYEH (1975), 'Perceiving that we Perceive', *The Philosophical Review* 84: 499–519.

KOSMAN, ARYEH (1987), 'Animals and Other Beings in Aristotle', in Allan Gotthelf and J. G. Lennox, eds., *Philosophical Issues in Aristotle's Biology* (Cambridge: Cambridge University Press), 360–91.

KOSMAN, ARYEH (1992) [1995], 'What does the Maker Mind Make?', in Nussbaum and Rorty (1995) [1992], 343–58.

LANG, H. S. (1980), 'On Memory: Aristotle's Corrections of Plato', *Journal of the History of Philosophy* 18: 379–93.

LEAR, JONATHAN (1982), 'Aristotle's Philosophy of Mathematics', *The Philosophical Review* 91: 161–92.

LEWIS, FRANK, A. (1996), 'Self-Knowledge in Aristotle', *Topoi* 15: 39–58.

LEWIS, FRANK, A. (2003), 'Is There Room for Anaxagoras in an Aristotelian Theory of Mind?', *Oxford Studies in Ancient Philosophy*, 25: 89–129.

LLOYD, A. C. (1979), 'Was Aristotle's Theory of Perception Lockean?', *Ratio* 21: 135–48.

LLOYD, G. E. R. (1996), 'The Varieties of Perception', in G. E. R. Lloyd, *Aristotelian Explorations* (Cambridge: Cambridge University Press), 126–37.

LONG, A. A. (1966), 'Thinking and Sense-Perception in Empedocles: Mysticism or Materialism?', *Classical Quarterly*, n.s. 16, 256–76.

LOWE, MALCOLM (1983), 'Aristotle on Kinds of Thinking', *Phronesis* 28: 17–30.

LYCOS, K. (1964), 'Aristotle and Plato on "Appearing"', *Mind* 73: 496–514.

MAGEE, JOSEPH M. (2000), 'Sense Organs and the Activity of Sensation in Aristotle'. *Phronesis* 45: 306–30.

MATTHEWS, GARETH (1977), 'Consciousness and Life', *Philosophy* 52: 13–26.

MATTHEWS, GARETH (1992) [1995], '*De anima* 2.2–4 and the Meaning of Life', in Nussbaum and Rorty (1995) [1992], 185–93.

MAUDLIN, T. (1986), '*De anima* 3.1: Is Any Sense Missing?', *Phronesis* 31: 51–67.

MILLER, FRED, D. (1999), 'Aristotle's Philosophy of Perception', *Proceedings of the Boston Area Colloquium in Ancient Philosophy* 15: 177–213.

MILLER, FRED, D. (2012), 'Aristotle on the Separability of Mind', in C. Shields, ed., *The Oxford Handbook of Aristotle* (Oxford: Oxford University Press), 306–39.

MIRUS, CHRISTOPHER, V. (2001), 'Homonymy and the Matter of a Living Body', *Ancient Philosophy* 21: 357–73.

MODRAK, DEBORAH (1981a), '*Koinê aisthêsis* and the Discrimination of Sensible Difference in *De anima* iii.2'. *Canadian Journal of Philosophy* 11: 404–23.

MODRAK, DEBORAH (1981b), 'An Aristotelian Theory of Consciousness?', *Ancient Philosophy* 1: 160–70.

MODRAK, DEBORAH (1987), 'Aristotle on Thinking', *Proceedings of the Boston Area Colloquium in Ancient Philosophy* 2: 209–41.

MOSS, JESSICA (2009), '"Akrasia" and Perceptual Illusion', *Archiv für Geschichte der Philosophie* 91: 119–56.

NUSSBAUM, MARTHA, C. (1978a), 'Aristotle on Teleological Explanation', in Nussbaum (1978), 59–106.

NUSSBAUM, MARTHA, C. (1978b), 'The *Sumphuton Pneuma* and the *De Motu Animalium*'s Account of Soul and Body', in Nussbaum (1978), 143–64.

NUSSBAUM, MARTHA, C. (1984), 'Aristotelian Dualism: Reply to Howard Robinson', *Oxford Studies in Ancient Philosophy* 2: 197–207.

NUSSBAUM, MARTHA, C. and PUTNAM, HILARY (1992) [1995], 'Changing Aristotle's Mind', in Nussbaum and Rorty (1995) [1992], 27–56.

OSBORNE, C. (1983), 'Aristotle, *De Anima* 3, 2: How do We Perceive that We See and Hear?', *Classical Quarterly* 33: 401–11.

OWENS, JOSEPH (1976), 'A Note on Aristotle, *De Anima* 3.4, 429b9', *Phoenix* 30: 107–88.

OWENS, JOSEPH (1981) [1976], 'Aristotle: Cognition a Way of Being', *Canadian Journal of Philosophy* 6 (1976): 1–11, repr. in John R. Catan, ed., *Aristotle: The Collected Papers of Joseph Owens* (Albany, NY: State University of New York Press), 74–80.

OWENS, JOSEPH (1982), 'Aristotle on Common Sensibles and Incidental Perception', *Phoenix* 36: 215–36.

POLITIS, VASILIS. (2001), 'Aristotle's Account of the Intellect as Pure Capacity', *Ancient Philosophy* 21: 375–402.

PRICE, A. W. (1996), 'Aristotelian Perceptions'. *Proceedings of the Boston Area Colloquium in Ancient Philosophy* 12: 285–309.

PRICE, A. W. (2008), 'The Practical Syllogism in Aristotle: a New Interpretation', *Logical Analysis and the History of Philosophy* 11: 151–62.

PRITZL, KURT (1984), 'The Cognition of Indivisibles and the Argument of *De Anima* 3.4–8', *Proceedings of the American Catholic Philosophical Association* 58: 140–50.

RENEHAN, ROBERT (1996), 'Aristotelian Explications and Emendations: II. Passages from the *De Anima, De Partibus Animalium, De Generatione Animalium, De Motu Animalium, Politics,* and *Nicomachean Ethics*', *Classical Philology* 91: 223–46.

RICHARDSON, HENRY, S. (1992) [1995], 'Desire and the Good in *De anima*', in Nussbaum and Rorty (1995) [1992], 381–99.

RIST, JOHN (1966), 'Notes on *De Anima* 3.5', *Classical Philology* 61: 8–20.

ROBINSON, H. M. (1978), 'Mind and Body in Aristotle', *Classical Quarterly*, n.s. 28: 105–24.

ROBINSON, H. M. (1983), 'Aristotelian Dualism', *Oxford Studies in Ancient Philosophy* 1: 123–44.

ROSEN, S. H. (1961), 'Thought and Touch: A Note on Aristotle's *De anima*', *Phronesis* 6: 127–37.

SCALTSAS, T. (1996), 'Biological Matter and Perceptual Powers in Aristotle's *De anima*', *Topoi* 15: 25–37.

SCHEITER, KRISANNA (2012), 'Images, Appearnce, and Phantasia in Aristotle', *Phronesis* 57: 251–78.

SCHILLER, J. (1975), 'Aristotle and the Concept of Awareness in Sense-Perception', *Journal of the History of Philosophy* 13: 283–96.

407

SCHOFIELD, MALCOLM. [1978] (1995), 'Aristotle on the Imagination', in Lloyd and Owen (1978), 99–141, repr. in Nussbaum and Rorty (1995) [1992], 249–77.

SHIELDS, CHRISTOPHER (1988a), 'Soul and Body in Aristotle', *Oxford Studies in Ancient Philosophy* 6: 103–37.

SHIELDS, CHRISTOPHER (1988b), 'Soul as Subject in Aristotle's *De anima*', *Classical Quarterly* 38: 140–49, repr. in A. Preus and J. Anton, eds., *Readings in Ancient Greek Philosophy* vol. v (Albany, NY: SUNY Press, 1992), 231–45.

SHIELDS, CHRISTOPHER (1990), 'The First Functionalist', in J.-C. Smith, ed., *The Historical Foundations of Cognitive Science*, (Dordrecht: Kluwer Academic Publishers), 19–33.

SHIELDS, CHRISTOPHER (1993), 'The Homonymy of the Body in Aristotle', *Archiv für Geschiche der Philosophie* 75: 1–30.

SHIELDS, CHRISTOPHER (1994), 'Mind and Motion in Aristotle', in Gill and Lennox (1994), 117–33.

SHIELDS, CHRISTOPHER (1995), 'Intentionality and Isomorphism in Aristotle', *Proceedings of the Boston Area Colloquium in Ancient Philosophy* 11: 307–30.

SHIELDS, CHRISTOPHER (2009), 'The Priority of Soul in Aristotle's *De Anima*: Mistaking Categories?', in D. Frede and B. Reis, eds., *Body and Soul in Ancient Philosophy* (Berlin: De Gruyter), 156–68.

SHIELDS, CHRISTOPHER (2010), 'Plato's Divided Soul', in M. McPherran, ed., *The Cambridge Companion to Plato's Republic* (Cambridge: Cambridge University Press), 147–70; repr. in K. Corcilius and D. Perler, eds., *Partitioning the Soul: Ancient Medieval, and Early Modern Debates* (Berlin: De Gruyter, 2014), 15–38.

SHIELDS, CHRISTOPHER (2013), 'The Science of Soul in Aristotle's *Ethics*', in K. M. Nielsen and D. Henry, eds., *Bridging the Gap between Aristotle's Science and Ethics* (Cambridge: Cambridge University Press), 232–53.

SHIELDS, CHRISTOPHER (2014), 'Virtual Presence: Psychic Mereology in Francisco Suárez', in K. Corcilius and D. Perler, eds., *Partitioning the Soul: Ancient Medieval, and Early Modern Debates* (Berlin: De Gruyter, 2014), 199–219.

SHIELDS, CHRISTOPHER (forthcoming), 'Some Medieval Powers', in J. T. Paasch and Richard Cross, eds., *The Routledge Companion to Medieval Philosophy* (Routledge: London).

SHOREY, PAUL (1901), 'Aristotle's *De Anima*', *American Journal of Philology* xxii: 149–64.

SILVERMAN, A. (1989), 'Color and Color–Perception in Aristotle's *De anima*', *Ancient Philosophy* 9: 271–92.

SISKO, JOHN (1996), 'Material Alteration and Cognitive Activity in Aristotle's De anima', *Phronesis* 41: 138–57.

SISKO, JOHN (1997), 'Space, Time, and Phantasms in Aristotle, *De memoria* 2, 452b7–25', *Classical Quarterly* 47: 167–75.

SISKO, JOHN (1998), 'Alteration and Quasi-Alteration: A Critical Notice of Stephen Everson, *Aristotle on Perception*', *Oxford Studies in Ancient Philosophy* 16: 331–52.

SISKO, JOHN (1999), 'On Separating the Intellect from the Body: Aristotle's *De Anima* iii.4, 429a20–b5', *Archiv für Geschichte der Philosophie* 81: 249–67.

SISKO, JOHN (2000), 'Aristotle's *Nous* and the Modern Mind', *Proceedings of the Boston Area Colloquium in Ancient Philosophy* 16: 177–98.

SLAKEY, T. J. (1961), 'Aristotle on Sense Perception', *The Philosophical Review* 70: 470–84.

SOLMSEN, F. (1961), '*Aisthêsis* in Aristotle and Epicurus', *Mededelingen der Koninklijke Nederlandse Akademie van Wetenschappen, Afd. Letterkunde*, n.r. 24/8: 241–62.

SORABJI, RICHARD (1971) [1979], 'Aristotle on Demarcating the Five Senses', *The Philosophical Review* 80: 55–79, repr. in Barnes, Schofield, and Sorabji (1979), 76–92.

SORABJI, RICHARD (1972), 'Aristotle, Mathematics, and Colour', *Classical Quarterly* 22: 293–308.

SORABJI, RICHARD (1974) [1979], 'Body and Soul in Aristotle', *Philosophy* 49: 63–89, in Barnes, Schofield, and Sorabji (1979), 42–64.

SORABJI, RICHARD (1991), 'From Aristotle to Brentano: The Development of the Concept of Intentionality', *Oxford Studies in Ancient Philosophy*, suppl. vol.: 227–59.

SORABJI, RICHARD (1992) [1995], 'Intentionality and Physiological Processes: Aristotle's Theory of Sense–Perception', in Nussbaum and Rorty (1995) [1992], 195–225.

SORABJI, RICHARD (2001), 'Aristotle on Sensory Processes and Intentionality: A Reply to Burnyeat', in Dominik Perler, ed., *Ancient and Medieval Theories of Intentionality*, 49–61 (= *Studien und Texte zur Geistesgeschichte des Mittelalters* (Bd 76. Leiden: Brill)).

STRIKER, GISELA (1996), 'Emotions in Context: Aristotle's Treatment of the Passions in the *Rhetoric* and his Moral Psychology', in A. Rorty, *Essays on Aristotle's Rhetoric* (Berkeley, CA: University of California Press: 1996), 286–302.

TAYLOR, C. C. W. (1983), 'The Arguments in the Phaedo Concerning the Thesis that the Soul is a *Harmonia*', in J. Anton and A. Preus, ed., *Essays in Ancient Greek Philosophy II*, (Albany, NY: SUNY Press), 217–231.

THEILER, WILLY (1958), 'Review of Ross, *De Anima* (OCT: 1956)', *Gnomon* 30: 443–45.

TRACY, THEODORE (1982), 'The Soul/Boatman Analogy in Aristotle's *De anima*', *Classical Philology* 77: 97–112.

TRACY, THEODORE (1983), 'Heart and Soul in Aristotle', in J. Anton and A. Preus, eds., *Essays in Ancient Greek Philosophy*, Vol. 2 (Albany, NY: SUNY Press), 321–39.

TRACY, THEODORE (1986), 'Two Views of the Soul: Aristotle and Descartes', *Illinois Classical Studies* 11: 247–64.

TURNBULL, R. G. (1978), 'The Role of the "Special Sensibles" in the Perception Theories of Plato and Aristotle', in P. K. Machamer and R. G. Turnbull, eds., *Studies in Perception: Interrelations in the History of Philosophy and Science* (Columbus, OH: Ohio State University Press), 3–26.

WARD, JULIE (1988), 'Perception and Λόγος in *De Anima* ii 12', *Ancient Philosophy* 8: 217–33.

WARD, JULIE (1996), 'Souls and Figures: Defining the Soul in "*De anima*" ii 3', *Ancient Philosophy* 16: 113–28.

WATSON, G. (1982), 'Phantasia in Aristotle, *De Anima* 3.3', *Classical Quarterly* 32: 100–13.

WEBB, P. (1982), 'Bodily Structure and Psychic Faculties in Aristotle's Theory of Perception', *Hermes* 110: 25–50.

WEDIN, MICHAEL (1989), 'Aristotle on the Mechanics of Thought', *Ancient Philosophy* 9: 67–86.

WEDIN, MICHAEL (1992), 'Content and Cause in the Aristotelian Mind', in Ellis (1992), 75–91.

WEDIN, MICHAEL (1994), 'Aristotle on the Mind's Self-Motion', in Gill and Lennox (1994), 81–116.

WEDIN, MICHAEL (1995), 'Keeping the Matter in Mind: Aristotle on the Passions and the Soul', *Pacific Philosophical Quarterly* 76: 183–221.

WEDIN, MICHAEL (1996), 'Aristotle on How to Define a Psychological State', *Topoi* 15: 11–24.

WHITE, KEVIN (1985), 'The Meaning of *Phantasia* in Aristotle's *De Anima*, III, 3–8', *Dialogue* 24: 483–505.

WHITING, JENNIFER (1992), 'Living Bodies', in Nussbaum and Rorty (1995) [1992], 75–91.

WILKES, KATHLEEN (1978), 'Mind Undermined', Chapter 7, *Physicalism* (London: Routledge & Keegan Paul), 114–35.

WILKES, KATHLEEN (1992) [1995], '*Psuchê* versus the Mind', in Nussbaum and Rorty (1995) [1992], 109–27.

WILLIAMS, BERNARD (1986), 'Hylomorphism', *Oxford Studies in Ancient Philosophy* 4: 189–99.

WILLIAMS, C. J. F. (1965), 'Form and Sensation', *Proceedings of the Aristotelian Society*, suppl. 39: 139–54.

WITT, CHARLOTTE (1996), 'Aristotelian Perceptions', *Proceedings of the Boston Area Colloquium in Ancient Philosophy* 12: 310–16.

WOOLF, RAPHAEL (1999), 'The Coloration of Aristotelian Eye-Jelly: A note on *On Dreams* 459b–460a', *Journal of the History of Philosophy* 37: 385–91.

# INDEX

An asterisk (*) indicates a full or central discussion. Page numbers given in **bold** **type** indicate a discussion in the text. Pages numbers given in *italics* indicate a glossary entry.

Printed and bound by CPI Group (UK) Ltd, Croydon, CR0 4YY